AQA AS PE

NESTA WIGGINS-JAMES
ROB JAMES
GRAHAM THOMPSON

WITHDRAWN

www.heinemann.co.uk

✓ Free online support
✓ Useful weblinks
✓ 24 hour online ordering

01865 888080

Heinemann is an imprint of Pearson Education Limited, a company incorporated in England and Wales, having its registered office at Edinburgh Gate, Harlow, Essex, CM20 2JE. Registered company number: 872828

www.heinemann.co.uk

Heinemann is a registered trademark of Pearson Education Limited

Text © Pearson Education Limited 2008

First published 2008

12 11 10 09
10 9 8 7 6 5 4 3

British Library Cataloguing in Publication Data
A catalogue record for this book is available from the British Library
.
ISBN 978 0 435499 48 8

Designed by Wooden Ark Studios
Typeset by HL Studios
Original illustrations © Pearson Education Limited 2008
Cover design by Wooden Ark Studios
Cover photo © Polka Dot Images/Jupiter Images
Printed in China (GCC/03)

Websites
The websites used in this book were correct and up-to-date at the time of publication. It is essential for tutors to preview each website before using it in class so as to ensure that the URL is still accurate, relevant and appropriate. We suggest that tutors bookmark useful websites and consider enabling students to access them through the school/college intranet.

Contents

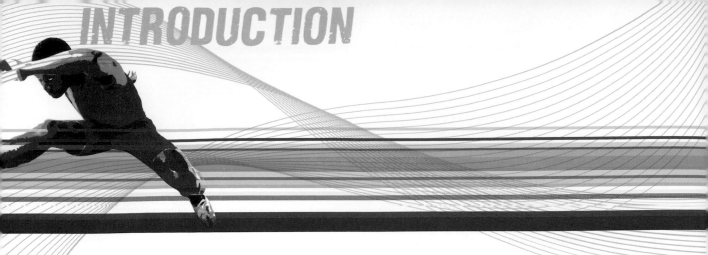

This book has been specifically written for those students following the AQA AS Physical Education course. This text will support and reinforce the teaching that you receive in your centre and will help you apply your understanding of theory to practical performance. The content of this book is presented in a form that is identical to the AQA specification and is arranged under the same sections and subheadings.

Specification at a glance

There are two units you must complete in order to gain your AS Physical Education. Unit 1 is assessed by written examination, while Unit 2 is the more practically based unit, assessed by your teachers in the first instance, and then subject to an external moderation by the examination board.

Unit 1 – Opportunities for and the effects of leading a healthy and active lifestyle		
2 hour written examination	84 marks available	60% AS marks 30% A Level marks

Section A	Section B
This section requires the candidates to answer six structured questions on: • Applied exercise physiology • Skill Acquisition • Opportunities for participation (two questions on each)	One extended question on the application of theoretical knowledge to a practical situation

Unit 2 – Analysis and evaluation of physical activity as a performer and/or in adopted roles
Candidates are assessed on their ability to perform, analyse and evaluate the execution of core skills/ techniques in isolation and in structured practice as either: *A player/performer and in an adopted role* **or** *in two adopted roles*

Internal assessment with external moderation	100 marks available	40% AS marks 20% A Level marks

Section A	Section B
Assessment of your ability in a choice of two from three roles (performer, coach or official)	The application of theoretical factors which improve performance. You are assessed on this element through the Section B question on the Unit 1 paper

There are four sections to this book, three for Unit 1 and one for Unit 2. The sections are divided into a number of chapters which, as well as giving you the exact information you need to be successful, provide a number of different features that will help you achieve your potential. These are outlined below:

Learning outcomes – these help to ensure you understand fully the content of the chapter. When you have completed a particular topic area, make sure you can achieve each learning objective stated. These will also prove invaluable when preparing for your examination – you should collate all the learning objectives stated and tick them off as you prepare

Tasks – these are designed to help you understand and apply your knowledge in a way similar to the requirements of your final examination

Athlete profiles – these profiles will help you understand how world-class performers have put theory you have studied into practice

Key terms – definitions and explanations of important terminology that you should be using in your written answers

Exam tips – essential bits of exam technique and advice that should help you beat the examiner

Apply it – this feature will help you place theory work into a practical context

Take it further! – if you've found everything too easy this feature should help exercise your brain and challenge you a little more

Remember – some useful ways to help you retain important bits of information

Hotlinks – these give you some ideas where you can find out more information on particular topics and so should encourage independence of learning. Be aware however that sometimes hotlinks are associated with an activity.

The ExamCafé

In addition to these features that occur throughout each chapter, this book is unique in that it contains an Exam**Café**. The Exam**Café** includes a number of **Revise as you go** questions and a **Summary checklist** of the key points of information from the chapter. In addition at the end of each section on applied exercise physiology, skill acquisition and opportunities for participation there will be some general revision guidelines for that particular topic as well as some marked past paper questions which have the added benefit of an examiner commentary.

The Exam**Café** has been specifically written to help you improve your examination performance so do pay particular attention to the advice offered here!

We hope you enjoy this book and that it increases your appetite to learn more about physical education and sport.

NJ, RJ, GT

Relax and prepare

Maximising learning capacity

The human brain is a complex organ that allows us to think, move, feel, see, hear, taste, and smell. It controls our body and receives, analyses and stores information (our memories).

Your brain is made up of approximately 15 billion brain cells joined together by interconnecting pathways. We actually access very little of our brain power and we must train the brain if we are to maximise our potential. The brain is divided into two halves known as hemispheres. The right side is your creative brain that deals with shapes and patterns, pictures and visual awareness. The left side of the brain is more logical dealing with numbers, words and language. If we can engage both sides of the brain at once when studying we can increase our brain power and memory capacity.

Use your whole brain!

There are essentially three ways or avenues that information can reach the brain:
- through sight (visually)
- through sound (auditory)
- through physical movement (kinaesthetic).

Many of us might favour learning through one method but we should aim to use all three avenues.

If we can use all three we will be able to learn more effectively retaining up to 90 per cent of information presented. Compare that to 60 per cent if doing (physically moving) alone, 50 per cent using solely visual stimuli or 20 per cent using solely auditory cues.

So when learning or revising make sure you try to present the information in the following ways:
- **Draw it!** (visual) – use mind maps and posters
- **Describe it!** out loud if necessary (auditory) – use audio tapes, podcasts and mnemonics
- **Do it!** (kinaesthetic) – make models, jigsaws or even move around while learning.

Building learning capacity

Some studies have shown that successful learners have similar characteristics and these are outlined below. You are encouraged to develop some or all of these when studying for your AS qualification.

Fig. Generalised characteristics of learners based on G Claxton's Positive Learning Dispositions (2006)

Getting started...

TASK

Match each of the characteristics of learners to each of the statements below:

- I love learning new things
- I'm willing to have a go at something new
- If something is hard, I keep at it until I've got it
- I can blot out distractions when concentrating
- I like to think how things could be different
- My head is full of questions
- I think about how I can improve what I have done
- I think how I can apply new things I've learned
- I like exploring things with other people
- I wonder how things seem to other people.

Ask yourself the questions in the context of each of the characteristics; if it sounds like you then you are on your way to being a successful learner. If it doesn't sound anything like you at all, then you can work on these particular characteristics to try to improve them and in the process improve your learning capacity.

What's so different about AS?

It is harder than GCSE: You might find yourself tempted to put in minimal effort particularly if you did okay in your GCSEs by not revising.

It is not a memory test: While it is true that you will need to remember a lot of information, the exams are testing whether you can apply the relevant information in answering the question.

It requires longer answers: You could give quite brief answers to some of the questions but you will not get good marks unless you fully answer the question and possibly give an extended detailed response.

Get the result!

Examiner's tips

1. Read the questions thoroughly so that you understand what they are asking you and what you have to do.
2. Relate your answer to the number of marks available for that question. Remember that you usually have to make one point in your answer for each mark that is available.
3. Wherever possible, apply theory to a practical activity and make sure that you name that activity.
4. Make sure that in your anatomy and physiology, and skill answers you use the appropriate technical terms.
5. Make sure that you plan the use of your time properly.
6. In the exam you will write your answers on the question paper. The number of lines available gives you an indication of the length of answer required.
7. Make sure that you revise all aspects of each area. Do not think that just because a topic was in a previous exam it will not be in yours.
8. When you are happy that you know what the question is asking underline or highlight all the question cues and key words; only then should you put pen to paper and attempt an answer. The table opposite lists some common question cues, or doing words, together with an idea of the requirements from the candidate in their answer.

Get the result!

Question cues/ doing words	What you need to do ...
Account for	Explain, clarify, give reasons
Analyse	Resolve into its component parts, examine critically
Assess	Determine the value of, weigh up
Compare	Look for similarities and differences between examples, perhaps reach conclusion about which is preferable and justify this clearly
Contrast	Set in opposition in order to bring out the differences sharply
Compare and contrast	Find some points of common ground between x and y and show where or how they differ
Criticise	Make a judgement backed by a discussion of the evidence of reasoning involved about the merit of theories or opinions or about the truth assertions
Define	State the exact meaning of a word or phrase, in some cases it may be necessary or desirable to examine different possible or often-used definitions
Describe	Give a detailed account of
Discuss	Explain, then give two sides of the issue and any implications

Question cues/ doing words	What you need to do ...
Distinguish/ Differentiate between	Look for differences between
Evaluate	Make an appraisal of the worth/validity/ effectiveness of something in the light of its truth or usefulness
Explain	Give details about how and why something is so
To what extent	Usually involves looking at evidence/ arguments for and against and weighing them up
Illustrate	Make clear and explicit, usually requires the use of carefully chosen examples
Justify	Show adequate grounds for decisions or conclusions and answer the main objections likely to be made about them
Outline	Give the main features or general principles of a subject omitting minor details and emphasising structure and arrangement
State	Present in a brief, clear form
Summarise	Give a concise, clear explanation or account of the topic, presenting the chief factors and omitting minor details and examples
What arguments can be made for and against this view	Look at both sides of this argument

Get the result!

Finally, why not try to apply the ten 'habits of success' to your study of Physical Education?

What's the habit	Apply the habit	Top tip
Take responsibility for yourself	Be proactive, take responsibility for your life. Only you can change your studying behaviour	If it's to be, it's up to me
Be resilient and persistent	Never give up, always keep trying even if things are hard. Learn from your mistakes	If at first you don't succeed try, try and try again. There's no such thing as failure only feedback!
Be optimistic	Look for the positive outcomes from all actions	Always look on the bright side of life!
Have confidence and self-belief	Believe in yourself and your talents.	Say to yourself, 'I'm brilliant!'
Have self-discipline	Learn to wait for things you want (delayed gratification)	No pain, no gain!
Take some risks	Stretch yourself. It's good to venture outside your comfort zone	Challenge yourself
Set yourself some learning goals	Write down your goals and keep a note of your progress towards them	Don't forget your goals need to be SMARTER (specific, measurable, agreed, realistic, time-bound, exciting and recorded)
Make a plan and prioritise tasks	Be organised and make a list of what you need to get done	Never put off what can be done today
Work with others	Take notice of what successful students do and copy them!	Listen and learn
Be good to yourself	Get enough sleep and don't party too hard! Exercise	A healthy body makes for a healthy mind

UNIT 1

Opportunities for and the effects of leading a healthy and active lifestyle

Section 1: *Applied Exercise Physiology*

Health, exercise and fitness

Introduction

In order to improve your athletic performance, it will undoubtedly be necessary to improve some aspects of your fitness. This can obviously be achieved by following a well-structured training programme. However, in order to design this training programme so that it improves the necessary dimensions of your fitness, you will need to gather some information regarding exactly where your fitness strengths and weaknesses lie. This can be achieved by carrying out a battery of fitness tests, which will provide you with some accurate data upon which to base the design of your training programme.

The main body of this chapter considers definitions of health and fitness and their various components.

Defining fitness

What is 'fitness'? Exercise physiologists have struggled for many years to come up with an acceptable definition of fitness. This is mainly because fitness means so many different things to different people. For you or me, being fit might mean being able to cope with the demands of playing a game of squash

once or twice a week. However, for somebody like Paula Radcliffe, being fit might be the state when she is at her peak, ready to compete and break a world record in the marathon!

Even elite athletes have a different concept of what it means to be fit. A 100m sprinter, for example, requires completely different dimensions of fitness (speed, power, reaction time) from a marathon runner (cardiorespiratory/aerobic

Figs. 1.01 and 1.02 A marathon runner will have very different fitness requirements from those of a 100m sprinter

endurance, muscular endurance), so their definitions of fitness will be completely different. One thing that is certain, however, is that elite levels of participation require higher levels of fitness than recreational levels.

When considering our levels of fitness, we must first ask ourselves the question, 'Exactly what are we trying to be fit for?' Only then can we consider exactly how fit we are.

In an attempt to give an all-encompassing definition that meets the requirements of all levels of fitness, whether you are a world-class athlete or a recreational badminton player, we might come up with the following definitions: **'the ability to carry out everyday activities without undue fatigue'**, or **'the ability to meet the demands of your environment or lifestyle'**. For a trained athlete, then, being fit means being able to cope with the demands of an activity or competition without becoming so fatigued that you can no longer perform the required skills of the activity.

EXAM TIP:

Make sure you can distinguish between the definitions of fitness and health for your examination.

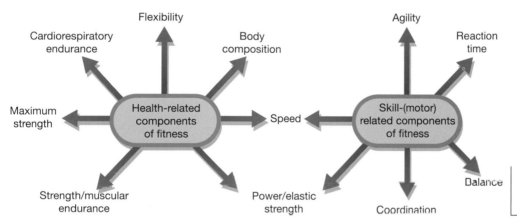

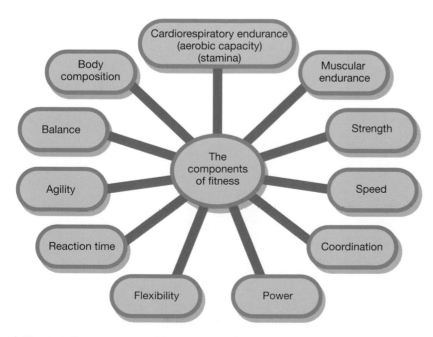

Fig. 1.03 Health-related and skill-related components of fitness

Fig. 1.04 The components of fitness required for your examination

Defining health

The above definitions of fitness, however, should never be confused with 'health'. Health has at its core physical, mental and emotional dimensions that allow a person to lead an active and contented lifestyle. A simple definition that is often cited is: **'a state of physical and social and mental well-being, where we are free from disease'**. Considering the terms 'fitness' and 'health' together, it is now possible to see that an athlete may well be physically fit, but if they are suffering from a mental illness such as depression, they can be classed as unhealthy.

The dimensions or components of fitness

A person's overall level of fitness is made up of many sub-components or dimensions. Some are classed as **health-related components** and others **skill-related**. Both types, however, are required in all sports, but depending upon the activity, the relative importance of each may differ. Figure 1.03 categorises the various dimensions into health-related and skill-related components. Note that speed and power can be categorised under both headings.

Figure 1.04 outlines the actual components of fitness that you will be required to know for your examination.

Stamina or cardiorespiratory endurance (aerobic capacity)

Cardiorespiratory endurance or **aerobic capacity** can be defined as: '**the ability of the cardiovascular and respiratory systems to take in and transport oxygen to the working muscles where it can be utilised and aerobic performance maintained**'.

Aerobic performance consists of sub-maximal exercise where the activity is of a continuous nature such as long-distance running, swimming and cycling. A triathlete requires high amounts of cardiorespiratory endurance, whereas a weightlifter requires very little.

Cardiorespiratory endurance also helps in multiple sprint-type activities and games such as soccer, rugby and hockey since it will help the performer to withstand fatigue, recover during periods of less intense activity and so last the duration of the game.

Several factors influence a person's cardiorespiratory endurance, these include:

- the efficiency of gaseous exchange – both at the lungs and at the muscle cells

Fig. 1.05 A distance runner such as Mo Farah will require high levels of cardiorespiratory endurance

- the effectiveness of oxygen transport from the lungs to the muscle cells
- the ability of the muscle cells to utilise oxygen that they receive.

With reference to the above factors, we might expect a performer with high cardiorespiratory endurance or aerobic capacity, such as the triathlete, to possess the following:

- a greater capillarisation of the alveoli and muscles
- a greater concentration of red blood cells, and therefore haemoglobin, in the blood, which helps to transport the oxygen to the working muscles
- a greater proportion of **slow oxidative muscle fibres (type 1)**
- a greater concentration of myoglobin within the muscle cell, which helps to store the oxygen and transport it to the **mitochondria**
- a greater number and size of mitochondria, which can utilise the oxygen to provide energy.

KEY TERMS

Slow oxidative muscle fibres (type 1):
muscle fibres that are designed for endurance and are able to produce a large amount of energy over a long period of time assuming that oxygen is present

Mitochondria:
the site of energy production under aerobic conditions (when oxygen is present)

Testing stamina/cardiorespiratory endurance

Tests designed to measure stamina include:

- the multi-stage fitness test
- the Harvard step test
- the PWC170 cycle ergometer test
- the Cooper 12 minute run test.

For a detailed explanation on the testing procedure and comments on the validity and reliability of each of these tests please refer to the fitness testing section in Chapter 6.

Most tests of cardiorespiratory endurance seek to discover a person's VO_2max or **maximal oxygen uptake**. This is defined as '**the maximal volume of oxygen that a person can take in, transport and utilise per minute, and is usually measured in ml/kg/min (millilitres of oxygen consumed per kilogram of body weight per minute) or more simply l/min**'.

TASK 1.02

Starting with the greatest, place the following activities in order of expected VO_2max scores:

- rower
- 200m swimmer
- cross-country skier
- weightlifter
- 10,000m runner
- 400m runner.

Activity	Male (ml/kg/min)	Female (ml/kg/min)
Triathlete	80	72
Marathon runner	78	68
Distance swimmer	72	64
Middle distance runner (800m–1500m)	72	63
Games player	66	56
Gymnast	56	47
Weightlifter	52	43

Table 1.01 Typical VO_2max scores for a range of sporting activities

Strength

Strength is the ability of the body to apply a force against a resistance. During sporting activity, this resistance may vary. For example, while running, the resistance that you are working against is your own body weight; a swimmer applies force to the water and a shot putter obviously must apply force to the shot, which is acting as the resistance.

However, when we are analysing strength during sporting performance, it is how we apply strength that is of most interest. Take the example of the shot putter: when putting the shot, the performer must apply strength rapidly over a very short space of time. Compare this to the swimmer, who might need to apply force to the water over a much longer period of time. Different terms are used to explain more clearly the exact type of strength that we require for our particular sporting activity:

- maximum strength
- elastic strength (also known as power)
- strength endurance (also known as muscular endurance).

Maximum strength

'The maximum force that can be developed in a muscle or group of muscles during a single maximal contraction.'

(This definition also tends to be the universal definition of strength.)

Maximum strength is dependent upon several factors, which include:

- the cross-sectional area of muscle – the greater the cross-sectional area of pure muscle mass, the stronger the performer
- the amount of fast twitch muscle fibre – **fast twitch glycolytic (FTG) muscle fibres (type 2b)** are designed more for maximum strength.

A good example of a performer who requires a lot of maximum strength is a weightlifter.

Elastic strength

'The ability to overcome a resistance rapidly and prepare the muscle quickly for a sequential contraction of equal force.'

A performer with high amounts of elastic strength should also possess a high proportion of fast twitch glycolytic (FTG) muscle fibres (type 2b) since the thick myelin sheath that surrounds these fibres allows the motor neurone to conduct the impulse to the muscle more rapidly. This ensures a faster rate of muscle contraction.

Fig. 1.06 A triple jumper requires high amounts of elastic strength

Sports performers who require high levels of elastic strength include sprinters, triple jumpers, and gymnasts.

Strength endurance

'The ability of a muscle or group of muscles to undergo repeated contractions and withstand fatigue.'

For this type of strength, a performer will require a high proportion of **fast oxidative glycolytic (FOG) muscle fibres (type 2a),** which can withstand fatigue much better than fast twitch glycolytic (FTG) muscle fibres (type 2b). Such sports performers include swimmers, rowers or even Olympic kayakers.

KEY TERMS

Fast twitch glycolytic (FTG) muscle fibres (type 2b):
muscle fibres designed for very high intensity, power-based activities such as sprinting, throwing and jumping

Fast oxidative glycolytic (FOG) muscle fibres (type 2a):
fast twitch muscle fibres that pick up certain slow twitch characteristics so that they can withstand fatigue for longer

TASK 1.03

Copy out Table 1.02. For each of the activities listed, state which type of strength is most likely to be required by the performer by placing a tick in the appropriate column.

Joint	Maximum strength	Elastic strength	Strength endurance
400m swim			
Throwing the javelin			
110m hurdles			
Weightlifting			
Track cycling			
Gymnastic floor routine			

Table 1.02

Testing strength

Tests designed to measure strength include:

- one repetition maximum test (1RM)
- the handgrip dynamometer test
- 25m hop test (elastic strength).

For a detailed explanation on the testing procedure and comments on the validity and reliability of each of these tests please refer to the fitness testing section in Chapter 6.

Muscular endurance or strength endurance

'The ability of a muscle or group of muscles to sustain repeated contractions against a resistance for an extended period of time.'

Muscular endurance is a major component of fitness in those activities where the performer must work at medium to high intensity for periods of up to five or six minutes. A good example is competitive rowing or swimming where muscles of both the upper and lower body are required to work repeatedly for the duration of the event. Performers with high levels of muscular endurance will possess both fast (type 2a) and slow (type 1) twitch muscle fibres and will be able to withstand high levels of lactic acid so that they can avoid delay and fatigue.

Testing muscular endurance

Tests designed to measure muscular endurance include:

- the NCF abdominal conditioning test
- the modified pull up test.

For a detailed explanation on the testing procedure and comments on the validity and reliability of each of these tests please refer to the fitness testing section in Chapter 6.

Power (also known as explosive strength)

'The amount of work done per unit of time or the rate at which we apply strength.'

A performer with high amounts of power can exert a great force over a very short period of time. A gymnast performing a vault or a hammer thrower launching the hammer, for example, requires a great deal of power. Powerful athletes should possess a high proportion of fast twitch glycolytic (FTG) muscle fibres (type 2b) since the thick myelin sheath that surrounds these fibres allows the motor neurone to conduct the impulse to the muscle more rapidly. This enables the neuromuscular system to recruit the fast twitch fibres as rapidly as possible.

Testing power

Tests designed to measure power include:

- the Wingate cycle test
- the standing vertical jump test (Sargent jump)
- the standing broad jump test.

For a detailed explanation on the testing procedure and comments on the validity and reliability of each of these tests please refer to the fitness testing section in Chapter 6.

Speed

Speed is a major factor in the successful performance of many sporting activities. From high intensity explosive activities such as sprinting, to a rugby player making a break, you simply cannot beat speed.

For your study, there are two aspects of speed that you need to be aware of. The first is concerned with moving the whole body from one point to another in the quickest time possible (**the maximum rate that a person can move over a specific distance**), for example when performing a 100m sprint. The other type of speed is concerned with moving perhaps just one body part quickly (**the ability to put body parts into motion quickly**), for example when throwing the javelin where the speed at which the arm moves is of supreme importance.

Fig. 1.07 Speed is not solely about how quickly we can move the whole body from one point to another. It is also concerned with how quickly we can put specific body parts into action. When throwing the javelin for example, a 'fast arm' is essential to successful performance

As with other components of fitness, speed is largely in our genes. However, some determining factors include:

- a high number of fast twitch glycolytic (FTG) muscle fibres (type 2b) within the muscle
- high stores of **phosphocreatine** within the muscle. This is the fuel used to help muscle contraction during very high intensity activities such as sprinting
- highly effective lever systems, which put limbs into motion quickly.

Testing speed

There most commonly used test of speed is:

- the 30m sprint test.

For a detailed explanation on the testing procedure and comments on the validity and reliability of this test please refer to the fitness testing section in Chapter 6.

Flexibility

'The range of movement possible at a joint.'

Flexibility is an important component of fitness for all sporting activities, from gymnastics and trampolining through to football and hockey. This is because flexibility not only helps in the prevention of injuries, but it also helps us perform some skills more successfully and helps in the generation of faster and more powerful muscular contractions. It is therefore essential that the training programme of any athlete includes sessions on improving their flexibility and mobility.

Two types of flexibility have been identified:

- **static flexibility**
- **dynamic flexibility.**

KEY TERMS

Static flexibility:
the range of movement about a joint when the muscles surrounding the joint are slowly lengthened

Dynamic flexibility:
this considers the speed at which body parts are moved about the joint, e.g. a trampolinist performing a straddle jump would demonstrate dynamic flexibility

Factors that help determine flexibility include:

- the elasticity of the ligaments and tendons surrounding the joint – the more elastic these soft tissues, the more movement they will allow at the joint
- the strength of the muscles surrounding the joint, in particular the **antagonist** muscle – stronger muscles can restrict movement and lead to a more stable joint, therefore limiting flexibility
- the type of joint, e.g. the ball and socket joint of the shoulder has a greater **range of movement (ROM)** than the hinge joint of the knee since the shoulder is designed for mobility while the knee is designed for stability
- the temperature of the muscles and connective tissues – the warmer the better
- the age of the performer – we generally lose flexibility and mobility as we get older due to our soft tissues becoming less elastic
- the sex of the performer – females tend to have greater flexibility than their male counterparts.

Fig. 1.08 A gymnast such as Beth Tweddle requires high levels of flexibility to enable her to perform a wide range of gymnastic skills

Testing flexibility

Tests designed to measure flexibility include:

- the sit and reach test
- **goniometer** measurement
- shoulder flexibility test.

For a detailed explanation on the testing procedure and comments on the validity and reliability of each of these tests please refer to the fitness testing section in Chapter 6.

KEY TERM

Goniometer:
an instrument used to measure angular displacement and flexibility

TASK 1.04

Copy out Table 1.03. For each of the activities listed, rate on the scale of 1–10 the flexibility requirements of the stated activity (1 = low flexibility requirement, 10 = high flexibility requirement). Write a sentence on each activity justifying your answer.

Sporting activity	Scale									
Volleyball player	1	2	3	4	5	6	7	8	9	10
Judo player	1	2	3	4	5	6	7	8	9	10
Gymnast	1	2	3	4	5	6	7	8	9	10
Javelin thrower	1	2	3	4	5	6	7	8	9	10
Hockey player	1	2	3	4	5	6	7	8	9	10
Trampolinist	1	2	3	4	5	6	7	8	9	10

Table 1.03

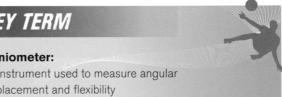

Body composition

'The relative components of total body mass in terms of fat mass and lean body mass or fat-free mass.'

Body composition is concerned with ensuring that the performer has an appropriate percentage of lean body mass for their particular activity. Although each sport may have a slightly different requirement in terms of body composition, in general it is safe to say the less body fat, the better. Excess body fat is really dead weight that must be carried around, which is energy inefficient. Lean body mass is much more desirable for those activities that require both cardiovascular and muscular endurance, such as distance running and rowing, since more oxygen can be directed to the working muscles. Ideal body fat percentages for males and females are 14–17 per cent and 24–29 per cent respectively.

Testing body composition

Tests designed to measure body composition include:

- skinfold measurement
- biolectric impedance
- hydrostatic weighing/densiometry
- body mass index (BMI).

For a detailed explanation on the testing procedure and comments on the validity and reliability of each of these tests please refer to the fitness testing section in Chapter 6.

Agility

'The ability to move and change direction and position of the body quickly while maintaining good body control and without loss of speed.'

Most sporting activity is not performed in a straight line, and multi-directional movement and rapid changes of direction are often needed. Take the position of centre in netball, for example. Successful performance relies on the performer being able to move into a space and lose defenders, which can only be accomplished through dodging and changing

Fig. 1.09 In most invasion games agility is a key component of fitness

direction at speed. Performers in most games will become better if they develop their agility, whether it be a basketball player cutting in to the basket or a squash player moving into position quickly to play a shot. Agility is closely linked to balance, since the key to improving agility is to minimise the loss of speed while shifting the body's centre of mass.

Testing agility

Tests designed to measure agility include:

- the Illinois agility run test
- the hexagon jump test.

For a detailed explanation on the testing procedure and comments on the validity and reliability of each of these tests please refer to the fitness testing section in Chapter 6.

Balance

'The maintenance of the body's centre of mass over the base of support.'

Few sporting activities require us to stand still, yet balance is an essential component in the effective performance of most sports. This is because balance can be either static or dynamic. **Static balance** can be seen when a gymnast is stationary, maintaining their **centre of mass (COM)** over their base of support when performing a handstand or an arabesque, for example.

Dynamic balance, on the other hand, involves the maintenance of a balanced position while moving. For example when a gymnast performs a cartwheel the hips (COM) must remain over the hands (base of support) throughout the movement. Dynamic balance can also be seen in the rugby player who must maintain balance while sidestepping or, remain on their feet when being tackled.

Balance depends upon the coordinated actions of the sensory functions of our ears, eyes and proprioceptors.

KEY TERM

Centre of mass (COM):
the point at which the body is balanced in all directions. In humans, the centre of mass is not fixed but moves according to the positioning of the limbs

Testing balance

Tests designed to measure balance include:

- the standing stork test
- balance boards.

For a detailed explanation on the testing procedure and comments on the validity and reliability of each of these tests please refer to the fitness testing section in Chapter 6.

Coordination

'An organised working together of muscles and groups of muscles aimed at bringing about a purposeful movement such as running or swimming' or 'the patterning of one's own body movements to environmental objects and surfaces...'

Coordination is required in all sporting activity. When serving in tennis for example, the tennis player must coordinate the toss of the ball with one hand with the striking of the ball with the racket head at the optimum position. Similarly, a water polo player must focus on passing the ball or shooting with their arms, while vigorously performing an 'egg-beater' leg kick under the water, all at the same time.

Aspects of coordination

- **General** – possession of fundamental skills such as walking, running and jumping
- **Specific** – possession of sport or exercise-based skills that can be developed through practice; adapting to unusual positions
- **Kinaesthetic differentiation** – ability to correctly adjust muscle tension for the desired outcome, e.g. knowing how hard to strike a ball
- **Orientation in time and space** – the ability to concentrate optimally and consistently on varying stimuli
- **Reactive ability** – producing fast reactions to unexpected situations
- **Rhythm/synchronisation** getting the timing right and feeling the action, e.g. striking a moving ball

KEY TERM

Kinaesthetic:
the ability of the body to receive and respond to stimuli, knowing which part of the body is moving, where it is moving and how it is moving

Tests of coordination

Tests designed to measure coordination include:

- the alternate hand ball toss test
- light board test.

For a detailed explanation on the testing procedure and comments on the validity and reliability of each of these tests please refer to the fitness testing section in Chapter 6.

Reaction time

'The time taken to initiate a response to a given stimulus.'

Quite simply reaction time is the ability to respond quickly to a stimulus and can determine success or failure. Colin Jackson was one of the fastest starters in the world. He contributed much of his success to getting a good start – in fact he coined the phrase 'going on the B' of the 'bang' of the gun.

Reaction time is dependent upon the ability of an individual to process information they see (visual) or hear (aural) and initiate a response. Reaction time can be subdivided into:

- Simple reaction time – this involves the movement response time to a single stimulus, e.g. reacting to the starter's pistol in swimming
- Choice reaction time – this is the movement response time to one stimulus or more that requires a choice of action. This type of response can be improved with practice and training.

Tests of reaction time

Tests designed to measure reaction time include:

- visual reaction time tests
- ruler drop test
- light board test.

For a detailed explanation on the testing procedure and comments on the validity and reliability of each of these tests please refer to the fitness testing section in Chapter 6.

The effect of lifestyle choices on health and fitness

We lead increasingly busy lives which means that we do not always look after our bodies as well as we should. Whether it is the stress imposed from studying or working relentlessly, or simply partying too hard, the lifestyle choices we make can seriously compromise our health and fitness.

Fig. 1.10 Smoking and drinking can have serious effects on your health

Lifestyle choices

The following section considers four key lifestyle factors that can have a significant impact upon health and fitness. Read each entry and discuss the impact of each with your classmates. In particular, consider how the negative impact of each factor can be addressed to give a positive influence on health and fitness.

Physical activity/exercise

It is now universally recognised that physically active people are healthier and fitter than their less active counterparts. Physical inactivity is a major risk factor in the development of coronary heart disease (CHD). In fact, in 2002 the World Health Organization reported that over 20 per cent of all CHD and 10 per cent of stroke cases were down to physical inactivity. Interestingly physical inactivity is defined by the World Health Organization as less than 2.5 hours per week of moderate intensity exercise or 1 hour per week of vigorous activity.

In 2002 the government's Strategy Unit proposed to increase the proportion of the adult population who participate in 30 minutes of moderate physical activity, five or more times per week to 70 per cent by 2020. Currently only 37 per cent of men and 24 per cent of women are meeting the physical activity guidelines.

In 2004 the Department of Health recommended that all children and young people aged between 5 and 18 participate in physical activity of at least moderate intensity for 1 hour per day – currently 70 per cent of boys and 61 per cent of girls are achieving these guideline levels. When it comes to organised Physical Education, the government propose to increase the proportion of school children in England who spend a minimum of 2 hours each week on high-quality sport from 25 per cent in 2002 to 85 per cent in 2008.

There are many factors that contribute to physical inactivity including the increased time spent on sedentary activities including watching television or playing video games, increased car ownership and a significant fall in the amount of walking and cycling undertaken.

The benefits of exercise to an individual are well documented and are dealt with in each of the following chapters. The diseases attributable to physical inactivity include cardiovascular diseases (including CHD), obesity and diabetes. It is estimated that physical inactivity costs the NHS as much as £1 billion per year!

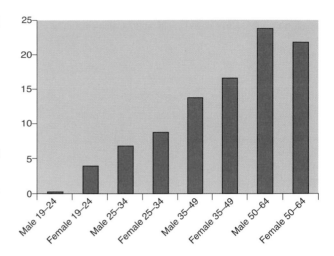

Fig. 1.11 Graph to show percentage of adults eating the recommended five or more portions of fruit and vegetables a day
Source: British Heart Foundation (2001)

KEY TERMS

Saturated fat:
fat that is usually solid at room temperature and found in foods from animal meats, dairy products and some vegetables. This is considered to be less healthy than unsaturated fat and is associated with high cholesterol levels

Unsaturated fat:
fat that is liquid at room temperature and found in vegetable oils. If only one of the chemical bonds is unsaturated it is called monounsaturated fat and if many are unsaturated it is called polyunsaturated fat

Diet

A well-balanced diet is essential for effective performance in sport and general well-being. A diet rich in fruit and vegetables and complex carbohydrates can increase longevity and ward off chronic diseases such as cardiovascular disease, obesity and some cancers, while a diet high in fat, particularly **saturated fat**, salt and simple carbohydrates (such as sugars) increase the risk of these chronic diseases significantly.

A poor diet, coupled with inactivity, can lead to individuals becoming overweight or even obese which is an excessive accumulation of body fat and usually diagnosed with a body mass index score of 30 or more. In 2005, the proportion of men and women classified as overweight (a BMI of 25–29 kg/m^2) was 44 per cent and 35 per cent respectively and the corresponding obesity rate (a BMI of 30+ kg/m^2) is 23 per cent and 24 per cent.

Of more concern perhaps is the 33 per cent of boys and 35 per cent of girls in England aged between 2 and 15 years that are classified as either overweight or obese. In Chapter 2 you will learn how some basic knowledge of the body's metabolism and a consideration of the energy balance can go some way in addressing the issue of obesity.

Simple guidelines to improve the health of the nation through diet include reducing our fat intake (particularly saturated fat), a reduction in salt intake, and an increase in the consumption of fruit, vegetables and complex carbohydrates. In 2005 the Department of Health produced the paper *Choosing a better diet: a food and health action plan* in which they set out their targets (see Table 1.04).

Nutrient	Recommended intake
Total fat	To maintain the average total intake of fat at 32% of food energy
Saturated fat	To reduce the average total intake of saturated fat to 10% of food energy
Fruit and vegetables	To increase the average consumption of a variety of fruit and vegetables to at least 5 portions per day
Fibre	To increase the average intake of dietary fibre to 18g per day
Sugar	To reduce the average intake of added sugars to 11% of food energy
Salt	To reduce the average intake of salt to 6g per day by 2010

Table 1.04 Guidelines to improve the health of the nation through diet   *Source: Department of Health (2005)*

Work/life balance

Undoubtedly the imbalance between work life and home life can lead to excessive levels of stress. Everyone has stressors in their lives but how we deal with these seem to be all important in our ability to cope with stress and the impact it has on our health. Stress is the psychological and physiological response to something that upsets our individual balance and often requires an adjustment or action to take place. Essentially stress is part of the body's defence mechanism. When faced with a threat the body's fight or flight response kicks in and floods the body with stress hormones including **adrenaline** and **cortisol** which prepare us to stand our ground and battle it out or run away. This was highly appropriate for our cave-dwelling ancestors facing life-or-death situations but not really for the day-to-day life of the modern world. Unfortunately the body makes no distinction between having to meet an approaching deadline, preparing for examinations or defending territory. The main problem with the stress response of the body is that the more it is triggered the harder it is to deactivate. So even if the immediate situation has passed, the stress hormones in the body, heart rate and blood pressure remain elevated. This takes a heavy toll on the body and can contribute to chronic illnesses such as cardiovascular disease.

Table 1.05 considers some common day-to-day causes of stress, health implications and some simple ways to combat or cope with stress more effectively.

REMEMBER!

Lifestyle choices that can impact upon our health and fitness include:
- physical activity/ exercise
- diet
- work/life balance
- quantity and quality of sleep
- smoking
- alchohol cosumption
- recreational drug use.

Causes of stress	Impact of stress on health	Coping with stress
• **Work stressors** e.g. workload, job dissatisfaction, insufficient pay, conflict • **Family/ relationship stressors** e.g. disagreements with spouses, children, caring for ill family members • **Social stressors,** e.g. financial pressures, isolation, lack of social support • **Environmental stressors,** e.g. noise from neighbours, pollution, crime	• **Cardiovascular diseases,** e.g: coronary heart disease, high blood pressure • **Ulcers** • **Irritable bowel syndrome** • **Diabetes** • **Obesity** • **Autoimmune diseases** • **Skin conditions** • **Migraines**	• **Acknowledge the stressors in your life** • **Relaxation techniques,** e.g. imagery, controlled breathing • **Prioritise your time** • **Exercise** • **Eat healthily** • **Get a good night's sleep** • **Stay away from depressants** (alcohol) **and stimulants** (smoking and caffeine)

Table 1.05 Common causes of modern-day stress and some coping strategies

Smoking

The dangers of smoking are well known. Smoking can increase the risk of some forms of cardiovascular disease by up to 400 per cent, not to mention the hugely inflated risk of developing lung cancer. In fact, it is estimated that smoking causes over 30,000 deaths a year from cardiovascular disease in the UK. Although the proportion of cigarette smokers has been decreasing, 26 per cent of men and 23 per cent of women in Britain still smoke. These factors alone decrease your levels of general well-being, health and fitness.

Smoking particularly impacts negatively on levels of aerobic fitness for two main reasons:

1. **Restricted transport of oxygen**
   Carbon monoxide contained in cigarette smoke combines with haemoglobin and restricts oxygen absorption, making less available to the muscles

2. **Narrowing of respiratory airways**
   Inflammation of the lining of the respiratory airways and alveoli can restrict the passage of air and impede gaseous exchange and therefore the movement of oxygen into the blood stream.

There is good news however! Stopping smoking can have an immediate positive impact on your health. Within 20 minutes of finishing your last cigarette blood pressure and pulse rate return to normal. After just one day your risk of a heart attack decreases. After three months circulation improves and after just one year the risk of coronary heart disease is just half that of a continuing smoker. It may take up to 15 years of smoking cessation to minimise the risk of coronary heart disease to that of a person who has never smoked – but the impact on your health and fitness make it worthwhile.

ATHLETE PROFILE

Fig. 1.12 Stephanie competes in the Women's 1500 metres

Stephanie Twell is an up and coming middle distance runner. She is hotly tipped to represent Britain in the 2012 Olympic Games. She has recently finished studying A Level Physical Education at a sixth form college. Here Stephanie describes how an understanding of fitness has helped her and her coach in improving her performances.

Stephanie believes that her level of performance is dependent upon a number of specific components of fitness. By focusing her training on particular components of fitness (both strengths and weaknesses) at the right time of the training year, Stephanie can continue to improve her performance. Cardiovascular and muscular endurance are the two components of fitness that Stephanie cites as being the most important while speed, and particularly speed endurance, is essential towards the end of any race. However, Stephanie's training will also incorporate a wide range of different strength and conditioning activities from core stability work to plyometrics.

Refresh your memory

Revision checklist

Make sure you know the following:

▷ Fitness is difficult to define as being fit means different things to different people

▷ Fitness is the ability to carry out everyday activities without undue fatigue

▷ Health is a state of physical, social and mental well-being where we are free from disease

▷ It is possible to be fit but unhealthy

▷ There are two divisions of fitness: health-related and skill-related components

▷ For your exam you need to know definitions and contributory factors to the following health-related components of fitness: stamina (cardiorespiratory endurance), muscular endurance, strength, speed, power and flexibility

▷ Stamina (cardiorespiratory endurance) is 'the ability of the cardiovascular and respiratory systems to take in and transport oxygen to the working muscles where it can be utilised and aerobic performance maintained'

▷ Muscular endurance is 'the ability of a muscle or group of muscles to undergo repeated contractions and withstand fatigue'

▷ There are three elements to strength: maximum strength, elastic strength and strength endurance

▷ Maximum strength is 'the maximum force that can be developed in a muscle or group of muscles during a single maximal contraction'

▷ Elastic strength is 'the ability to overcome a resistance rapidly and prepare the muscle quickly for a sequential contraction of equal force'

▷ Strength endurance is 'the ability of a muscle or group of muscles to undergo repeated contractions and withstand fatigue'

▷ There are two elements to speed: 'the maximum rate that a person can move over a specific distance' or the 'ability to put body parts into motion quickly'

▷ Power is 'the amount of work done per unit of time' – it is the rate at which we apply strength

▷ Flexibility is 'the range of motion possible at a joint'

▷ Two types of flexibility have been identified: static and dynamic flexibility

▷ For your exam you need to know definitions and contributory factors to the following skill-related components of fitness: reaction time, agility, coordination and balance

- Reaction time is 'the time taken to initiate a response to a given stimulus'

- Agility is 'the ability to move and change direction and position of the body quickly while maintaining good body control and without loss of speed'

- Coordination is 'an organised working together of muscles and groups of muscles aimed at bringing about a purposeful movement such as running or swimming'

- Balance is 'the maintenance of the body's centre of mass over the base of support'

▷ We all make certain lifestyle choices that can adversely affect our health and fitness. These lifestyle choices include: physical activity, diet, work/life balance, quality of sleep, smoking, alcohol consumption and recreational drug use

Revise as you go

1. Define each of the following:
   (a) fitness
   (b) health.

2. Explain the division of the term fitness into health-related and skill (motor)-related components.

3. Define VO_2max. What factors determine the VO_2max of a performer?

4. Give examples of two sporting performers who require high levels of each of the following components of fitness:
   (a) muscular endurance
   (b) cardiorespiratory endurance (aerobic capacity)
   (c) power.

5. Provide a definition each of the following types of strength:
   (a) maximum strength
   (b) elastic strength
   (c) strength endurance.

6. Give an example of a sports performer who will require each of the types of strength in Question 5.

7. Define flexibility. What factors contribute to the flexibility of a performer?

8. Discuss the following statement. '*Skill-related components of fitness are far more important in determining the level of competence of a sports performer than health-related components of fitness.*'

CHAPTER 2

Nutrition

– eating for performance

LEARNING OBJECTIVES:

By the end of this chapter you should be able to:

▶ *identify the seven classes of food and their exercise-related function: carbohydrates, fats, proteins, vitamins, minerals, dietary fibre and water*

▶ *explain what constitutes a balanced diet*

▶ *explain the concept of energy balance*

▶ *identify the difference in dietary composition between endurance athletes and power athletes*

▶ *define the condition of obesity and appreciate the limitations in the definitions*

▶ *identify measures of body composition and nutritional suitability.*

Introduction

Whether we are following an exercise programme for health-related reasons or for high-level competition one thing is certain; a well-constructed diet is essential for optimal performance. What we eat, how much we eat and when we eat are all important factors to consider and can have a significant impact upon performance and recovery. If you get the balance right then you should have plenty of energy to train but get it wrong and you will be left behind feeling constantly tired and unable to compete effectively. This chapter will discuss the components of a healthy, balanced diet and give tips and advice on eating for performance.

There is no 'one-size-fits-all' diet when it comes to sports performers – quite simply different activities require a different dietary composition. We will consider the various dietary needs of performers, with a particular focus on the difference in dietary composition between endurance and power athletes.

The chapter will also touch on how a carefully constructed diet, together with a considered approach to exercise, can help combat the increased incidence of childhood and adult **obesity**.

Components of a balanced diet

We need a variety of different nutrients each day to keep us fit and healthy. The food we eat contains these essential nutrients. However, as no one food contains all the nutrients we need, it is essential that we eat a variety of foods from each of the major food groups below, daily. The essential nutrients are:

- carbohydrates
- fats
- proteins
- vitamins
- minerals
- dietary fibre
- water.

These nutrients will ensure that the systems and cells of the body function efficiently. They will provide the body with the energy required to perform, enable the body to grow and repair following training, as well as keep illness and disease at bay.

Carbohydrates, fats and proteins are termed **macronutrients** and are the energy providers while vitamins and minerals are **micronutrients** which perform a range of metabolic functions within cells.

KEY TERM

Obesity:
an accumulation of excess body fat to an extent that may impair health

Macronutrients:

elements from your diet that provide energy including fats, carbohydrates and proteins. They are termed macronutrients because we need more than just a few grams of these daily

Micronutrients:

elements from your diet that perform a range of metabolic functions within cells. They are termed micronutrients because we need these in relatively small quantities

Glycogen:

the stored form of carbohydrate in the muscles and liver

Glucose:

the sugar molecule which is broken down to release energy for exercise

Adipose tissue:

fatty tissue stored beneath the skin and around some vital organs

Glycaemic index (GI):

a measure of the effect different foods have on your blood glucose levels

Simple carbohydrates	Complex carbohydrates
Sugars and jams	Potatoes
Sweets and confectionery	Pasta
Fruit	Bread
Soft drinks	Nuts and pulses

Table 2.01 Examples of carbohydrates

Fig. 2.01 Good sources of carbohydrate in the diet include brown rice, bread, whole wheat pasta, potatoes and cereals

Carbohydrates

Carbohydrates can be divided into simple and complex forms. Examples of each type are shown in Table 2.01.

Carbohydrates are stored in the muscles and liver as **glycogen**. The glycogen storage capacity of the body is about 350g in the muscles, 100g in the liver and approximately 5–10g in the blood as **glucose**. Once this capacity is exceeded, excess carbohydrates are readily converted to fat and stored as **adipose tissue**. This helps to explain how the body's fat content can increase when excess carbohydrates (particularly simple carbohydrates) are consumed.

All carbohydrates (stored as glycogen) are eventually turned into glucose which is subsequently broken down to release the energy needed for exercise. Energy derived from glucose is particularly useful in activities that are of high intensity as it can be accessed relatively quickly. The rate at which carbohydrates are converted into glucose varies depending on the type of carbohydrate consumed. The **glycaemic index (GI)** is a measure of the effect different foods have on blood glucose levels. Foods with a high GI provide a rapid surge in blood glucose levels, while those with a low GI release their energy more slowly. We might expect increases in blood glucose that accompany consumption of high GI foods to be useful in providing energy – but in fact they only give a relatively fleeting high and in the long run will be detrimental to performance. This is because, in order to maintain blood glucose levels within a 'healthy' range, the pancreas releases insulin which carries the glucose out of the blood and into the cells. Excessive consumption of high GI foods results in an increased release of insulin which, in fact, causes blood glucose levels to fall rapidly. Although there is room for some foods with a high GI in everybody's diet, a large proportion of an athlete's carbohydrate intake should come from foods that have a low GI such as nuts and pulses. These are converted into glucose at a much slower rate, so blood glucose levels are sustained over a much longer period.

TASK 2.01

Compile a table which shows foodstuffs with a high GI and those with a low GI.

Low GI (best for sustained energy)	High GI (only give an immediate energy buzz)

Table 2.02

Functions of carbohydrates in exercise

The primary function of carbohydrates in exercise is to provide a continuous supply of energy to the cells and working muscles. Carbohydrates also allow the nervous system to function properly.

Fats

Fats are the major source of energy in the body at rest and during low-intensity exercise, and are therefore essential for good health. There are three main types of fats:

- **Saturated fats** – found in meats and dairy products (such as butter and cheese). These have no role in keeping the body healthy when eaten excessively. They can raise **cholesterol** levels and increase the risk of obesity and heart disease
- **Monounsaturated fats** – found in olive oil, avocados and some nuts such as peanuts. These fats can actually reduce cholesterol levels and therefore reduce the risk of heart disease
- **Polyunsaturated fats** – found in soya beans, sunflower and corn oils and some nuts and seeds. These can also help to reduce cholesterol and reduce the risk of heart disease, although less effectively than monounsaturated fats.

The Department of Health recommends a fat intake of no more than 32 per cent of total calories (a maximum of 10 per cent from saturated fats, 12 per cent monounsaturated fats and a maximum of 10 per cent from polyunsaturated fats.)

Furthermore a healthy diet should also include some foods rich in **Omega 3 fatty acids** (found in oily fish) and **Omega 6 fatty acids** (in olive oil and sunflower oil). However **trans fats** and **hydrogenated oils** should be avoided at all costs as they can increase cholesterol levels and also increase the risk of obesity and heart disease.

Fats in the body are stored as **triglycerides** in the adipose tissue and skeletal muscle. Energy from triglycerides is released through the **oxidation** of **free fatty acids**. This is a relatively slow process and can therefore only provide the body with its energy requirements at rest or during low to moderate intensities of exercise.

Functions of fats in exercise

- Fats are the main energy source for the body at rest and during light to moderate exercise
- Fats absorb fat-soluble vitamins (A, D, E and K) which contribute to the release of energy by forming parts of **enzymes**.
- Fats form a layer of insulation which can help keep the body warm when exercising in cold environments, such as in open water swimming
- Fats form a protective layer around vital organs such as the heart, liver and spleen.

Cholesterol:
a fat-like substance that is essential for maintaining health but which cannot be made by the body, however, high concentrations in the blood increase the risk of heart disease

Omega 3 and 6 fatty acids:
fatty acids (found in fish oil and linseed oil, respectively) that are essential for maintaining health but cannot be made by the body

Hydrogenated oils and trans fats:
oils that are hydrogenated are transformed from their normal liquid state into solids, to make margarine for instance. The unsaturated oil is converted to a saturated fat and its polyunsaturated benefits are removed. It is formed into a trans fat, these can be found in a wide array of processed foods including biscuits and other baked foods. An excess of trans fats in the diet is thought to raise the cholesterol level in the bloodstream

Triglycerides:
the form in which most fat is stored in the body

Oxidation:
oxidation of saturated fat provides the body with the energy it needs to function

Adrenaline:
a hormone produced in response to low blood glucose, exercise and stress

Cortisol:
a steroid hormone produced in response to stress

Free fatty acids (FFAs):
the components of fat that are used by the body to provide energy when at rest or during low/moderate exercise

Enzyme:
a protein that helps to speed up the rate of chemical reactions in the body

Amino acids:
the main components of protein that ultimately contribute to the growth and repair of the body's tissues and promote recovery of the body following exercise

Proteins

Proteins are the third and final energy-providing nutrient. It is thought however, that only about a

During endurance exercise such as a triathlon, the body will use a mixture of both glycogen and fats. This is due to the low solubility of fats in the blood which means that transportation to the muscle is too slow for them to be used on their own. One explanation of a marathon runner hitting the wall is that glycogen stores have been fully depleted and the body tries to use fat as a sole source of energy.

Through endurance training the body can become more adept at utilising fatty acids as a fuel and, therefore, rely less on glycogen. This is known as glycogen sparing and allows the limited stores of glycogen to be used for more intense periods of endurance performance.

maximum of 10 per cent of the energy released during exercise is derived from it and this is only true when participating in endurance activities exceeding 1 hour. Proteins also provide the **amino acids** required for the creation of all enzymes and some hormones.

Amino acids are the building blocks of protein and are used in the growth and repair of the body's cells and tissues, including skeletal muscle. There are about 20 different kinds of amino acid in the body, most of which the body can synthesise and manufacture, however the nine essential amino acids can only come from the food we eat. Protein-rich foods include lean red meats, fish, poultry, beans and lentils. Therefore it is essential that the athlete consumes sufficient protein to promote recovery following training. As a guide, it is suggested a protein intake of 10–15 per cent of total calories should suffice.

Functions of proteins in exercise

- Proteins provide the amino acids required for the growth and repair of cells and tissues such as skeletal muscle
- Proteins provide the amino acids necessary for the manufacture of enzymes and hormones used in the production of energy

- Proteins provide the amino acids necessary for the manufacture of **haemoglobin** and **myoglobin** – essential for oxygen transport
- Proteins can provide energy during endurance-based activities.

KEY TERMS

Haemoglobin:
an iron-based protein in the blood that transports oxygen and carbon dioxide to and from the muscle cells

Myoglobin:
a protein in muscle cells that stores and transports oxygen

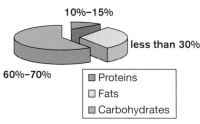

10%–15%

less than 30%

60%–70%

- Proteins
- Fats
- Carbohydrates

Fig. 2.02 The suggested contribution of energy providing nutrients to a healthy diet

Vitamins

Vitamins are chemical compounds which help to convert food fuels into energy, support the immune system, and help the brain to function properly. Although vitamins themselves contain no usable energy, they form components of enzymes which help to release energy from our main energy providers – carbohydrates and fats.

The body is not able to produce most of the vitamins required to maintain health (with the exception of vitamin D and K), so they must be consumed in our diet. A variety of foods are good sources of vitamins, including fresh fruit and vegetables, cereals, eggs, fish and meat.

Each vitamin has a particular function and individual requirements depend very much on a person's age, sex, state of health and exercise levels.

A word on vitamin supplementation

Although there is a wide range of vitamin supplements available on the market, nutrition experts suggest that supplementation should not be necessary in a healthy balanced diet. Despite this some athletes insist on taking megadoses of up to 100 times the **recommended daily allowance (RDA)** in the hope of bringing about improved performance. In fact, such practice can be harmful to the performer in the long run and can cause health complications, and performance to suffer.

Functions of vitamins in exercise

- Vitamins help to release energy from the breakdown and synthesis of carbohydrates, fats and proteins
- Vitamins promote a healthy immune system and thus enable performers to train to the best of their ability and to recover more quickly.

KEY TERMS

Recommended Daily Allowances (RDAs):
set by the EU, RDAs are estimates of the necessary nutrient requirements to meet the needs of the majority of the population

Adenosine triphosphate (ATP):
a high energy compound found in all muscle cells which is broken down to release energy for all purposes

Minerals

Minerals are inorganic compounds found in the body that are vital for effective cell functioning. We gain minerals almost exclusively from the food and water we consume. Although minerals are only required in relatively small amounts in the body (hence the reason why they fall into the category of micronutrient) they have a wide range of roles which can have a significant impact on the performer. A variety of foods are good sources of minerals, including fresh fruit and vegetables, cereals, eggs, meat and fish.

Functions of minerals in exercise

- Calcium contributes to the formation of bones and teeth as well as playing a vital role in muscle contraction and nerve transmission
- Phosphorous is an essential component of **adenosine triphosphate** and **creatine phosphate** both high energy compounds in the body
- Iron is a major component of haemoglobin and myoglobin, our oxygen transporters in the body
- Sodium, potassium, and chlorine form **electrolytes** which help to maintain the correct rate of exchange of nutrients and waste products into and out of the muscle cells.

Fig. 2.03 Taking on fluids during competition and training is essential to prevent dehydration and to facilitate optimal performance

KEY TERM

Creatine phosphate:
a compound found in the muscle cells which is broken down by enzymes to quickly replenish ATP stores

Electrolytes:
substances that help to maintain the optimum rate of exchange of nutrients and waste products into and out of the muscle cells

Water

Up to 60 per cent of a person's body weight is comprised of water. Drinking water is therefore an essential daily activity since nearly all processes in the body take place in a watery medium. Blood plasma is composed predominantly of water and it is this that is responsible for transporting oxygen and the energy-providing nutrients: glucose and fatty acids. Plasma also carries hormones and removes waste products such as carbon dioxide and lactic acid. Water is also responsible for temperature regulation of the body, particularly while exercising. So it is fair to say that water is critical for effective sporting performance.

Sweating is a mechanism by which the body seeks to maintain core body temperature. Typically we can lose 500ml of water every half an hour, although this can increase depending upon the heat, humidity and exercise intensity. Losing the equivalent

of 2 per cent of your body weight as sweat can impair performance by up to 10–20 per cent. If you do not replace the lost water your core body temperature will rise which brings with it a number of performance inhibitors. The blood becomes 'thicker' or more viscous which slows down the flow to the working muscles. To try to compensate, the heart beats faster, putting the body under greater stress. The loss of electrolytes through sweating can cause fatigue and cramps so it is essential that performers remain hydrated. The best rehydrater is water itself, which is easily absorbed into the bloodstream. Water should be taken before, during and following training. For competitions or training sessions lasting in excess of one hour, drinks containing carbohydrates can be taken, which not only keep the body hydrated, but also give an energy boost. Isotonic drinks can also be taken which can help to replace electrolytes lost through sweating and prevent irritations such as muscle cramps.

Functions of water in exercise

- Water forms the foundation of the body's transport network so is responsible for transporting oxygen, nutrients and hormones to the body's cells and the removing of harmful waste products such as carbon dioxide and water
- Water helps to regulate and maintain core body temperature through sweating.

Dietary fibre

An essential ingredient in every athlete's diet, fibre helps the digestive system to function properly by absorbing water and helping the passage of food through the gut. In doing so it prevents constipation and promotes a healthy bowel. Good sources of fibre are found in whole wheat bread, brown rice and vegetables. Some soluble fibres found in pulses, fruit and vegetables can also reduce cholesterol levels and control blood glucose levels by slowing down the absorption of glucose. According to the Department of Health, an athlete's diet should consist of between 18g and 24g of fibre per day.

Functions of fibre in exercise

- Insoluble fibre absorbs water in the intestine which helps to excrete waste from the body
- Soluble fibres contribute to lowering cholesterol in the blood by minimising the absorption of fat and cholesterol from foodstuffs
- Soluble fibre can also maintain blood glucose levels by reducing the rate of glucose absorption.

A balanced diet

We've all heard about eating a balanced diet but what does this actually mean for the sportsperson? A balanced diet is as important as any training undertaken to help optimise performance, whatever your sport.

What constitutes a balanced diet?

A single food group does not give you all the nutrients you need. In fact the more varied your diet the more likely it is that you are fulfilling and meeting all your dietary requirements.

Table 2.03 outlines the essential nutrients and their role in sporting performance.

The nutrition pyramid

The nutrition pyramid is a guide to how much of each food group or nutrient a performer should be eating.

The food groups towards the base of the pyramid represent the nutrients that should make up the majority of your diet (i.e. fresh fruit and vegetables and carbohydrate-rich foods), while those towards the top of the pyramid represent those nutrients that should be consumed in smaller quantities. Figure 2.04 identifies the types of food that fall into each group and gives an indication as to the amount that should be consumed in the athlete's diet.

The athlete's diet

While it is important that all performers have a balanced diet, there is not one all-encompassing diet that is appropriate for every performer. In fact runners, swimmers, cyclists and even gym enthusiasts will each have different dietary requirements. So diet plans need to be tailor-made to the exact requirements of the given sport or activity. In this section we will consider the difference in diet composition between endurance and power athletes in particular.

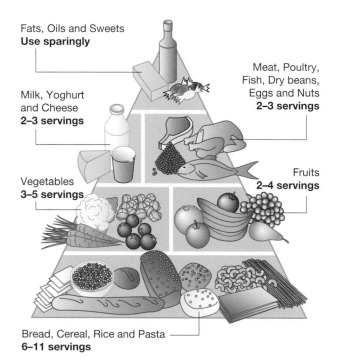

Fats, Oils and Sweets
Use sparingly

Meat, Poultry, Fish, Dry beans, Eggs and Nuts
2–3 servings

Milk, Yoghurt and Cheese
2–3 servings

Fruits
2–4 servings

Vegetables
3–5 servings

Bread, Cereal, Rice and Pasta
6–11 servings

Fig. 2.04 The food pyramid shows the recommended daily intake of nutrients

APPLY IT!

Most experts recommend an intake of 1.4–1.8g of protein per kg of body weight per day.

Nutrient	Sports-related role	Preferred sources
Fat	The preferred energy source during low intensity/ aerobic exercise. It is used in conjunction with glycogen	Meat, dairy products, olive and sunflower oil, avocados, nuts
Carbohydrate	Main energy source. Used in nearly all physical activity. Regular intake helps to build up and maintain glycogen stores	Pasta, rice, bread, potatoes, fruit
Protein	Helps repair and replace muscle tissue. Can provide some energy	Meat, fish, eggs, milk, cheese, nuts, pulses
Water	Helps to prevent dehydration	Water in drinks and foods and specialised sports drinks
Vitamins	Aids energy release and maintains a healthy immune system	Fresh fruit and vegetables, cereals, eggs, meat and fish
Minerals	Essential for muscle contraction, oxygen transport and helps in the exchange of nutrients into and out of the muscle cell	Fresh fruit and vegetables, cereals, eggs, meat and fish
Dietary fibre	Maintains health and vitality, maintains blood glucose levels	Fruit and vegetables, wholegrain cereals, nuts, pulses

Table 2.03 Essential nutrients and their role in sporting performance

Endurance performers

Endurance athletes, such as marathon runners, require many calories in order to sustain the volume of training they undertake. As with other athletes endurance performers need to follow a balanced diet but because of the extra calories burned each day endurance athletes in particular benefit from eating energy-rich, fuel-efficient complex carbohydrate meals which maintain levels of muscle glycogen. If muscle glycogen breakdown exceeds its replacement, glycogen stores become depleted. The result is fatigue and inability to maintain training and racing intensity. So in order to replenish and maintain glycogen stores, the endurance athlete's diet needs to be carbohydrate-rich. Carbohydrates should therefore make up 60–70 per cent of total calories.

Water is another essential nutrient of an endurance performer's diet. The marathon runner, for example, should drink a lot more than the 2–3 litres suggested for the typical adult. It is recommended that 15 minutes before training or competition performers drink 400–500ml, while during exercise they drink 150–200ml every 15–20 minutes. Fluid replacement should obviously continue during the recovery period. Sports drinks are often used by endurance performers during training and recovery to maintain blood glucose levels, replace lost fluids and electrolytes. This ensures optimum performance during the activity and facilitates recovery.

To aid the recovery process further and to ensure the endurance performer can keep up with the physically demanding training programme, approximately 10–15 per cent of his or her diet should be comprised of protein, which you will recall facilitates muscle (tissue) growth and repair.

The marathon runner not only has to think about what to eat and drink before the training run or competition, but also during and following it. Replacing your glycogen stores after a run is crucial if you want to train well the following day. The 'carbohydrate window' is the period of time after exercise when the muscles are most receptive to refuelling with glycogen. This typically occurs within the first 30 minutes of the cessation of exercise. Endurance athletes should therefore get into the habit of having a high carbohydrate drink or snack, which ideally also contains some protein, in order to speed up glycogen recovery.

TAKE IT FURTHER

Find out how and why some endurance performers follow a programme of carbohydrate (glycogen) loading. Critically evaluate the process by considering both the perceived benefits and arguments against following such a programme.

Power athletes

Power athletes, such as sprinters or javelin throwers, have different dietary requirements from those of endurance performers because their events rely mainly on speed, strength and power as opposed to cardiovascular and muscular endurance. Both protein and carbohydrates are key nutrients when planning the diet of the power performer. Carbohydrate remains the main energy provider to fuel the muscles during power-based training such as lifting weights. During an intense weight training session more than half of the stores of muscle glycogen can be depleted and needs to be replenished following the session. By eating plenty of carbohydrates muscle glycogen reserves are maintained and most of the protein consumed can

be focused on repairing and building new muscle tissue. If insufficient carbohydrate is consumed, glycogen stores will be depleted quickly and some protein will be required to meet the energy deficit and thus diverted away from building muscle.

During recovery periods between training, protein is introduced to muscle fibres, making the muscle fibres thicker and stronger. Protein is therefore a vital part of the power athlete's diet. Amino acids – the building blocks of protein – are used to repair the muscle fibres that have been damaged during the workout.

A word on protein supplementation

Assuming a well-balanced diet, protein supplementation should not be necessary for any athlete. However, supplements may be able to make up a protein shortfall in the diets of those athletes in heavy training or who are vegetarian. Protein or meal replacement shakes may also be useful for those who have trouble fitting regular meals into busy schedules.

TASK 2.02

1. Use a website, such as the English Institute of Sport (www.eis2win.co.uk), and research the dietary guidelines for a range of different performers.
2. Summarise the dietary advice given by the experts for both endurance and power performers before, during and after competition or training. Don't forget to consider the most important nutrient – water!

ATHLETE PROFILE

Undoubtedly a major consideration for athletes such as Stephanie Twell is their diet. There is no 'one-size-fits-all' diet. Every performer is different. Take Paula Radcliffe for instance: she has a wheat intolerance and so must avoid pasta and bread – common sources of carbohydrate for most athletes. Paula must, therefore, get her carbohydrates from other food sources. Whereas for Kelly Holmes a diet of lots of chicken, fish, vegetables and a plentiful supply of carbohydrates, such as rice, to fuel her body during the heavy training and competition season was normal. Stephanie Twell consumes anything from between 4 and 8 litres of water a day depending upon the volume of training she is undertaking. However, it is clear that elite performers more or less universally agree that eating little and often is far better for their lifestyle than eating three square meals a day.

The energy balance

Everybody has different energy needs which tend to be influenced by number of different factors such as:

- age
- sex
- build
- metabolic rate
- type of exercise
- frequency of exercise
- intensity of exercise.

The more vigorous the exercise you do, the greater the energy demands. Each unit of energy is represented by a calorie; the amount of heat required to raise 1g of water by 1°C.

As long as the number of calories consumed equals the number of calories burned, then the performer should maintain their body weight. This is referred to as a **neutral energy balance** and is the aim for most performers. If the number of calories consumed exceeds the number of calories expended then a **positive energy balance** occurs; weight is gained and fat stores increased. A **negative energy balance** occurs when less calories are consumed than expended. Energy stored as glycogen and fat can be used to make up the calorie deficiency causing a reduction in body fat, resulting in weight loss. Figure 2.05 illustrates the energy balance equation.

In most instances athletes will wish to keep their body weight stable, where energy input = energy output. Occasionally however, they may wish to increase or decrease their weight (for example, when wishing to make a weight category in Judo a player may need to restrict his/her caloric intake in the days leading up to the event) and so must make the necessary adjustments to their calorie intake and/or expenditure.

KEY TERM

Calorie:
a calorie is the amount of heat required to raise 1g of water by 1°C

REMEMBER!

The kilocalorie (kc), equivalent to 1000 calories, is often substituted for the calorie.

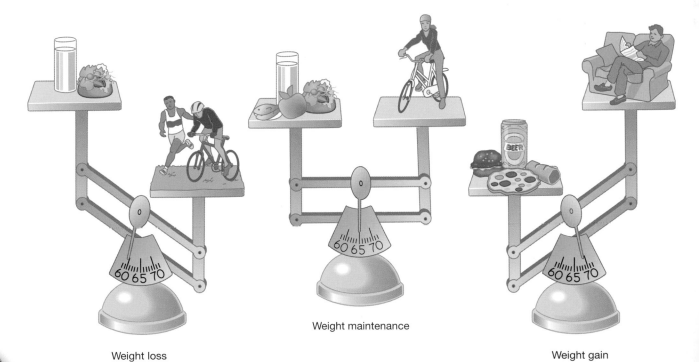

Weight maintenance

Weight loss

Weight gain

Fig. 2.05 The energy balance equation

Body composition

'The relative components of total body mass in terms of fat mass and lean body mass or fat-free mass.'

Body composition is concerned with ensuring that the performer has an appropriate percentage of lean body mass for their particular activity. Although each sport may have a slightly different requirement in terms of body composition, in general it is safe to say the less body fat, the better. Excess body fat is really dead weight that must be carried around, which is energy-inefficient. Lean body mass is much more desirable for those activities that require both cardiovascular and muscular endurance, such as distance running and rowing, since more oxygen can be directed to the working muscles. Ideal body fat percentages for males and females are 14–17 per cent and 24–29 per cent respectively.

The relative shape of the body or **somatotype** is also linked to body composition. Somatotyping, however, is more concerned with whether our body shape is suited to the activity that we are performing. For example, an ideal body shape for a high jumper is to be very tall and lean, while a male gymnast needs to be very muscular with broad shoulders and a narrow waist. A performer's body shape can be categorised according to three extreme somatotypes:

- **mesomorph:** wedge-shaped body, broad shoulders and narrow hips, very muscular with little body fat
- **endomorph:** pear-shaped body, wide hips with narrow shoulders, fat distributed around the stomach, thighs and upper arms
- **ectomorph:** narrow shoulders and hips, little muscle or fat.

In reality, everybody is part endomorph, part mesomorph and part ectomorph, but the relative contribution each makes to our body shape is very individual and differs from performer to performer.

Testing body composition

Tests designed to measure body composition include:

- skinfold measurement
- biolectric impedance
- hydrostatic weighing/densiometry
- body mass index (BMI).

 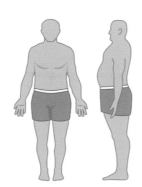 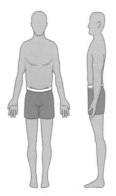

Extreme mesomorph   Extreme endomorph   Extreme ectomorph

Fig. 2.06 The three extreme somatotypes

Performing the skinfold measurement test	
Facilities and equipment needed	Calibrated skinfold callipers
Testing procedure	All measurements should be taken from the right-hand side of the body. The thickness of four skinfolds around the body are taken at: • triceps • biceps • subscapular • suprailiac spine. The tester pinches the skin and subcutaneous adipose tissue (being careful to avoid pinching any muscle) and applies the callipers 1cm below and at right angles to the pinch
Data collected	The sum of the found skinfold measurements in mm
Main strengths of the test	• Easy testing procedure • Little equipment needed • Scores can be used to identify changes in body fat over time
Main limitations of the test	• Does not convert into a percentage of body fat • Inaccuracies can occur in determining the exact site at which to perform the skinfold measurement • Pinching muscle tissue can distort the scores • It only considers subcutaneous fat
Validity of the test	Skinfold measurement can only predict the percentage of body fat and is therefore not particularly valid. However, some studies have shown a standard error of measurement +/− 3.5 per cent when compared to other methods of determining body fat percentage
Reliability of the test	Measurements can vary from tester to tester. Assuming the same person is carrying out the test each time, it can be reliable

Table 2.04 Skinfold measurement

TASK 2.03

True somatotypes are rare. In reality, we are a mixture of all three. Copy out the delta graph and place the listed sporting activities on the graph:
• high jumper
• male gymnast
• weightlifter
• basketball player
• distance runner
• sumo wrestler.

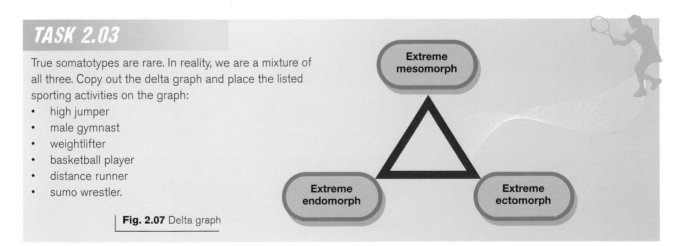

Fig. 2.07 Delta graph

Name of test	Brief description of the test	Strengths of the test	Limitations of the test	Validity of the test	Reliability of the test
Biolectric impedance	A small electrical current is passed through the body. Since fat offers greater resistance to the flow of the electrical current, it can be predicted that the greater the current needed, the greater the percentage of body fat	This test gives accurate predictions of body fat percentage	Equipment can be expensive (although it is getting cheaper)	Validity correlations are quite high when compared to hydrostatic weighing	Reliability is high if laboratory equipment is used. However, cheaper handheld 'home' devices can give distorted readings
Hydrostatic weighing (densiometry)	The body is submerged in water. By dividing the body mass of the subject by the volume of water displaced when immersed, body density can be calculated: $$\text{Body density} = \frac{\text{Mass}}{\text{Volume}}$$ Body density can be used to predict the body fat percentage. (NB Air trapped in the airways and intestines must be accounted for.) The body weighs less in water than out of water because fat floats. A large amount of fat mass will make the body lighter in water. The greater the difference between weight in water and weight out of water, the higher the percentage of body fat	This test gives accurate predictions of body fat percentage	• Can normally only be performed in a laboratory so it is not very practical • Some performers may suffer anxiety from being immersed in water	This is considered to be one of the most accurate measures of the percentage of body fat of the performer	Reliability is high due to the objective nature of this assessment
Body mass index (BMI)	A simple calculation is performed: $$BMI = \frac{\text{Weight in kg}}{(\text{Height in m})^2}$$	A simple calculation to perform	Does not consider lean body mass – just total body mass	Very poor validity as it only considers total body mass. No distinction is made between fat mass and lean body mass	High reliability. The calculation should come up with the same result all the time assuming no change in height or body mass

Table 2.05 Other tests of body composition

TASK 2.04

1. Calculate your body mass index (BMI).
2. Compare your result to those of the rest of your group.
3. Comment upon your findings.

Obesity

Obesity can be defined as: **'an accumulation of excess body fat to an extent that may impair health'.**

A person is classed as being overweight if they have a body mass index (BMI) of 25 or more, and obese with a BMI of 30 or more. We must however be a little careful of using BMI as an indicator of obesity as it fails to take account of lean body mass. It is possible therefore for a muscular, healthy individual with low body fat to be classed as obese using the BMI formula.

Over 30,000 deaths per year in England alone can be attributed to obesity and its associated health problems. In the last 25 years adult obesity rates have quadrupled with 23 per cent now being classified as obese and 40 per cent overweight. This pattern is repeated when we consider children. The number of obese children has increased three-fold over the past 20 years. Now 10 per cent of 6-year-olds and 17 per cent of 15-year-olds are obese.

Fig. 2.08 A performer, such as a weightlifter, can be classed as obese as the BMI fails to take account of lean body mass

REMEMBER!

A person is classified as obese with a BMI of 30+.

Causes of obesity

- **Over-consumption** – The average portion size has increased significantly over the past quarter century, which when coupled with the individual eating foodstuffs packed with calories (i.e. those composed of fat and refined sugar) contributes significantly to the onset of obesity.

- **Reduced energy expenditure/exercise** – We lead a much more sedentary lifestyle today than 20 years ago. The service industry has taken over from more active jobs in agriculture and manufacturing. The number of children who walk or cycle to school has reduced considerably over the past 20 years. Playing fields have been sold off to developers and built upon and the sedentary nature of computer games has also meant that playing a virtual game of football has superseded playing the game for real.

- **The imbalance between calorie intake and calorie expenditure** – When calorie intake is greater than calorie output or expenditure then a positive energy balance is created, where weight is gained and fat stores increased.

- **Eating a poor diet** – Consuming food high in fat, refined sugar and salt (commonly referred to as junk food) is certainly a contributory factor in the obesity epidemic!

- **Genetic causes** – For the minority of obese individuals heredity factors may be a contributory cause. However, the very rapid growth in obesity over the past 20 or so years would suggest that genetics cannot be a significant factor.

- **Socio-economic factors** – The incidence of obesity is greatest in low income groups. This could be due to a number of economic factors such as the higher costs associated with healthy eating and the costs linked to participation in physical activity.

Fig. 2.09 Consumption of junk food high in fat and refined sugars contributes to the onset of obesity

Associated health risks of obesity

Obesity is considered a chronic disease. It has many serious long-term consequences and is a rapidly growing problem for the UK health service.

In particular, obesity is associated with increased risk of:

- coronary heart disease (CHD), angina and heart attacks
- vascular diseases such as high blood pressure (hypertension) and varicose veins
- strokes
- diabetes
- osteoarthritis
- some cancers such as colon cancer
- psychological disorders such as depression.

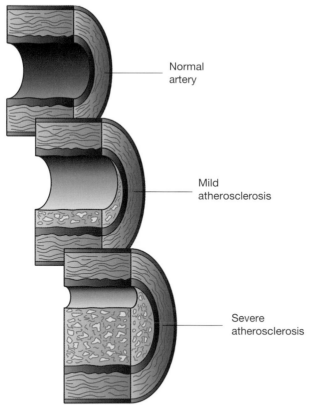

Normal artery

Mild atherosclerosis

Severe atherosclerosis

Fig. 2.10 How poor nutrition can lead to cardiovascular diseases such as atherosclerosis

TASK 2.05

Find out a little more about each of the above health conditions associated with obesity.

HOT LINKS

Use a website such as that of The British Heart Foundation (www.bhf.org.uk) and summarise key points of advice on how to maintain a healthy heart and prevent many of the health risks associated with obesity.

TAKE IT FURTHER

Design a health promotion leaflet that outlines the dangers of obesity and gives suggestions for leading a more active lifestyle.

Preventing obesity

Society, and parents in particular, have an important role to play in the prevention of obesity.

The number of fat cells in the body are determined only during infancy (0–2 yrs) and during puberty. The number formed during this time appears to depend upon our eating habits. Eating a lot of junk food during these critical childhood years will cause the number of fat cells to proliferate and grow rapidly. Once fat cells have been produced in the body we cannot get rid of them, furthermore they are likely to increase in size as we get older. This is why overweight children tend to turn into overweight or obese adults. As the number of fat cells are only formed during these critical years it is important to keep them to a minimum by following a healthy diet and maintaining a neutral energy balance. It is essential of course to couple a healthy diet with an appropriate exercise regime. Recently the government has increased the minimum time requirement of physical education in schools to two hours per week. The long-term ambition, by 2010, is to offer all children at least four hours of sport every week, made up of:

- at least two hours of high-quality PE and sport at schools – with the expectation that this will be delivered totally within the curriculum; and
- an additional two or more hours beyond the school day delivered by a range of school, community and club providers.

At home children should be encouraged to take up more physical activity, such as cycling.

Fig. 2.11 Physical activity can go some way to preventing obesity

TASK 2.06

1. What general nutritional advice would you give to an obese adult who wished to lose weight?
2. From what you have learned in Chapter 1, and with reference to information contained in Chapter 6, prescribe a 6-week exercise programme for an obese adult.
   a) What factors do you need to consider in preparing the programme?
   b) How would you apply the principles of training?
   c) State the type of exercises you would include and give reasons for your choices.

APPLY IT!

Childhood obesity is rising at an alarming rate in the UK. The Carnegie summer fat camp was first set up in Leeds in1999 in an attempt to slow down the incidence of obesity in children. It aims to provide children with a number of skills to enable them to achieve a permanent change in their lifestyle. This is achieved by teaching the child about the role of exercise and portion control, as well as providing a sensible low fat diet. The programme seems to have been a terrific success, as of the 40 teenagers who took part in the first fat camp, 85 per cent maintained their weight loss long after leaving.

Refresh your memory

Revision checklist

Make sure you know the following:

▷ There are seven components of a healthy diet: carbohydrates, fats, proteins, vitamins, minerals, dietary fibre and water

▷ Carbohydrates, fats and proteins are the energy providers and are termed macronutrients

▷ Vitamins and minerals are termed micronutrients

▷ Carbohydrates are stored in the muscles and liver as glycogen

▷ In total, the body is only able to store about 450g of glycogen, which equates to approximately 90 minutes worth of exercise

▷ The glycaemic index is a measure of the effect different foods have on blood glucose; foods with a high GI provide a rapid surge in blood glucose while those with a low GI provide a steady release of glucose into the blood over a longer period of time

▷ The primary function of carbohydrates is to provide energy. They are also vital for the effective functioning of the nervous system

▷ Fats in the body are stored as triglycerides which break down into free fatty acids. Energy is then released through the oxidation of the free fatty acids

▷ Foods high in monounsaturated and polyunsaturated fats are preferable to those high in saturated fat

▷ Fats are the main energy for the body at rest and during light to moderate exercise. They also help to protect our organs and keep us warm when we are exercising in warm environments

▷ Proteins are found in meat, fish and beans and are predominantly used in the body for the growth and repair of tissues and cells

- ▷ Proteins provide the amino acids necessary for the manufacture of enzymes, hormones and the oxygen transporters, haemoglobin and myoglobin

- ▷ Vitamins form components of enzymes which help to release the energy from the food we consume

- ▷ Most of the vitamins we need can only come from the food we eat. Good sources of vitamins include fresh fruit and vegetables, eggs, fish and meat

- ▷ Vitamin supplementation should not really be necessary given the consumption of a healthy balanced diet

- ▷ Minerals are vital for effective cell functioning and have a wide range of roles

- ▷ Calcium contributes to bone density; phosphorous is an essential component of our energy currency ATP; iron is a significant component of haemoglobin and myoglobin – our oxygen transporters; sodium, potassium and chlorine form electrolytes which help in the exchange of nutrients and waste products

- ▷ Water is crucial for effective sports performance as it is the main constituent of blood plasma and helps in the regulation of the body's temperature

- ▷ Dehydration of as little as 2 per cent of a performer's body weight can impair performance by up to 10–20 per cent

- ▷ The best rehydrater is water itself, which is easily absorbed into the blood stream

- ▷ Fibre helps the digestive system to function properly by absorbing water and helping the passage of food through the gut

- ▷ A balanced diet should include all seven nutrients. The composition of a balanced diet can be further illustrated by a nutrition pyramid

- ▷ The dietary requirements of different sports performers is dependent upon the specific characteristics of each activity. For example, endurance performers should have a carbohydrate-rich diet. However, power athletes should ensure that, in addition to a high carbohydrate intake, they also consume sufficient protein to aid the growth and repair of tissues and cells

- The energy balance considers the level of energy input versus energy expenditure. The energy balance can be positive, negative or neutral

- In most instances athletes will wish to keep their body weight stable and so favour a neutral energy balance where energy input = energy output

- Body composition is the relative components of total body mass in terms of fat mass and lean body mass or fat-free mass

- Body composition can determine the relative shape of the body known as somatotype

- Obesity is the accumulation of excess body fat to an extent that may impair health

- A person is classed as obese when the body mass index (BMI) exceeds 30

- There are many factors that can contribute to obesity, but the key factor is the imbalance between calorie intake and calorie expenditure

- Obesity can lead to a number of associated health risks including coronary heart disease (CHD), vascular diseases and diabetes

- Society needs to take an active role in preventing obesity. We need to put an end to poor eating habits and more physical activity should be encouraged both at home and at school

Revise as you go

1. Name the seven categories of nutrient.

2. Outline the three types of macronutrient and explain the specific exercise-related function of each.

3. Explain the exercise-related functions of vitamins and minerals.

4. Explain what is meant by glycogen and explain why this is beneficial to the endurance performer.

5. Discuss the value of using protein supplements to enhance performance in both power-based and endurance-based activity.

6. What nutritional advice would you give to a marathon runner regarding dietary manipulation in the run up to a competition?

7. Why is remaining hydrated so important to the sports performer?

8. Critically evaluate the use of the body mass index (BMI) as a measure of obesity.

9. Outline the main causes of obesity.

10. What advice would you give to a group of overweight children in an attempt to prevent them from becoming obese?

CHAPTER 3

The respiratory system

– pulmonary function and gaseous exchange

LEARNING OBJECTIVES:

By the end of this chapter you should be able to:

▶ describe the structure and function of the respiratory system

▶ explain the mechanics of breathing during a) inspiration and b) expiration, making reference to the different respiratory muscles involved

▶ give definitions and values for the major respiratory volumes and capacities at rest and during exercise

▶ interpret a spirometer trace

▶ explain the principles of diffusion and the importance of partial pressure in the process of gaseous exchange

▶ describe the process of gaseous exchange at a) the lungs and b) the tissues and muscles

▶ describe the effects of training on lung volumes and capacities and gaseous exchange

▶ explain the importance of carbon dioxide in the control of breathing

▶ explain what is meant by the arterial venous oxygen difference (a-vO$_2$ diff) and state how it differs during exercise from resting values.

Introduction

Successful endurance performance requires the delivery of sufficient oxygen to our muscles to produce the energy which fuels muscle contraction. At the same time, carbon dioxide produced by the muscles must be cleared and removed from the body. The primary function of the respiratory system is therefore to bring oxygen into our bodies so it can be delivered to our muscles and tissues, and to rid us of excess carbon dioxide. It has a dual function of supplying essential nutrients to the working muscles yet also being a waste disposal system.

EXAM TIP:

You must be able to show an understanding of the very close relationship and interaction of the cardiovascular and respiratory system in your examination.

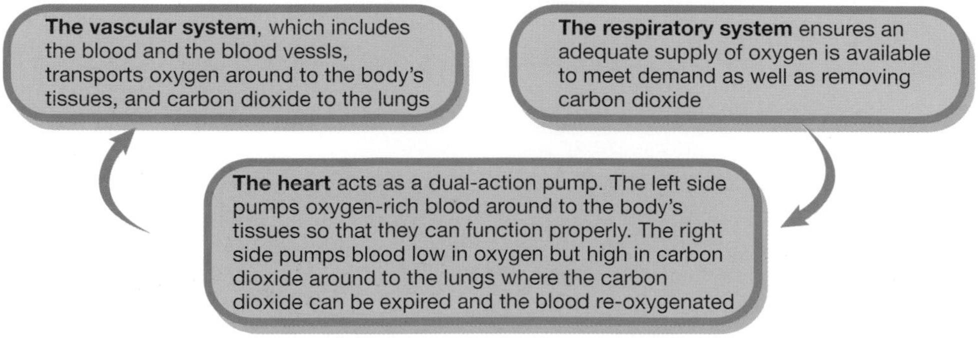

The vascular system, which includes the blood and the blood vessls, transports oxygen around to the body's tissues, and carbon dioxide to the lungs

The respiratory system ensures an adequate supply of oxygen is available to meet demand as well as removing carbon dioxide

The heart acts as a dual-action pump. The left side pumps oxygen-rich blood around to the body's tissues so that they can function properly. The right side pumps blood low in oxygen but high in carbon dioxide around to the lungs where the carbon dioxide can be expired and the blood re-oxygenated

Fig. 3.01 The interaction of the cardiovascular and respiratory systems

The structure of the respiratory system

Figure 3.02 shows the main structures of the respiratory system.

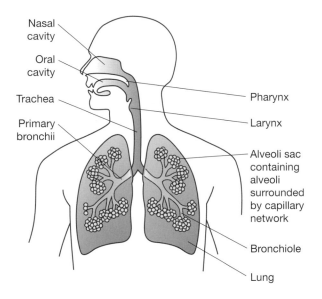

Nasal cavity

Oral cavity

Trachea

Primary bronchii

Pharynx

Larynx

Alveoli sac containing alveoli surrounded by capillary network

Bronchiole

Lung

Fig. 3.02 The structures of the respiratory system

TASK 3.01

1. Describe how the structure of the lungs is adapted to absorb oxygen.
2. Describe the pathway taken by a molecule of oxygen as it passes from the atmosphere to the blood in the lungs.

The mechanics of breathing

Inspiration

Inspiration, or breathing in, is an active process that requires the contraction of certain muscles. The **external intercostal muscles**, which lie between each pair of ribs, contract during inspiration, causing the ribcage to move upwards and outwards. At the same time, the **diaphragm**, which forms the floor of the thoracic cavity, contracts downwards and flattens. These actions together cause an overall increase in the size of the thoracic cavity and therefore a decrease in the pressure within the lungs (since the pressure of a given volume of gas is created by the number of molecules of gas present and the size of the area they occupy). In fact, the pressure within the lungs during inspiration falls below the external or atmospheric pressure, and since gases will always move from areas of high pressure to areas of low pressure, air is drawn into the lungs.

During exercise, when the rate and depth of breathing increase, inspiration is aided by certain accessory muscles, which include the **sternocleidomastoid**, the **scalenes** and the **pectoralis minor** (see Fig. 3.04).

Expiration

Expiration, or breathing out, during normal quiet breathing is a passive process since no muscular contractions are involved. It depends upon two factors:

1. the elastic recoil of the lungs and thoracic tissues
2. the relaxation of the inspiratory muscles, i.e. the external intercostal muscles and the diaphragm.

As the external intercostal muscles relax, the ribcage moves downwards and inwards, taking up its original position, while the diaphragm relaxes into its resting dome shape. These movements decrease the size of the thoracic cavity, increasing the pressure within the lungs so that it becomes greater than external or atmospheric pressure. Once again, because gases will move from an area of high pressure to an area of low pressure, air is forced out of the lungs.

Expiration becomes active, however, during exercise, when breathing rates are increased. In this instance, expiration is aided by the **internal intercostal muscles** and the abdominal muscles, which pull the ribcage down more quickly and with greater force. Table 3.01 summarises the respiratory muscles used at rest and during exercise (Figures 3.03 and 3.04).

	Rest	Exercise
Inspiration	Contraction of external intercostal muscles and diaphragm	Contraction of external intercostal muscles, diaphragm, sternocleidomastoid, scalenes and pectoralis minor
Expiration	Relaxation of external intercostal muscles and diaphragm	Contraction of internal intercostal muscles and abdominals

Table 3.01 Respiratory muscles used at rest and during exercise

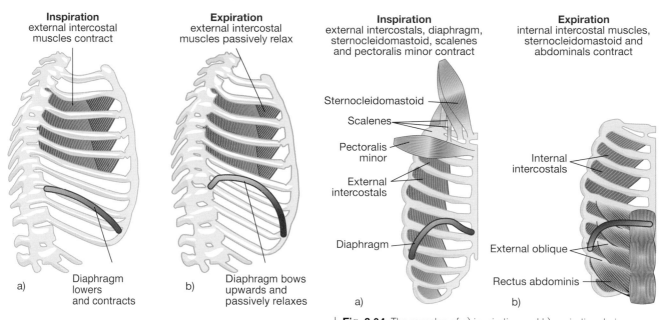

Fig. 3.03 The muscles of a) inspiration and b) expiration at rest

Fig. 3.04 The muscles of a) inspiration and b) expiration during exercise

TASK 3.02

1. Place the following stages in the correct order to describe the mechanics of inspiration.
   - Thoracic cavity volume increases.
   - Diaphragm and external intercostal muscles contract.
   - Air rushes into the lungs.
   - Pressure within the lungs becomes lower than atmospheric air outside the body.
   - Diaphragm flattens while the ribcage moves upwards and outwards.
2. Place the following stages in the correct order to describe the mechanics of expiration during exercise.
   - Diaphragm pushed upwards while the ribcage moves inwards and downwards.
   - Air is forced out of the lungs.
   - Thoracic cavity volume decreases.
   - Pressure inside the lungs increases above that of atmospheric pressure outside the lungs.
   - Internal intercostal muscles contract, along with the abdominals.

EXAM TIP:

For your examination, you may be asked to describe the path an oxygen molecule takes on its journey into the blood stream, stating what respiratory structures it passes through.

EXAM TIP:

For your examination, make sure you know the muscles of respiration at rest and during exercise.

Lung volumes and capacities

Lung volumes

The process of inspiration and expiration causes volumes of air to enter and leave the lungs. These volumes of air vary depending upon the size, height, health and sex of an individual, and the values can alter significantly from rest to exercise. Below is an explanation of each of the lung volumes that you need to know for your examination. Make sure you can give a definition of each, as well as an approximate value at rest and how they change during exercise. This is shown in Table 3.02.

APPLY IT!

To help you understand the different lung volumes, have a go at the following activity.
1. Breathe in as you would normally during normal resting conditions. The volume of air you have just inspired is known as the **tidal volume** and equates to approximately 500ml.
2. Now breathe out as you would normally (you have just expelled $500cm^3$/ml or your tidal volume), but before you breathe in again, try to force all the remaining air out of your lungs. This extra volume of air that you have just expired is known as the **expiratory reserve volume** and can measure as much as 1200ml.
3. Now breathe in once more as you did in step 1, but before you breathe out again, continue to breathe in until you have completely filled your lungs. This extra volume of inspired air over and above your tidal volume is known as your **inspiratory reserve volume** and can reach values of 3100ml.
One other volume that you need to be aware of is the **residual volume**. This is about 1200ml of air that remains in the lungs following maximal expiration to prevent the lungs from collapsing. Unlike the other lung volumes, this does not change during exercise.

EXAM TIP:

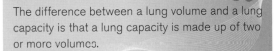

The difference between a lung volume and a lung capacity is that a lung capacity is made up of two or more volumes.

Lung volume or capacity	Definition	Typical value at rest	Change during exercise
Tidal volume (TV)	Volume inspired or expired per breath	500ml	Increase
Inspiratory reserve volume (IRV)	Maximal volume inspired following end of resting inspiration	3100ml	Decrease
Expiratory reserve volume (ERV)	Maximal volume expired following end of resting expiration	1200ml	Decrease
Residual volume (RV) TLC − VC	Volume of air remaining in the lungs at the end of maximal expiration	1200ml	Remains the same
Inspiratory capacity (IC) TV + IRV	Maximum volume of air inspired from resting expiratory levels	3600ml	Increase
Vital capacity (VC) IRV + TV + ERV	The maximum volume of air forcibly expired following maximal inspiration	5000 ml	Slight decrease
Total lung capacity (TLC) VC + RV	The volume of air that is in the lungs following maximal inspiration	6000ml	Slight decrease
Minute ventilation (VE) TV x f	The volume of air inspired or expired per minute	7500ml	Dramatic increase

Table 3.02 Definitions of lung volumes and capacities, showing typical resting values and changes that occur during exercise

Lung capacities

Lung capacities result from adding two or more lung volumes together. For example, the **inspiratory capacity** is the sum of tidal volume and inspiratory reserve volume (IC = TV + IRV) and is equal to approximately 3600ml. **Vital capacity** is the sum of the inspiratory reserve volume, tidal volume and the expiratory reserve volume (VC = IRV + TV + ERV) and is typically about 5000ml of air. Essentially, your vital capacity is the maximum amount of air that you can breathe in and out during one inspiration and expiration. One final capacity is the **total lung capacity**, which is basically the sum of all the lung volumes: inspiratory reserve volume, tidal volume, expiratory reserve volume, and residual volume (TLC = IRV + TV + ERV + RV). Total lung capacity averages between 5000ml to 6000ml but generally varies between individuals depending upon their size, height, health and sex.

TAKE IT FURTHER

Free divers such as Tom Sietas can often remain underwater for as long as 9 minutes. What physiological reasons could possibly explain this?

TASK 3.03

Do the following lung volumes increase, decrease or remain the same during exercise?
a) Tidal volume
b) Inspiratory reserve volume
c) Expiratory reserve volume.

Lung volumes and capacities of individuals are easily measured using an instrument called a **spirometer**. A spirometer produces a chart known as a spirometer trace that clearly identifies the performer's lung function. An example of a trace is shown in Figure 3.05.

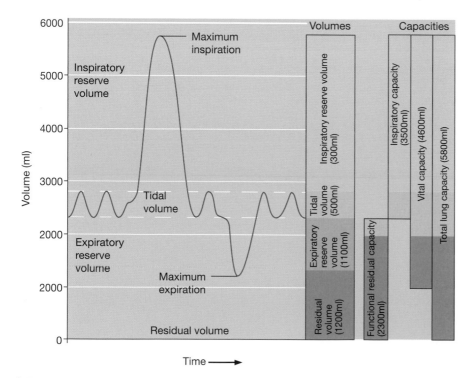

Fig. 3.05 A spirometer trace showing respiratory volumes and capacities

EXAM TIP:

You will need to be able to identify each lung volume and capacity labelled on the spirometer trace for your examination.

TASK 3.04

In the spirometer shown in Figure 3.06, a person breathes through a tube connected to an oxygen-containing chamber that floats on a tank of water. The chamber falls during inhalation and rises during exhalation. A container of soda lime is used to absorb all the carbon dioxide in the exhaled air.

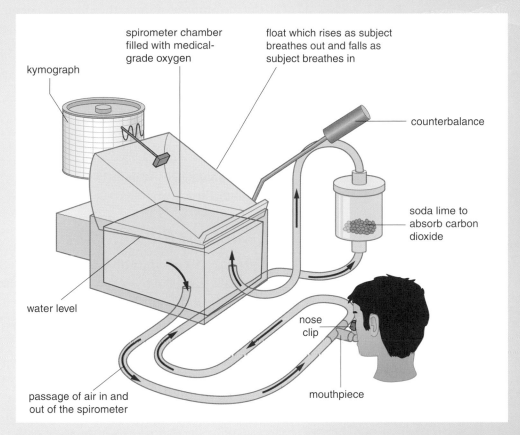

kymograph

spirometer chamber filled with medical-grade oxygen

float which rises as subject breathes out and falls as subject breathes in

counterbalance

soda lime to absorb carbon dioxide

water level

nose clip

passage of air in and out of the spirometer

mouthpiece

Fig. 3.06 A spirometer

1. Record the weight and height of your subject.
2. Ensure that the spirometer is set up and calibrated correctly.
3. Sit the subject down and place the clean mouthpiece in the subject's mouth, and clip on the nose clip. Leave the two-way tap closed for the time being.
4. When ready to proceed, open the tap just as the subject is finishing exhaling normally.
5. Instruct the subject to breathe normally for about a minute or so.
6. After a minute of normal breathing, instruct the subject to breathe in as deeply as possible and then resume normal breathing.
7. After three or four more breaths, ask the subject to breathe out as much as possible and then to resume normal breathing for a minute or so.
8. Remove the spirometer trace and label the following:
   a) tidal volume (TV)
   b) inspiratory reserve volume (IRV)
   c) expiratory reserve volume (ERV)
   d) vital capacity (VC).
9. From the spirometer trace, calculate the following volumes:
   a) tidal volume (TV)
   b) inspiratory reserve volume (IRV)
   c) expiratory reserve volume (ERV).
10. What is the subject's vital capacity?
11. Estimate the total lung capacity of the subject.
    Hint: A reasonably accurate method of estimating the total lung capacity is to multiply the expiratory reserve volume by six.
12. Now calculate the subject's residual volume (TLC − VC).

TAKE IT FURTHER

Collate all of the data collected by the rest of your group and record the sport or activity that each subject participates in most often. Investigate whether there is any correlation between lung volumes and selected sport or activity.

TASK 3.05

Figure 3.07 shows a spirometer trace. Copy out the trace.

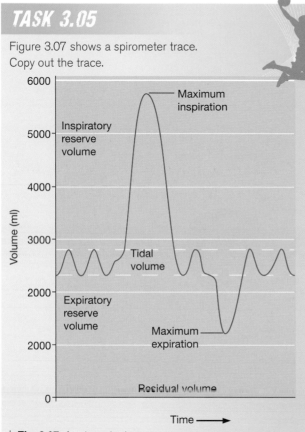

Fig. 3.07 A spirometer trace

1. On your spirometer trace, draw a line to show what would happen to tidal volume if the subject commenced exercise.
2. Write down what happens to:
   a) tidal volume
   b) inspiratory reserve volume
   c) expiratory reserve volume.

Minute ventilation

Minute ventilation (VE), or minute volume, is the volume of air breathed in **or** out per minute. It is calculated by multiplying a person's tidal volume (TV) by the number of times they breathe per minute or breathing rate (f). At rest, based on average figures for tidal volume and breathing rate, this will be:

Minute ventilation (VE)	=	Tidal volume (TV)	×	Breathing rate (f)
	=	500ml	×	15
	=	7500ml/min (7.5l/min)		

However, minute ventilation will increase significantly during exercise.

Ventilation during exercise

During exercise, both the rate (frequency) and depth (tidal volume) of breathing increases in direct proportion to the intensity of the activity. This is in order to satisfy the demand by the working muscles for oxygen and to remove the carbon dioxide and **lactic acid** that has been produced as a consequence of **tissue respiration**. Tidal volume increases by utilising both the inspiratory and expiratory reserve volumes – consequently, both these volumes decrease during exercise.

The tidal volume, however, increases its usage of the overall vital capacity six-fold from about 10 per cent at rest to 60 per cent during exercise. It is not energy-efficient for tidal volume to utilise 100 per cent of the vital capacity during exercise as this will substantially increase oxygen demand of the respiratory muscles.

KEY TERMS

Lactic acid:
a substance formed when insufficient oxygen is available to meet the demands of the exercise. It can cause muscle fatigue if it is allowed to accumulate

Tissue respiration:
the process of energy creation through the oxidation of food fuels. It produces energy, carbon dioxide and water

The spirometer trace you completed in Task 3.05 illustrates the increase in tidal volume and the subsequent decrease in both inspiratory and expiratory reserve volumes during exercise.

Minute ventilation (VE) during exercise therefore increases dramatically – up to 20 or 30 times resting values:

Minute ventilation (VE)	=	Tidal volume (TV)	×	Breathing rate (f)
	=	3000ml	×	50
	=	150,000ml/min (150l/min)		

Figures 3.08a and 3.08b compare the changes in minute ventilation (VE) during sub-maximal (low intensity) and maximal (high intensity) exercise. In your exam, you may be required to explain the patterns of the two graphs, so take a few moments now to study them both.

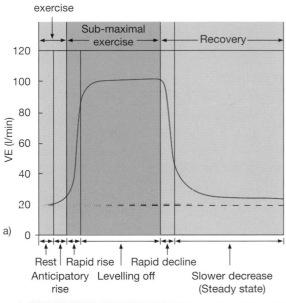

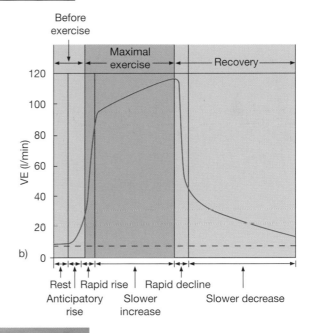

Fig. 3.08 Minute ventilation response to a) sub-maximal exercise, such as an athlete running and b) maximal exercise, such as a speed cyclist

TASK 3.06

1. Write down the equation used to calculate minute ventilation.
2. Calculate the minute ventilation of an athlete at rest assuming she has a tidal volume of 500ml and a respiration rate of fourteen breaths per minute.
3. Now calculate the tidal volume of the same athlete during maximal exercise where her minute ventilation is 125,000ml/min and her respiration rate is 50 breaths per minute.

EXAM TIP:

The units of pressure are millimetres of mercury (mmHg) and sometimes you may see pressure measured as kilopascals (kPa)

Gaseous exchange – the exchange of respiratory gases

You should now understand how inspiration and expiration move air into and out of the body, but more importantly, you need to discover how oxygen and carbon dioxide are actually exchanged.

There are two sites for gaseous exchange in the body:

1. between the air in the **alveoli** of the lungs and the blood in the surrounding alveolar capillaries
2. between the tissues/muscles of the body and the surrounding blood capillaries.

To fully understand the process of gaseous exchange, you need to know a little about pressures of gases or partial pressures.

Partial pressures

Each gas that exists within a mixture of gases has its own pressure that it exerts, and it behaves as if no other gas is present. The **partial** (part) **pressure (p)** of a gas is therefore the pressure that is exerted by the individual gas when it exists within a mixture of gases. The gas will exert a pressure that is proportional to its concentration within the whole gas. For example:

atmospheric pressure is composed of three main gases: nitrogen (approximately 79 per cent), oxygen (approximately 21 per cent) and carbon dioxide (approximately 0.03 per cent). Together they exert a pressure of 760mmHg:

$$\text{Atmospheric pressure (760mmHg)} = pN_2 + pO_2 + pCO_2$$

KEY TERMS

Partial pressure (p):
the pressure that is exerted by an individual gas when it exists within a mixture of gases

Diffusion:
the movement of gases from a higher partial pressure to a lower partial pressure until equilibrium is reached. The difference in high and lower partial pressure creates a pressure or diffusion gradient. The larger the gradient, the greater the diffusion

Alveolus (alveoli)
a tiny air sac in the lungs

ATHLETE PROFILE

In 2008 Oxford beat Cambridge in the University Boat Race by 16 seconds, the equivalent of six boat lengths. The crew no doubt put this down to the high volume and intensity of training they did in preparation for the competition. As part of their training, however, the crew incorporated inspiratory muscle training into their daily training routine. The breathing trainer is a handheld respiratory muscle trainer which you breathe through for a few minutes twice a day. It is a form of resistance training and, just like all other methods of resistance training, the respiratory muscles adapt to the increased resistance by increasing in strength. This is thought to increase lung volumes and capacities, allowing more oxygen to enter the body and more effective removal of waste products.

	Atmospheric air (sea level)	Alveolar air	Deoxygenated blood	Oxygenated blood	Muscle cells
pO_2	160mmHg	105mmHg	40mmHg	105mmHg	40mmHg
pCO_2	0.3mmHg	40mmHg	45mmHg	40mmHg	45mmHg

Table 3.03 Partial pressures of oxygen and carbon dioxide in atmospheric air, alveolar air, blood and muscle cells

If we want to find out the pressure exerted by an individual gas and we know its fractional concentration, then we only need to perform a simple calculation. Using the above example, if we want to calculate the partial pressure of oxygen within the atmosphere, then we would perform the following calculation:

Partial pressure of gas (p)	=	Barometric pressure	×	Fractional concentration
pO_2	=	760mmHg	×	0.21
pO_2	=	159.6mmHg		

So why is a knowledge of partial pressure so important? You will recall that gases move from areas of high pressure to areas of low pressure.

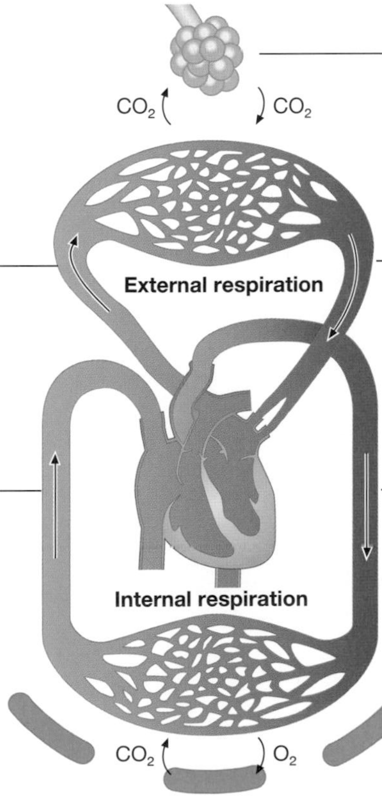

Knowledge of the partial pressures of oxygen and carbon dioxide at various sites of the body will explain the movement or **diffusion** of these two gases either into and out of the blood at the alveoli or into and out of the muscle tissue.

Gaseous exchange at the alveoli (external respiration)

Gaseous exchange at the alveoli involves the movement of oxygen and carbon dioxide between the alveoli of the lungs and the surrounding alveolar capillaries. The object of this exchange is quite simply to convert deoxygenated blood returning from the body into oxygenated blood. As blood circulates through the alveolar capillaries, oxygen is picked up from the alveoli and carbon dioxide is lost to them so that it can be expired.

Blood entering the alveolar capillaries has a low partial pressure of oxygen (40mmHg) when compared to that of alveoli (105mmHg) (Fig. 3.09). Consequently, a diffusion gradient of 65mmHg is created (105mmHg–40mmHg), causing oxygen to diffuse from the alveoli into the capillary blood. This process continues until the pressure on both sides of the respiratory membrane is equal. In the meantime, the partial pressure of carbon dioxide within the blood entering alveolar capillaries is relatively high (45mmHg) when compared to that in the alveoli

Atmospheric air
$pO_2 = 159$
$pCO_2 = 0.3$

CO_2 CO_2

External respiration

1 Alveolar air
$pO_2 = 105$
$pCO_2 = 40$

6 Pulmonary arteries
$pO_2 = 40$
$pCO_2 = 46$

2 Pulmonary veins
$pO_2 = 100$
$pCO_2 = 40$

5 Systemic veins
$pO_2 = 40$
$pCO_2 = 46$

3 Systemic arteries
$pO_2 = 100$
$pCO_2 = 40$

Internal respiration

CO_2 O_2

4 Tissues
$pO_2 = 40$
$pCO_2 = 46$

Fig. 3.09 Partial pressures of oxygen and carbon dioxide at various sites around the body

(40mmHg). Once again, a diffusion gradient of 5mmHg is created (45mmHg–40mmHg), enabling carbon dioxide to diffuse from the capillary blood into the alveoli until the pressure on both sides of the respiratory membrane, once again, becomes equal.

Diffusion of gases at the alveoli (Fig. 3.10) is facilitated by several structural features of the respiratory system:

- the respiratory (alveolar capillary) membrane is very thin, which means that the diffusion distance between the air in the alveoli and the blood is very short
- the numerous alveoli create a very large surface area over which diffusion can take place
- the alveoli are surrounded by a vast network of capillaries, which further provides a huge surface area for gaseous exchange
- the diameter of the capillaries is slightly narrower than the area of a red blood cell. This has two effects: a) it causes the shape of the red blood cell to become slightly distorted, increasing its surface area, and b) it forces the blood cells to flow through the capillary slowly in single file. Both these factors maximise the exposure that the red blood cell has to oxygen.

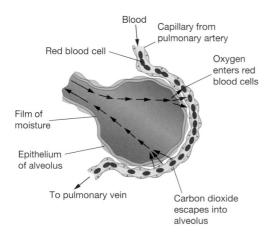

Fig. 3.10 Diffusion of gases in an alveolus

HOT LINKS

To view an animation of the diffusion process visit www.coolschool.ca/lor/BI12/unit4/U04L03/diffusion.swf

TASK 3.07

Name four factors that influence the rate of gaseous diffusion across the respiratory membrane in the alveoli.

TAKE IT FURTHER

Using websites such as www.quit-smoking-stop.com and www.asthma.org.uk, research the effects that smoking and respiratory complications, such as asthma, have on lung function. What advice might you give to an asthmatic child who was keen to participate fully in sporting activity?

Gaseous exchange at the tissues (internal respiration)

You should recall that gaseous exchange at the lungs was determined by the relative partial pressures of oxygen and carbon dioxide. Similarly, gaseous exchange at the tissues is governed by the partial pressure gradients of these two respiratory gases. At the tissue–capillary membranes surrounding the muscles, the pO_2 in the capillary (105mmHg) is greater than that in the tissues (40mmHg), therefore oxygen diffuses from the blood into the muscle tissue along a diffusion gradient of 65mmHg, until equilibrium is reached. Conversely, the pCO_2 in the tissues (45mmHg) is higher than that in the capillary blood (40mmHg), causing movement of carbon dioxide from the muscle into the bloodstream.

There are several factors that make gaseous exchange so effective at the muscles and tissues:

- the diffusion gradient along which oxygen travels from the blood into the muscle cell is relatively large (65mmHg)
- myoglobin within the muscle cell has a much higher affinity for oxygen than haemoglobin and therefore attracts oxygen to it
- the diameter of the capillaries is very narrow which forces blood cells to travel through them slowly in single file maximising the diffusion of gases across the cell wall
- the extensive network of capillaries surrounding the tissues provides a huge surface area for the exchange of oxygen and carbon dioxide
- capillary walls are just one cell in thickness which means the diffusion distance for oxygen and carbon dioxide is very short.

APPLY IT!

Note that during normal resting conditions, the expiratory control centre is not involved in the process of expiration. Expiration at rest is a passive process that occurs when the inspiratory muscles relax.

The control of respiration

Breathing happens automatically and is under the influence of the respiratory control centre (RCC) located in the medulla oblongata of the brain. This control centre has two areas, both of which are under involuntary nervous control:

- the **inspiratory control centre (ICC)**
- the **expiratory control centre (ECC)**.

Breathing patterns at rest

During normal resting conditions, it is the inspiratory control centre that determines the basic rhythm of breathing. Inspiration is initiated when nerve impulses from the inspiratory control centre are sent via the phrenic and intercostal nerves to the diaphragm and external intercostal muscles respectively. These nerve impulses last for about

two seconds and cause the inspiratory muscles to contract, thus enabling inspiration. You will recall that expiration at rest is a passive process. After the two seconds of inspiration, stimulation of the respiratory muscles ceases and the inspiratory muscles relax, causing expiration. Expiration at rest typically lasts three seconds.

Breathing patterns during exercise

During exercise, the rate and depth of breathing both increase. This increased rate of ventilation, however, causes impulses from the inspiratory control centre to activate the expiratory control centre so that the duration of inspiration is reduced and the rate of breathing can be increased further. Impulses from the expiratory control centre stimulate the internal intercostal muscles and the abdominal muscles, which decrease the size of the thoracic cavity and cause forced expiration.

TAKE IT FURTHER

Figure 3.11 illustrates the blood pH of a marathon runner following the start of a race. We might normally expect blood pH to decrease during exercise, which stimulates the respiratory rate to increase.

Suggest an explanation for the increased pH values following the start of the race.

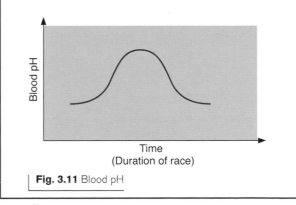

Fig. 3.11 Blood pH

Factors affecting the respiratory control centre (RCC)

Several factors (see Fig. 3.12) can influence the basic rate and depth of breathing so that oxygen and carbon dioxide content and acidity levels of the blood are maintained at acceptable levels. These factors include:

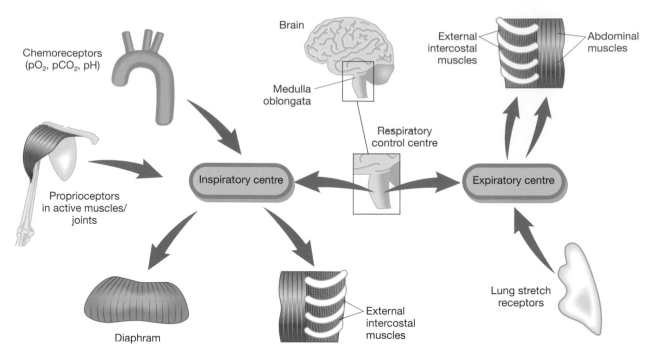

Fig. 3.12 Factors affecting the respiratory control centre (RCC)

- a **low blood pH** (increase in blood acidity) resulting from an increase in plasma concentration of carbon dioxide and lactic acid production, which together stimulate the respiratory control centre, causing an increase in the ventilation rate

- **chemoreceptors** located in the aorta and carotid arteries. Together with the chemosensitive area of the medulla, they detect changes in the concentration of carbon dioxide and oxygen levels in the blood. When stimulated (that is, when pCO_2 is high and pO_2 is low), nerve impulses are sent to the brain, causing the rate of inspiration to increase

- **mechanoreceptors** and **proprioceptors** located in the muscles and joints stimulate the respiratory control centre to increase the rate and depth of breathing as soon as exercise commences

- **stretch receptors** in the walls of the bronchi and bronchioles are stimulated when over-inflation of the lungs occurs. These receptors send impulses to the respiratory control centre, causing inspiration to stop and expiration to occur. This safety mechanism, which prevents over-inflation of the lungs, is known as the **Hering-Breur reflex**.

- **thermoreceptors** detect increases in body temperature that accompany exercise. This will cause the respiratory rate to increase.

Fig. 3.13 Did you know that at the last Olympics synchronised swimmers had the second biggest aerobic capacities after long distance runners?

The effects of training upon lung function

A prolonged period of aerobic training creates an improvement in lung function. This is due to several factors including:

- small increases in lung volumes and capacities
- improved transport of respiratory gases, oxygen and carbon dioxide
- more efficient gaseous exchange at the alveoli and tissues
- improved uptake of oxygen by the muscles.

Small increases in lung volumes and capacities

Although total lung capacity remains unchanged following training, there are some small changes to other lung volumes and capacities:

- tidal volume remains unchanged at rest and during sub-maximal exercise but does appear to increase during high-intensity maximal exercise. This ensures as much oxygen as possible is being taken into the lungs with each breath and as much carbon dioxide expelled as possible
- vital capacity also increases slightly, which causes a small decrease in the residual volume.

These increases in lung volumes can be accounted for by the increased strength of the respiratory muscles following training.

Improved transport of the respiratory gases

- Prolonged endurance training can cause changes in the composition of the blood. These changes include an increase in the total volume of the blood (primarily due to an increase in blood plasma volume) and an increase in the number of red blood cells (erythrocytes), which leads to an increase in the content of haemoglobin. These changes provide for increased oxygen delivery to the working muscles and improved removal of carbon dioxide.

- The increase in blood plasma volume also means that the blood becomes less viscous, i.e. it flows more freely. Lower blood viscosity means that there is less resistance to blood flow and an improved blood supply to the working muscles.

More efficient gaseous exchange at the alveoli and tissues

- Capillary density (which refers to the number of capillaries that surround the alveoli and skeletal muscle) increases substantially following endurance training, providing for a greater opportunity for gaseous exchange to take place. This enhances the supply of oxygen to, and the removal of carbon dioxide from, the working muscle.
- Endurance athletes also appear to have enhanced blood flow to the lungs (pulmonary blood flow), which, together with an increase in maximal minute ventilation, causes a significant increase in pulmonary diffusion, i.e. gaseous exchange at the alveoli, once again ensuring maximum exchange of oxygen and carbon dioxide.

Improved uptake of oxygen by the muscles

- Endurance training improves the ability of skeletal muscle to extract oxygen from the blood. This is largely the result of increased mitochondrial density and myoglobin content within the muscle cell, which will cause an improvement in an athlete's **maximum oxygen uptake** or VO_2max by about 10–20 per cent.
- The enhanced oxygen extraction by skeletal muscle also causes an increase in the arterial venous oxygen difference (a-vO_2 diff).

KEY TERM

Maximum oxygen uptake (VO$_2$max):
the maximum volume of oxygen that can be utilised by the working muscles per minute. It is a measure of aerobic capacity

Refresh your memory

Revision checklist

Make sure you know the following:

▷ Inspiration at rest relies on the contraction of the external intercostal muscles and diaphragm

▷ Inspiration during exercise requires the additional support and contraction of the sternocleidomastoid, the scalenes and the pectoralis minor

▷ Expiration at rest is a passive process – it is simply relaxation of the external intercostals and diaphragm

▷ Expiration during exercise, however, involves the contraction of the internal intercostals and the abdominals

▷ Tidal volume is the volume of air inspired or expired per breath

▷ During exercise tidal volume increases while inspiratory reserve volume and expiratory reserve volume decrease

▷ Minute ventilation is the volume of air breathed in or out per minute – an average resting value for minute ventilation is 7.5l/min

▷ Minute ventilation increases significantly during exercise – up to 150l/min

▷ There are two sites for gaseous exchange in the body: 1) at the alveoli 2) at the muscle cells

▷ Partial pressure is the pressure exerted by an individual gas when it occurs in a mixture of gases

▷ Differences between partial pressures of individual gases creates a diffusion gradient which facilitates gaseous exchange

▷ Blood entering the tissue-capillaries has a high oxygen content (pO_2 of 105mmHg) compared to that in the tissue cells (pO_2 40mmHg). Oxygen therefore diffuses from the blood into the muscle tissue

▷ Blood entering the tissue-capillaries has a relatively low carbon dioxide content (pCO_2 of 40mmHg) compared to that in the tissue cells (pCO_2 45mmHg). Carbon dioxide therefore diffuses from the muscle tissue into the blood

- ▷ Breathing is controlled by the respiratory control centre (RCC)

- ▷ Factors that cause the rate and depth of breathing to increase include a low blood pH caused by a high concentration of carbon dioxide and lactic acid (detected by chemoreceptors), movement (detected by mechanoreceptors and proprioceptors) and an increase in body temperature (detected by thermoreceptors)

- ▷ Training can improve lung function due to the small increases in lung volumes and capacities, the improved transport of respiratory gases, the more efficient gaseous exchange at the alveoli and tissues and the improved uptake of oxygen that results from the training programme

Revise as you go

1. Outline the path of inspired air from the nasal passages to the alveoli. State the respiratory structures it travels through on its journey.

2. Name the respiratory muscles of inspiration and expiration a) at rest and b) during exercise. What is the effect of long term endurance training upon them?

3. Define the term 'partial pressure'. Explain the importance of partial pressure in gaseous exchange.

4. Give typical values of pO_2 and pCO_2 in a) the alveoli following inspiration b) the deoxygenated blood returning to the alveoli c) the oxygenated blood arriving at the tissues d) the muscle cell.

5. Define the following lung volumes and capacities: a) tidal volume; b) inspiratory reserve volume: c) vital capacity; d) residual volume.

6. What happens to the following during exercise a) tidal volume b) inspiratory reserve volume and c) expiratory reserve volume?

7. State the equation that you would use to calculate minute ventilation. Give typical values of minute ventilation: a) at rest and b) during exercise.

8. Sketch a graph to illustrate minute ventilation during: a) sub-maximal exercise and b) maximal exercise. Explain the shape of both curves. You will need to consider the pattern before, during and following exercise.

9. Explain the importance of plasma carbon dioxide in the control of respiration. What other factors affect the respiratory control centre during exercise?

10. How does aerobic training enhance respiratory functioning?

CHAPTER 4

The cardiovascular system

– cardiac function and the transport of gases in the blood

LEARNING OBJECTIVES:

By the end of this chapter you should be able to:

- describe how the heart is structured in relation to its function as a dual-action pump
- explain the events of the cardiac cycle in relation to the conduction system of the heart
- define heart rate, stroke volume and cardiac output, giving typical resting values and describing the effects of varying workloads upon them
- draw and label the expected heart rate curves for sub-maximal and maximal workloads
- differentiate between pulmonary and systemic circulation
- name and describe the structure of the blood vessels, identifying their main features in relation to their respective functions

- explain the importance of blood pressure in relation to the redistribution of blood during exercise
- describe the mechanisms of venous return
- explain the regulation and control of the heart rate through neural and hormonal means
- describe the effects of training on cardiac functioning
- explain what is meant by the terms 'bradycardia' and 'cardiac hypertrophy'.
- explain what is meant by the arterial venous oxygen difference (a-vO_2 diff) and state how it differs during exercise from resting values
- state how oxygen and carbon dioxide are transported in the body
- explain the effect of exercise upon the dissociation of oxygen from haemoglobin at the tissues.

Introduction

The body has its own unique plumbing system that ensures that all parts of the body receive an adequate supply of blood. At the centre of this operation is the heart, an efficient muscular pump made out of specialist cardiac tissue that works continuously. The blood vessels act as an extensive network of pipes, which extend into and reach all parts of the body to feed the living tissues with blood.

The blood nourishes these tissues, feeding them with the oxygen and nutrients they require as well as removing any waste products that have been produced. Together the heart, blood vessels and the blood form the cardiovascular system, and this works in conjunction with the respiratory system (see Chapter 3) to maintain a constant supply of oxygen to the muscles both at rest and during exercise. In this chapter you will see how the maintenance and control of the blood supply is the major determining factor in the effective and successful performance of **aerobic** or endurance-based **exercise**.

KEY TERM

Aerobic exercise:
exercise that is su b-maximal and requires oxygen

REMEMBER!

The three components of the cardiovascular system are:
- the heart – the muscular pump
- blood vessels – the body's blood pipeline
- blood – the river of life that transports all the nutrients and hormones necessary to stay alive.

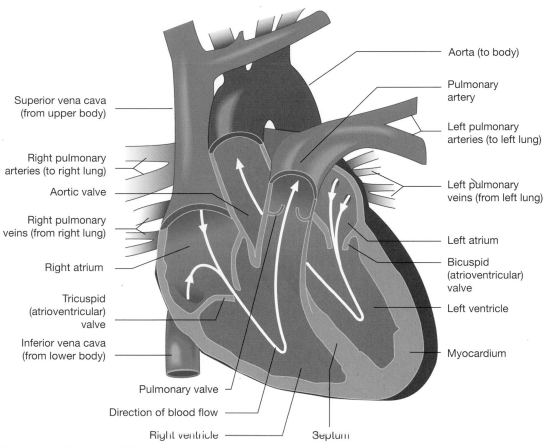

Superior vena cava
(from upper body)

Right pulmonary
arteries (to right lung)

Aortic valve

Right pulmonary
veins (from right lung)

Right atrium

Tricuspid
(atrioventricular)
valve

Inferior vena cava
(from lower body)

Pulmonary valve

Direction of blood flow

Right ventricle

Aorta (to body)

Pulmonary
artery

Left pulmonary
arteries (to left lung)

Left pulmonary
veins (from left lung)

Left atrium

Bicuspid
(atrioventricular)
valve

Left ventricle

Myocardium

Septum

Fig. 4.01 The anatomical structure of the heart

The structure of the heart

You will recall from your previous study that the heart is structured as a dual-purpose pump. The left side of the heart (on the right as you look at it) is responsible for pumping oxygen-rich blood around the whole of the body, while the right side pumps blood that is low in oxygen around to the lungs where it can be re-oxygenated and returned to the left side of the heart. To ensure this process functions as effectively as possible, there are many anatomical structures of the heart which are illustrated in Figure 4.01.

To help understand the anatomy of the heart you will now be taken on

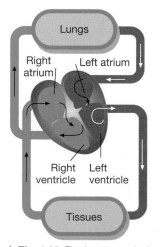

Fig. 4.02 The heart as a dual-action pump

a journey through it. Make a note of the key structures and their functions as you go.

Blood low in oxygen returns from the body to the right atrium via the superior (upper body) and inferior (lower body) vena cava. At the same time, oxygen-rich blood returns to the left atrium from the lungs via the pulmonary veins. The atria are the top two chambers of the heart. You will see from Figure 4.01 that they are separated by a thick muscular wall that runs through the middle of the heart, known as the septum. This enables the two pumps to function separately – thus enabling the heart to be dual purpose (Fig. 4.02).

Blood will eventually start to enter the larger lower chambers of the heart, called the right and left **ventricles**. In doing so, it passes the **atrioventricular** (**AV**) valves. The right AV valve is the **tricuspid valve** and the left AV valve is the **bicuspid valve**. The purpose of these valves is not merely to separate the atria from the ventricles but also to ensure that the blood can only flow in one direction through the heart. When the ventricles contract, blood on the right side of the heart is forced through the semi-lunar pulmonary valve into the pulmonary artery from where it travels towards the lungs. Meanwhile, blood from the left ventricle enters the aorta via the semi-lunar aortic valve. The aorta branches into many different arteries, which then transport the blood around the whole body. Once again, the semi-lunar valves ensure the unidirectional flow of blood, preventing backflow of blood into the heart.

As the left side of the heart is responsible for pumping blood around the whole body, the wall of cardiac tissue (**myocardium**) surrounding the left ventricle is much thicker than that on the right side of the heart.

The conduction system of the heart

Cardiac tissue is extremely specialised. To start with, it is '**myogenic**', which means that it can generate its own electrical impulses and does not require stimulation by the brain. It also possesses an intricate network of nerves. Together, these two factors ensure an efficient flow of blood through the heart and around the body.

KEY TERMS

Myocardium:
cardiac muscle that makes up the heart

Myogenic:
the ability of the heart to produce its own impulses

The cardiac impulse originates from the **sinoatrial node** (**SA node**). This is a specialised area of cardiac muscle fibres located in the muscular wall of the right atrium and acts as the heart's intrinsic pacemaker. Once the SA node has emitted the electrical impulse, it rapidly spreads throughout both atria, creating a wave of excitation and causing them both to contract. The impulse then arrives at and activates another specialised area of cardiac tissue known as the **atrioventricular node** (**AV node**). The AV node initially delays the transmission of the cardiac impulse from spreading to the ventricles (for approx 0.1 seconds). This enables the atria to contract fully before ventricular contraction begins. After this short delay, the impulse is sent down the septum of the heart via the **bundle of HIS** and throughout the muscular walls of the ventricles via **Purkinje fibres**. Both ventricles now contract, forcing the blood out of the heart and around the body. Figure 4.03 traces the journey of an impulse through the heart's conduction system. Take a few minutes to familiarise yourself with the components of this system.

TASK 4.01

Copy and complete Table 4.01, identifying the relevant function for each anatomical structure of the heart in the list.

Structure of the heart	Function
Aorta	
AV bicuspid valve	
Right ventricle	
Pulmonary vein	
Septum	

Table 4.01

EXAM TIP:

Remember that the heart requires its own blood supply. It achieves this via the coronary arteries, which feed the myocardium with oxygen and other nutrients to keep it pumping continuously.

HOT LINKS

View an animation of the conduction system of the heart at www.bostonscientific.com/templatedata/imports/HTML/CRM/heart/interact_8.html

The cardiac cycle

The cardiac cycle refers to the electrical and mechanical events that take place in the heart during one complete heartbeat. Typically, at rest, one complete heartbeat will occur every 0.8 seconds and occurs approximately 72 times per minute. During this time, the heart will at first relax and fill with blood – known as the **diastolic phase** – and then contract, forcing blood from one part of the heart to another or forcing blood out of the heart altogether – this is referred to as the **systolic phase**.

It is possible to summarise the cardiac cycle into four stages:

Fig. 4.03 The journey of an electrical impulse through the heart's conduction system

Stage 1	Atrial diastole	0.5 seconds
Stage 2	Ventricular diastole	
Stage 3	Atrial systole	0.3 seconds
Stage 4	Ventricular systole	

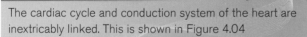

REMEMBER!

The cardiac cycle and conduction system of the heart are inextricably linked. This is shown in Figure 4.04

The control of the heart rate

It was stated earlier that the heart is myogenic – it generates its own impulses from its own intrinsic pacemaker, the sinoatrial node (SA node). However, the rate at which cardiac impulses are fired can be altered and controlled by mechanisms external to the heart. During exercise, for example, the heart rate must increase and the SA node must fire impulses more rapidly in order to meet the body's demands for oxygen. It is able to do this through two main regulatory mechanisms:

- **neural control mechanism**
- **hormonal control mechanism**.

Stage of cardiac cycle	Description	Action of valves
Atrial diastole (relaxation)	Atria fill with blood	Atrioventricular valves are closed Semi-lunar valves are open
Ventricular diastole (relaxation)	Rising pressure in the atria causes the AV valves to open and the ventricles to fill with blood	Atrioventricular valves open Semi-lunar valves are closed
Atrial systole (contraction)	Atria contract, forcing blood into the ventricles	Atrioventricular valves open Semi-lunar valves are closed
Ventricular systole (contraction)	Ventricles contract, increasing pressure in the ventricles, and forcing blood into the aorta and pulmonary artery	Atrioventricular valves are forced to close

Table 4.02 A summary of the events of the cardiac cycle

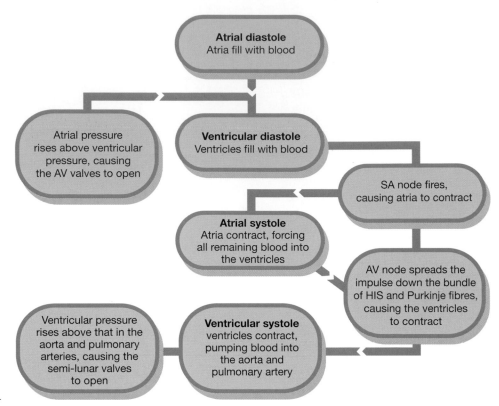

Fig. 4.04 The events of the cardiac cycle linked to the conduction system of the heart

Central to the regulation of the heart rate is the **cardiac control centre** (**CCC**) (see Fig. 4.04), situated in the **medulla oblongata**. Forming part of the **autonomic nervous system**, the CCC is under involuntary control and is made up of two components:

1. the **sympathetic nervous system** or cardio-acceleratory centre, which, as the name suggests, is responsible for increasing heart rate
2. the **parasympathetic nervous system** or cardio-inhibitory centre, which is the heart's braking system, returning heart rate back to normal resting levels.

KEY TERMS

Medulla oblongata:
part of the brain that controls such functions as heart and respiratory rate

Autonomic nervous system:
the self-governing or involuntary component of the nervous system. It transmits nerve impulses from the central nervous system to the heart, lungs and smooth muscle without our conscious control

Both the sympathetic and parasympathetic systems act upon the SA node and will cause the heart rate to increase or decrease respectively, depending upon the requirements of the body.

Neural control of the heart

The cardiac control centre receives information from different sensory receptors around the body which include:

- **mechanoreceptors and proprioceptors –** these inform the CCC of the extent of movement that is taking place within the muscles and tendons. Exercise brings about an increase in muscular activity, which requires an increase in heart rate.
- **chemoreceptors** – these are specialised cells that detect changes in the pH of the blood. They are located in the aorta and carotid arteries of the neck and provide information to the CCC concerning the concentration of carbon dioxide, lactic acid and oxygen in the blood. Increases in carbon dioxide and lactic acid that accompany exercise will cause the pH of the blood to fall and cause the heart rate to increase.

- **baroreceptors** – these are stretch receptors that exist in the walls of the aorta, venae cavae and carotid arteries. They detect increases in blood flow and therefore blood pressure within these vessels. If these stretch receptors within the venae cavae are stimulated, then the CCC causes an increase in heart rate, which in turn causes an increase in cardiac output.

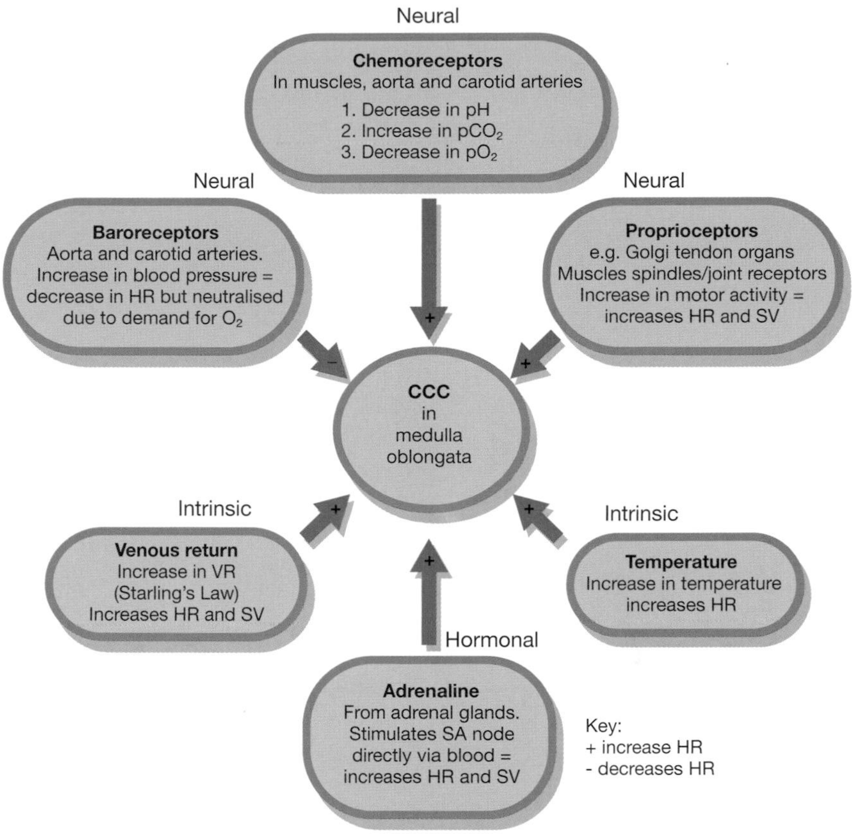

During strenuous exercise, the CCC responds to information from the mechanoreceptors, chemoreceptors and baroreceptors by stimulating the SA node via the sympathetic or cardiac acceleratory nerve, which causes the heart rate and stroke volume to increase. Once exercise stops, the stimulation of the SA node by the sympathetic nerve reduces and allows the parasympathetic vagus nerve to take over, causing a decrease in the heart rate. The more stimulation of the SA node by the vagus nerve, the quicker the heart rate will return to normal resting levels.

Neural

Chemoreceptors
In muscles, aorta and carotid arteries
1. Decrease in pH
2. Increase in pCO_2
3. Decrease in pO_2

Neural

Baroreceptors
Aorta and carotid arteries.
Increase in blood pressure =
decrease in HR but neutralised
due to demand for O_2

Neural

Proprioceptors
e.g. Golgi tendon organs
Muscles spindles/joint receptors
Increase in motor activity =
increases HR and SV

CCC
in
medulla
oblongata

Intrinsic

Venous return
Increase in VR
(Starling's Law)
Increases HR and SV

Intrinsic

Temperature
Increase in temperature
increases HR

Hormonal

Adrenaline
From adrenal glands.
Stimulates SA node
directly via blood =
increases HR and SV

Key:
+ increase HR
- decreases HR

Fig. 4.05 A summary of factors affecting the cardiac control centre (CCC)

Hormonal control of heart rate

You may have experienced the feeling of 'butterflies' together with an increase in your heart rate prior to an important competition. This anticipatory response or rise is largely due to the hormone **adrenaline**, which is released by the adrenal glands into the bloodstream during times of stress. It prepares the body for the impending exercise by increasing heart rate and strength of ventricular contraction, and consequently forms part of the sympathetic system. During exercise, adrenaline (and its close relative **noradrenaline**) can aid the body's response to exercise by:

- increasing heart rate and rate of respiration
- constricting blood vessels, which increases blood pressure, helping blood to reach the active muscles
- increasing blood glucose levels by stimulating the breakdown of glycogen in the liver. This helps to fuel muscular contraction.

KEY TERMS

Chemoreceptors:
receptors in the body that are sensitive to changes in the acidity of the blood. In particular, they monitor levels of carbon dioxide and lactic acid in the blood

Baroreceptors:
receptors in the body that monitor the degree of stretch of various blood vessels (carotid arteries, aorta, venae cavae). The level of stretch can give an indication of blood pressure

Adrenaline:
hormone responsible for increasing heart rate and the strength of ventricular contraction

Nordrenaline:
hormone responsible for transmitting nerve impulses

It was established earlier that following exercise, stimulation of the SA node by the sympathetic nerve decreases, which allows the parasympathetic nerve to take over, causing the heart rate to fall. It is the action of another hormone, **acetylcholine**, released by parasympathetic nerves, that in fact causes this decrease in heart rate.

TASK 4.02

In your own words, explain the antagonistic action of the sympathetic and parasympathetic nerves in the regulation of heart rate during and following exercise.

Cardiac dynamics and performance

The performance of the heart is largely dependent upon two variables that work together to optimise cardiac functioning. These two variables are:

* **stroke volume** (**SV**)
* **heart rate** (**HR**).

Stroke volume

Stroke volume is '**the volume of blood pumped out of the heart per beat**'. It usually refers to the blood ejected from the left ventricle and is measured in millilitres (ml) or cm³. A typical value of stroke volume at rest is about 75ml, but this can increase significantly in a trained athlete.

Stroke volume is determined by several factors:

* **venous return** – the volume of blood returning to the right atrium. The greater the venous return, the greater the stroke volume since more blood is available to be pumped out
* **the elasticity of cardiac fibres** (sometimes referred to as pre-load) – this refers to the degree of stretch of cardiac tissue just prior to contraction. The greater the stretch of the cardiac fibres, the greater the force of contraction, which can further increase the stroke volume. This is also known as the **Frank-Starling mechanism** (Starling's Law).

* **the contractility of cardiac tissue** – with increased contractility, a greater force of contraction can occur, which can cause an increase in stroke volume. This results partly due to an increased **ejection fraction**. The ejection fraction is the percentage of blood actually pumped out of the left ventricle per contraction. It is determined by dividing the stroke volume by the end-diastolic volume and is expressed as a percentage. At rest, the ejection fraction is about 55 per cent (meaning that 45 per cent of blood that enters the heart remains in it), but this can increase to over 85 per cent during exercise.

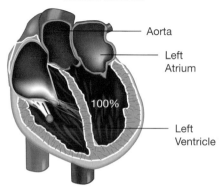

Normal diastole

- Aorta
- Left Atrium
- 100%
- Left Ventricle

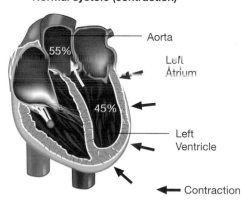

Normal systole (contraction)

- Aorta
- 55%
- Left Atrium
- 45%
- Left Ventricle
- ← Contraction

Fig. 4.06 This is the heart of a performer with an ejection fraction of 55%

KEY TERM

Acetylcholine:
hormone responsible for transmitting nerve inpulses

Frank-Starling mechanism (Starling's Law):
the mechanism by which an increase in venous return leads to a stronger ventricular contraction and a consequential increase in stroke volume

Ejection fraction:
the percentage of blood actually pumped out of the left ventricle per contraction

Bradycardia:
the reduction of resting heart rate to below 60 beats per minute. This usually accompanies endurance training

Heart rate

The heart rate represents the number of complete cardiac cycles and therefore the number of times the left ventricle ejects blood into the aorta per minute. The average resting heart rate of a human is 72 beats per minute, but this can vary tremendously depending upon levels of fitness. We might expect, for example, an elite endurance athlete to have a resting heart rate of below 60 beats per minute. When this happens, **bradycardia** is said to have taken place.

It is possible to measure your heart rate by palpating your radial or carotid arteries. This is referred to as your **pulse rate**.

TAKE IT FURTHER

1. Measure and record the resting heart rates of your classmates together with the sport or activity they participate in the most.
2. Is there any correlation between choice of sport/ activity and resting heart rate?
3. Attempt to explain any relationship you find.

Cardiac output

Cardiac output reflects the relationship between stroke volume and heart rate. It is defined as the volume of blood ejected by the heart per minute and measured in litres per minute (l/min) or dm^3. It is the product of stroke volume and heart rate and can be expressed as:

$$\text{cardiac output (Q)} = \text{stroke volume (SV)} \times \text{heart rate (HR)}$$

This relationship shows that if there is an increase in either stroke volume or heart rate (or both), then cardiac output will increase. This will be discussed further in the following section when we will investigate the response of the heart to exercise. Table 4.03 gives expected values for cardiac output, stroke volume and heart rate.

Cardiac output	=	stroke volume × heart rate	
Definition	The volume of blood ejected from the heart per minute	The volume of blood ejected from the heart per beat	The number of cardiac cycles per minute
Untrained subject	Five litres or dm^3 per minute	70ml or cm^3	72bpm
Trained subject	Five litres or dm^3 per minute	85ml or cm^3	60bpm

Table 4.03 Typical values for cardiac output, stroke volume and heart rate at rest

Cardiac dynamics during exercise

During exercise, the body's muscles demand more oxygen. Consequently, the heart must work harder in order to ensure that sufficient oxygen is delivered by the blood to the working muscles, and that waste products such as carbon dioxide and lactic acid are removed. You will recall that:

$$\text{cardiac output (Q)} = \text{stroke volume (SV)} \times \text{heart rate (HR)}$$

It is now necessary to consider what happens to each of these variables during exercise.

EXAM TIP:

Sometimes you will see volumes of blood measured in litres or dm^3. For the purpose of your study, these measures are effectively the same so that 1 litre = $1 dm^3$.

Heart rate response to exercise

You are aware that when we exercise, heart rate increases, but the extent of the increase is largely dependent upon exercise intensity. Typically, heart rate increases linearly in direct proportion to exercise intensity so that the harder you are working, the higher your heart rate will be (see Fig. 4.07). This proportional increase in heart rate will continue until you approach your maximum heart rate (this can be calculated by subtracting your age from 220). However, we do not always perform exercise of increasing intensity. During **sub-maximal exercise**, where exercise is performed at constant intensity over a prolonged period of time such as a 1500m swim, you might expect heart rate to plateau into a **steady state** for much of the swim. This steady state represents the point where oxygen demand is being met by oxygen supply and the exercise should therefore be relatively comfortable. Figure 4.08 illustrates typical heart rate curves for maximal and sub-maximal exercise. Make sure that you are able to draw and label these curves.

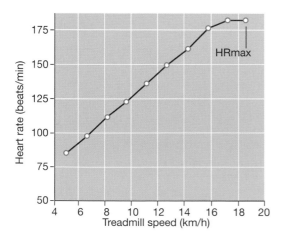

Fig. 4.07 The response of the heart to exercise

You will note that, just prior to exercise, heart rate increases even though the exercise is yet to commence. This phenomenon is known as the **anticipatory rise** and represents the heart's preparation for the forthcoming activity. It results from the release of hormones such as adrenaline, which causes the SA node to increase the heart rate. You will also note that following exercise, the heart rate takes a while to return to its resting level; this represents the body's recovery period. During this phase, the heart rate must remain slightly elevated in order to rid the body of waste products such as lactic acid.

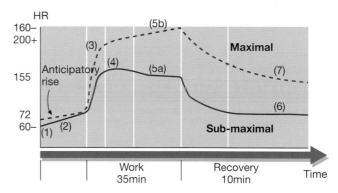

(1) resting HR (5a) steady state
(2) anticipatory rise (5b) slower increase
(3) rapid increase (6) quick recovery to resting HR
(4) plateau (7) much slower return to resting HR.

Fig. 4.08 heart rate response to maximal and sub-maximal exercise

Fig. 4.09 World class rowers are exceptionally fit. They are able to push themselves almost to their maximum during competition and can reach heart rates that the average human will never achieve

	Resting heart rate	Sub-maximal	Maximal
Trained	40–60bpm	140bpm	180bpm
Untrained	60–80bpm (average 72bpm)	110bpm	220 minus age

Table 4.04 Heart rate values at rest and during exercise for trained and untrained subjects

TASK 4.03

1. On a piece of graph paper, plot the data from Table 4.05, which illustrates the pattern of heart rate for rowers Pinsent and Cracknell during the Olympic final. Place heart rate along the y-axis (vertical axis) and distance covered along the x-axis (horizontal axis).
2. Explain the pattern of heart rate response that the graph illustrates.
3. Draw and label the expected heart rate curve for a hockey outfield player during a hockey match. Give a brief explanation of the curve you have drawn.

Matthew Pinsent	Heart rate	James Cracknell	Heart rate
Resting HR	45	Resting HR	40
Just prior to the start	55	Just prior to the start	50
500m into race	160	500m into race	155
1000m into race	160	1000m into race	155
1500m into race	160	1500m into race	155
1750m into race	190	1750m into race	185
2000m – the finish	190	2000m – the finish	185

Table 4.05 Heart rate of Olympic rowers

Stroke volume response to exercise

You will recall that stroke volume is the volume of blood pumped out of the heart with each contraction. As with heart rate, stroke volume increases linearly with increasing intensity, but only up to 40 60 per cent of maximum effort. After this point, stroke volume plateaus (see Fig. 4.10). One reason for this is the shorter diastolic phase (ventricular filling) that results from the significantly increased heart rate near maximal effort.

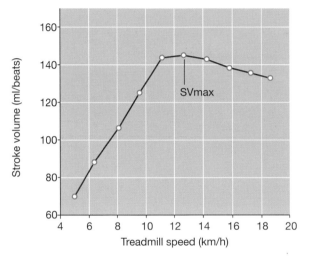

Fig. 4.10 The relationship between stroke volume and exercise intensity

Stroke volume is able to increase during exercise for several reasons:

- **increased venous return** – this is the volume of blood that returns from the body to the right side of the heart. During exercise, the venous return significantly increases due to a mechanism termed the **muscle pump**, where skeletal muscles squeeze blood back towards the heart (this will be explained a little later in this chapter)
- **the Frank-Starling mechanism (Starling's Law)** – this mechanism basically suggests that when the heart ventricles stretch more, then they can contract with greater force and therefore pump more blood out of the heart. With increased venous return, more blood enters the ventricles during the diastolic phase, which causes them to stretch more and thus contract more forcefully.

TASK 4.04

Study the data in Table 4.06. Suggest reasons why stroke volume does not change significantly between sub-maximal and maximal exercise.

	Resting stroke volume	Sub-maximal exercise	Maximal exercise
Trained	80–110ml	160–200ml	160–200ml
Untrained	60–80ml	100–120ml	100–120ml

Table 4.06 Stroke volume values at rest and during exercise for trained and untrained subjects

The reduced heart rate that is experienced by the trained athlete also allows a greater time for the ventricles to fill with blood, increasing the degree of stretch by the cardiac tissue and causing the stroke volume of these trained individuals to increase.

Cardiac output response to exercise

You will recall that cardiac output is the volume of blood pumped out of the heart per minute and is the product of heart rate and stroke volume (cardiac output (Q) = stroke volume (SV) × heart rate (HR)). As such, the response of cardiac output during exercise is easy to predict. You have just discovered that during exercise, both heart rate and stroke volume increase linearly with increasing exercise intensity. Consequently, the pattern of cardiac output

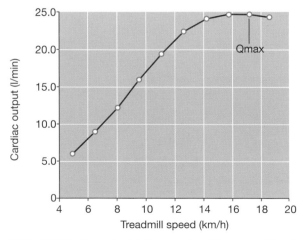

Fig. 4.11 Cardiac output during exercise of increasing intensity

during exercise is the same and will continue to increase linearly until maximum exercise capacity, where it will plateau. This is shown in Figure 4.11.

Cardiac output represents the ability of the heart to circulate blood around the body, delivering oxygen to the working muscles. During maximum exercise, cardiac output may reach values of between four to eight times resting values and is therefore a major factor in determining endurance capacity.

TASK 4.05

1. Draw a graph representing the changes in cardiac output that might occur during sub-maximal exercise.
2. Exercise the line graph you have drawn.

	Resting cardiac output	Sub-maximal exercise	Maximal exercise
Trained	5/min	15–20l/min	30–40l/min
Untrained	5l/min	10–15l/min	20–30l/min

Table 4.07 Cardiac output values at rest and during exercise for trained and untrained subjects (approximate values)

Cardiovascular drift

Cardiovascular drift is the phenomenon whereby heart rate 'drifts' upwards over time despite the performer working at a constant rate. Cardiovascular drift typically occurs in warmer environments and is thought to link to the sweating response of the body and the associated redistribution of blood to the peripheral circulatory system (i.e. to the skin). Sweating reduces the volume of blood returning to the heart, which has the knock-on effect of reducing stroke volume (remember Starling's Law of the heart!). The heart rate increases to compensate for the reduced stroke volume in order to maintain cardiac output at constant levels.

TAKE IT FURTHER

Jess competed in a 10k road race on a surprisingly hot day. She felt uncomfortable throughout the race and her finish time was unusually slow for Jess.
What could account for Jess's disappointing performance?

REMEMBER!

- Dehydration by 3–5 per cent of body weight during exercise also reduces blood volume by approximately 3–5 per cent.
- To reduce the effects of cardiovascular drift, whatever exercise you are performing it is essential to remain hydrated in order to maintain blood volume.

Fig. 4.12 Remaining hydrated can reduce the effects of
cardiovascular drift

Circulation – the vascular system

Blood is transported around the body by a
continuous network of blood vessels, which make
up the vascular system. Essentially there are two
circulatory networks forming a double circuit:

- **systemic circulation** – oxygenated blood from
  the left ventricle is transported to the
  whole of the body's tissues by a network
  of arteries and arterioles. Oxygen is
  extracted and deoxygenated blood is
  returned to the right side of the heart
  via veins
- **pulmonary circulation**
  – deoxygenated blood from the right
  ventricle is transported to the lungs
  via the pulmonary artery where it is
  re-saturated with oxygen and returned
  to the left side of the heart via the
  pulmonary vein

This double circuit ensures that the blood is
continually re-saturated with oxygen and
delivered to the working muscles, while
carbon dioxide can be expelled from the
body. Figure 4.13 illustrates the double
circulatory system.

Vessels of circulation

There are several different types of blood
vessel, each with a specific purpose
(Fig. 4.14). They include:

- arteries and arterioles
- capillaries
- veins and venules.

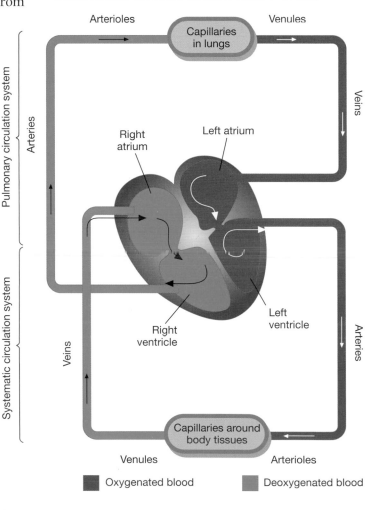

Fig. 4.13 The double circulatory system showing systemic and pulmonary
circuits

Arteries and arterioles

Arteries and arterioles are the vessels that carry blood away from the heart, supplying the body's tissues with oxygenated blood. The main artery of the body is the aorta, which has a very large cross-sectional area, but as arteries get further away from the heart, they branch into smaller vessels, each with a smaller cross-sectional area. The very smallest arteries are known as arterioles. Since arteries and arterioles carry blood at high pressure, their walls are made up of elastic fibres that enable them to stretch and withstand the pumping action of the heart. When the heart contracts, it sends a volume of blood into the aorta, which stretches to accommodate the surge of blood. This stretching and recoiling is repeated along the arterial network, generating a wave of pressure that you can palpate (feel). This is your pulse, which can be felt at several different points in the body.

The elastic walls of arterioles also serve another very important purpose. During exercise, there is competition for blood between the body's muscles and organs. By contracting the elastic fibres within their walls, arterioles can **vasoconstrict**, reducing their diameter and cross-sectional area. This means that they can reduce the amount of blood flowing to various inactive organs of the body. Conversely,

arterioles supplying blood to the working muscles of the body can relax the elastic fibres within their walls, causing them to **vasodilate**, increasing the cross-sectional area of the vessel. This means that more blood, and therefore more oxygen, can reach these exercising tissues. This mechanism of blood redistribution is known as the **vascular shunt** (this will be revisited later in this chapter).

Capillaries

Blood from the arterioles will eventually enter the extensive network of capillaries that surround all tissues. Capillary walls are just one cell in thickness, which means that the diffusion distance for oxygen and other nutrients is very short. Exchange of gases and other nutrients is further enhanced by the very narrow diameter of the capillaries. Blood cells must travel through the narrow capillaries in single file, which means that blood flow is relatively slow, maximising the diffusion of nutrients across the cell walls. The vast number of capillaries surrounding the tissues also provides a huge surface area for the exchange of nutrients into and out of the blood.

Veins and venules

Blood from the capillaries is transported back towards the heart via a network of small venules, which join together to form larger vessels called veins. Veins carry deoxygenated blood back to the heart at low pressure. The walls of the veins are less elastic than arteries but do contain a very thin layer of involuntary muscle, which, when stimulated, can help return the blood back to the heart.

KEY TERMS

Vasoconstrict:
a reduction in the diameter of artery and arteriole walls. It results in increased blood pressure and helps to speed the flow of blood around the body

Vasodilate:
an increase in the diameter of artery and arteriole walls. It can lead to a decrease in blood pressure

Vascular shunt:
the redistribution of blood around the body so that the working muscles receive an increased proportion. This is achieved through the vasoconstriction and vasodilation of blood vessels

Pocket valves:
structures that exist within the veins which aid the return of the blood to the heart, ensuring that there is no backflow

The return of blood back to the heart (venous return) is aided by **pocket valves** that exist in the veins, ensuring the unidirectional flow of blood towards the heart and preventing backflow. At rest, the veins act as a reservoir of blood, containing up to 70 per cent of the blood at any one time. This means there is a large reserve to draw upon when we start exercising and accounts partly for the dramatic increase in cardiac output during the first few minutes of activity.

REMEMBER!

Blood vessels are structured to perform particular functions.

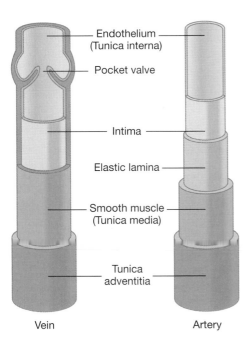

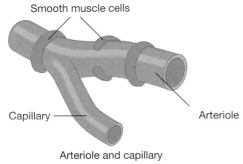

Fig. 4.14 The structure of the blood vessels

TASK 4.07

Complete Table 4.08, linking blood vessel structure to its function.

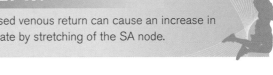

	Structure	Function
Arteries/ arterioles		
Capillaries		
Veins/ venules		

Table 4.08

APPLY IT!

Increased venous return can cause an increase in heart rate by stretching of the SA node.

TAKE IT FURTHER

Using information from Chapter 1 and Chapter 6, plan a training programme designed to enhance the pulmonary functioning and gaseous exchange, and cardiac dynamics and performance of a marathon runner. Make sure you include relevant fitness tests, principles of training and a number of different training methods. Justify the content of your training programme with regard to the respiratory and cardiovascular adaptations expected.

HOT LINKS

Using websites such as www.educypedia.be/education/respiratory.htm and www.britishtriathlon.org to help in your research, write an extended answer on how the effective functioning of the respiratory and cardiovascular systems can contribute to the successful performance of a triathlete such as Andrew Johns.

The venous return mechanism

Venous return is the term used to define the volume of blood that returns to the right side of the heart via the venules, veins and venae cavae. You discovered earlier that at rest up to 70 per cent of the total volume of blood is held in the veins. This pool of blood acts as a large reservoir or storage depot that can be drawn upon quickly when the need arises, such as during exercise.

You will also recall that stroke volume is dependent upon venous return. This means that if we can increase the volume of blood returning to the heart (venous return), then stroke volume and therefore cardiac output will also increase. Hence, if blood flow is to increase during exercise, then venous return must increase. However, the pumping action of the heart is spent by the time the blood reaches the veins and consequently blood travels in the veins at relatively low pressure which is sufficient to maintain stroke volume at rest but inadequate for the demands of the body during exercise.

The body has therefore developed several mechanisms to help improve the flow of blood back to the heart and enhance stroke volume (Fig. 4.15).

- The **skeletal muscle pump** (Fig. 4.15b)
Because the walls of the veins are relatively thin, the contraction and relaxation of muscles during exercise create a massaging effect on them, which squeezes and pumps blood back towards

the heart. This is aided by the pocket valves located inside the veins.

- **Pocket valves** (Fig. 4.15a)
The pocket valves that exist within the veins snap shut, ensuring that there is no backflow of blood and that the flow is one way, back towards the heart.

- **Smooth muscle within veins** (Fig. 4.15c)
Located within the walls of the veins is a very thin layer of smooth muscle that can work in conjunction with the muscle pump to squeeze blood back towards the heart.

- The **respiratory pump**
The increased rate and depth of breathing that accompanies exercise creates pressure changes within the thorax and abdomen. On breathing in, increased pressure in the abdomen compresses the veins and squeezes blood into the veins that supply the heart.

- **Gravity**
Gravity assists the flow of blood from the upper extremities of the body into the superior vena cava and then into the right atrium.

The mechanisms of venous return are essential in maintaining cardiac output during exercise. It is important to note, however, that by completing a cool down following exercise, venous return can be maintained, which can prevent the 'pooling' of the

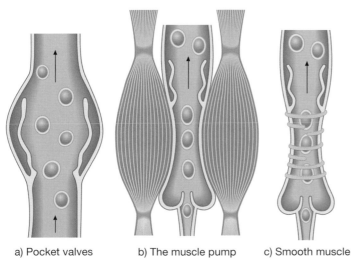

a) Pocket valves   b) The muscle pump   c) Smooth muscle

Fig 4.15 Venous return mechanisms

REMEMBER!

The venous return mechanism is particularly important at the start of exercise in order to increase stroke volume and cardiac output!

APPLY IT!

With up to 70 per cent of the blood held in the veins at rest, the action of the skeletal muscle pump as exercise commences causes a huge increase in the stroke volume and cardiac output.

blood in the veins. The cool down has the effect of maintaining the muscle pump and cardiac output. A reduced cardiac output following exercise can reduce blood flow to the brain and increase the likelihood of dizziness or even fainting.

The redistribution of blood during exercise

As we begin to exercise, the destination of our blood flow changes dramatically. Through vasomotor control and the action of the sympathetic nervous system, blood can be diverted away from non-essential tissues and organs and redirected towards those active during exercise. From Table 4.09 and Figure 4.16, you can see that at rest only about 20 per cent of the total cardiac output is distributed to the muscles, with the majority going to the liver, kidneys and intestines. However, during maximal exercise, the active working muscles may receive as much as 85–90 per cent of the total blood flow, leaving only 10–15 per cent to supply the remaining organs and tissues.

This redistribution of blood flow during exercise results from the **vasoconstriction** or narrowing of arterioles supplying organs such as the intestines, liver and kidneys, and **vasodilation** or opening of the arterioles supplying the more active working muscles. This mechanism is known as the **vascular shunt** and is aided by the presence of a small ring of smooth muscle that exists on the arterioles at the point of entry to the capillary network. These **pre-capillary sphincters** regulate blood flow into the capillaries by either vasoconstricting (narrowing) or vasodilating (opening).

KEY TERM

Pre-capillary sphincter:
a ring of muscle located at the entrance to the capillary bed which regulates the amount of blood flowing into it

The redirection of blood flow is important to the performer for several reasons:

- it increases oxygen supply to the working muscles
- it provides the working muscles with the necessary fuels to contract (glucose and fatty acids)
- it removes carbon dioxide and lactic acid from the muscles
- it helps maintain body temperature and rids the body of excess heat produced during exercise.

Destination	Rest	Maximal exercise
Muscle	20%	88%
Brain	15%	3%
Heart	5%	4%
Skin	10%	3%
Liver and intestines	30%	1%
Kidneys	20%	1%

Table 4.09 The distribution of cardiac output during rest and maximal exercise

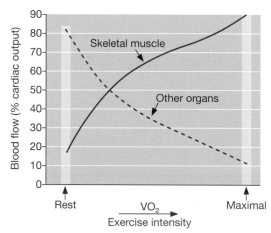

Fig. 4.16 The redistribution of blood flow during exercise

The control of blood redistribution – vasomotor control

The vascular shunt mechanism is regulated by the process of **vasomotor control**. The vasomotor centre is located in the medulla oblongata of the brain. Chemical changes in the blood that result from the onset of exercise (namely increases in carbon dioxide and lactic acid, and low oxygen concentration) are detected by **chemoreceptors**, which inform the vasomotor centre to stimulate the sympathetic nerves located in the smooth muscular walls of the blood vessels. The sympathetic nerves will cause vasoconstriction of those arterioles and pre-capillary sphincters supplying non-essential muscles and organs, decreasing blood flow to these areas. At the same time, vasodilation of arterioles that are supplying the more active working muscles (including the heart) occurs, which will increase blood flow to them. The process of vasomotor control is entirely involuntary and occurs more or less immediately, ensuring that the areas of the body in most need receive the necessary amount of blood and nutrients.

Blood pressure and blood velocity

Blood pressure is the driving force that moves the blood through our circulatory systems and can be defined as 'the force exerted by the blood on the inside walls of the blood vessels'. As the heart pumps blood around the body, the blood vessels offer resistance to the flow of blood, which generates pressure within the circulatory system. The two main determining factors of blood pressure are:

- blood flow (cardiac output)
- peripheral resistance (resistance offered to the flow of blood due to friction). Resistance is related to three factors:
  1. **blood viscosity** (the relative thickness of the blood)
  2. blood vessel length
  3. blood vessel diameter.

The relationship can be expressed as follows:

blood pressure =
cardiac output × peripheral resistance

KEY TERM

Blood viscosity:
a term used to describe the relative thickness of the blood. If the blood is very viscous, it has a high amount of blood cells to plasma and consequently does not flow very quickly

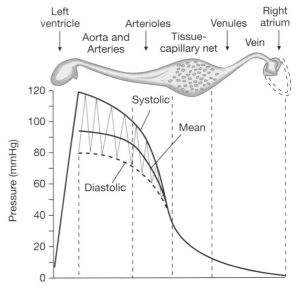

Fig. 4.17 Blood pressure at various points of the circulatory system

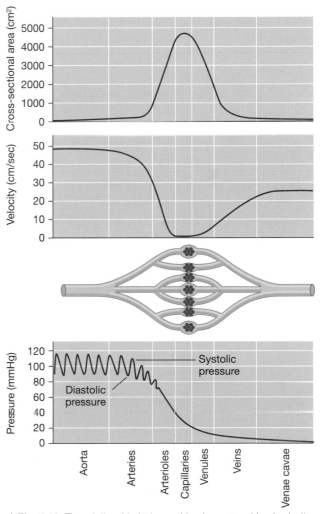

Fig. 4.18 The relationship between blood pressure, blood velocity and total cross-sectional area of blood vessels

The pressure within the system fluctuates in line with the events of the cardiac cycle. The highest blood pressure is seen in arteries close to the heart (aorta) during ventricular systole and is termed '**systolic blood pressure**', while the lowest is recorded when the ventricles are relaxing (ventricular diastole) and is known as '**diastolic blood pressure**'.

Blood pressure reduces the further the blood travels away from the left ventricle. Hence it is greatest in the aorta, lower in the arteries, arterioles and capillaries, lower still in the venules and veins, and at its lowest in the venae cavae as it enters the right atrium of the heart.

As the blood flows away from the heart through the arteries, mean (average) blood pressure falls progressively (Fig. 4.20). This is partly due to the decreasing effect of the pumping action of the heart but also because there is an increase in the total cross-sectional area of blood vessels as the numbers of arterioles and capillaries increase. This will have the effect of reducing peripheral resistance. Accompanying this increase in total cross-sectional area is a decrease in blood velocity. Thus the velocity of the blood decreases the further away from the heart it gets, so that by the time it reaches the capillaries, the blood is travelling very slowly indeed (Fig. 4.18). This slow movement of blood along the capillaries is essential for the effective diffusion of gases and other nutrients into and out of the blood.

However, as the blood enters the venules and veins, blood velocity increases again as the total cross-sectional area of these vessels decreases. The venous return mechanisms outlined earlier also help in increasing the velocity of the blood in the veins.

Measurement of blood pressure

Blood pressure is usually measured in the left brachial artery by a blood pressure meter or 'sphygmomanometer', although simple readings can be given using a digital blood pressure recorder. A pressure cuff is wrapped around the upper arm and inflated to stop the flow of blood into the brachial artery. At this point, a reading is taken which represents the systolic blood pressure – the force

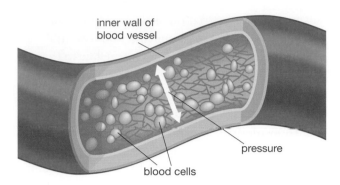

Fig. 4.19 Blood pressure is the force exerted by the blood on the inner walls of the blood vessels

with which blood is pushing against the arterial walls during ventricular contraction. As the cuff is slowly deflated blood will surge through the artery and a second reading is taken. This reading is the diastolic blood pressure and represents the force of the blood in the arteries during ventricular relaxation. A stethoscope is used to listen to the blood pumping through the artery. These pumping sounds register on a gauge attached to the cuff.

The two readings are expressed as follows:

$$\frac{\text{Systolic pressure}}{\text{Diastolic pressure}}$$

The blood pressure reading for an average healthy adult is generally regarded as being:

$$\frac{120\text{mmHg}}{80\text{mmHg}}$$

The effects of exercise upon blood pressure

Performing aerobic exercise, such as a long distance run or a distance swim, causes systolic blood pressure to increase (usually in direct proportion to the exercise intensity). Systolic pressure can rise from its resting value of 120mmHg to values approaching 200mmHg. This increase results largely from the increase in cardiac output and the vasoconstriction of arterioles that help the vascular shunting of blood towards the working muscles. However, once steady state is reached, systolic blood pressure may, in fact, start to gradually decrease due to the arteriole dilation supplying the working muscles. This has the effect of reducing the total peripheral resistance, thereby lowering **mean blood pressure** to only just above that of resting levels. The diastolic pressure changes little during this endurance type activity.

During exercise that is more anaerobic or that which involves more **isometric** type muscle contractions such as weightlifting, the changes in blood pressure are very different. In this instance, both systolic and diastolic blood pressures rise significantly, largely due to the performer holding their breath, which increases the pressure within the thorax and abdomen and squeezes on the peripheral blood vessels, increasing overall mean blood pressure.

KEY TERMS

Mean blood pressure:
the average value of systolic and diastolic pressures

Isometric exercise:
exercise that involves static muscle contractions (i.e. where the muscle length remains the same during contraction). For example, the abdominal muscles work isometrically when performing a one repetitions maximum on the bench press

TASK 4.08

Explain what happens to the systolic pressure of an athlete before, during and following a 10k run. Explain how blood pressure is regulated in each case.

The control and regulation of blood pressure

The maintenance of blood pressure within a normal range is essential for healthy living. Whereas high blood pressure can damage organs such as the heart and the brain, low pressure can starve the body's tissues of oxygen and other nutrients. It is the role of the vasomotor centre to regulate blood pressure. Pressure receptors or baroreceptors located in the aorta and carotid arteries monitor the blood pressure and feed this sensory information to the vasomotor centre in the medulla oblongata. If blood

pressure is too high, then the vasomotor centre will decrease sympathetic stimulation of the arterioles, resulting in vasodilation and a decrease in blood pressure. On the other hand, if blood pressure is too low and an increase in blood pressure is required, then the vasomotor centre will increase sympathetic stimulation, causing vasoconstriction of arterioles.

The vasomotor centre works in conjunction with the cardiac control centre, which will help maintain blood pressure by either increasing or decreasing cardiac output accordingly.

REMEMBER!

A healthy blood pressure reading is considered to be
$$\frac{120\text{mmHg}}{80\text{mmHg}}$$

TAKE IT FURTHER

Under the guidance of your teacher investigate the blood pressure of your PE group both at rest and following a period of intense exercise.

Follow the procedure below:
1. Wrap the cuff of a digital blood pressure meter or sphygmomanometer around the brachial artery of the left arm, whilst the palm of the hand is facing upwards and the arm relaxed.
2. Pump air into the cuff up to approximately 190–200mmHg
3. Slowly release the air inside the cuff by pressing the attachment on the bulb. The systolic pressure can now be read and recorded.
4. Continue to release air from the cuff until the diastolic pressure is displayed on the screen. Record the diastolic pressure.
5. Your blood pressure is recorded by placing the systolic pressure reading over the diastolic reading:
$$\frac{\text{Systolic}}{\text{Diastolic}}$$
6. Follow the above procedure after completing 2 minutes of intense exercise.
7. Now take your reading immediately after a series of dumb-bell bicep curls.
8. Account for any differences in your results.

TASK 4.09

Write out these statements, stating clearly whether they are true or false.

1. Stroke volume is the difference between end-diastolic and end-systolic volume in the heart.
2. During the cardiac cycle, the semi-lunar valves open because the pressure in the left ventricle is less than the pressure in the aorta.
3. Sympathetic stimulation of the heart causes both the heart rate and force of ventricular contraction to increase.
4. Veins possess larger amounts of elastic fibres than any of the other blood vessels. This helps in the venous return mechanism.
5. Blood pressure is lowest in the capillaries because their total cross-sectional area is much greater than the aorta.

TAKE IT FURTHER

Investigate the changes in blood pressure during the following types of exercise!
- endurance exercise
- resistance training

Account for the changes identified.

The transport of oxygen

When oxygen from the alveoli diffuses across the alveolar capillary membrane, it enters the bloodstream. It is the function of the blood to transport oxygen and it does this in two ways:

1. 97 per cent is carried in chemical combination with **haemoglobin** (a red iron-based pigment found in red blood cells)
2. 3 per cent is dissolved in the blood plasma (oxygen is not very soluble in water and therefore this figure is relatively low).

When oxygen combines with haemoglobin, it forms **oxy-haemoglobin**:

$$\text{Hb (haemoglobin)} + O_2 \text{ (oxygen)} = HbO_2 \text{ (oxy-haemoglobin)}.$$

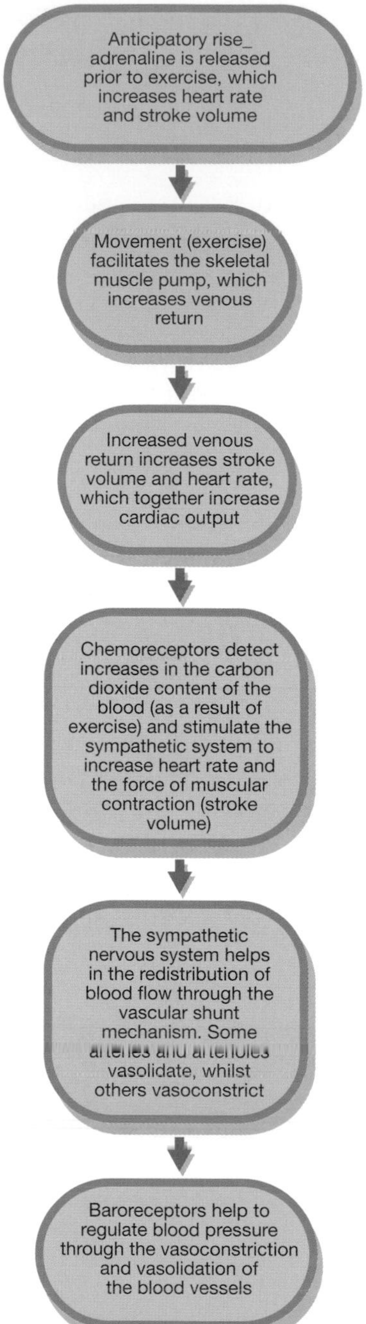

Anticipatory rise_ adrenaline is released prior to exercise, which increases heart rate and stroke volume

Movement (exercise) facilitates the skeletal muscle pump, which increases venous return

Increased venous return increases stroke volume and heart rate, which together increase cardiac output

Chemoreceptors detect increases in the carbon dioxide content of the blood (as a result of exercise) and stimulate the sympathetic system to increase heart rate and the force of muscular contraction (stroke volume)

The sympathetic nervous system helps in the redistribution of blood flow through the vascular shunt mechanism. Some arteries and arterioles vasolidate, whilst others vasoconstrict

Baroreceptors help to regulate blood pressure through the vasoconstriction and vasolidation of the blood vessels

Fig. 4.20 Putting it all together – what happens to the cardiovascular system when we exercise

Haemoglobin has a very high affinity for oxygen, each molecule combining with four molecules of oxygen so that:

$$Hb + 4O_2 = HbO_8$$

The most important factor that determines how much oxygen combines with haemoglobin is the partial pressure of oxygen (pO_2). When the pO_2 of blood is high, such as in the alveolar capillaries of the lungs, haemoglobin readily combines with large amounts of oxygen until it becomes almost fully saturated (96 per cent). When the pO_2 of blood is low, such as in the capillaries of the contracting muscles, oxygen is released by the haemoglobin. This oxygen can now be used by the respiring tissues and muscles. This dissociation of oxygen from haemoglobin occurs since the reaction stated above is easily reversible and is represented by the oxy-haemoglobin dissociation curve.

KEY TERMS

Haemoglobin (Hb):
a respiratory pigment of the blood found in all red blood cells which attaches to and helps transport oxygen (and carbon dioxide) around the body

Oxy-haemoglobin (HbO$_2$):
haemoglobin combined with oxygen

The oxy-haemoglobin dissociation curve

An oxy-haemoglobin dissociation curve (Fig. 4.21) represents the amount of haemoglobin saturated

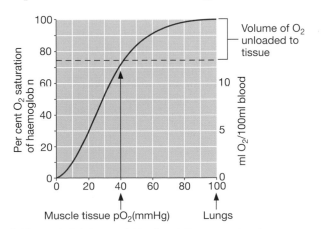

Fig. 4.21 Oxy-haemoglobin dissociation curve at rest

with oxygen as it passes through areas of the body that have very different partial pressures of oxygen (pO_2).

You will note that the oxy-haemoglobin dissociation curve is 'S'-shaped. This 'S'-shaped curve means that relatively small changes in the pO_2 can result in a large uptake or association of oxygen at the lungs and a large dissociation at the muscles/tissues.

Now look at Figure 4.22. Note that at very low partial pressures of oxygen, which we would expect at the respiring muscles, the percentage saturation of haemoglobin is very low – approximately 20 per cent, the remaining 76 per cent has been released to the muscles for energy production. At very high partial pressures of oxygen, as we find in the lungs, the haemoglobin is 96–98 per cent saturated.

TASK 4.10

1. What effect does an increase in the carbon dioxide partial pressure have on the oxygen-carrying capacity of haemoglobin?
2. State where in the human body the partial pressure of oxygen and carbon dioxide is likely to be a) high and b) low.

Partial pressure	Oxygen	Carbon dioxide
High		
Low		

Table 4.10

Exercise and the Bohr effect

During exercise, when the muscles require more oxygen, the dissociation of oxygen from haemoglobin occurs more readily, causing a shift of the oxy-haemoglobin dissociation curve to the right. This is known as the **Bohr effect** and frees up more oxygen, which can then be utilised by the working muscles for energy production.

There are several reasons for this:

- increases in carbon dioxide and in lactic acid production that accompanies muscular contraction, which causes

- an increase in acidity of the blood (lower pH)
- increases in blood and muscle temperature resulting from energy released as heat during muscular contraction.

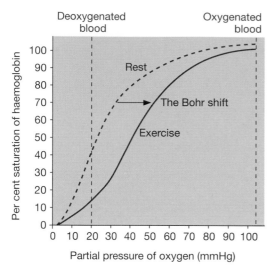

Fig. 4.22 The Bohr effect

All these factors inform the body that the muscles require more oxygen and cause the dissociation of oxygen from haemoglobin. The Bohr shift is illustrated in Figure 4.22.

One further method the body has of ensuring that the muscles are constantly supplied with adequate amounts of oxygen is through the respiratory pigment **myoglobin**. Myoglobin is another iron-based protein similar to haemoglobin, but it is only found in skeletal muscles. It has a much higher affinity for oxygen than haemoglobin and acts as an oxygen store, saturating itself with oxygen that has dissociated from haemoglobin. You will notice from Figure 4.23 that the myoglobin curve

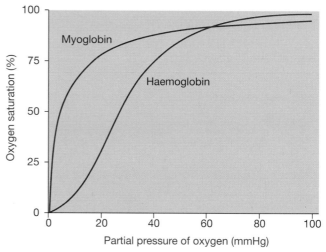

Fig. 4.23 Oxy-myoglobin saturation

HOT LINKS

To view an animation of oxy-haemoglobin dissociation curve visit www.getbodysmart.com/ap/respiratorysystem/physiology/gases/hbsaturation/animation.html

TASK 4.11

From Figure 4.23, state the partial pressure of oxygen at 25 per cent, 50 per cent and 96 per cent saturation during resting conditions.

lies well to the left of our regular oxy-haemoglobin dissociation curve. This means that even at very low partial pressures of oxygen, it remains relatively saturated. So, even if the percentage saturation of haemoglobin is low, myoglobin still has oxygen available to supply the working muscles, which can be quickly exploited.

KEY TERMS

The Bohr effect:
a shift in the oxy-haemoglobin dissociation curve to the right resulting from a lower blood pH. This is due to the increased levels of carbon dioxide that accompany exercise and free up oxygen which can then be used by the working muscles

Myoglobin:
a respiratory pigment that acts as a store of oxygen within the muscle cell

EXAM TIP:

Be sure to understand that increased blood acidity leads to a decrease in the pH.

The arterial venous oxygen difference (a-vO₂ diff)

The arterial venous oxygen difference represents how much oxygen is actually extracted and utilised by the muscles. It is measured by analysing the difference in oxygen content of the blood in the arteries leaving the lungs and that in the mixed venous blood returning to the lungs. We have already established that after flowing through the alveolar capillaries, blood is 96 per cent saturated with oxygen. During resting conditions, blood returning to the alveoli via the pulmonary artery is still 70 per cent saturated with oxygen. This suggests that at rest our muscles only use about 25 per cent of the oxygen delivered to them. This difference actually equates to about 4–5ml of oxygen per 100ml of blood.

During intense exercise, however, this difference can increase three-fold to about 15ml of oxygen per 100ml of blood and reflects an increased uptake of oxygen by the working muscles.

The transport of carbon dioxide

Like oxygen, carbon dioxide is transported around the body by the blood. It is carried in several forms:

- **70 per cent** is transported in the blood as hydrogen carbonate (**bicarbonate**) **ions**. Carbon dioxide produced by the muscles diffuses into the tissue capillaries and enters the red blood stream where it combines with water to form carbonic acid:

$$CO_2 + H_2O \rightarrow H_2CO_3$$

However, carbonic acid is a weak acid and quickly dissociates into hydrogen ions (H+) and hydrogen carbonate or bicarbonate ions (HCO₃⁻):

$$H_2CO_3 \rightarrow H^+ + HCO_3^-$$

The complete reaction is more accurately written as:

$$CO_2 + H_2O \rightarrow H_2CO_3 \rightarrow H^+ + HCO_3^-$$

It is in this form that the majority of carbon dioxide is transported back around to the lungs and expired.

- **23 per cent** combines with haemoglobin in the red blood cells to form carbaminohaemoglobin:

$$CO_2 + Hb \rightarrow HbCO_2$$

This reaction relies on the partial pressure of carbon dioxide (pCO₂) so that at the tissues where pCO₂ is high, haemoglobin and carbon dioxide readily combine, while at the alveoli, the relatively low pCO₂ causes haemoglobin and carbon dioxide to dissociate.

- **7 per cent** is dissolved in the **plasma** of the blood.

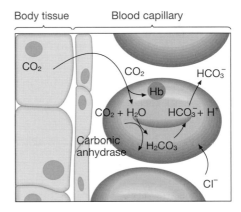

Fig. 4.24 The majority of carbon dioxide is transported in the blood as bicarbonate ions and carbonic acid

KEY TERMS

Bicarbonate ions (HCO₃⁻):
an ion formed as a result of the dissociation of carbonic acid. This is how much of the carbon dioxide produced in the body is transported in the blood to the lungs where it is expired

Plasma:
the fluid component of the blood

TAKE IT FURTHER

Describe how carbon dioxide is transported in the blood during a game of netball. Explain the role carbon dioxide plays in the control of heart rate during the match. Explain the term buffering and how it occurs in the body.

Training effects upon the heart – athlete's heart

Training can induce structural and functional changes to the heart that lead to greater efficiency and improved performance. Endurance training, for example, can cause the heart to enlarge, undergoing **hypertrophy**. This is particularly true of the ventricular cavities, which increase in size, enabling them to fill with more blood during the diastolic phase of the cardiac cycle. This condition leads to a greater stroke volume and a reduced resting heart rate (**bradycardia**). Resistance or strength training, on the other hand, causes a thickening of the ventricular myocardium (the heart muscle), which increases the force of heart contractions, which in turn increases stroke volume. Both types of athletes will also experience improved contractility of the heart. Consequently, the **ejection fraction** (the percentage of blood that enters the left ventricle, which is actually pumped out per beat) will increase (from 60 per cent up to 85 per cent).

Cardiac hypertrophy enables the trained heart to beat less frequently both at rest (bradycardia) and during sub-maximal exercise (see Fig. 4.26). This is due to increased activity of parasympathetic nerves slowing the heart rate down. This results in a greater filling of the heart during the diastolic phase of the cardiac cycle and therefore, according to Starling's Law, an increase in stroke volume.

There is also increased **capillarisation** of the heart (cardiac) muscle itself, which facilitates the diffusion of oxygen into the myocardium.

The adaptations of the heart following a period of training can be summarised as follows:

- cardiac hypertrophy (enlargement of the heart)
- increased contractility (strength of contraction)
- increased stroke volume
- increased maximum cardiac output (although cardiac output at rest and sub-maximal levels remain unchanged)
- increased ejection fraction
- bradycardia (lower resting heart rate)
- greater diastolic filling of the ventricles
- increased capillarisation.

TASK 4.12

Outline the expected adaptive responses to the cardiovascular system of a runner training for their first triathlon.

Fig. 4.25 A marathon runner's cardiovascular system will adapt in response to the training they undertake

KEY TERMS

Cardiac hypertrophy:
the enlargement of the heart muscle in response to training

Buffering:
the ability of the body to keep acidity levels (blood pH) within acceptable limits

REMEMBER!

Following a period of training cardiac output will only increase during exercise. Resting cardiac output remains the same.

Training effects upon the vascular system

Endurance training will also improve the efficiency of the body's vascular system. This ensures that when exercising, the working muscles receive the necessary oxygen and other nutrients to sustain the workload, and that any fatiguing waste products can be removed. The primary effect of endurance training on an athlete's vascular system is that there is increased blood flow to the muscles. This results partly from the cardiac adaptations outlined above but also by:

- the increased capillarisation of the muscles, enabling a greater surface area for gaseous exchange
- improved ability of arterioles to vasoconstrict and vasodilate, which means that blood redistribution is more effective, ensuring the working muscles receive the greatest supply of blood
- increased blood volume making more blood, and therefore oxygen, available to the working muscles.

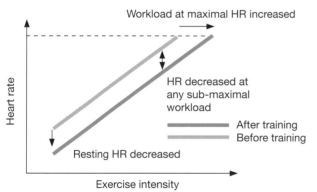

Fig. 4.26 Training effects on the heart rate/workload relationship

Other adaptations of the vascular system that enable a performer to continue exercising for longer include:

- improved transport of the respiratory gases
- changes in the composition of the blood caused by prolonged endurance training. These changes include an increase in the total volume of the blood (primarily due to an increase in blood plasma volume) and an increase in the number of red blood cells (erythrocytes), which leads to an increase in the content of haemoglobin. These changes provide for increased oxygen delivery to the working muscles and improved removal of carbon dioxide.

- the blood becomes less viscous, that is, it flows more freely, because of the increase in blood plasma volume. Lower blood viscosity means that there is less resistance to blood flow and an improved blood supply to the working muscles.
- an increase in red blood cell count, and therefore haemoglobin content, which enhances the oxygen-carrying capacity of the blood
- the blood becomes more efficient at removing waste products such as carbon dioxide and lactic acid. This is known as **buffering**.
- resting blood pressure can be reduced.

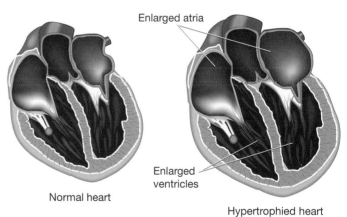

Fig. 4.27 Endurance training can bring about cardiac hypertrophy by enlargement of the ventricular chambers of the heart

TAKE IT FURTHER

Using information from Chapter 1 and Chapter 6, plan a training programme designed to enhance the cardiovascular functioning of a hockey player. Make sure you include relevant fitness tests, principles of training and a number of different training methods in your programme. Justify the content of your training programme with regard to the cardiovascular adaptations expected.

Exam**Café**
Relax, refresh, result!

Refresh your memory

Revision checklist

Make sure you know the following:

Heart

▷ The cardiovascular system consists of the heart, blood vessels and blood

▷ The unique structure of the heart enables it to act as a dual-action pump

▷ The valves of the heart ensure that the blood can only flow in one direction

▷ The heart is myogenic which means that it can produce its own impulses

▷ Impulses originate from the SA node which then spread across the atria causing them to contract. The AV node directs the impulse down the bundle of HIS and through the Purkinje fibres which causes contraction of the ventricles

▷ The cardiac cycle refers to the electrical and mechanical events of one heartbeat and on average takes place 72 times per minute

▷ There are four stages to the cardiac cycle: atrial diastole where the atria (top chambers) fill with blood; ventricular diastole where the ventricles (bottom chambers) fill with blood; atrial systole when the atria contract forcing all remaining blood into the ventricles and ventricular systole which forces blood out of the heart and into the circulatory system

▷ The heart is regulated by the cardiac control centre which is sited in the medulla oblongata in the brain

▷ The sympathetic and parasympathetic nervous systems work antagonistically to speed up and slow down heart rate, respectively

▷ Neural control of the heart is governed by information from mechanoreceptors and proprioceptors which detect movement; chemoreceptors which detect changes in blood pH largely in response to changes in carbon dioxide and lactic acid production; and baroreceptors which are sensitive to changes in blood pressure

▷ Hormonal control of the heart results from adrenaline and noradrenaline which stimulates the heart to beat faster and acetylcholine which helps return heart rate to normal resting levels following exercise

▷ Stroke volume is the volume of blood pumped out of the heart per beat. It is determined by venous return, elasticity of cardiac fibres and contractility of the heart. Stroke volume is governed by Starlings Law of the heart

▷ Heart rate represents the number of times the heart beats per minute

▷ Cardiac output is the volume of blood ejected by the heart per minute and is the product of stroke volume and heart rate:

　　　Cardiac output = Stroke volume x Heart rate

▷ The anticipatory rise is the pre-exercise increase in heart rate due to the effects of adrenaline

▷ During sub-maximal exercise heart rate will plateau and enter 'steady state'

▷ During maximal exercise heart rate will continue to increase throughout the duration of the activity

▷ Stroke volume increases during exercise because of the associated increase in venous return and the Frank-Starling mechanism (Starling's Law)

▷ Cardiovascular drift is the increase in heart rate when performing an endurance activity at constant intensity. We would normally expect heart rate to enter steady state but the fluid loss resulting from sweating reduces blood plasma volume and consequently venous return. The heart rate increases to compensate for the reduced venous return even though exercise intensity remains constant

Vascular system

▷ The vascular system is composed of the blood and the network of blood vessels

▷ There are two circulatory networks: the systemic network (where blood is directed to the muscles and tissues of the body) and the pulmonary network (blood is directed from the heart to the lungs and back to heart again)

▷ The vessels of circulation include arteries, arterioles, capillaries, venules and veins

▷ Each type of vessel has a particular role to play and is structured to fulfil that role effectively

▷ Blood returning to the right side of the heart is known as venous return

▷ Venous return ultimately determines stroke volume (Starling's Law of the heart)

▷ The venous return mechanism helps to maximise the amount of blood that returns to the right side of the heart and includes the muscle pump, pocket valves, the respiratory pump, smooth muscle and gravity

- During exercise blood is redistributed to the working muscles and diverted away from inconsequential organs and tissues. It does this through the vascular shunt mechanism

- Vascular shunt is controlled by the vasomotor centre and involves the vasoconstriction of blood vessels supplying the muscles and tissues not required and the vasodilation of those blood vessels supplying the working muscles

- The vascular shunt mechanism is aided by the action of pre-capillary sphincters

- Blood pressure is the force exerted by the blood on the inside walls of the blood vessels

- The two main determining factors of blood pressure are cardiac output and the resistance to blood flow offered by the blood vessels

- Blood pressure is greatest in the aorta and reduces the further the blood travels away from the left ventricle

- Blood pressure is measured using a sphygnomonometer

- There are two components to a blood pressure reading: systolic pressure (when the heart is contracting) and diastolic pressure (whilst the heart is relaxing)

- During aerobic type activity mean blood pressure may only increase slightly however during very explosive anaerobic activity both systolic and diastolic pressures rise significantly

- 97 per cent of oxygen is transported in chemical combination with haemoglobin while the other 3 per cent is dissolved in the blood's plasma

- The oxy-haemoglobin dissociation curve shows the amount of haemoglobin saturated with oxygen as it flows around the body

- During exercise there is a shift in the oxy-haemoglobin dissociation curve to the right. This is known as the Bohr shift and explains why more oxygen is released by haemoglobin to feed the working muscles during the exercise period

- 70 per cent of carbon dioxide is transported as hydrogen carbonate (bicarbonate) ions in the blood; 23 per cent combines with haemoglobin (carbaminohaemoglobin) and 7 per cent is dissolved in the blood's plasma

- The arterio-venous oxygen difference (a-vO$_2$ diff) represents the volume of oxygen actually extracted from the blood and used by the muscles and tissues of the body

- Training can induce structural and functional changes to the heart. Cardiac hypertrophy is the enlargement of the heart that accompanies training and bradycardia is the associated reduction in resting heart rate

- Training can induce structural and functional changes to the vascular system. These changes include: capillarisation, improved vasoconstriction and dilation, increased blood volume and the maintenance of blood pressure within the 'healthy' range

Revise as you go

1. Which blood vessels carry:

   a) oxygenated blood from the lungs to the heart

   b) deoxygenated blood from the heart to the lungs?

2. Define 'stroke volume', 'heart rate' and 'cardiac output'. State how they are related.

3. Give typical values at rest and during exercise for:

   a) stroke volume

   b) heart rate

   c) cardiac output.

   How might these differ for a trained athlete?

4. What is the Frank-Starling mechanism?

5. Briefly outline the conduction system of the heart.

6. Explain the events of the cardiac cycle.

7. Sketch the expected heart rate response for:

   a) sub-maximal exercise

   b) maximal exercise.

8. Explain the function of the sympathetic and parasympathetic nervous systems. How do they regulate the heart rate?

9. Define venous return. Explain the mechanisms of venous return.

10. Sketch a graph to show the relationship between blood pressure, blood vessel cross-sectional area and blood velocity.

11. Explain the ways in which oxygen and carbon dioxide are transported in the body.

12. Give three factors that cause oxygen to dissociate from haemoglobin during exercise.

13. Explain the role played by blood carbon dioxide in the control of heart rate.

14. Briefly outline some of the physiological adaptations that we might expect to see as a result of endurance training on:

    a) the heart

    b) the vascular system.

CHAPTER 5

Joints, muscles and mechanics

– an analysis of human movement in sporting activity

Introduction

The human body is an amazing machine. At the centre of its operations is movement, which occurs as a result of two of its systems working together: the skeletal and muscular systems. The muscles are the engines of movement, which power the levers or bones of the body and enable us to move. This chapter will investigate the structure and function of each of these systems and look at how they interact to produce coordinated movements from a smooth sprinting action to a powerful tennis serve. The main focus of this chapter is therefore movement analysis and the knowledge you acquire from this chapter will help you describe and explain your sporting performances.

The skeletal system

The skeletal system is made up of approximately 206 bones, which are joined together by **ligaments** to provide a framework of support for our muscles. The skeleton ensures the body can stand erect and maintain posture as well as providing protection for our vital organs. Bones also store essential minerals as well as being a centre for blood production. Another important function of the skeleton is that bones act as a system of **levers** that muscles can put into action to enable movement. Figure 5.02 identifies the names of those bones of the skeleton that are required for your study. Familiarise yourself with the names and location of these bones and then attempt Task 5.01 on page 86.

The skeleton can be divided into two basic sections known as the **axial** and **appendicular** Skeletons. The **axial skeleton** consists of the bones that form the head, neck and trunk and houses

EXAM TIP:

Make sure you use the appropriate technical terminology in your written exam.

the vertebral column, rib cage and sternum. These bones are **unshaded** in Figure 5.01. The bones that form the axial skeleton together form the main support and stabilising structure of the body. The **appendicular skeleton** consists of the shoulder girdle (including the scapula and clavicle) together with the bones of the arm and hands, as well as the hip girdle with the bones of the leg and feet. These bones are **shaded** in Figure 5.01. The majority of sporting movements are a result of moving the bones of the appendicular skeleton.

REMEMBER!

Exercise increases the strength of bones by the laying down of calcium along the lines of stress imposed.

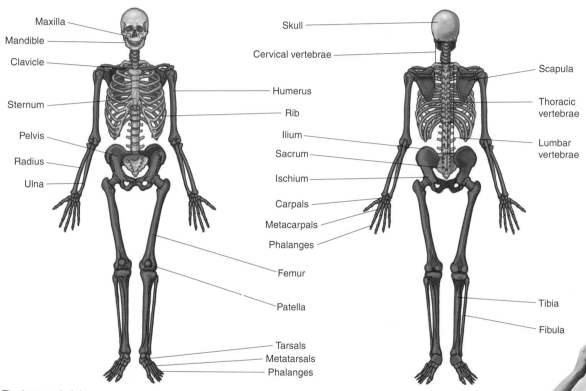

Fig. 5.01 The human skeleton

ATHLETE PROFILE

Elite performers such as Stephanie Twell will require a sound level of understanding of human movement if they are to optimise their performance. A knowledge of how the muscles work and the range of movement that is taking place at joints can help to refine and fine-tune an athlete's technique. Centres such as those of the English Institute of Sport can help in the analysis of movement and the identification of weaknesses in a performer's technique. Through biomechanical analysis, for example, an athlete's performance is assessed and problems diagnosed that might limit sporting potential. In close consultation with the athlete's coach, training programmes can be modified to incorporate activities which might help rectify the problem. A common problem for some middle-distance runners is over-pronation, where the feet roll inwards when striking the track. Over-pronation shifts the forces produced when running out of line and creates wasted energy making the runner's action very inefficient. Biomechanical analysis of the runner's gait can diagnose this problem and then remedies can be suggested to resolve the problem and hopefully improve performance.

TASK 5.01

Using a partner's body as a model, correctly locate and label as many bones of their skeleton as possible. Use a stopwatch to time each other to see who can name the most bones in the quickest time.

TASK 5.02

Summarise the main functions of the skeleton.

The articular system – joints

Joints are formed wherever two or more bones meet and are the only places in the body where movement can take place. The site at which bones move against one another is sometimes called an articulation, but this term can only really be used of joints which allow movement. These are called **synovial** or freely movable joints, and enable us to perform a wide range of movements. Fixed or immovable joints are called **fibrous joints**. Their role is to prevent any movement at the point at which two bones meet. A good example of this is where the bony plates of the skull meet. **Cartilaginous** or slightly movable joints are so called because they only allow a small degree of movement. The best examples of these in the human body are between the adjacent vertebrae of the spinal column. However, it is synovial joints that you must mainly focus on for your examination.

Synovial joints

Synovial joints are categorised according to the range of movement possible at each. This is largely determined by the shapes of the articulating surfaces of the bones within the joint capsule, and the position and number of ligaments that surround the joint.

All synovial joints possess several defining features (Fig. 5.02). These include:

- a **joint capsule**: a tough connective tissue that surrounds and encases the bones of the joint
- a **joint cavity**: filled with synovial fluid which helps to lubricate the joint
- a **synovial membrane**: this lines the inside of the joint capsule and secretes the synovial fluid
- **articular (hyaline) cartilage:** a smooth slippery cartilage that covers the ends of the articulating bones preventing friction and general wear and tear.

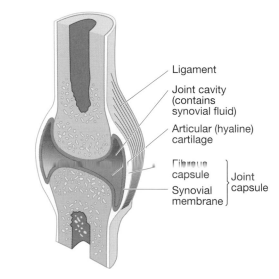

Ligament

Joint cavity (contains synovial fluid)

Articular (hyaline) cartilage

Fibrous capsule ⎤
                  ⎬ Joint
Synovial membrane ⎦ capsule

Fig. 5.02 A typical synovial joint

TASK 5.03

1. Fig. 5.03 illustrates a typical synovial joint. Name the structures A to E.
2. State whether the functions of the above features are to increase protection, stability or mobility.
3. Several other features of a synovial joint include **ligaments, bursae, menisci** and **pads of fat**. Find out the role of each in the joint. For each feature state whether they are there to increase protection, stability or mobility.

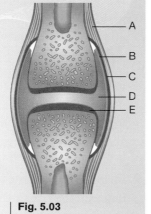

Fig. 5.03

KEY TERMS

Bursae:
small sacs of synovial fluid located at points of friction in and around the joint capsule

Meniscus (pl. menisci):
discs of cartilage found between the articulating surfaces of the bones in the knee joint. They prevent wear and tear of the bones and help in shock absorption

Pads of fat:
fatty tissue located in the joints to give added protection

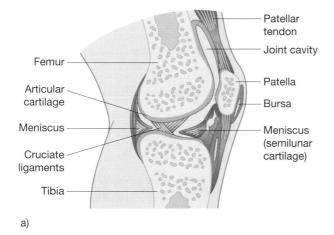

a)

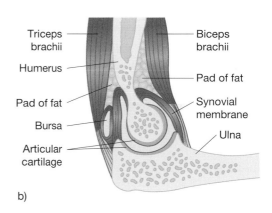

b)

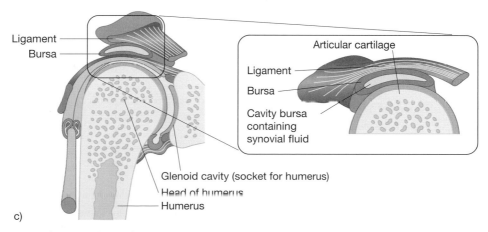

c)

Fig. 5.04 a) The knee joint; b) the elbow joint; c) the shoulder joint

Copy out the statements A–D then match the terms below with the correct definitions.
- Appendicular skeleton
- Axial skeleton
- Fibrous joint
- Cartilaginous joint
- Synovial joint

_____

A. The main axis of the body, which includes the bones of the skull, spine and rib cage

_____

B. Joints which do not allow any movement, such as those between the plates of the skull

_____

C. Joints which only allow a small degree of movement, such as those found between the vertebrae

_____

D. The bones of the limbs, together with the bones of the shoulder and hip girdles.

Types of synovial joint

The shapes of articulating surfaces at a joint can vary tremendously and can determine the range of movement that occurs. Synovial joints are therefore categorised according to the shape of these articulating surfaces. There are six types of synovial joint. These are outlined below and illustrated in Figure 5.05:

a) **Ball and socket joint:** these joints offer the widest range of movement. The head of one bone fits snugly into the cup-shaped cavity of another. Movement at these joints occurs, in all three planes allowing side-to-side, back and forth and rotational movements. Examples include the shoulder and hip joints.

b) **Hinge joint:** these joints offer back and forth movement only in one plane. Here bony protrusions called **condyles** articulate in depressions of a second articulating bone. Hinge joints also possess an intricate network of ligaments which restrict movement, but make the joint very stable. Examples include the knee and elbow joint.

c) **Pivot joint**: pivot joints allow rotational movement only in one plane. Typically the structure of a pivot joint includes the head or 'peg' of one bone articulating in a deep depression or socket of a second bone. Examples include the radio-ulnar joint and between the atlas and axis vertebrae.

d) **Gliding joint**: these joints offer movement in two planes, back and forth and side-to-side movement. Typically they occur where the articulating bones have flat surfaces that can slide past each other. Movement at these joints is limited by the action of ligaments. Examples include between the carpal bones of the wrist and between the ribs and thoracic vertebrae.

e) **Saddle joint**: a saddle joint permits side-to-side and back and forth, but no rotational, movement. Two saddle-shaped articulating surfaces of adjacent bones (either concave or convex) 'fit' together at right angles to allow movement in these two planes. A good example can be found in the thumb at the site where the carpal and metacarpal meet.

f) **Condyloid joint (ellipsoid)**: this is very similar to a hinge joint, but instead of having movement restricted to one plane, side-to-side movement can also take place. The bony projections (condyles) of one bone articulate with hollow depressions of another. A good example includes the radio-carpal joint – where the radius articulates with the carpals at the wrist.

1. Name the bones that articulate at the following joints:
   a) the shoulder joint
   b) the elbow joint
   c) the hip joint
   d) the knee joint
   e) the ankle joint.
2. When performing the butterfly stroke in swimming, the knee joint and shoulder joint are central to the performance. Briefly outline the structure of each joint and suggest how this structure suits the particular function of each joint in this activity.

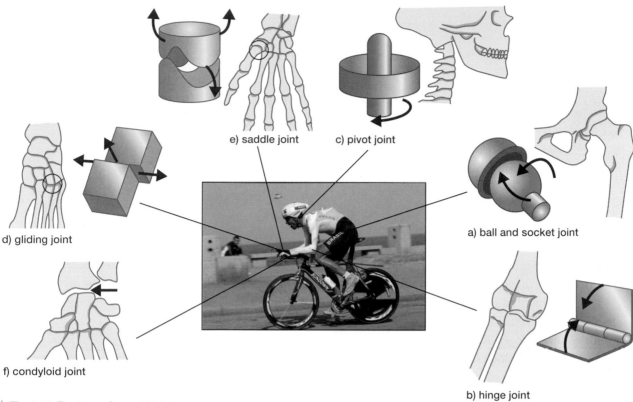

Fig. 5.05 The types of synovial joint

Terms of movement

In order to describe the movements of the body special terms are used to explain the movements that take place. Using these terms correctly when studying movement analysis will help you tremendously in your examination. This language covers three main areas:

* planes of the body
* terms of movement or 'movement patterns'
* axes of the body.

Planes of the body

To aid our understanding of movement it is useful to describe the body as having a series of 'planes' or imaginary flat surfaces (think of them as panes of glass) running through the body within which different types of movement takes place. There are three such planes:

* the **sagittal (median) plane** divides the body vertically into left and right sides
* the **frontal (coronal) plane** divides the body vertically into front and back sections
* the **transverse (horizontal)** plane divides the body into top and bottom halves and runs horizontally parallel to the ground.

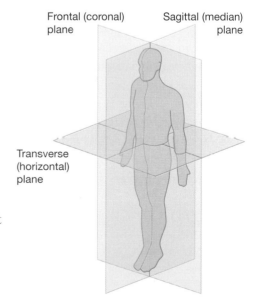

Fig. 5.06 Planes of the human body

a)   b)

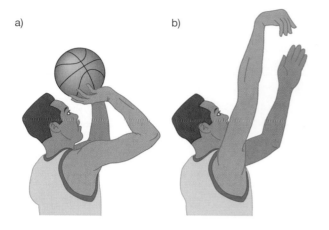

Fig. 5.07 a) flexion and b) extension at the elbow during a set shot in basketball

Terms of movement – movement patterns and joint actions

There are many different types of movement possible at synovial joints. You may remember that the movements permitted at any particular joint are largely determined by the joint structure. Some joints (the ball and socket joints) are designed to allow a wide range of movement while others (hinge joints) are designed more for stability, which limits the amount of movement possible. Movements at synovial joints can be classified according to how the movement relates to the **anatomical position**.

Movement patterns typically occur in pairs because if we can perform a movement at a joint in one direction, we must be able to return the body

part to its original starting position, which requires movement in the opposite direction.

For your AS course it is important that you can identify the movement patterns and the planes in which each movement occurs. For ease, therefore, each pair of movement patterns has been categorised according to the relevant plane of movement.

Movements in the sagittal (median) plane

The sagittal plane divides the body down the middle into left and right halves. The following movements are parallel to this plane and are therefore said to take place within it.

- **Flexion and extension**
  Flexion and extension are distinctive to the sagittal plane (see Fig. 5.07). **Flexion** typically occurs when there is a decrease in angle between the articulating bones of a joint, and there is a movement forward from the anatomical position. For example, bending the arm at the elbow during the upward phase of a bicep curl or bringing the arm forward at the shoulder joint. There are, however, one or two exceptions where flexion occurs with a movement backwards from the anatomical position. These include bending the leg at the knee and dorsiflexion (see below) of the ankle, which brings the foot up towards the shin. **Extension** is usually any straightening movement that brings a body part backwards from its anatomical position. Extension will cause an increase in angle between the articulating bones at a joint, for example when lowering the barbell, during a bicep curl at the elbow. Once again, extension at the knee and plantar flexion at the ankle are exceptions, where extension brings the body part forward from the anatomical position. A continuation of extension beyond the anatomical position is sometimes referred to as **hyperextension.**

- **Plantar flexion and dorsiflexion**
  Plantar flexion is unique to the ankle joint and is characterised by the pointing of the toes. More

simply, it is extension at the ankle joint. Plantar flexion occurs at the ankle when performing a handstand, ensuring a neat body line. Flexion at the ankle joint is termed **dorsiflexion** and occurs when there is a decrease in angle between the tibia and the foot for example, if you walk on your heels.

Movements in the frontal (coronal) plane

The frontal plane divides the body down the middle into front and back halves. The following movements are parallel to this plane and are therefore said to take place within it.

- **Abduction and adduction**
  Abduction and adduction are distinctive to the frontal plane. **Abduction** is any movement that takes a body part away from the midline of the body. For example, when raising the arm out sideways at the shoulder when performing 'the crucifix' on the rings apparatus in gymnastics. **Adduction** involves the movement of a body part towards the midline of the body. Taking our earlier example, adduction will occur when lowering the arm back to the sides of the body.
- **Lateral flexion**
  The movement of the head or bending of the trunk sideways away from the midline of the body is termed lateral flexion.
- **Inversion and eversion**
  Abduction and adduction of the foot are termed eversion and inversion respectively. **Eversion** of the foot is characterised by turning the sole of the foot laterally outwards, for example during the 'kicking' phase of a breaststroke leg kick. **Inversion** takes place when the sole of the foot is turned towards the midline of the body. This

might happen when placing spin on a ball by kicking it with the outside of the foot.
- **Elevation and depression**
  Movement of the scapula upwards, for example when shrugging the shoulders, is termed **elevation**. This can be seen in the sporting arena when shooting in netball or basketball. When the scapulae are lowered back down **depression** occurs.

Movements in the transverse (horizontal) plane

The transverse plane divides the body across the middle into upper and lower halves (Fig. 5.06). The following movements are parallel to and are therefore said to take place within this plane.

- **Lateral and medial rotation**
  Rotation of a joint occurs when a bone moves about its longitudinal axis. **Medial rotation** is rotation that occurs towards the midline of the body from the anatomical position. When swimming butterfly, for example, medial rotation at the shoulder takes place when the arms enter the water. **Lateral rotation** on the other hand occurs when there is rotation of a body part towards the outside of the body from the anatomical position. For example, when preparing to put top spin on a tennis ball, lateral rotation must first take place at the shoulder joint.
- **Pronation and supination**
  Rotation at the radio-ulnar joint is uniquely termed pronation or supination. **Pronation** is a form of medial rotation characterised by the turning of the palm of the hand to face downwards or backwards. Pronation will take place when placing top spin on a tennis ball. **Supination** of the radio-ulnar joint involves lateral rotation and will typically have occurred when the palm is facing upwards or forwards. When performing a 'dig' in volleyball, the forearms and palms of the hands will be facing upwards, so supination has occurred.

KEY TERM

Abduction/adduction:
muscles that cause abduction are called abductors
Muscles that cause adduction are called adductors

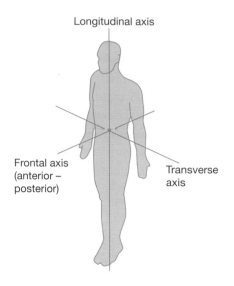

Longitudinal axis

Frontal axis
(anterior –
posterior)

Transverse
axis

Fig 5.08 The axes of the body

- **Horizontal abduction and adduction**
  Abduction and adduction in the horizontal plane is termed horizontal abduction and horizontal adduction. These movements can be demonstrated by raising your arm out in front of

you, so that your arm is parallel to the ground; this is flexion of the shoulder. Now move your arm towards the outside of the body, keeping it parallel to the ground; this is **horizontal abduction**. From here, move your arm towards the midline of your body, You have just performed **horizontal adduction** of the shoulder. Perhaps the best example of horizontal abduction and horizontal adduction is during the preparation and execution phases respectively of a discus throw. Sometimes horizontal abduction is referred to as horizontal extension and horizontal adduction is referred to as horizontal flexion.

There are several other movement patterns that take place in the body. One in particular that is necessary for your study is **circumduction**. Circumduction is said to occur when the distal end of a body part can describe a circle. Essentially circumduction is a combination of flexion, extension, abduction and adduction, but can only truly happen at the ball and socket joints of the shoulder and hip. Circumduction occurs in two planes of movement; the sagittal and frontal planes. Circumduction occurs at the shoulder when a bowler delivers the ball in cricket.

TASK 5.06

Working with a partner, identify the movement patterns that occur at each of the joints outlined in Table 5.01. Once you have worked out these movements, complete the table in your student workbook. For each movement pattern identified, think of a relevant sporting example for each and write it in the third column of the table. An example for the hip joint has been completed to help you make a start.

Joint	Movement Patterns	Relevant sporting example
Hip	1 Flexion 2 Extension 3 Abduction 4 Adduction 5 Medial Rotation 6 Lateral Rotation 7 Circumduction	1 During the downward phase of a leg squat 2 When driving out of the blocks during a sprint start
Knee		
Ankle		
Shoulder		
Elbow		
Radio-ulnar		
Wrist		

Table 5.01

Axes of the body

Just as the earth rotates about its axis, articulating bones at the joints must rotate about one of three body axes. Like the body planes these can also be viewed as a series of imaginary lines (this time think of them as poles) which run through the body. For movement to occur in the sagittal plane, rotation about the **horizontal axis** (transverse axis) must take place. This enables the movements of flexion and extension to occur (see page 90 for a description of these types of movement).

Movement in the frontal plane takes place about the **anterio-posterior axis** (frontal axis), enabling the movements of abduction and adduction, as well as some other associated movements, which are outlined below.

Finally, movement in the transverse plane takes place about the **longitudinal axis**, enabling rotational movement to take place.

Fig 5.09 A high diver will need to rotate around all three axes of the body

REMEMBER!

The axis of rotation is always at right angles to the plane in which the movement occurs.

APPLY IT!

Movement can take place about more than one axis and in more than one plane. Think of the high diver performing a full twisting dive in Figure 5.09.

TASK 5.07

For each of the actions stated below, state the axis and plane in which the movement takes place.

Movement	Plane	Axis of rotation
A cartwheel		
A backward somersault		
An ice skater spinning		
A full twisting somersault		

Table 5.02

TASK 5.08

Write out the following statements, stating clearly beside them whether they are TRUE or FALSE.
1. The cruciate ligaments help to stabilise the knee joint.
2. The radio-ulnar joint is just another name for the elbow joint.
3. A front somersault takes place in the sagittal plane.
4. Horizontal abduction is also known as horizontal flexion.
5. The movements of flexion and extension take place about the horizontal axis.

TAKE IT FURTHER

1. Use a website such as BBC Sport Academy (news.bbc.co.uk/sport1/hi/academy/default.stm) and research the technical model of a chosen skill.
2. Compare the technical model to a live performance of the same skill demonstrated by a friend. Using correct terminology (i.e. flexion, extension, etc.) comment upon the similarities of and differences between the two performances. What accounts for the differences in the performances? Can these be overcome? How?

Muscles – the engines of movement

The body possesses three types of muscle tissue: **skeletal muscle**, **cardiac muscle** and **smooth muscle**. Cardiac and smooth muscle are **involuntary**, working outside our conscious control and are found in the heart and blood vessels respectively (smooth muscle is also found in the intestines and bladder). Skeletal muscle, however, is attached to the skeleton and is under our **voluntary control**. Consequently it enables voluntary movement to take place. In addition to movement, skeletal muscle also helps to support and maintain the posture of the body through **muscle tone**, and produces heat, keeping the body warm through contraction. Since the focus of this chapter is an analysis of human movement, we will only be considering skeletal muscle in the following discussion.

At the end of this section you should be able to locate some of the major skeletal muscles in the body, explain the function of each and apply this to a range of sporting performances.

Skeletal muscle

The human body contains in excess of 600 skeletal muscles, which contain contractile units that are able to convert chemical energy into mechanical energy, and therefore facilitate movement. Skeletal muscle is attached to the skeleton via **tendons**, which transmit the muscular 'pull' to the bones, causing them to move. Typically a muscle will have two or more attachments onto the skeleton (via tendons). The attachment of the muscle on to a bone nearer the midline of the body (the proximal end), is known as an **origin**. This is normally a flat, relatively stable bone. The attachment at the distal end of the bone, furthest away from the midline of the body is known as the **insertion**, and is typically attached to the bone that the muscle puts into action. Figure 5.10 shows the origin and insertion of the biceps brachii and triceps brachii muscles.

Figure 5.11 illustrates the locations and functions of the major muscles that you are required

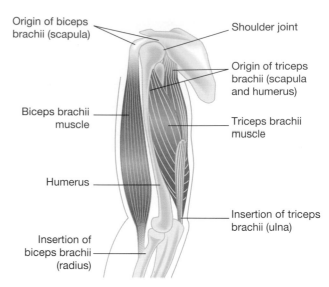

Fig. 5.10 The origin and insertion of the biceps brachii and triceps brachii muscles

to know for this AS course. Learning them all may seem a bit daunting, but by reading over them regularly you will be surprised at how quickly you will be able to recall them.

REMEMBER!

The origins of the muscles of the trunk are always the superior attachment (closer to the head) while the insertion will always be the inferior attachment (closer to the foot).

REMEMBER!

By rule of thumb, the insertion of a muscle is on the bone that moves, while the origin of the muscle is on the nearest flat bone.

HOT LINKS

www.bbc.co.uk/science/humanbody/
www.innerbody.com/htm/body.html
www.getbodysmart.com/
Visit one or all of the above websites to test your knowledge of the function and location of muscles in the body.

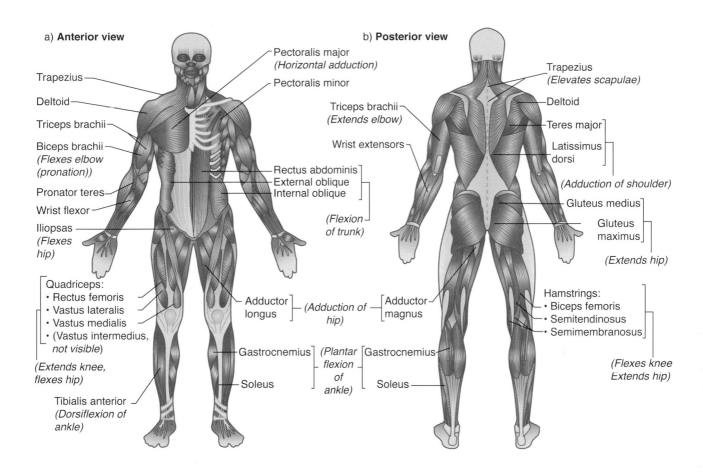

Fig. 5.11 Location and function of major muscles of the body, showing an anterior and posterior view

The coordination of movement – antagonistic muscle action

For smooth coordinated movements to occur, skeletal muscles need to cooperate and work together. Because muscles can only pull, and not push, they generally work in pairs, with the help of several other muscles, to ensure that the desired movements take place as effectively as possible. For any particular movement, therefore, muscles will take up one of several roles.

The muscle that is directly responsible for the desired movement at a joint will typically shorten, and is known as the **agonist** or **prime mover**. To assist this movement, the other muscle of the pair will lengthen and act as an **antagonist**. During the upward phase of a bicep curl, for example, flexion occurs at the elbow joint; the biceps brachii are the muscles directly responsible for this movement and therefore shorten. They are the agonists. The triceps brachii are the antagonists and lengthen. However several other muscles will ensure that this movement occurs smoothly. The trapezius will stabilise the scapula, upon which the origin of the biceps brachii attaches. This ensures that the biceps have something solid to pull against when contracting. The role of the trapezius in this instance is as a **fixator** muscle. Meanwhile other muscles will be preventing any other undesired movements in the body. In the example of the upward phase of a bicep curl, the deltoid neutralises any unwanted movement at the shoulder joint. In this instance the deltoid is known as a **neutraliser** or **synergist**.

Now study Figure 5.12, which illustrates the antagonistic muscle action occurring at the elbow joint during the upward phase of a bicep curl.

During a tricep extension, the tricep brachii is the agonist and the biceps brachii becomes

the antagonist. In this exercise, the neutraliser and fixator remain as the deltoid and trapezius respectively.

During the downward phase of a leg squat, the quadriceps group is the agonist, even though flexion is occurring at the knee. This controls the movement and prevents the body from collapsing to the floor.

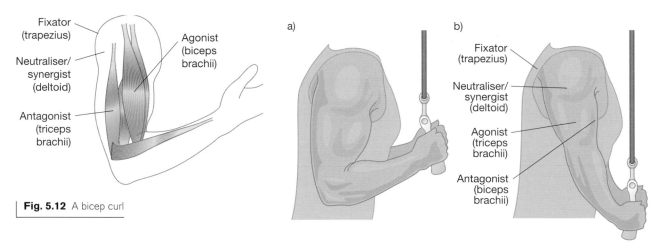

Fig. 5.12 A bicep curl

Fig. 5.13 The roles of the muscles during a triceps extension exercise

TASK 5.09

Research the Internet for suitable images of an athlete putting the shot and a player kicking a rugby ball. Label the photos with the correct roles of the muscles in each phase of the movement. Briefly explain your diagrams.

REMEMBER!

Be aware that sometimes the roles of the muscles do not reverse for opposite movements – this is especially true for downward movements such as performing squats or running a marathon.

KEY TERM

Flexors/extensors:
muscles that cause flexion are known as flexors
muscles that cause extension are called extensors

APPLY IT!

During the downward phase of a bicep curl the bicep remains as the agonist, but lengthens as it contracts. In doing so it acts like a brake to control the forearm as it lowers. Similarly, during the downward phase of a leg squat the quadriceps group is the agonist, even thought flexion occurs at the knee. This controls the movement, and prevents the body from collapsing to the floor.

TASK 5.10

Working with a partner, investigate the anatomical movements outlined in Table 5.03.
Complete the table, filling in the agonist and antagonist for each movement identified.

Joint	Movement Patterns	Agonist	Antagonist
Elbow	Flexion		
Elbow	Extension		
Radio-ulnar	Pronation		
Radio-ulnar	Supination		
Shoulder	Flexion		
Shoulder	Extension		
Shoulder	Abduction		
Shoulder	Adduction		
Trunk (lumbar)	Flexion		
Trunk (lumbar)	Extension		
Trunk (lumbar)	Lateral flexion		
Hip	Flexion		
Hip	Extension		
Hip	Abduction		
Hip	Adduction		
Knee	Flexion		
Knee	Extension		
Ankle	Plantar flexion		
Ankle	Dorsi flexion		

Table 5.03

Types of muscular contraction

Muscles have different contraction capacities, depending upon the role they are playing in the movement.

- The agonist muscle will generally shorten and fatten while contracting, drawing the insertion of the muscle towards the origin. This is **isotonic** concentric contraction. The triceps brachii undergo **concentric** contraction during the upward phase of a press-up.
- Sometimes muscles will contract while lengthening, acting like a brake to control the movement. When a muscle contracts while

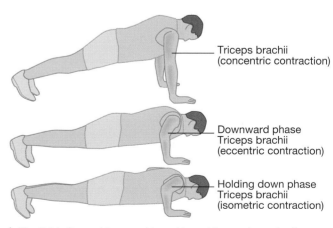

Triceps brachii
(concentric contraction)

Downward phase
Triceps brachii
(eccentric contraction)

Holding down phase
Triceps brachii
(isometric contraction)

Fig. 5.14 Concentric, eccentric and isometric muscle contraction during a press-up

lengthening **isotonic eccentric** contraction is taking place. The triceps brachii will undergo eccentric contraction during the downward phase of a press-up.

- A third type of muscle contraction occurs when there is an increase in muscle tension, but no visible movement of the muscle taking place. This is **isometric muscle contraction** and will invariably occur when a muscle is acting as a fixator or neutraliser.

In the example of a press-up the deltoids will work isometrically. We may also see isometric contraction taking place if the muscle is exerting a force against a resistance that it cannot overcome, for example, when pushing against a wall or remaining stationary in the press-up position.

REMEMBER!

Muscles can either contract concentrically (shorten), eccentrically (lengthen) or isometrically (remain the same length).

KEY TERMS

Isotonic contraction:
an isotonic contraction involves some visible movement of the muscle. This can be either shortening (concentric) or lengthening (eccentric)

Isometric contraction:
an isometric contraction occurs when a muscle is contracting but there is no visible movement of the main bulk of the muscle or muscle belly

TASK 5.11

1. Perform a bicep curl.
2. Observe the movement occurring in the biceps brachii and triceps brachii during both the upward and downward phases of the curl.
3. Now hold the barbell so that your elbows are held at 90°. Note the action of the triceps and biceps brachii.
4. Now complete the table below in your student workbook.

Phase of bicep curl	Action of bicep brachii	Action of tricep brachii
Upward		
Downward		
Elbow held at 90°		

Table 5.04

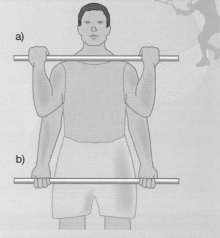

Fig. 5.15 A bicep curl being performed: a) upward phase and b) downward phase

TASK 5.12

Copy out and complete the passage below, filling in the blanks using the words listed in the box. You may use some of the words more than once.

> antagonistically, isometrically, agonists, eccentrically, shortens, lengthening, concentric

Eccentric contraction occurs when a muscle contracts while _____. Concentric contraction occurs when a muscle _____ while contracting. During the upward phase of a press-up the triceps brachii are the main _____ at the elbow and the biceps brachii are working _____. The type of contraction taking place in the triceps brachii is _____ contraction. During the downward phase of the press-up the triceps remain as the main _____ but this time contract _____. This controls the movement during the downward phase. When holding the press-up in the down position, muscles acting on the elbows are working _____.

Joint	Action	Plane	Muscles used
Shoulder	Flexion	Median	Anterior deltoid Pectoralis major
	Extension	Median	Posterior deltoid Latissimus dorsi Teres major
	Adduction	Frontal	Latissimus dorsi Pectoralis major Teres major Teres minor
	Abduction	Frontal	Medial deltoid Supraspinatus
	Horizontal adduction	Horizontal	Pectoralis major Anterior deltoid
	Horizontal abduction	Horizontal	Posterior deltoid Trapezius Latissimus dorsi
	Medial rotation	Horizontal	Subscapularis
	Lateral rotation	Horizontal	Infraspinatus Teres minor
Elbow	Flexion	Median	Biceps brachii Brachialis brachioradialis
	Extension	Median	Triceps brachii
Radio-ulnar	Pronation	Horizontal	Pronator teres brachioradialis
	Supination	Horizontal	Biceps brachii Supinator
Wrist	Flexion	Median	Wrist flexors
	Extension	Median	Wrist extensors
Hip	Flexion	Median	Psoas } Iliopsoas Iliacus Rectus femoris
	Extension	Median	Gluteus maximus Biceps femoris Semimembranosus Semitendinosus Gluteus medius
	Abduction	Frontal	Gluteus medius Gluteus minimus Tensor fasciae latae

Table 5.05 Summary of the main functions of the major muscles working at each joint

Joint	Action	Plane	Muscles used
Hip	Adduction	Frontal	Adductor magnus Adductor brevis Adductor longus gracilis
	Medial rotation	Horizontal	Gluteus medius Gluteus minimus Tensor fasciae latae
	Lateral rotation	Horizontal	Gluteus maximus Adductors
Knee	Flexion	Median	Hamstrings (semitendinosus, semimembranosus, biceps femoris) Gastrocnemius
	Extension	Median	Quadriceps (rectus femoris, vastus medialis, vastus lateralis, vastus intermedius) Tensor fasciae latae
Ankle	Dorsi flexion	Median	Tibialis anterior Extensor digitorum longus
	Plantar flexion	Median	Gastrocnemius Soleus Flexor digitorum longus
	Inversion	Frontal	Tibialis anterior Flexor digitorum longus
	Eversion	Frontal	Peroneus longus Peroneus brevis Extensor digitorum longus
Movement of the trunk	Flexion	Median	Rectus abdominus Internal obliques External obliques
	Extension	Median	Erector spinae Spinalis
	Lateral flexion	Frontal	Internal obliques Rectus abdominus Erector spinae
	Rotation		External obliques Rectus abdominus Erector spinae
Movement of the scapulae	Elevation	Frontal	Levator scapulae Trapezius Rhomboids
	Depression	Frontal	Lower trapezius Pectoralis minor

Table 5.05 Summary of the main functions of the major muscles working at each joint

Muscle functions

Table 5.05 summarises the major functions of the muscles that surround each joint. You will need to study this so that you have a good understanding of the functions of these muscle functions.

Levers of the body

We established earlier in this chapter that in order for us to perform sporting movements – from kicking a rugby ball to serving in tennis – the bones of the skeleton act as a series of levers against which the muscles can pull. Levers are relatively simple mechanisms that involve a rigid bar rotating about a fixed point when a force or effort is applied to overcome a resistance.

Levers in the body can help us to:

- maintain balance
- give greater speed to an object by throwing it or kicking it
- overcome a heavy resistance with little effort
- give a wider range of movement.

There are three components to every lever system:

1. An **effort point (E)** – in the human body this will be the point at which the force supplied by a contracting muscle is applied, i.e. the insertion of the muscle
2. A pivot point or **fulcrum (F)** – in the human body this will be the joint itself
3. A resistance point or **load (L)** – this may simply be the weight of the lever or body part or indeed an object that we are trying to move.

There are three types (classes) of lever system found in the human body: first, second and third. Each has a particular function, whether it be to increase the amount of resistance that can be overcome by a given force, or to increase the speed of an object. A lever system is classified according to the relative positions of the effort, fulcrum and load, the three components listed above. Look at the information in Table 5.06 which explains the function of each class of lever.

Two other important features of lever systems are the **effort arm** and the **resistance arm.** The effort arm (also known as the **force arm**) is the name given to the shortest perpendicular distance between the fulcrum and the application of the effort. The resistance arm refers to the shortest perpendicular distance between the fulcrum and the resistance.

Figure 5.17 illustrates a first class lever system operating at the elbow. Here the longer resistance arm cannot move as heavy a load but gives greater speed to the system. When the resistance arm is greater than the effort arm the lever system is at a **mechanical disadvantage**. Figure 5.18 shows a second class lever system, but the longer effort arm allows for more force to be developed and a large load can be moved over a short distance. This is known as **mechanical advantage**.

REMEMBER!

Most lever systems used in the human body are third class lever systems.

The vast majority of levers in the human body are **third class levers** which are better suited to increasing the body's ability to move quickly, rather than to improving its ability to move heavy loads. This is because in third class levers the resistance arm is always greater than the effort arm, and therefore mechanical disadvantage exists.

REMEMBER!

If you are having difficulty in working out what class of lever is operating at a particular joint, try to work out the middle component. Once you have this you will be able to determine the lever system working using the following rhyme: '…for 1, 2, 3 think F, L, E…' Where F is the middle component of a first class lever, L for a second class lever and E for a third class lever system.

KEY TERMS

Mechanical disadvantage:
mechanical disadvantage occurs in a lever system when the resistance arm is longer than the force arm. This means that the lever system cannot move as heavy a load but can do it faster

Mechanical advantage:
occurs in a lever system when the force arm is longer than the resistance arm. This means that the lever system can move a large load over a short distance

The body's levers can be made even more effective by using striking implements such as rackets, oars and ski poles. In essence these are extensions of the body's third class levers, increasing the length of the resistance arm of the lever and consequently the speed at the end of it. Keeping the arm extended when bowling a cricket ball or during a tennis serve will maximise the length of the resistance arm and allow more force to be exerted.

Tall tennis players have an advantage when serving, as they have very long levers and can impose a great deal of speed onto the tennis ball.

TASK 5.13

Copy out the following passage about lever systems and fill in the missing words.
You may use some of the words from the box more than once and your own words where a phrase is necessary.

load, bones, fulcrum, joints, effort, jumping, throwing, kicking

In the human body the _____ act as levers and the _____ act as fulcra in order to enhance movement. There are three components to every lever system; an _____ force, a _____ force and a pivot or _____. There are three types or classes of lever – first, second and third class. In a first class lever the _____ lies between the _____ and the _____. An example of this in the human body is the _____. In a second class lever the _____ lies between the _____ and the _____. An example from sport when this lever system operates is _____ _____. In a third class lever system the _____ lies between the _____ and the _____. This is the most popular class of lever system in the human body. An example from the sporting arena when a third class lever operates is _____ _____. The term mechanical disadvantage when applied to a lever system refers to _____ _____ _____ _____.

Class of lever	Positions of components	Example in the human body	Function
First class lever	E F L 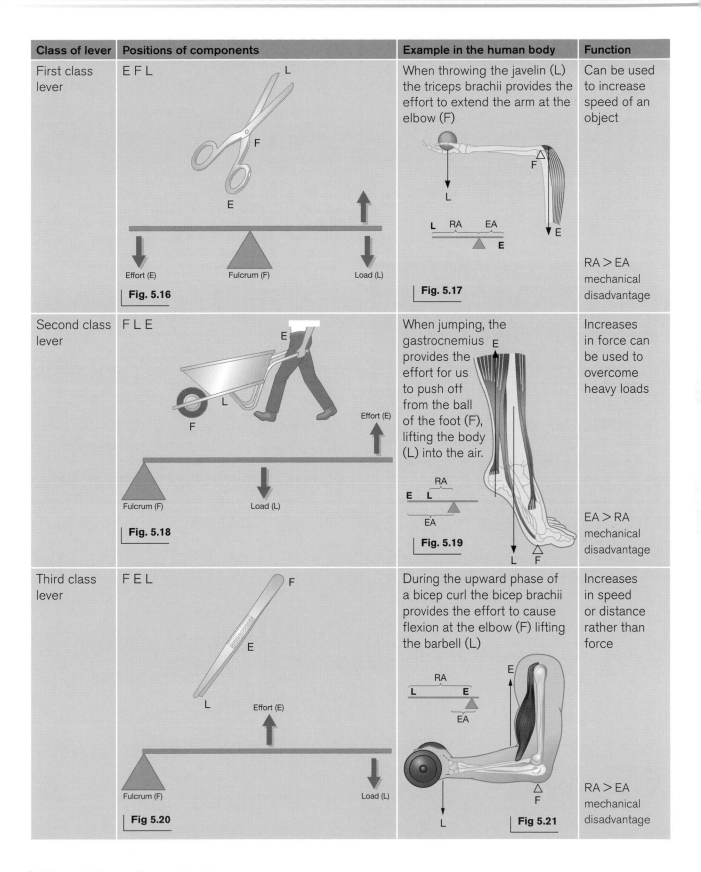 Effort (E) Fulcrum (F) Load (L) **Fig. 5.16**	When throwing the javelin (L) the triceps brachii provides the effort to extend the arm at the elbow (F) L RA EA **E** **Fig. 5.17**	Can be used to increase speed of an object RA > EA mechanical disadvantage
Second class lever	F L E Fulcrum (F) Load (L) Effort (E) **Fig. 5.18**	When jumping, the gastrocnemius provides the effort for us to push off from the ball of the foot (F), lifting the body (L) into the air. E L RA EA **Fig. 5.19**	Increases in force can be used to overcome heavy loads EA > RA mechanical disadvantage
Third class lever	F E L Fulcrum (F) Effort (E) Load (L) **Fig 5.20**	During the upward phase of a bicep curl the bicep brachii provides the effort to cause flexion at the elbow (F) lifting the barbell (L) L RA E EA **Fig 5.21**	Increases in speed or distance rather than force RA > EA mechanical disadvantage

Table 5.06 Classes of levers in the body

TAKE IT FURTHER

1. A comparison of bone measurements – identify the following points on a partner:
   - the acromion process of the scapula
   - the olecranon process at the elbow
   - the styloid process at the wrist
   - the greater trochanter of the femur
   - the femoral condyle of the knee joint
   - lateral malleolus of the fibula.
2. Using a tape measure, measure the distance between the points listed in the table below:

Name	Height	Favoured sporting activity

Body measurement	Length
Acromion process to olecranon process	
Olecranon process to styloid process	
Greater trochanter to femoral condyle	
Femoral condyle to malleolus	

Table 5.07

3. Copy out and complete the table, recording the results of your fellow classmates.
4. Comment upon the results of your group. You may wish to consider the following questions.
   - Does the length of lever determine which sports people participate in?
   - Is there any difference between male and female scores?
   - In which activities do the players benefit from having longer limbs?
   - In which sports do the players benefit from having shorter limbs?

TASK 5.15

Name and sketch the lever system that is in operation in each of the following examples:
a) at the ankle during the take-off phase of a long jump
b) at the elbow when throwing the javelin
c) at the knee when kicking a football.

TASK 5.16

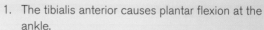

Write out the following statements, stating clearly beside them, whether they are TRUE or FALSE.
1. The tibialis anterior causes plantar flexion at the ankle.
2. The gluteus maximus causes extension at the hip.
3. The origin of the gastrocnemius muscle is on the femur.
4. When performing a leg squat, the quadriceps muscle group are the agonist in both the downward and upward phases of the movement.
5. When performing a press-up the triceps brachii are the agonists in both the downward and upward phases of the movement.
6. When jumping, a first class lever system operates at the ankle joint.

TASK 5.14

Draw a simple second class lever system from the human body. On your diagram label the effort arm and the resistance arm. Which is longer? What does this tell you about the function of second class lever systems?

Putting it all together – movement analysis

You now have all the information that you need to carry out a full movement analysis of a wide range of skills. To help you remember the key features of a movement analysis, ask yourself the questions outlined below:

- What bones are articulating?
- At what type of joint is the movement taking place?
- What movement pattern or joint action is happening?
- In which plane and about which axis is the movement taking place?
- What is the name and function of the muscle contracting?
- How is the muscle contracting?
- Which lever system is operating?

EXAM TIP:

In your examination it may be easier to draw up a movement analysis table to help your explanation and description of movement taking place.

TAKE IT FURTHER

An extended writing task
In order to maximise the effectiveness of movement within the context of a sporting activity, performers will experience a range of training methods.
1. Select an action from an activity of your choice and suggest a method of training to:
   a) develop strength
   b) increase the range of movement possible at a joint.
2. Describe a number of different exercises for each method of training suggested.

You may find it useful to refer to information contained in Chapter 6.

The following section investigates a range of skills from a variety of sporting activities. For each skill a complete movement analysis has been undertaken. Your task is to study each completed skill and then complete a full analysis for:

a) leg action in jumping
b) arm action in throwing
c) leg action in kicking
d) the arm action during a tennis serve.

For the AQA specification you must be able to perform a movement analysis for each of the skills listed below.

- Leg action in running/sprinting (hip, knee and action)
- Leg action in squats (hip, knee and action)
- Leg action in kicking (hip, knee and action)
- Leg action in jumping (hip, knee and action)
- Arm/shoulder action in throwing (shoulder and elbow)
- Shoulder/arm action in racket strokes (shoulder and elbow)
- Arm action in press-ups (shoulder and elbow).

Joint	Phase of movement	Plane	Axis	Movement pattern	Muscles responsible	Role of muscle	Type of contraction	Lever system
HIP	Drive	Sagittal	Transverse	Extension/ hyperextension	Gluteal muscles Hamstring group	agonist	concentric	Third
	Recovery	Sagittal	Transverse	Flexion	Hip flexors (quadriceps and iliopsoas)	agonist	concentric	Third
KNEE	Drive	Sagittal	Transverse	Extension	Quadriceps group	agonist	concentric	Third
	Recovery	Sagittal	Transverse	Flexion	Hamstring group	agonist	concentric	Third
ANKLE	Drive	Sagittal	Transverse	Plantar flexion	Gastrocnemius	agonist	concentric	Second
	Recovery	Sagittal	Transverse	Dorsiflexion	Tibialis anterior	agonist	concentric	Second

Table 5.08 Analysis of leg action in sprinting/running

Joint	Phase of movement	Plane	Axis	Movement pattern	Muscles responsible	Role of muscle	Type of contraction	Lever system
HIP	Downward	Sagittal	Transverse	Flexion	Gluteal Muscles	agonist	Eccentric	Third
	Upward	Sagittal	Transverse	Extension	Gluteal Muscles	agonist	Concentric	Third
KNEE	Downward	Sagittal	Transverse	Flexion	Quadriceps group	agonist	Eccentric	Third
	Upward	Sagittal	Transverse	Extension	Quadriceps group	agonist	Concentric	Third
ANKLE	Downward	Sagittal	Transverse	Dorsi flexion	Gastrocnemius	agonist	Eccentric	Second
	Upward	Sagittal	Transverse	Plantar flexion	Gastrocnemius	agonist	Concentric	Second

Table 5.09 Analysis of leg action in a squat

Joint	Phase of movement	Plane	Axis	Movement pattern	Muscles responsible	Role of muscle	Type of contraction	Lever system
Elbow (Tricep press)	Downward	Sagittal	Transverse	Flexion	Triceps brachii	Agonist	Eccentric	First
	Upward	Sagittal	Transverse	Extension	Triceps brachii	Agonist	Concentric	First
Shoulder (Pec press)	Downward	Transverse	Longitudinal	Horizontal abduction	Pectoralis Major	Agonist	Eccentric	Third
	Upward	Transverse	Longitudinal	Horizontal adduction	Pectoralis Major	Agonist	Concentric	Third

Table 5.10 Analysis of arm action in a press-up

Leg action in sprinting/running

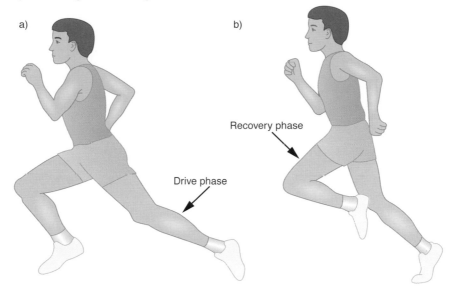

a)

b)

Recovery phase

Drive phase

Fig. 5.22 A running action: a) drive phase and b) recovery phase

Leg action in squats

You will note from Table 5.09 that the same muscle is responsible for both flexion and extension at each of the joints. This is because the action of a squat is in a **downward direction**, with the added force of gravity. In order to stop the body collapsing to the floor during this downward movement, the agonist muscle lengthens undergoing an eccentric contraction, which controls the movement and acts as a brake. A similar situation occurs in the arms during a press-up.

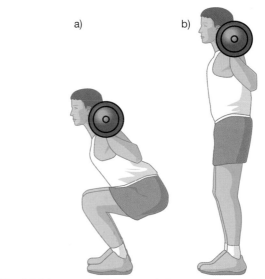

a)   b)

Fig. 5.23 Leg squats: a) downward phase and b) upward phase

Arm action in a press-up

Note that there are two different ways a press-up can be performed:

1. A tricep press is where hands are placed shoulder-width apart and predominantly works the triceps brachii
2. A 'pec' press is where hands are placed wider than shoulder width apart and predominantly works the pectoralis major.

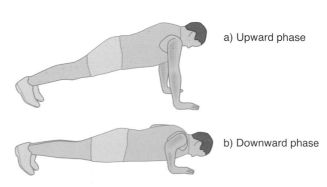

a) Upward phase

b) Downward phase

Fig. 5.24 A press-up

TASK 5.17

As part of a training programme to improve strength, a performer undertakes push-ups (press-ups). This movement involves a downward phase and an upward phase. Copy and complete Table 5.11 to identify the plane and axis, agonists, actions and types of contractions involved in the two phases.

Press-ups				
	Plane and axis	Agonist	Action	Type of contraction
Downward Phase				
Upward Phase				

Table 5.11

TAKE IT FURTHER

Draw a blank movement analysis table and complete a full movement analysis for each of the following:
a) the leg action in jumping
b) the arm action in throwing
c) the leg action in kicking
d) the arm action during a tennis serve.

Refresh your memory

Revision checklist

Make sure you know the following:

▷ The human skeleton consists of approximately 206 bones

▷ The axial skeleton consists of the head, neck and trunk

▷ The appendicular skeleton consists of all the bones of the limbs, together with their associated girdles

▷ Synovial joints are the freely-moveable joints used most in sporting activity

▷ There are six types of synovial joint: ball and socket, hinge, gliding, pivot, saddle and condyloid/ellipsoid

▷ Synovial joints possess a number of structures designed to facilitate movement or promote stability. These structures include: articular cartilage, synovial fluid, bursae, menisci, the joint capsule, ligaments

▷ All body movements take place along one of three planes of movement:
  - sagittal – Flexion/extension, plantar flexion/dorsiflexion
  - frontal – Abduction/adduction, lateral flexion, inversion/eversion, elevation/depression
  - transverse/horizontal – lateral/medial rotation, pronation/supination, horizontal adduction/horizontal abduction

▷ All body movement occurs about one of three axes of the body: frontal, transverse, or longitudinal

▷ The axis of rotation is always at right angles to the plane in which the movement occurs

▷ Skeletal muscles work together to produce coordinated movements. This is known as antagonistic muscle action where:
  - the agonist is the muscle responsible for the movement
  - the antagonist muscle works in opposition to the agonist, i.e. if the agonist shortens the antagonist lengthens, and vice versa
  - the fixator is a muscle that maintains a stable base against which the agonist can pull

▷ There are three types of muscular contraction:
  • Isotonic concentric – when the muscle shortens while contracting
  • Isotonic eccentric – when the muscle lengthens while contracting
  • Isometric contraction – when the muscle remains the same length, yet still contracts

▷ There are three types of lever in the body:
  Class 1 – which can move at great speeds but is relatively weak
  Class 2 – which is very strong and can overcome heavy loads
  Class 3 – which can be used to generate speed to a body part or object

▷ Most levers in the body are third class

▷ To complete a comprehensive movement analysis, the following information is required:
  a) What bones are articulating?
  b) At what joint is the movement taking place?
  c) What type is this joint?
  d) What movement pattern or joint action is occurring?
  e) In which plane, and about which axis, is the movement taking place?
  f) What is the name and function of the muscle contracting?
  g) How is the muscle contracting?
  h) Which lever system is operating?

Revise as you go

1. Identify the bones that articulate at:

   a) the shoulder joint

   b) the knee joint

   c) the ankle joint.

2. All of the following are features of a synovial joint. Explain the function of each: articular cartilage, joint capsule, synovial fluid, bursae.

3. State the types of synovial joint located at:

   a) the hip

   b) the knee

   c) the radio-ulnar

   d) ankle joints.

4. During the take off (execution phase) of a long jump, what are the movement patterns that occur at the hip, knee and ankle joints.

5. Which plane of movement:

   a) divides the body into left and right sections

   b) divides the body into front and back sections

   c) divides the body into top and bottom.

6. About which axis do we perform the following movements:

   a) flexion and extension

   b) abduction and adduction

   c) rotation.

7. State the muscle(s) that are responsible for performing the following movements:

   a) extension at the elbow

   b) abduction at the shoulder

   c) extension at the knee

   d) plantar flexion at the ankle

   e) extension at the hip.

8. During the action of a press-up, state the function of the triceps brachii in both the upwards and downwards phases.

9. Using one movement from a physical activity of your choice, explain what is meant by the term 'antagonistic muscle action'.

10. During the action of a leg squat the quadriceps group (rectus femoris, vastus lateralis, vastus medialis, vastus intermedius) will go through a period of eccentric contraction followed by a period of concentric contraction. Explain these terms using the example of a leg squat.

11. State the three components of a lever system.

12. Name the class of lever system that operates at:

    a) the ankle during the take off phase of a long jump

    b) the elbow when throwing a javelin

    c) the elbow when performing a bicep curl.

CHAPTER 6

Applied exercise physiology in practical situations

– Preparing for Section B – application of theoretical knowledge for effective performance

LEARNING OBJECTIVES:

By the end of this chapter you should be able to:

▶ name and explain the principles of training and apply them to a given performer

▶ calculate optimal training intensities through use of heart rate, the Borg scale and 1 rep max percentages

▶ identify and outline the testing procedure for at least one fitness test for each component of fitness

▶ discuss the reasons for fitness testing and the limitations of fitness tests

▶ comment on the validity and reliability of each fitness test

▶ explain the physiological value of a warm up and cool down

▶ design and justify a warm up and cool down for a given performer which includes a range of different stretching activities

▶ critically evaluate a number of different training methods and apply them to a given performer.

Introduction

Much of the content of this chapter you will acquire through your practical lessons in your school or college. However, this theoretical content will be assessed via an extended question in Section B of your Unit 1 written examination paper. You will be expected to apply your acquired knowledge to a practical scenario and the question will focus on the application and justification of that knowledge in the context of a performer, coach or official.

In order to maximise your performance it will be necessary for you to have an awareness and understanding of the factors that underpin a range of performers; and use the knowledge gained from this chapter to identify and justify strengths and weaknesses in their performance; and suggest appropriate strategies to enable an improvement in their performance.

Fitness testing

You will recall that in Chapter 1 we considered the different elements or components that contributed to an individual's overall level of fitness. In this section we will investigate how each of these components can be assessed and how the coach and athlete can use the information in the design of training programmes. However, in order to design the training programme so that it improves the required dimensions of fitness, it will be necessary to gather some information by carrying out a battery of tests to identify where exactly the strengths and weaknesses of the performer's fitness lie.

The first part of this chapter will therefore focus on fitness testing and protocols specific to each component.

Testing stamina/ cardiorespiratory endurance

Most tests of cardiorespiratory endurance seek to discover a person's **VO$_2$max** or maximal oxygen uptake. This is defined as **the maximal volume of oxygen that a person can take in, transport and utilise per minute**. It is usually measured in ml/kg/min (millilitres of oxygen consumed per kilogram of body weight per minute) or more simply l/min.

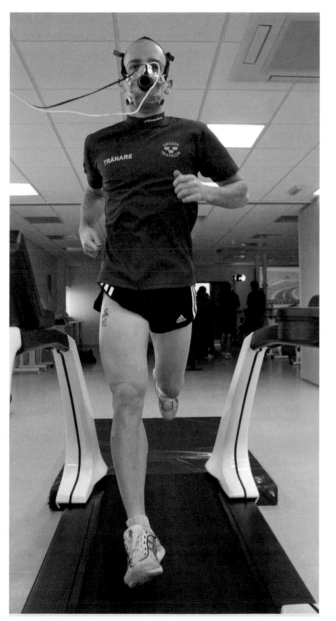

Fig. 6.01 Assessment of cardiorespiratory endurance (VO$_2$max) through direct gas analysis

KEY TERMS

Validity of testing:
the validity of a test assesses whether the test actually measures what it claims to measure

Reliability of testing:
the reliability of a test considers whether the test will produce the same or similar results when the test is repeated and where there has been no change in fitness levels

Direct tests:
these are the most accurate types of test since they give a direct or objective measure of a physiological factor linked to a particular dimension of fitness. For example, a treadmill test actually measures oxygen consumption in ml/kg/min

Indirect tests:
these are not as accurate as direct tests since they will only give a prediction of a physiological factor linked to the particular fitness dimension. For example the number of shuttles completed in the multi-stage fitness test can only be used to predict oxygen consumption

The most accurate measures of VO$_2$max are **direct tests** that are determined in the laboratory. **Direct gas analysis**, for example, involves a subject either running on a treadmill or cycling on an ergometer during a test that progresses in intensity until they reach exhaustion. Expired air samples are collected and analysed throughout the test to determine how much oxygen their muscles have extracted and utilised. However, these tests require access to a laboratory that possesses this rather expensive and hi-tech equipment, so some less expensive predictive tests (**indirect tests**) have been developed to estimate the performer's VO$_2$max.

EXAM TIP:

In your examination, make sure you are able to give a critical appraisal of a test for each component of fitness.

Performing the multi-stage fitness test	
Facilities and equipment needed	• A marked non-slip 20m track such as at a sports hall • Multi-stage fitness test CD and booklet
Testing procedure	Performers run the 20m distance in time to the bleeps emitted from the CD. They should aim to place their foot on or over the line as the bleep sounds. After every minute, the time interval between the bleeps decreases and the performer must increase his or her running speed accordingly. Performers must continue to run in time to the bleeps until they can no longer keep up (exhaustion). This is judged to be when the performer fails to make it to the line as the bleep sounds. At this point, the level and shuttle number attained are recorded
Data collected	The level and shuttle number recorded are compared to the booklet provided, which converts the level and shuttle number to give a prediction of VO_2max in ml/kg/min
Main strengths of the test	• Easy testing procedure • Standardised data that easily converts into a predicted VO_2max score • Large groups can be tested at the same time
Main limitations of the test	• The test is only a prediction of VO_2max, not an absolute measure • The test is maximal and to exhaustion, and is therefore dependent upon the performer's level of motivation • As the test involves a running action, it may favour runners. Test scores for swimmers and cyclists may be distorted
Validity of the test	As a predictor of VO_2max, the test is quite valid. Studies on its validity show correlation coefficients with direct gas analysis of between 0.87 and 0.93 with a standard error of approximately 3.5ml/kg/min
Reliability of the test	Because the test is maximal, it does depend upon the motivation levels of the performer at a given time. With this being equal, the multi-stage fitness test can be a fairly reliable test of VO_2max

Table 6.01 The multi-stage fitness test

The multi-stage fitness test

The multi-stage fitness test is a maximal progressive shuttle run test, so it gets harder and harder as the test progresses, that gives a prediction of the performer's VO_2max. Table 6.01 gives a detailed overview of the multi-stage fitness test.

Other tests

Table 6.02 shows some other commonly conducted fitness tests used to evaluate cardiorespiratory endurance. Study the table, taking time in particular to judge the strengths and limitations of each test.

EXAM TIP:

As a general rule, typical oxygen consumption for female performers is approximately 10ml/kg/min below that of their male counterparts.

TASK 6.01

Starting with the greatest, place the following activities in order of expected VO_2max scores:
• rower
• 200m swimmer
• cross-country skier
• weightlifter
• 10,000m runner
• 400m runner.

Activity	Male (ml/kg/min)	Female (ml/kg/min)
Triathlete	80	72
Marathon runner	78	68
Distance swimmer	72	64
Middle distance runner (800m–1500m)	72	63
Games player	66	56
Gymnast	56	47
Weightlifter	52	43

Table 6.02 Typical VO_2max scores for a range of sporting activities

Name of test	Brief description of the test	Strengths of the test	Limitations of the test	Validity of the test	Reliability of the test
Harvard step test	A performer steps up onto and down from a bench in time to a set rhythm for five minutes. Recovery heart rate is recorded and used to predict VO_2max	• Easy to use and organise • Little equipment needed	• Errors in recovery heart rate scores can occur when taking the pulse rate manually • The activity of stepping is not very specific to many sports • The equation used to predict VO_2max has been questioned • Some performers find it difficult to keep up • Some performers find it difficult to maintain the cadence (rate of stepping)	Some validity tests have shown that this test is a poor predictor of VO_2max with correlation coefficients of 0.2–0.5 when compared to laboratory measures	As this is a sub-maximal test, performers' motivation levels should not affect the results. Therefore, all things being equal, this test should be relatively reliable
PWC170 cycle ergometer test	Athletes perform three consecutive workloads on a cycle ergometer. Heart rate is measured each minute for four minutes for each workload. Target HRs for each workload are: W/load 1 (115–130) W/load 2 (130–145) W/load 3 (145–165). The HR for each workload is graphed and a line of best fit drawn. A workload that would elicit a HR of 170bpm can be extrapolated from the graph	• This is a sub-maximal test that does not require the subject to work to exhaustion • Cycle tests are good as the saddle supports the subject's weight	• As the test is performed on a cycle ergometer, it may favour cyclists. • Determining the line of best fit and extrapolating the workload at 170bpm can be open to error • Errors in recording heart rate can occur if performed manually	Some studies have shown a correlation coefficient of 0.9 when compared to laboratory studies and therefore demonstrates high validity	As this is a sub-maximal test, performers' motivation levels should not affect the results. Therefore, all things being equal, this test should be relatively reliable
Cooper 12 minute run test	Performers run as far as they can in twelve minutes. The distance covered in twelve minutes is recorded	• Simple to organise • Little equipment needed • Large groups can be tested at the same time	A maximal test that depends upon the performer's level of motivation	Cooper's equation to convert miles covered into a VO_2max score has been questioned. Studies on correlation coefficients range from 0.65–0.9 when compared to laboratory VO_2max scores	Because the test is maximal, it does depend upon the motivation level of the performer at a given time. With this being equal, the distance covered should be similar and the Cooper run is therefore a fairly reliable test

Table 6.03 Other tests of cardiorespiratory endurance (aerobic capacity)

One repetition maximum test (1RM test)

Performing the 1 repetition max test	
Facilities and equipment needed	A weights room with free weights or multi-gym facility
Testing procedure	Following a thorough warm up, the maximum weight that a performer can lift just once is determined by trial and error. After each attempt, the weight should be increased or decreased by about 5kg and a recovery period of two to three minutes given between each trial.
Data collected	The maximum weight that can be lifted just once (1RM). The weight can then be converted to a percentage of the performer's body mass in kg. That is: $\dfrac{\text{Weight lifted (kg)} \times 100}{\text{Body mass (kg)}}$
Main strengths of the test	• Easy testing procedure • Most muscle groups can be tested • Sport-specific actions can be tested
Main limitations of the test	• Requires access to weights or multi-gym facility • Performing maximal lifts increases the likelihood of injury • Only gives a general strength measure
Validity of the test	The data provided does not give precise data concerning the actual force generated within the muscle but can give a general evaluation of muscular strength
Reliability of the test	This test is very reliable since the maximum weight that can be lifted is often repeated

Table 6.04 One repetition maximum test (1RM)

Handgrip dynamometer test

Performing the handgrip dynamometer test	
Facilities and equipment needed	A handgrip dynamometer
Testing procedure	Having adjusted the grip for hand size, the performer holds the dynamometer in one hand at shoulder height. The subject brings the dynamometer down to their side while squeezing the handle. Record the highest reading from three attempts for both dominant and non-dominant hand
Data collected	Scores are recorded in kg
Main strengths of the test	• Easy testing procedure • Little equipment needed
Main limitations of the test	• Erroneous adjusting of the handgrip can affect the results • This test only gives an indication of the strength of the handgrip and forearm, and care should be taken if using handgrip scores to comment on general body strength
Validity of the test	As a measure of handgrip and forearm static strength, this test can be considered valid, but it is completely invalid as a measure of dynamic strength of other muscles around the body, e.g. leg strength.
Reliability of the test	This test is very reliable since the maximum handgrip score is often repeated, assuming appropriate adjustment of the handgrip

NB: Dynamometers have also been designed to test the strength of other areas of the body.

Table 6.05 Handgrip dynamometer test

Testing strength

Before you decide upon which test of strength to use, you must first decide upon which type of strength you wish to test: for example, maximum strength, elastic strength or strength endurance.

In this section we will start with tests of maximum strength, then we will consider the tests of strength endurance and elastic strength under the headings of 'muscular endurance' and 'power' later in this chapter.

There are two tests for maximum strength illustrated here. The 1 repetition maximum text (see Table 6.04) and the handgrip dynamometer test (see Table 6.05).

The NCF abdominal conditioning test

Muscular endurance or strength endurance

'The ability of a muscle or group of muscles to sustain repeated contractions against a resistance for an extended period of time.'

Muscular endurance is a major component of fitness in those activities where the performer must work at medium to high intensity for periods of up to five or six minutes. A good example is competitive rowing or swimming, where muscles of both the upper and lower body are required to work repeatedly for the duration of the event. Performers with high levels of muscular endurance will possess both fast (type 2a) and slow (type 1) twitch muscle fibres and will be able to withstand high levels of lactic acid so that they can avoid fatigue.

Performing the NCF abdominal conditioning test	
Facilities and equipment needed	NCF (National Coaching Foundation) abdominal conditioning CD, CD player, gymnasium floor, gym mats, stopwatch
Testing procedure	Thoroughly warm up. Follow the instructions on the CD. Subjects are required to perform as many sit-ups as possible while keeping in time with the signals emitted from the CD. A partner counts the number of sit-ups completed and times the duration of the work period. The test should be halted when the performer can no longer keep in time with the signals or when their technique deteriorates
Data collected	The number of sit-ups completed
Main strengths of the test	• Easy testing procedure • Large groups can be tested at once • Little equipment needed • The abdominal muscles are easily isolated
Main limitations of the test	• The test is maximal and therefore relies upon the motivation of the performer to work to exahustion • It is difficult to monitor the correct technique • Full sit-ups should not be completed on a regular basis due to excessive strain being placed on the lumbar region of the spine
Validity of the test	The test does isolate the abdominals, assuming the testing protocol is followed correctly. It is therefore a relatively valid test
Reliability of the test	Because the test is maximal, it does depend upon the motivation levels of the performer at a given time. With this being equal, the abdominal conditioning test can be a fairly reliable test of muscular endurance

Table 6.06 The NCF abdominal conditioning test

Stage	No. of sit-ups	Rating: males	Rating: females	Stage	No. of sit-ups	Rating: males	Rating: females
1	20	Poor	Poor	5	116	Good	Good
2	42	Poor	Fair	6	146	Good	Very good
3	64	Fair	Fair	7	180	Excellent	Excellent
4	89	Fair	Good	8	217	Excellent	Excellent

Table 6.07 Abdominal conditioning norms

Power (also known as explosive strength)

'The amount of work done per unit of time or the rate at which we apply strength'.

A performer with high amounts of power can exert a great force over a very short period of time. A gymnast performing a vault or a hammer thrower launching the hammer, for example, requires a great deal of power. Powerful athletes should possess a high proportion of **fast twitch glycolytic (FTG) muscle fibres (type 2b)**, since the thick myelin sheath that surrounds these fibres conducts the motor neurone to the muscle more rapidly. This enables the neuromuscular system to recruit the fast twitch fibres as rapidly as possible.

> ## KEY TERM
>
> **Fast twitch glycolytic (FTG) muscle fibres (type 2b):**
> a muscle fibre designed for very high intensity, power-based activities such as sprinting, throwing and jumping

Testing power

Since power is measured in watts, true tests of power must focus on the amount of work done by the body in a certain time. Perhaps the best test of anaerobic power is the Wingate cycle test (see Table 6.10) but a simple test of leg power is the standing (Sargent) vertical jump test (see Table 6.08). Power can also be measured in the 25m hop test.

The standing (Sargent) vertical jump test

Performing the standing (Sargent) vertical jump test	
Facilities and equipment needed	Gymnasium, jump board/wall, tape measure (or timing mats, which measure the time a subject spends in the air, can be used if available)
Testing procedure	Warm up thoroughly. The subject's standing reach is measured by his placing a mark on the jump board/wall. From a squatting position, the subject then jumps as high as he can, marking the jump board/wall at the top of the jump. The best score from three attempts can be recorded
Data collected	The difference in height between the standing reach and the jump mark is taken and recorded. This is known as the jump height. This can be used on its own and compared to norms or it can be converted into watts – the unit of power. Lewis's formula can be used to calculate power: Power (watts) = 21.72 × mass (kg) × jump height (m)
Main strengths of the test	• Quick and easy testing procedure • Little equipment needed
Main limitations of the test	• Many different techniques have been used to jump, including allowing a run-up, from a squatting position, use of arms and so on • Some subjects will find it difficult to time marking the board at the height of the jump
Validity of the test	The validity of Lewis's power formula has been questioned. If jump height is used without conversion, the test does give a good indirect prediction of leg power. When compared to the Wingate cycle test, studies have concluded a modest validity correlation coefficient of 0.78
Reliability of the test	The test is generally reliable (between 0.93 and 0.98) assuming the same technique is used

Table 6.08 The standing (Sargent) vertical jump test

Rating	Distance (cm): males	Distance (cm): females
Excellent	>59	>46
Good	51–9	36–46
Average	41–50	29–35
Poor	26–40	25–34
Very poor	<26	<24

Table 6.09 Vertical jump norms

The Wingate cycle test

Performing the Wingate cycle test	
Facilities and equipment needed	Monarch bicycle ergometer, weight stack (resistance), video recorder, stopwatch
Testing procedure	Thoroughly warm up. With a resistance of 75g per kg of body weight, the subject pedals flat out for a period of 30 seconds. Using a video recorder, the number of revolutions is counted for every five seconds of the test. The subject should then perform a cool down
Data collected	Peak power in watts, power decline, fatigue index, mean anaerobic capacity
Main strengths of the test	• Objective data collected • Aspects of power can be evaluated (see data collected)
Main limitations of the test	• The test is maximal and therefore relies upon the motivation of the performer to work to exhaustion • Expensive equipment needed • As it is a cycle test, it may favour cyclists
Validity of the test	When peak power from the Wingate cycle test has been compared to 50m spring times, the validity correlation coefficient of 0.91 is very high
Reliability of the test	This test is known for its reliability but, as it is a maximal test, it can depend on the subject's motivation level to perform the test

Table 6.10 The Wingate cycle test

The standing broad jump test

Performing the standing broad jump test	
Facilities and equipment needed	Gymnasium, mat, tape measure
Testing procedure	Warm up thoroughly. The subject jumps as far as possible (horizontally) with both feet kept together. Take-off must be with both feet and the distance between the start line and the nearest heel is recorded. The best score from three attempts can be recorded
Data collected	Distance jumped
Main strengths of the test	• Quick and easy testing procedure • Little equipment needed
Main limitations of the test	• This test only predicts leg power through distance jumped • Heavily dependent upon technique • Different techniques have been used including use of the arms, or hands clenched behind the subject's back
Validity of the test	There is no conversion into units of power (watts) although the distance jumped can give an indirect prediction of leg power
Reliability of the test	The test is generally reliable assuming the same technique is used

Table 6.11 The standing broad jump test

Rating	Distance (cm): males	Distance (cm): females
Excellent	>240	>190
Good	231–40	181–90
Average	221–30	171–80
Poor	211–20	161–70
Very poor	<211	<161

Table 6.12 Standing broad jump norms

Testing speed

Most tests of speed are sprint tests from a flying start. A flying start is preferred over a standing start since this eliminates the effect that **reaction** time might have on the scores. It is possible to conduct sprint tests over almost any distance from 10m to 50m, which helps make the test more specific to a particular performer. Table 6.13 gives an example of the 30m sprint test.

The 30m sprint test

Performing the 30m sprint test	
Facilities and equipment needed	A non-slip 30m track, tape measure, stopwatch (preferably sprint timing gates)
Testing procedure	Thoroughly warm up. From a 1m flying start, the time taken for the performer to cover the 30m distance is recorded
Data collected	Time taken in seconds to cover the 30m distance
Main strengths of the test	• Easy testing procedure • Little equipment needed
Main limitations of the test	• Manual timing can be affected by human error (timing gates should ideally be used over short distances) • Running surface and weather can affect the results • The test is not sport-specific. Most sporting activities are multi-directional and few require us to run in a straight line for 30m
Validity of the test	The sprint test is widely accepted as being a valid test of speed, especially when a flying start is used, which eliminates the effect of reaction time. When compared to other anaerobic tests, such as the Wingate cycle test, correlation coefficients of 0.89 have been shown
Reliability of the test	The use of timing gates greatly improves the reliability of this test to as much as 0.97

Table 6.13 The 30m sprint test

Rating	Time (secs): males	Time (secs): females
Excellent	<4.0	<4.5
Good	4.2-4.0	4.6-4.5
Average	4.4-4.3	4.8-4.7
Poor	4.6-4.5	5.0-4.9
Very poor	>4.6	>5.0

Table 6.14 30m sprint norms

Testing flexibility

Although it is difficult to measure the length of a muscle, most coaches accept that angular displacement at a joint is a good predictor of muscle length. Angular displacement at a joint can be measured using a modified protractor known as a goniometer. The centre of the **goniometer** is placed in the middle of the joint while the arms are aligned with each of the two body parts as they move. Angular displacement can then be assessed by measuring the degree of movement between the two body parts. The most widely used field test to assess flexibility, however, is the sit and reach test, which is outlined below.

The sit and reach test

Performing the sit and reach test	
Facilities and equipment needed	Sit and reach box (if this is not available, a bench and a metre rule can be used)
Testing procedure	Warm up thoroughly. In a sitting position with legs outstretched, knees locked and feet flat against the box (with shoes off), slowly reach forward and push the cursor along the calibrated part of the box and hold for a two second count. No bouncing or jerking is permitted and the fingertips of both hands must be level. Record the highest score from three attempts
Data collected	Distance (positive or negative) recorded from the calibrated part of the box or metre rule
Main strengths of the test	• Easy testing procedure • Little equipment needed
Main limitations of the test	• The test only measures flexibility of the lower back and hamstrings – it is difficult to isolate the hamstrings • The extent to which the performer has warmed up can affect the score when comparing against standard norms • Variations in limb length can make comparisons between performers difficult
Validity of the test	The validity of the test is questionable as it is difficult to isolate the hamstrings
Reliability of the test	The extent to which the performer has warmed up can affect the reliability of this test

Table 6.15 The sit and reach test

Rating	Distance (cm): males	Distance (cm): females
Excellent	>34	>38
Good	31–4	33–8
Average	27–30	29–32
Poor	<27	<29

Table 6.16 Sit and reach test norms

KEY TERM

Goniometer:
an instrument used to measure angular displacement and flexibility

TASK 6.02

Copy out Table 6.17. For each of the activities listed, rate on the scale of 1–10 the flexibility requirements of the stated activity (1 = low flexibility requirement, 10 = high flexibility requirement). Write a sentence on each activity justifying your answer.

Table 6.17

Sporting activity	Scale									
Volleyball player	1	2	3	4	5	6	7	8	9	10
Judo player	1	2	3	4	5	6	7	8	9	10
Gymnast	1	2	3	4	5	6	7	8	9	10
Javelin thrower	1	2	3	4	5	6	7	8	9	10
Hockey player	1	2	3	4	5	6	7	8	9	10
Trampolinist	1	2	3	4	5	6	7	8	9	10

Testing agility

There are several tests of agility. The most commonly used test is the Illinois agility run test. Other tests of agility include the 'T' drill test and the hexagon obstacle test.

Illinois agility run test

Performing the Illinois agility run test	
Facilities and equipment needed	A non-slip 10m x 5m area, tape measure, stopwatch (timing gates would be better), cones
Testing procedure	Warm up thoroughly. Mark out the 10m x 5m area as shown in the diagram (Figure 6.02). The subject lies face down at the starting position. At the signal, the performer moves onto his/her feet and completes the course, weaving in and out of the cones as quickly as possible
Data collected	Time taken in seconds to cover the course
Main strengths of the test	• Easy testing procedure • Little equipment needed • There is a lot of data available with which to compare results
Main limitations of the test	• Manual timing can be affected by human error • Running surface and weather can affect the results • The test is not sport-specific – the agility demands of many sports differ. A hockey player, for example, needs to control a ball with a stick while changing direction quickly
Validity of the test	Since agility is influenced by many factors including speed, balance and coordination, the validity of the test can be questioned
Reliability of the test	The use of timing gates greatly improves the reliability of this test

Table 6.18 Illinois agility run test

Rating	Time (secs): males	Time (secs): females
Excellent	<15.2	<17
Good	16.1–15.2	17.9–17
Average	18.1–16.2	21.7–18
Fair	18.3-18.2	23–21.8
Poor	>18.3	>23

Table 6.19 Illinois agility run test norms

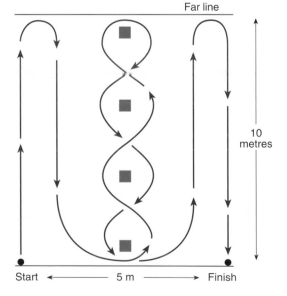

Fig. 6.02 Course for Illinois agility run test

TASK 6.03

All fitness tests should, where possible, be sport-specific. For a named activity of your choice, design a test of agility that is sport-specific. Once you have decided upon your test protocol, conduct your test with a group of students within your class. Complete a table, using the headings given below, and discuss your results with others within your class. Include a diagram of the layout of your test of agility.

• Facilities and equipment needed
• Testing procedure
• Data collected
• Main strengths of the test
• Main limitations of the test
• Validity of the test
• Reliability of the test.

Testing balance

Since dynamic balance is difficult to measure, most tests of balance evaluate static balance. One of the most common tests of balance is the standing stork test. Other tests of balance include the use of balance or 'wobble' boards.

HOT LINKS

Use a website such as www.topendsports.com to investigate the range of fitness tests available for each of the components of fitness required for your examination. Consider the validity, reliability and practicability of each test.

Fig. 6.03 The standing stork test

The standing stork test

Performing the standing stork test	
Facilities and equipment needed	A small non-slip area, stopwatch
Testing procedure	Stand comfortably on both feet with your hands on your hips. Lift one leg and place the toes of this foot against the knee of the other leg. On the signal, raise the heel of the straight leg and stand on your toes. Balance for as long as possible without letting the heel of the foot touch the floor or move the foot away from the knee of the balancing leg
Data collected	Time in balance in seconds
Main strengths of the test	• Easy testing procedure • Little equipment needed
Main limitations of the test	The test is not sport-specific. Most sporting activities require dynamic balance, not static balance
Validity of the test	For gymnasts and other activities where static balance is required, the correlation coefficient is high. However, most activities require dynamic balance and for this reason the validity of this test can be questioned
Reliability of the test	As results may vary, this test is not particularly reliable (especially as different results may be obtained for the left and right legs!)

Table 6.20 The standing stork test

A quick guide to fitness testing

Here are a few key points to consider before you embark on your chosen fitness tests.

Why conduct fitness tests?

Fitness testing should be an integral part of any athlete's training regime. In fact, testing should be the basis on which their training programme is designed! Fitness testing attempts to measure a performer's individual aspects of performance, with the overall aim of improving ability within each component. Think about what the likely benefits of fitness testing might be to both the coach and performer. Have you come up with some of these?

- identify strengths and weaknesses of the athlete
- monitor progress by comparing against previous test results or even the results of other performers
- enhance motivation – there is nothing more satisfying than seeing yourself improve
- provide information for the design and modification of training programmes – it can be used to measure the success of your current training programme
- talent identification and prediction of physiological potential – it can be used to steer the performer into the most appropriate sport or activity
- help performers set appropriate goals for fitness development.

Fitness tests, though, are not a magic potion; they will not in themselves create a better performer, they should merely be used as a tool, which, when used correctly, can provide the coach and athlete with valuable information to help them improve.

Limitations of fitness tests

For each of the fitness tests outlined in this chapter, some specific limitations have been highlighted. Below is a general summary of the key limitations to fitness testing.

- Many tests are not sport-specific. They do not replicate the specific movements or actions that are required by different activities.

- Many tests are predictive. They do not use direct measures and can therefore be inaccurate.
- Many tests do not consider the sporting environment or the competitive conditions of the activity.

Validity and reliability of testing

To be valid, a fitness test must measure what it claims to. For example, the sit and reach test may be a valid test of the flexibility at the hip, but not at the shoulder joint. The validity of a test is also improved if the test is sport-specific. If the test reflects or mimics one or two of the fitness requirements of that activity, then the **validity of the test** will be enhanced. A distance runner, for example, should perform a VO_2 max test that requires running rather than cycling; a squash player should perform a test of agility that requires sideways movement as well as sprinting forwards. Specificity and therefore validity of the test can also be improved by:

- testing the appropriate muscle groups
- testing the appropriate muscle fibre type
- testing the appropriate energy systems
- replicating the sporting environment (for example, a rugby player should perform a sprint test on grass wearing rugby kit and boots).

Reliability of a test is more concerned with the consistency and repeatability of the test results. If the test is reliable, then the same or very similar test results should be achieved when the test is repeated (assuming no change in fitness levels). There are several factors that can influence the reliability of fitness tests:

- sub-maximal tests are more reliable tests since the performer's motivation to work to exhaustion is not an issue
- the testing environment must be the same each time the test is conducted (for example, consider the weather if the test is to be conducted outside)
- the testing personnel and protocol must be standardised (for example, use timing gates rather than stopwatches in order to minimise human error).

A word on maximal and sub-maximal testing

Maximal tests such as the multi-stage fitness test and the Wingate cycle test require the athlete to work at maximum effort and are invariably tested to exhaustion. While this does give some truly objective data, it does pose some serious problems. Firstly, it is difficult to ensure that the performer is working at their maximum. This may often depend upon how the performer is feeling on the day and their motivation level to push themselves to exhaustion. This can result in some distorted evaluations of fitness. Secondly, there are some ethical considerations and dangers involved in forcing performers to work to their maximum since this can lead to over-exertion and injury.

Sub-maximal tests, such as the PWC170 test, are often favoured since they do not require the subject to work at maximal levels and the motivation of the performer is not an issue. Most sub-maximal tests rely on estimating or predicting maximum work capacity through extrapolation, using data achieved at sub-maximal levels. This, however, also poses some problems in terms of the validity and reliability of the tests used. The results extrapolated to determine work capacity at maximal levels are only estimates or predictions, so they are not totally objective. Also, measurement inaccuracies at sub-maximal levels can also produce large discrepancies in the results when extrapolated.

When selecting the battery of tests, it is necessary to choose tests that are wholly appropriate for the individual performer.

Other ethical considerations

- All performers should be screened before any kind of fitness testing can take place. This can be done through asking subjects to complete a 'Physical Activity Readiness Questionnaire' (PAR-Q).
- Tests should be selected that are appropriate for the subject's age, sex and current fitness level.

TASK 6.04

As you read through this chapter on fitness testing, complete the battery of fitness tests outlined in Table 6.21. Copy out and complete the accompanying table for your records.

Component of fitness	Recognised test	My score	My rating
Cardiorespiratory endurance (aerobic capacity)	Multi-stage fitness test		
Maximal strength	1. One repetition maximum test 2. Handgrip dynamometer		
Strength endurance (muscular endurance)	NCF abdominal conditioning test		
Elastic strength (power)	1. Wingate cycle test 2. The standing (Sargent) vertical jump test		
Speed	30m sprint test		
Flexibility	Sit and reach test		
Body composition	1. Skinfold measure 2. Bioelectric impedance		
Agility	Illinois agility run test		
Balance	The standing stork test		

Table 6.21

The principles of training

When planning training programmes, the coach and athlete must consider the principles of training. These are the guidelines that should underpin all training that is undertaken and if followed successfully the performer should gain maximum benefit from the training. Table 6.22 outlines the main principles of training and how each can be applies to a training programme.

REMEMBER!

To help remember all of these principles of training try to remember the acronym **SPORT FITT WIMP** where each letter represents the initial letter of a different principle!

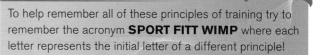

Principle of training	Explanation	Application
Specificity	All training must be relevant to the activity or sport. For example a cyclist must perform most of their training on a bike. There is of course some value in other forms of training, but the majority must be performed on the bicycle. Actions from the activity should also be replicated during training	Be sure to train the: • relevant muscles • energy systems • relevant fibre types • fitness components • use appropriate technique
Progression	As the body becomes better at coping with the training over time, greater demands must be made if improvement is tomade continue. This is often linked to overload and known as 'progressive overload'	Increase: • % HRmax • %1RM • duration • frequency of training

Table 6.22 Applying the principles of training

continued

Principle of training	Explanation	Application
Overload	If training is to have the required effect then the performer must find the training taxing. The level of training must be pitched at a level greater than the demands regularly encountered by the player. The old adage 'no pain, no gain' can be applied here!	• Use heart rate to gauge how hard you are working • Work at an appropriate % of max heart rate or 1RM • Increase the duration of the activity if needed
Reversibility	Use it or lose it! If the training load decreases or if training stops altogether then the benefits of the prior training can be lost	Unless injured, training should continue
Tedium (Variety)	Variety is the spice of life so make sure training sessions are varied using a range of different methods and intensities. Try to incorporate an element of fun into some sessions. This will hopefully prevent staleness and boredom and your athletes will keep coming back!	A swimmer will follow a programme that includes pool-based work and land-based training including weights work. Some pools even have the facility to play music underwater to keep boredom at bay!
FITT	F (Frequency) = How often we train I (Intensity) = How hard we train T (Time) = How long we train for T (Type) = What type of training we use	• Train 3–6 days/week • %HRmax or %1RM • 30mins–2hrs/session • Use the principle of specificity
Warm-up/ cool-down	Start as you mean to go on. A thorough warm-up and cool-down is an essential ingredient to every training session. This ensures you get the most out of the session and recover quickly for subsequent sessions	A warm-up will typically include 3 different stages: • Stage 1 pulse raiser • Stage 2 stretching activity • Stage 3 skill-related practices A cool-down will typically include only Stages 1 and 2
Individuality	Training programmes need to be tailor-made to meet the needs of individual performers. Athletes respond differently to the same training; what may help one athlete to improve may not help another. The coach must therefore be sympathetic to the individual performer – particularly if they are part of a training group.	Swimmers and athletes often train in small groups. Everybody will respond and adapt to the same training differently. It is essential, therefore, that the coach respects the particular needs of each person in the group so that they can focus on particular strengths or weaknesses, such as the start for a 100m sprinter
Moderation (Prevention of over-training and adequate recovery)	Sufficient recovery time must be built into the training programme to prevent over-training. Rest allows the body to overcompensate and adapt to the training, leading to improved performance. Over-training is characterised by muscular fatigue, illness and injury	Heavy training sessions should be followed by lighter sessions or even rest days. The ratio of 3:1 is often used to express the ratio of hard sessions to easy sessions within a week's training cycle
Periodisation	This is the organisation of the training programme into blocks. Each block may have a particular focus, such as the development of stamina or strength endurance. By following a periodised programme the performer is more likely to peak and avoid the scourge of many an athlete – over-training	A sprinter: • Preparation period (usually subdivided into 2 phases): development of aerobic and muscular endurance, max strength, followed by development of elastic strength, power and speed • Competition period (sometimes subdivided into 3 phases): development and maintenance of speed and power; technique work; tapering and peaking for competitions • Transition or recovery period (1 phase) active rest

Table 6.22 Applying the principles of training

TASK 6.05

For each of the principles of training outlined in Table 6.22 show how a coach can apply these to a marathon runner in training for the London marathon. Specificity has already been completed for you. Copy Table 6.23 out and follow a similar pattern for the remaining principles.

Principle of training	Applied to a marathon runner
Specificity	The coach will ensure that the runner's training programme will predominantly involve the action of running whether it be on the roads or on a running machine. In doing so they will train the required muscles of running and train the slow twitch muscle fibres of these muscles. The training should also improve the cardiovascular (stamina) and muscular endurance components of fitness. In doing so the efficiency of the aerobic system will improve so that the marathon runner can optimise their energy expenditure.

Table 6.23

Training intensities

One of the key principles of training is intensity. This is fundamental if the performer is to get the most out of the training. There are some simple steps that can be taken to ensure that a performer is training at the correct intensities, which are outlined below.

Heart rate training zones

For aerobic type activities such as long distance running and cycling, you can use heart rate training zones to gauge how hard you are working.

Simplified versions of this include working at a percentage of your maximum heart rate (HRmax). This can be calculated by subtracting your age from the figure 220:

maximum heart rate = 220 − age.

For a 16-year-old this would be:

HRmax = 220 − 16,

Therefore HRmax = 204 bpm

Depending upon the intensity of training required, a lower or higher percentage of this maximum heart rate can be used. Some guidelines are given below for low, moderate and high intensity exercise:

- Low intensity = 30–49% of HRmax
- Moderate intensity = 50–69% of HRmax
- High intensity = 70–85% HRmax

Assuming you wanted to work at moderate intensity your target heart rate should therefore lie between 50 per cent and 69 per cent of your HRmax. This should equate to a target heart rate zone of between 102bpm and 141bpm:

$0.5 \times 204 = 102$ bpm and $0.69 \times 204 = 141$ bpm

The closer to 141bpm, the harder you will be working. The great part about this is that you now have some objective data to ensure training is going to be effective.

This formula has been criticised however for being too simplistic, as it treats all people of the same age as the same and does not really take into account current fitness levels.

Karvonen therefore developed a more appropriate formula which takes account of individual levels of fitness as resting heart rates are required to work out an individual's training heart rate zone.

To calculate the heart rate training zones in this instance, you must first find your maximum heart rate reserve. This can be calculated by subtracting your resting heart rate from your maximum heart rate (maximum heart rate = 220 − age)

Maximum heart rate reserve	= HRmax − HRrest
	= 204 − 70
	= 134 bpm

For training to be effective Karvonen suggested a training intensity of between 60 and 75% of maximum heart rate reserve which in this case is between 150 and 171 bpm:

Lower training threshold	= 0.6 (Maximum HR reserve) + HRrest
	= (0.6 × 134) + 70
	=150 bpm
Higher training threshold	= 0.75 (Maximum HR reserve) + HRrest
	= (0.75 × 134) + 70
	=171 bpm

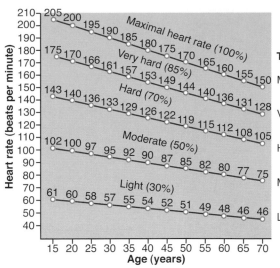

Fig. 6.04 Heart rate training zones

Target training zones (ACSM)

Maximal (220 — age) × 100%

Very hard (220 — age) × >85%

Hard (220 — age) × 70-84%

Moderate (220 — age) × 50-69%

Light (220 — age) × 30-40%

TASK 6.06

Using Karvonen's formula, calculate your training zone.

The Borg scale

The Borg rating of perceived exertion scale is a further method of determining exercise intensity. Perceived exertion is used widely by the coach and athlete during training sessions to ascertain how hard the athlete is working. It is centred around the physical feelings and sensations experienced by the performer and arises from the physiological responses of the body, such as muscle fatigue, sweating response, heart rate and respiratory responses. Quite simply, during the training session the performer rates their level of exertion by considering their levels of effort, signs of distress and fatigue. The main advantage of assessing intensity in this way is that it is quick and easy to report and does not require any form of equipment. Although there are a number of different perceived exertion scales, the most widely used is the 15 point Borg scale (which ranges from 6–20) illustrated in Table 6.24.

A distance runner who is required to train for 40 minutes at a moderate level of intensity should be targeting levels 12–14 on the scale. If however he or she perceives his/her breathing and muscle fatigue to be very light (9 or 10 on the scale) it is obvious he or she needs to increase the intensity. If on the other hand, the runner is breathing and sweating very heavily (17 or 18 on the scale) he or she may not be able to continue the activity for the entire 40 minutes and must therefore reduce the intensity so that it hits the 12–14 range on the scale.

Some studies undertaken to investigate the reliability of the Borg scale of perceived exertion have concluded that the correlation of the scale to the physiological responses of the body such as heart rate and %VO_2max is quite high.

Point scale	Perceived exertion
6	No exertion at all
7	Extremely light
8	
9	Very light (easy walking)
10	
11	Light
12	
13	Moderately hard (you feel tired but can continue)
14	
15	Hard
16	
17	Very hard (you feel very fatigued)
18	
19	Extremely hard (you cannot continue at this pace for much longer)
20	Maximal exertion (exhaustion)

Table 6.24 The 15-point Borg scale of perceived exertion

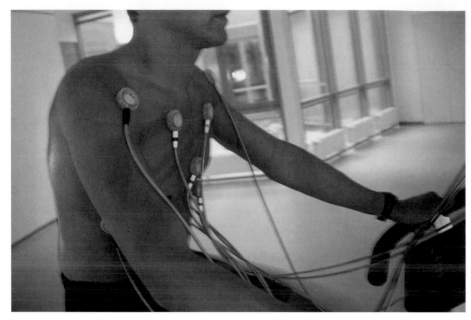

Fig. 6.05 An athlete must train at the correct intensity if physiological adaptation and performance improvement is to occur

Calculating the correct intensity when training for strength using weights

First of all you must decide upon the type of strength that you wish to improve. Remember there are three different types of strength: maximum strength, explosive strength (power) and strength endurance. The intensity at which you train will also depend upon you finding out your one repetition maximum (1RM). Once you have discovered this you will have the tools necessary to calculate an appropriate training intensity or load. The examples below give you a good guideline to follow for each type of strength.

Types of strength	Training intensity
Maximum strength	High load, low reps 5 sets × 6 reps × 85% 1RM
Elastic strength (power)	Moderate to high load (must be rapid contractions) 3 sets × 12 reps × 75% 1RM
Strength endurance (muscular endurance)	Light load/ high reps 3 sets × 20 reps × 50% 1RM

Table 6.25 The three different types of strength

TASK 6.07

Design a weight training programme for a classmate who is wanting to develop strength for a named activity. Make sure you clearly state how you will apply the principles of training and identify relevant strengthening exercises.

The warm-up and cool-down

Warm-ups and cool-downs are one of the most important of all principles of training. They should be performed not solely to prepare the body for exercise but they can also prevent injury and undue muscle soreness and discomfort following exercise. Table 6.25. highlights some of the key benefits of warm-ups and cool-downs.

The structure of the warm up

Your warm-up should consist of three distinct phases.

Stage 1 – The pulse raiser

A 5–10 minute period of light continuous exercise such as jogging or skipping is an excellent way to begin a warm-up. This will increase heart rate and body temperature and help redistribute blood to the working muscles. It is really important to undertake this stage first in order to maximise the effects of the succeeding stretching activities.

Stage 2 – Stretching activity

Once the muscles are warm, stretching activities can follow. Stretches should aim to take the muscles through their full range and each should be held for a minimum of 15 seconds. It may be necessary to replicate movements from the activity that follows to ensure that the muscles are fully prepared. A triple jumper for example may perform some bounding type activities.

There are several different types of stretching activity:

- **Active stretching** involves the performer undertaking a stretch with no external assistance
- **Passive stretching** typically involves the assistance of a partner or piece of equipment such as a towel. The partner helps to manoeuvre the performer's limbs into a position that the performer could not reach alone and a greater degree of stretch can therefore be achieved
- **Static stretching** tends to involve the lengthening of a muscle which is then held for a short period of time (15–20 seconds)
- **Ballistic stretching** usually involves bouncing into and out of a stretched position. It is not to be recommended for all performers as it uses the momentum of the body to force the muscle beyond its normal range of movement
- **Dynamic stretching** is not to be confused with ballistic stretching. Dynamic stretching involves taking the muscle through its full range of motion (the lengthening-shortening cycle) in a more controlled and gradual way. Slow lunges, and controlled arm and leg swings are good examples of dynamic stretching.

Fig. 6.06 A warm up should be performed before all training and competition to ensure optimal performance

Warm ups	Cool downs
• Improves oxygen delivery to the muscles, due to an increase in heart rate and dilation of blood vessels through the release of adrenaline and the vascular shunt mechanism • Increases venous return and therefore stroke volume through the action of the skeletal muscle pump • Increased temperature reduces the viscosity of the blood improving blood flow to the working muscles • Increased muscle temperatures improve the elasticity of muscle fibres, which can lead to a greater force and speed of contraction • Increased muscle temperature facilitates enzyme activity which ensures a readily available supply of energy to the muscles • Increased speed of nerve impulse transmission means that we become more alert, which can help us perform skills better • Can reduce DOMS (delayed onset of muscle soreness) which typically occurs 24–48 hrs following exercise	• Maintains cardiorespiratory functioning which helps to speed up the recovery process • Keeps capillaries and other blood vessels dilated, enabling the muscles to be flushed through with oxygen-rich blood which helps to remove fatiguing by-products, such as lactic acid and carbon dioxide which can act on our pain receptors • Maintains the venous return mechanism, thereby preventing blood pooling in the veins, which can cause dizziness if the exercise is stopped abruptly • It can help minimise the muscular pain associated with DOMS

Table 6.26 Summary of the benefits of the warm-ups and cool-downs

Principles of safe stretching practice

• Always ensure the body and muscles are fully warmed up before attempting to perform any form of stretching activity

• Always undergo static stretching before dynamic stretching activities
• Ballistic stretching activities should only be performed under the direct supervision of a qualified coach

Fig 6.07 A passive stretch with the aid of a dynaband

Fig 6.08 Static stretching involves the lengthening of a muscle which is then held for 15–20 seconds

- Dynamic stretching activities should gradually increase in intensity so that the muscles will eventually be taken through the movements that are to be experienced in the ensuing activity.

Stage 3 – Skill-related practices

The focus of this third phase of the warm up should be some kind of skills-related practice to improve the coordination of the neuromuscular systems. This might include shooting baskets in basketball, practising tumble turns in swimming or practising team plays such as corner kicks in football.

Methods of training

It is essential that the coach selects and employs the most appropriate type of training from those available to ensure that the training is successful. Table 6.27 outlines the main methods that can be used to improve a performer's fitness, and Figure 6.09 shows a suggested circuit for training.

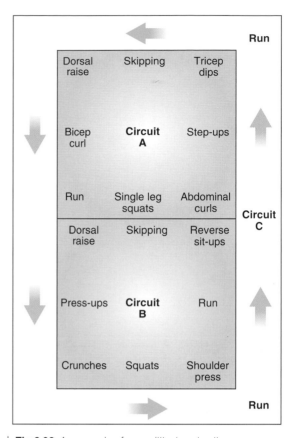

Fig 6.09 An example of a conditioning circuit

TASK 6.08

Design a warm up routine for a named physical activity of your choice. Make sure you give detailed information on the activities that you would include in each of the three phases of the warm up and support your answer with relevant diagrams where necessary. Justify the activities that you have included.

REMEMBER!

When applying methods of training in answering a question in section B of Unit 1 make sure you can:
- name a relevant method of training
- give a brief description of it
- state the main components of fitness improved
- give an example of a typical session
- comment upon the relative advantages and disadvantages of the training method selected.

TASK 6.09

Design a circuit training session for a named invasion game. Justify your choice of exercises included.

Table 6.27 The benefits of the different types of training

Type of training	Brief description	Major components of fitness stressed	Example of a session e.g. of a performer	Advantages	Disadvantages
Continuous training	Low intensity rhythmic exercise that uses large muscle groups. The intensity of the training should be between 60–85% HRmax and the duration of the session between 30 mins and 2 hours. Distance running, swimming and cycling are good examples of this	• Cardio - respiratory endurance • Muscular endurance	5–10k steady runs at 65% HRmax e.g. Paula Radcliffe (marathon)	• Time-efficient • Routine programmes are easy to follow • Less chance of injury due to lower intensities	• Can be monotonous • Athletes may need to train at higher intensities • May not be specific to some activities such as team sports
Fartlek training	A form of continuous training where the intensity or speed of the activity is varied throughout the session—from sprinting to walking. The beauty of this type of training is that it develops both aerobic and anaerobic fitness. It is ideal for games players	• Cardio-respiratory endurance • Muscular endurance • Speed	Jog at 60% HRmax 15 mins Sprint x 50m : jog x 150m Repeat 10 times Walk for 90 seconds Jog at 70% HRmax 5 mins Sprint x 200m Jog gently to finish e.g. Aaron Lennon (football)	• Adds variety of pace • Higher intensities can be achieved than in continuous training	• Not specific to all sports • Higher intensities may increase the risk of injury
Sprint interval training	An intermittent training regime that involves periods of alternating exercise and rest. Widely used in athletics and swimming the main benefit of this training method is its versatility, since there are many variables that can be altered in order to stress the required components of fitness. These variables include: • Distance of work period • Intensity of work period • The number of sets • The number of reps • Duration of rest period	• Speed • Power	3 sets x 10 reps x 30m sprints (wbr) 5 mins rest between sets e.g. Jason Gardener (100m sprint)	• Adds variety of pace and duration of work periods • Can be sport-specific, e.g. sprinting • Training at higher intensities leads to significant adaptation	• Requires a measured work distance (e.g. an athletics track) or timed duration • Resting periods need to be timed • More recovery time may be needed when compared to continuous training
Anaerobic Interval training		• Speed • Power • Muscular endurance	2 sets x 4 reps x 300m runs (90 secs rest, work relief) e.g. Chris Hoy (1km cycle time trial)		
Aerobic interval training		• Cardio-respiratory endurance • Muscular endurance	3 x 1000m runs (125% personal best time) work: relief ratio = $1\frac{1}{2}$ e.g. Mo Farah (5K/cross-country)		

Table 6.27 continued

Type of training	Brief description	Major components of fitness stressed	Example of a session	Advantages	Disadvantages
Weight training	An intermittent training method that uses free weights or resistance machines to overload the body. The resistance is determined by working as a percentage of your 1 rep max. and the session is divided into sets ad repetitions which can be manipulated to stress the required aspect of strength	• Maximum strength • Power • Muscular endurance	Maximum strength Heavy weights, low reps 5 sets × 6 reps × 85% 1RM e.g. Naim Suleymanoglu (weight lifting) Elastic strength (must be rapid contractions) 3 sets × 12 reps × 75% 1RM e.g. Jamie Noon (rugby) Strength endurance Light weights, high reps 3 sets × 20 reps × 50% 1RM e.g. Kirsty Balfour (swimming)	• The best method to improve all types of strength and power • Some actions can replicate sporting movements	• Greater risk of injury due to higher intensities • Specialised equipment is needed • Requires some knowledge of appropriate technique to ensure maximum development of the target muscle • More recovery time may be needed when compared to continuous training
Circuit training	A general conditioning activity in which a series of exercises are used to work different muscle groups. Exercises can be made activity or game-specific	• Muscular endurance • Cardio-respiratory endurance	See Fig 6.09 Circuit A = 8 exercises × 30 secs Circuit B = 8 exercises × 30 secs Circuit C = Run for 4 mins Total = 12 mins Repeat 2 or 3 times e.g. Kelly Sotherton (heptathlon)	• Large numbers can perform at once • Can be tailored to meet the needs of particular sports • Can develop a number of components of fitness, e.g. muscular endurance and cv endurance	• Need access to equipment and large facility • Does not produce maximal improvements in strength or cv fitness • General circuits may not meet the needs of some activities

Table 6.27 continued

Type of training	Brief description	Major components of fitness stressed	Example of a session	Advantages	Disadvantages
Plyometrics	A type of training that involves an eccentric muscle contraction followed immediately by a concentric contraction. When the quadriceps lengthen, for example when jumping down from a box top, it pre-loads the muscle and initiates the stretch reflex which causes a rapid and forceful concentric contraction	• Power • Strength • Speed	A plyometrics circuit to include depth jumping, hopping, skipping, press-ups with claps, throwing and catching a medicine ball e.g. Phillips Idowu (triple jump)	• Excellent method of developing power and elastic strength • Can develop power in both upper and lower body • Activities can be made to replicate actions from sport	• The high intensity activities can increase the risk of injury • Appropriate technique is essential to the prevention of injury • More recovery time may be needed when compared to continuous training
PNF (proprioceptive neuromuscular facilitation)	A stretching technique that seeks to inhibit the stretch reflex that occurs when a muscle is stretched to its limit. By isometrically contracting the muscle that is being stretched (usually with the aid of a partner), the stretch reflex is diminished and a greater stretch can occur.	• Flexibility	With the aid of a partner stretch the muscle to it's limit. Isometrically contract the muscle for a minimum of 6 seconds (this can be achieved through pushing against your partner) Relax the muscle When the stretch is performed a second time the range of movement should have increased e.g. Beth Tweddle (gymnastics)	• The best method of improving flexibility and therefore increasing the range of movement possible about a joint • Can also help improve speed and elastic strength of a performer	• Must be done with the assistance of a partner • Can only be performed under the watchful eye of a trained coach • Extreme flexibility can lead to joint instability and increase the risk of injury
SAQ (speed, agility and quickness)	A type of training designed to improve the speed, agility and quickness of performers, particularly games players	• Speed • Agility • Power	Training activities include: Ladder drills Resistance drills eg: parachute runs, bungee rope runs Plyometric drills e.g. Peter Nicol (squash)	• A wide variety of activities can be used • Can be sport-specific • Activities can develop speed, agility and power simultaneously	• Requires specialist equipment

Refresh your memory

Revision checklist

The knowledge acquired from this chapter will be assessed in section B of your Unit 1 written paper.

Make sure you know the following:

▷ Fitness testing is an essential ingredient in the design of training programmes

▷ Suitable tests for stamina/cardiorespiratory endurance include: direct gas analysis, the multi-stage fitness test, Cooper 12 minute run test

▷ Suitable tests of strength include: 1 rep max test and the handgrip dynamometer

▷ Suitable tests of muscular endurance include: the abdominal conditioning test

▷ Suitable tests of speed include: 30m sprint test

▷ Suitable tests of flexibility include: goniometer measurements, sit and reach test

▷ Suitable tests of agility include: the Illinois agility run test

▷ Suitable tests of balance include: the standing stork test

▷ Suitable tests of coordination include: the hexagon test, the alternate hand ball toss test

▷ Suitable tests of reaction time include: visual reaction time tests, ruler drop test

▷ The validity of testing assesses whether a test actually measures what it claims to

▷ The reliability of testing considers whether a test will produce the same or very similar results when the test is repeated

▷ When planning fitness tests it is necessary to consider issues such as the choice of maximal or sub-maximal tests

▷ The principles of training should be followed if training is to be successful

▷ SPORT FITT WIMP is an acronym that can be used to help you remember each of the principles of training

- ▷ The Karvonen formula can be used to calculate appropriate heart rate training intensities for aerobic-type activities

- ▷ The Borg scale is a perceived exertion rating and can be used to determine appropriate training intensities

- ▷ When weight training the 1 repetition maximum should be used to gauge the correct intensity for development of maximum, elastic or strength endurance

- ▷ A warm up should be completed before and a cool down following every training session

- ▷ A warm up should consist of three distinct phases: a pulse raiser, followed by stretching activities and finishing with some skill-related practice

- ▷ There are many different types of training at the disposal of the coach and athlete. It is essential that appropriate methods are selected for inclusion in the training programme

- ▷ When applying methods of training in answering an examination question from section B of Unit 1, make sure you can: name a relevant method of training, give a brief description of it, state the main components of fitness improved, give an example of a typical session and comment upon the relative advantages and disadvantages of the training method selected

Revise as you go

1. Explain why fitness testing is necessary for both the coach and athlete.

2. Critically evaluate the multi-stage fitness test as a test of cardiorespiratory endurance.

3. Validity and reliability are important in any test. How would you ensure that an investigation was both valid and reliable?

4. Apply the principle of specificity to a shot putter who is preparing for a major championships.

5. What are the physiological reasons behind a) a warm up and b) a cool down?

6. Using Karvonen's formula calculate the heart rate training zone for a 38-year-old triathlete who has a resting heart rate of 56 bpm.

7. What weight training exercises would you include for a swimmer wanting to improve the strength endurance of their shoulders and upper back muscles? Name each strengthening exercise and state the intensity (resistance), number of sets and number of repetitions you would advise.

8. Justify the methods of training that you would employ to develop the elastic strength of the quadriceps, gluteals, hamstrings and calf muscles of a triple jumper. Try to give some specific examples of exercises that you would include in your programme.

9. Outline the stretching technique of proprioceptive neuromuscular facilitation.

10. How would an interval training session for a 100m sprinter differ from that of a 400m runner?

Get the result!

Examination question

In what ways should the diet of a marathon runner differ from that of a weight lifter? Give reasons for your answer.   (3 marks)

Model answer

Student answer (A grade)

A marathon runner needs to supply energy to the working muscles for a long period of time. The muscles will use both fatty acids and glycogen during the run so the marathon runner must ensure that muscular stores of these nutrients are maximised before the run.

The marathon runner will need to consume a diet high in carbohydrates which ensures an adequate supply of energy for training and competition.

Typically the contribution of carbohydrate to the marathon runners diet should be around 65–70 per cent of total calories consumed. Prior to competition marathon a runner may attempt to maximise his/her stores of glycogen through carbohydrate or glycogen loading. A weightlifter will also need to have a high carbohydrate diet to enable them to train and recover quickly. However their diet will consist of a lot more protein than a marathon runner. This protein helps to repair the muscle and tendon damage caused by lifting very heavy weights , consequently the protein helps the muscle mass to increase.

Typically the protein intake for a weightlifter should be between 15–20 per cent.

Examiner says:
The candidate has correctly identified the fuels used by a marathon runner and the specific exercise-related roles of these nutrients, i.e. energy creation.

Examiner says:
A direct comparison between the weightlifter and marathon runner has been made here and the candidate has correctly identified the importance of protein to a weightlifter's diet.

Examiner says:
The correct contribution of carbohydrate to a marathon runner's diet has been accurately stated.

What physiological benefits are gained by making sure a performer's diet contains sufficient iron and calcium?

(2 marks)

Model answer

Student answer (A grade)

Iron and calcium are two important minerals needed in our diet. Iron is found in all blood cells as haemoglobin which helps to transport oxygen around the body.

Calcium is needed for healthy bones and teeth. Iron can be acquired by eating red meats, wholegrain cereals and green leafy vegetables while calcium can be found in milk, dairy products and nuts and seeds.

Examiner says:

The candidate has shown some extended knowledge here by stating good sources of iron and calcium.

Examiner says:

The candidate has correctly identified the physiological benefits of having a diet rich in protein and calcium.

Examiner says

Before answering the question make sure you read the question 2 or 3 times first. When you are happy that you know what the question is asking underline or highlight **all** the question cues and key words; only then should you put pen to paper and attempt an answer.

Compare the expected pattern of heart rate of an athlete completing a steady 5K run and a basketball player during a match. Account for any similarities and differences.

Model answer

Student answer (A grade)

The expected heart rate patterns of an athlete completing a 5K run and a basketball player are likely to be quite different because of the different demands of the two activities.

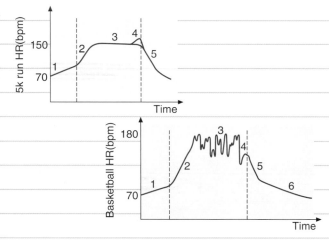

Examiner says:

It is a good idea to sketch heart rate graphs to help in your explanation. Label them clearly and refer the examiner to the graphs as this candidate has done.

Examiner says:

In this first part of the answer the candidate has considered the similarities between the two patterns of heart rate.

Examiner says:

Here the candidate has not only described the pattern but has also offered an explanation as to the reasons behind the pattern.

Immediately before the commencement of both activities I would expect to see a slight increase in heart rate. This is known as the anticipatory rise and results from the release of adrenaline that helps prepare the body for the ensuing exercise. (see stage 1 on both graphs). As both activities begin I would expect the heart rate of both individuals to rise rapidly (stage 2 on both graphs). This is to make sure that sufficient blood and nutrients can reach the working muscles. This is where the similarities would seem to end as during the remainder of the activities, I would expect the patterns of heart rate to be quite different. The heart rate of the athlete would plateau and reach steady state (stage 3).

This is where the demands of the muscles for oxygen are being met by supply and so heart rate does not need to increase further. I would expect this steady state to continue for the remainder of the event or until the 5K runner increases the intensity of the exercise or their running speed, when sprinting to the finish line for example (stage 4).

I would expect the heart rate of the basketball player, on the other hand to fluctuate much more throughout the duration of the match depending upon the levels of intensity they are working at (stage 3). When performing a full court press for example the effort level is high and the demands on the muscles greater. Heart rate therefore needs to increase to meet these demands and supply sufficient oxygen and other nutrients. During less intense periods of the game, for example, during time outs or when jogging back into position the demands on the body are less and heart rate will fall slightly.

Immediately following both activities I would expect heart rate to fall rapidly (stage 5) but I would doubt heart rate would return straight back to normal as it takes a while to clear waste products such as lactic acid. Lactic acid is a product of anaerobic exercise and since basketball has a greater anaerobic component to it than a 5K run (which is predominantly aerobic) I would expect heart rate to remain elevated for longer and take longer to return back to normal (stage 6).

Examiner's tip

When sketching heart rate or oxygen consumption curves make sure you begin the sketch some way up the y (vertical) axis and not from the origin. Drawing from the origin would assume a heart rate of 0bpm and an oxygen consumption of 0l/min ... i.e. the subject is dead!!!

Examination question

You have been asked to develop the skills and fitness of a group of A Level Physical Education students who wish to improve their performance in a team game.

Explain why you would need to use the principles of training when developing a training programme to improve the fitness of the A level Physical Education students.

Model answer

Student answer (A grade)

The principles of training are essentially the rules of training that must be followed if the training is going to be of benefit to the performer and physiological adaptation is to occur. The principles can be summarised in the acronym SPORT FITT WIMP and applied to the PE class as follows:

Specificity requires all training that is undertaken to be relevant to the activity; this can include training the necessary muscles and energy systems. If I were wanting to improve the aerobic fitness of the A level PE students, I would ensure that some endurance-based work to stress the aerobic energy system was included.

Progression requires exercise to increase in intensity as the training programme progresses. As the weeks of training passed I would encourage the PE students to train at a slightly higher percentage of their maximum heart rate.

Overload involves the body undergoing some form of stress and discomfort during the training session — there is no gain without pain! To ensure overload I would make the students

Examiner says:

A good definition of the principles of training given here by the candidate which serves as a good introduction.

Examiner says:

The candidate has clearly identified and explained each of the principles of training. They have related how they would apply each principle to the group of PE students throughout their answer which is essential if they are to achieve top bar marks.

relate their training intensity to a perceived exertion scale such as the Borg scale.

Reversibility infers that once the training programme stops all the gains from the previous training will eventually be lost. I would make sure that there are no significant breaks in training or a significant reduction in intensity when training the PE students.

Tedium should encourage the coach to make training sessions varied and exciting for the performer so that motivation is maintained. So that the A level PE students do not get bored, I will vary the training sessions so that it includes continuous training, Fartlek, cross country, aerobic interval training and circuit training. I might also encourage them to listen to music while training.

The FITT principle requires the coach and performer to consider the Frequency, Intensity, time (duration) of training sessions and the type or method of training used.

The WIMP principle reminds the coach to start every session with a warm-up and cool-down (Warm-up/Cool-down), to treat everybody as individuals (Individuality), to not train people too hard so that they are liable to overtraining syndrome (Moderation) and to have some long-term training goal and base the training around that (Periodisation).

If these principles of training are followed I would expect the group of A level PE students to adapt physiologically and improve their aerobic performance.

This is a really good answer for this section B question. Section B is marked in levels with band descriptors. The band descriptors for this 8-point question are below along with the mark scheme. Once you have studied the mark scheme have a go at marking this answer yourself.

Band Range	Band descriptors
7–8	• Addresses all of the question • Has accessed at least 7 points from the mark scheme • Few errors in their spelling, punctuation and grammar, and correct use of technical language
5–6	• Addresses most of the question • Has accessed at least 5 points from the mark scheme • Few errors in their spelling, punctuation and grammar, demonstrates use of technical language although sometimes inaccurately
3–4	• Addresses one area of the question • Has accessed at least 3 points from the mark scheme • Errors in spelling, punctuation and grammar and little use of technical language
1–2	• Attempted to address one area of the question • Has accessed at least 1 point from the mark scheme • Major errors in spelling, punctuation and grammar, with no use of technical language

1. Specific – need to make movements/energy systems same as activity

2. Example of activity/exercise that is specific

3. Progressive – improving fitness requires more intensity in exercises

4. Example of how to make training programme progressive

5. Overload – must stress body to produce adaptations

6. Example of how to incorporate overload into the programme

7. Reversibility – too much rest/not regularly enough means fitness deteriorates

8. Example of strategy to prevent reversibility

9. Tedium – without variety – boredom/loss of motivation

10. Example of how to prevent tedium in the programme

11. Identifying SPORT but not explaining

12. FITT principle

UNIT 1

Opportunities for and the effects of leading a healthy and active lifestyle

Section 2: *Skill acquisition*

Introduction

The terms 'skill' and 'ability' are frequently used to describe sporting performance, but are their full meanings actually understood and used in the correct contexts? Hopefully, as you are studying the AS Physical Education course, you will have already developed a wide variety of skills and are applying them effectively both in practice and competitive situations. There are many skills we use daily without even thinking about them because, as we develop and refine such skills, they become second nature to us, or autonomous. For example, writing your name, using mobile phones to text a message and using money to pay for goods. All of these are skills and have developed over time through practice.

During this chapter you will develop an understanding of the relationship between the different terms and how this subsequently affects the development of skill in different performers. As a result, you should be able to answer the question, 'What makes one performer more skilful than another?'

Although some definitions are given, you will not be expected to learn and quote specific examples, merely to interpret and explain them, using appropriate examples to support your answers.

The nature of a skilled performance

We all possess and can execute a variety of skills, even though some people may appear to be more skilled than others. We can all run, throw, catch, aim, dodge and jump. But what makes one performance more highly skilled than another? How can we recognise these skilled performances and justify our reasons?

TASK 7.01

1. List five skills you use daily (they do not have to be of a sporting nature).
2. List five skills you can apply to a variety of sports (generic skills).
3. List five skills you use that are sport-specific.
4. Compare and contrast your lists with other students. Have you all listed similar skills?

APPLY IT!

Construct your own definition of a 'skill' and compose it with other students in your group.

Look at the skills you listed in Task 7.01. They probably fall into one of three categories:

- some may be a single act, for example a cricket stroke or netball shot
- others may be a series of actions linking with other players and requiring an assessment of the situation, for example a passage of play involving dribbling and passing to create a scoring opportunity
- others may be linked to the quality of the performance and application of techniques within the sporting environment. For example, assessing the effectiveness and/or outcome of the actions when compared to previous performances, either personally, or when compared to others (for example, a gymnastic sequence).

Characteristics of skill

All skilled performances have similar characteristics, even though they may appear totally different in nature. For example, how can the performances of a trampolinist, a volleyball setter, a hurdler and a rugby union prop forward be compared and regarded as skilful? While each may be different in terms of technique and outcome, the characteristics associated with a skilful performance are common to all.

There are many popular definitions of the term 'skill', several of which are outlined below. When you are reading each one, try to highlight similar characteristics to those identified in Task 7.02.

'Skill is the learned ability to bring about predetermined results with maximum certainty, often with the minimum outlay of time or energy or both.'

Knapp

'Skill is an organised, coordinated activity in relation to an object or situation which involves a whole chain of sensory, central and motor mechanisms.'

Welford

'While the task can be physical or mental, one generally thinks of skill as some type of manipulative efficiency. A skilled movement is one in which a predetermined objective is accomplished with maximum efficiency with a minimum outlay of energy. A skilful movement does not just happen. There must be a conscious effort on the part of the performer in order to execute a skill.'

Robb

Hopefully, by comparing the list of characteristics linked to the photographs and reading the definitions, similarities can be seen. Therefore we can conclusively say that a skilled action is:

TASK 7.02

Using the photographs of Jonny Wilkinson and Tiger Woods, or by observing a short video clip of a high-quality sporting event, list at least five words to describe their best performance. Compare your words with those listed by other students.

Fig. 7.01

Fig. 7.02

- **learned** – it requires practice and develops through experience. Being skilled involves a permanent change in behaviour that will stand the test of time
- **goal-directed/has an end result** – each skill has a predetermined objective at the beginning of the movement
- **consistent** – the phrase 'maximum certainty' is a key element, reflecting the ability of the performer to repeat the skill despite differing environmental conditions
- **efficient** – the actions are performed with coordination and precision using the required amount of energy necessary
- **fluent** – the actions appear to flow naturally rather than be forced, with good balance and timing
- **recognisable/linked to a technical model** – the skill is instantly recognisable and its execution can be compared to other performers, allowing an analysis of performance to occur
- **aesthetic** – the execution of the skill is pleasing to observe, appearing controlled and effective within the context of the situation.

Types of skills

In order to become an effective performer, there are a variety of different types of skills that need to be mastered and applied to sporting situations. You will already use the types of skills outlined below, but their application may be one reason to explain how performers reach different levels of competence.

The types of skills are:

- **cognitive** – skills that involve thought processes and intellectual ability. Examples include devising appropriate strategies and tactics to outwit an opponent, calculating scores, split times or interpreting data
- **motor** – skills that involve physical movement and muscular control linked to a specific objective. Examples include a high jump, kicking a ball or badminton serves
- **perceptual** – skills that involve the detection and interpretation of stimuli from the environment.

This may differ between performers, referees and coaches, who may all observe the same situation but focus on different cues and consequently arrive at a different conclusion. For example, during a netball match, players have to quickly analyse the location of teammates, the opposition and their own location on court before deciding on the most effective skill to execute. Those who can do this quickly will develop into the better performers

- **psychomotor** – also known as perceptual motor skills. These skills are a combination of the perceptual and motor skills outlined above and are the type most frequently used during sporting performance. They involve the interpretation of environmental stimuli and the execution of movement. For example, during a rugby match, a player who receives the ball will have to analyse the situation, decide if the best option is to pass, run with the ball or kick and then execute the movement, while constantly updating new stimuli and modifying their actions as needed.

Often these skills can be viewed as a never-ending cycle during the course of the performance, as illustrated in Figure 7.03.

TASK 7.03

For your chosen activity, identify when each type of skill would be used during a personal performance.

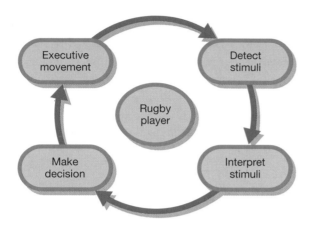

Fig. 7.03 A rugby player uses all the types of skill during a match

Classification of skills

When analysing skills, it is useful to be able to group together those that may have similar characteristics. This allows the teacher or coach to study the general requirements of a skill and select the appropriate method of practice and learning environment. The process for classifying skills is commonly based on the use of a continuum, or sliding scale. This allows a general interpretation of the characteristics of the skills to take place and for several skills to be compared at the same time.

Many of the skills you will analyse may have components that could fall into both extremes of the **continuum**, but for the purpose of this course, it is advisable to analyse the overall movement action rather than subroutines. For example, a bowling action of a cricketer should be viewed as a whole, not merely the wrist action during release of the ball.

Numerous classifications have been proposed, but your studies have to limit the number to four. You are expected to have knowledge of the characteristics of each, give suitable examples to illustrate your understanding and justify your reasons. The classification groups of continua are:

- open/closed continuum
- gross/fine continuum
- self-paced/externally-paced continuum
- discrete/serial/continuous continuum.

KEY TERM

Continuum:
a sequence of gradations between two extremes

ATHLETE PROFILE

Claire Vigrass is a young 'real tennis' player who has competed at international level for several years. She participates in both the singles and doubles events, but to date has experienced greater success at the former. She is the 2008 United States Ladies Open Champion and currently ranked in the world's top five players. She is hoping to turn professional in the future. Claire is a talented performer in several sports including netball, athletics and real tennis because her abilities allow her to effectively complete the skills required. However, some of her natural abilities have allowed her, through training, to develop the specific skills required to excel in the sport of real tennis. In terms of **gross motor abilities** she has very good **explosive strength** allowing her to play shots with considerable force. She also has high levels of **dynamic strength** allowing her to execute shots during prolonged rallies. Other abilities include good **trunk strength**, so she can maintain good posture and transfer power when playing both forehand and backhand drives, as well as excellent **flexibility** to move around the court and return difficult shots.
Claire's **perceptual motor abilities** are possibly the more important factors that have enabled her to reach the elite level. She has excellent **coordination** and **control precision**, so that shots are played with accuracy. The nature of real tennis means that the ball can bounce in unpredictable ways, but her **reaction time** and **response orientation** allow her to make quick decisions and select the most appropriate shot to play. She also relies on her **speed** around the court, her **manual dexterity** to alter her grip on the racket as required and her ability to **aim** accurately to place the ball where she wants to, either when serving or when playing a particular shot, which may win the point.

Open/closed continuum

This continuum is based on the influence the environment has on the production of the skilled movement. Any number of factors may influence the performance, for example the position of other players, your own position, proximity of the crowd, playing conditions, surface/facilities and so on (see Table 7.01).

There are examples of closed skills being executed within a mainly open environment. A tennis player completing the serve (closed skill) has to consider the position of their opponent, even though they are not directly influencing the skill action itself. Similarly, a player taking a penalty or free throw is executing a closed skill during a break from the usual unpredictable environment.

Fig. 7.04 A tennis rally is an example of an open skill

Fig. 7.05 A dive is an example of a closed skill

Open skills are directly affected by the environment because:	Closed skills are not directly affected by the environment because:
• the environment is unstable and changing • the environment is not predictable • the skills require constant adjustment to suit the situation • the skills are perceptual and involve decision making • they are usually externally paced • decisions need to be made quickly	• the environment is stable and constant • the environment is predictable • the skills can be repeated consistently when learned or habitual • the skills are pre-learned in a set routine and require minimal adjustment • they are usually self-paced • decisions are pre-planned

APPLY IT!

A tennis player receiving the ball must evaluate the speed and direction of the ball, his or her own location on court and that of the opponent, the nature of the surface and the opponent's strength before deciding which shot to play: making it an open skill.

A springboard diver will experience the same conditions each time he or she competes. The particular dive is selected based on the tariff required, and the dive is performed without the influence of any other competitor: making it a closed skill.

Table 7.01 Open and closed skills

Fig. 7.07 Throwing the dart is an example of a fine skill

Fig. 7.06 A basketball lay-up shot is an example of a gross skill

Fig. 7.08 The spin bowler's action is an example of a fine skill within a gross skill because of the action of the wrist and fingers

Gross/fine continuum

This continuum is based on the amount of muscular movement and the precision required during the execution of the skill (see Table 7.02). Many skills combine the two elements during different phases of the action. For example, a cricket bowler's run-up would be classed as a gross skill, while the delivery action of the wrist and hand would be classed as a fine skill.

Gross skills involve:	Fine skills involve:
• large muscular movements • large muscle groups	• small muscular movements • small muscle groups
Accuracy and precision are not necessarily a high priority	Accuracy and precision are vital factors

APPLY IT!

Running, throwing, jumping or kicking a ball are gross motor skills.	A snooker shot, throwing a dart or the wrist and finger action of a cricketer when bowling are fine skills.

Table 7.02 Gross and fine skills

Fig. 7.09 A gymnast uses self-paced skills

Fig. 7.10 A hockey player depends on externally-paced skills

Self-paced/externally-paced continuum

This continuum is based on the amount of control the performer has over the execution and timing of the movement (see Table 7.03). This is based on two factors: the timing and initiation of the movement, and the actual speed/rate of the movement.

EXAM TIP:

If asked for an example to illustrate your answer, be specific – do not just name a sport, give a definite skill or situation.

Self-paced skills involve:	Externally-paced skills involve:
• performer controls the start of the movement	• performer initiates the start of the movement, based on other people's actions or changing events in the environment
• performer controls the speed of the movement	• performer changes the speed of the movement in relation to other people's actions or changing events in the environment
• usually *closed* skills	• usually *open* skills

APPLY IT!

A gymnastic routine, golf swing or long jump involve self-paced skills.	Sailing, receiving a pass or a sprint start involve externally-paced skills.

Table 7.03 Self-paced and externally-paced skills

Discrete skills involve:	Serial skills involve:	Continuous skills involve:
• a clear beginning and end • short time duration for completion • to repeat the skill, it must be started again	• a linked series of discrete skills • set order or sequence for each subroutine	• no clear beginning or end • extended time duration • the end of one movement is the start of the next

APPLY IT!

A cricket shot, kicking a ball, tennis shot, somersault or catching an object involve discrete skills.	A triple jump, canoe slalom race, gymnastic routine or basketball lay-up involve serial skills.	Swimming, cycling or running involve continuous skills.

Table 7.04 Discrete, serial and continuous skills

Discrete/serial/continuous continuum

This continuum is based on the relationship between the subroutines and identification of the beginning and end of the movement (see Table 7.04).

Characteristics of abilities

The terms 'skill' and 'ability' are often used in the same context and are interlinked but are, in fact, different in their meanings. We now know that a 'skill' is a learned action, but our 'abilities' actually allow us to perform the skills effectively. Below are two definitions of the term 'ability'.

'An inherited, relatively enduring trait that underlies or supports various kinds of motor and cognitive activities or skills. Abilities are thought of as being largely genetically determined.'

Schmidt

'Abilities are enduring characteristics which underlie a person's potential to acquire skill in one sport or another.'

Sharp

From these definitions, we can identify generally agreed characteristics of abilities.

- They are **genetic/innate** – our abilities are inherited from our parents.
- They are **enduring** – they remain relatively stable over time, but some development can occur due to training and exercise.
- **Ability underpins skill** – various abilities combine, which allow movement to occur.

TASK 7.04

Place the skills listed below in each of the four continua described above. Justify your reasons for each decision.

• Basketball set shot	• Cycling race
• Receiving a pass in netball	• Gymnastic vault
• High jump	• Hockey dribble
• Tennis rally shot	• Snooker

The terms 'skill' and 'ability' must be regarded as different. Without the necessary levels of specific ability, it would not be possible to excel in a given activity. For example, a springboard diver requires high levels of flexibility, power and coordination, while a marathon runner requires high levels of stamina, with limited levels of the diver's necessary abilities. Performers often possess a general level of each type of ability, but to progress to the highest levels of competition, specific abilities are required for each skill. They should be viewed as the building blocks of movement patterns, but a limiting factor of performance. In other words, if the performer does not have the innate abilities required for a particular skill, they will never achieve excellence.

EXAM TIPS:

When asked to outline the abilities required for a skill, explain why they are needed.

When asked to 'list', 'state' or 'name' the abilities required for a skill, the examiner will usually only accept the first answers if a specific number of abilities are requested.

SKILL ACQUISITION

Gross motor abilities

Static strength – the maximum force that can be exerted against an external object, for example weightlifter holding bar above the head

Explosive strength – the ability to exert a powerful burst of energy during a short period of time, for example shot put

Dynamic strength – the ability to perform repeated muscular contractions over a period of time, for example press-ups

Trunk strength – the amount of strength in the abdominal region, for example sit-ups

Stamina – the ability to maintain maximum effort when using the cardiorespiratory system, for example marathon, triathlon

Gross body equilibrium – the ability to maintain balance, for example dribbling a basketball or doing a handstand

Gross body coordination – the ability to coordinate several parts of the body while moving, for example a gymnastic sequence

Extent flexibility – the ability to flex or stretch the back and trunk muscles as far as possible in any direction, for example a walkover

Dynamic flexibility – the ability to make repeated, rapid flexing movements, for example hurdling

Perceptual motor abilities

Multi-limb coordination – the ability to coordinate the movement of several limbs at the same time

Control precision – the ability to perform precise, controlled movement involving large muscle groups

Response orientation – the ability to make quick decisions when faced with numerous options (choice reaction time)

Reaction time – the ability to respond as quickly as possible to the stimulus

Speed of movement – the ability to make gross, rapid movements

Rate control – the ability to alter the speed and direction of the movement precisely

Finger dexterity – the ability to manipulate small objects accurately with the fingers

Manual dexterity – the ability to make hand-arm movements while using an object accurately at speed

Hand-arm steadiness – the ability to make accurate hand-arm movements when strength and speed are not always needed

Wrist-finger speed – the ability to move the fingers and wrist quickly

Aiming – the ability to aim at small objects accurately

Fig. 7.11 Gross and perceptual motor abilities

156

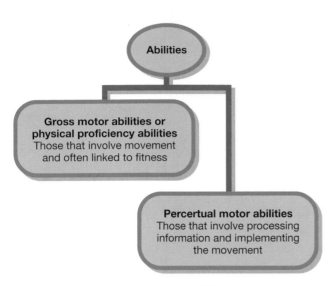

Fig. 7.12 Fleishman's classification of abilities

Types of abilities

Numerous classifications are used to analyse and categorise abilities. One of the most frequently used is that proposed by Fleishman, who subdivided abilities into two categories (Fig. 7.12). Each of the categories is outlined in greater detail in Figure 7.11.

The relationship between skill and ability

In order to perform any skill, we require specific abilities to execute the movement effectively. Talent Identification Programmes (TIP) attempt to measure a person's natural abilities and try to find a corresponding activity that may then allow them to develop into a high-level performer. This alone does not guarantee success, as effective coaching, training and competition programmes are also required to nurture and refine genetic natural abilities. The key factor to remember is that **abilities are skill-specific**.

Another limiting factor of performance may be the range of abilities a performer possesses. Just because they have high levels of one type of ability, it does not mean they will necessarily have corresponding levels in all areas. For example, an athlete may have a fast reaction time and good speed but may also have poor response orientation

TASK 7.05

1. For the two activities listed below, list the five most important gross motor abilities and perceptual motor abilities required to produce a high level of performance. Justify your reasons for their inclusion.
   a) Trampolining   b) Netball
2. Repeat the task for your own chosen activity.

and manual dexterity, which would limit their effectiveness as a games player.

Many skills require similar abilities and often transfer between skills does occur. For example, a decathlete requires speed, explosive strength, flexibility, coordination and good reaction time. These qualities are also required for the sport of bobsleigh, and numerous athletes have been successful performers in both sports.

APPLY IT!

In an attempt to achieve the goal of Team GB reaching 4th place in the medal table at the 2012 London Olympics, several programmes have been introduced to identify suitable performers who may have the required abilities to excel in particular activities. For example, the Sporting Giants programme is a joint initiative between UK Sport, the English Institute of Sport and the Olympic sports of Rowing, Handball and Volleyball to identify particularly tall athletes from all over the country with the ability to take to the international sporting stage in 2012.

The partners launched the appeal to the young, tall and athletically gifted of the British public and the response was overwhelming. Around 3800 people between the ages of 16 and 25, taller than 180 cm (women) and 190.5 cm (men) applied for the chance to take their place on the world class sporting pathway.

Measuring abilities

Numerous tests have been devised to measure levels of ability, some of which you may experience during your practical lessons. Such tests not only allow potential talent spotting to occur, but are a vital aspect in the construction and monitoring of training programmes. A more comprehensive explanation of the tests can be found in Chapter 6.

Refresh your memory

Revision checklist

Make sure you know the following:

▷ Skills are learned behaviour and are refined via practice

▷ Skills are consistent, appear effortless, involve decision making and have a pre-determined objective

▷ Skills can be cognitive (thinking), perceptual (interpreting and analysing) and motor (movement). Sports skills are often referred to as psychomotor skills

▷ Classification systems consider the common characteristics of skills

▷ A continuum is a more effective tool in classifying skills

▷ Abilities are innate, enduring qualities or capacities

▷ Abilities are task-specific. Specific skills need different abilities

▷ Abilities underpin skill development

▷ 'Gross motor abilities' involve movement and are linked to fitness

▷ 'Psychomotor abilities' involve processing information and executing the movement

▷ Abilities underpin skill. Specific abilities are required to perform specific skills

Revise as you go

1. State three characteristics of a skilled movement.

2. What do 'cognitive' skills involve?

3. Why are 'perceptual' skills important when taking part in a sporting activity?

4. What are 'motor' skills?

5. What type of skill involves no interference from the local environment?

6. Name the type of skill which has a clear beginning and end.

7. Explain what is meant by the term 'self-paced' skill.

8. What type of skill has several discrete elements or subroutines linked together to form an integrated sequence?

9. Explain the term 'open' skill.

10. Name the type of skill which involves large muscle movement during its execution.

11. Name the type of skill which has no definite beginning or end.

12. Explain the term 'fine' skill.

13. Outline the characteristics of a 'simple' skill.

14. What is an 'externally-paced' skill?

15. What is the difference between 'skill' and 'ability'?

16. Explain the term 'psychomotor/perceptual motor ability'.

17. Explain the term 'gross motor ability'.

18. Why are 'abilities' task specific?

19. Name three gross motor abilities required to excel in the sport of long jumping.

20. List three psychomotor abilities required to play hockey.

CHAPTER 8

Information processing

LEARNING OBJECTIVES:

By the end of this chapter you should be able to:

▸ outline the basic stages of recognised information processing models

▸ explain the stages involved in the memory process

▸ discuss factors that affect decision making, including reaction time, Hick's Law and the psychological refractory period

▸ explain the function and value of feedback

▸ explain the term 'motor programme' and identify specific subroutines

▸ understand how movement is controlled with reference to the open and closed loop theory

▸ apply the knowledge of motor control to practical situations.

Introduction

One of the key aspects of this chapter is to understand how you gather, interpret and make use of the various pieces of information your senses are constantly gathering. The effectiveness of your information processing system is a vital factor in your ability as an individual and can have a big impact on the level of your performance. Often it is not the most skilful performer who succeeds, but the one who is most able to identify the relevant cues, ignore those that are irrelevant and, based on that information, select the appropriate action in the quickest time.

For each of the areas outlined in the learning objectives above, you will be expected to explain its characteristics, give practical applications of its use and discuss its various advantages and disadvantages. You will also be expected to explain how each of the processes may be maximised using relevant practical examples.

As with previous chapters, often the best way to gain a fuller understanding of each topic may be to refer back to personal experience and then apply some of the acquired knowledge to your current performances.

Models of information processing

The majority of the models of information processing are based on the assumption that our brain functions in a similar fashion to that of a computer and as such works in stages to arrive at the output phase.

The main stages involved are:

- **input** – information is gathered from the **environment/display**. This is also referred to as **stimulus identification** – information is collected from the display via the sensory system. This involves the performer using his or her **perceptual mechanism**. Any information deemed irrelevant is filtered via **selective attention** to increase the speed of the decision-making process. For example, a netball player will gather information regarding the speed and direction of the ball, the location of teammates and opponents, personal location on court and specific strategies being adapted. Shouts from spectators and location of the umpire will be ignored as this will slow down the decision making process

- **decision making** – gathered information is used to formulate a **motor programme**. This is also referred to as **response identification** – the relevant information is assessed and a decision made based on previous experience using the **translatory mechanism**, which is stored in the memory. For example, the netball player will decide upon a particular type of pass to use to a specific player
- **output** – motor programme is completed by the performer. This is also referred to as **response programming** – the motor programme is completed via the **effector mechanism** and the muscular system. For example, the netball player completes the pass to her teammate.

Whiting's model

One of the models most commonly used to illustrate information processing is Whiting's.

The input is gathered via three forms of receptors in the sensory system (Fig. 8.01):

- **exteroceptors** – information gathered from outside the body – extrinsic, for example sight, sound, touch, smell and taste (the first three are the most important to sports performers)
- **proprioceptors** – information gathered from inside the body via nerve receptors in the muscles and joints – intrinsic, for example the feeling of the movement or kinaesthetic awareness
- **interoceptors** – information from the internal organs, which is passed to the central nervous system, to control functions such as blood flow, blood pressure and body temperature.

KEY TERMS

Display:
the physical environment surrounding the performer, containing various stimuli or cues, from which the performer has to select those that are relevant at the time

Selective attention:
a process that filters irrelevant information gathered by the sensory system and prioritiises the stimuli that can affect the particular situation

Motor programme:
organises a series of subroutines into the correct sequence to perform a movement, adapting it to changes in the environment. They are based on a hierarchical structure, involving movements that are autonomous at the lower level with more complete subroutines at the peak

Perceptual mechanism:
the interpretation and analysis of information gathered from the environment by the sensory system

Translatory mechanism:
uses the information gathered from the environment and makes the appropriate decision

Effector mechanism:
transfers the decision that has been made to the muscular system via motor nerves

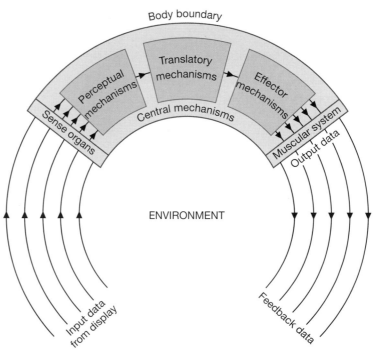

Fig. 8.01 Whiting's model

The intensity of the stimulus can affect the ease of 'signal detection' and the resultant motor programme; that is, if the stimulus is easier to detect, usually the motor programme can be initiated sooner. Often the teacher or coach may modify the situation to make the identification of cues easier.

TASK 8.01

1. Play a game of your choice but inhibit the sensory system to limit the amount of information received. For example, wear earplugs, an eye patch, blinkers, thick gloves, and so on. Do not restrict all your senses at once!
2. Alternate the inhibition. Discuss the effects and implications on performance with a partner.

The central mechanisms on Whiting's model are as outlined previously, and the final stages involve the performer receiving feedback about his or her performance. This can be received either extrinsically or intrinsically (see page 161), allowing adjustments to be made when required and retention of the information in the memory for future reference.

It must be remembered that although Figure 8.01 represents a static situation, our environment and the components of the model are constantly changing and being updated. It is dynamic in nature.

TASK 8.02

For each of the major sensory exteroceptors (vision, auditory and touch), suggest ways in which the intensity of the stimulus may be altered to aid the detection of the stimulus and processing of information.

TASK 8.03

Another well-known model of information processing was proposed by Welford (1968). Find a diagram of Welford's model then compare and contrast its similarities and terminology with Whiting's model.

Memory

Memory is a key element in information processing. Learning is concerned with acquiring relatively permanent changes in behaviour, therefore this information must be stored in some way allowing us to recall it when needed. When performing in a sporting environment, we are always making decisions based on the current situation and our previous experience, allowing us to make the correct choice based on our own strengths and weaknesses. The faster the information can be retrieved, the faster the decision can be made and executed.

Memory is subdivided into three components and their relationship is illustrated in Figure 8.02.

APPLY IT!

Practise drawing the memory model diagram (Fig. 8.02) including the correct number and direction of the respective arrows.

Short-term sensory store (STSS)

The **short-term sensory store** collects all the information entering the body via the sensory system. It has a huge capacity to receive information but can only retain it for a short period of time – up to one second before it is lost. The information is prioritised and irrelevant stimuli are discarded. This process is known as **selective attention**

Selective attention allows the performer to gather only important information and consequently speeds up the decision-making time. Many theories suggest there is only a limited amount of information that can be processed at any one time and by focusing on a smaller number of cues, we react faster to them. For example, a tennis player will attempt to focus on the ball, his position on court and his opponent. He will attempt to ignore the crowd, advertising boards and the consequences of the match. Often a performer with the ability to focus and block out distractions will be more effective than a potentially more skilful player who cannot concentrate fully. Sometimes athletes have referred to this as 'tunnel vision'.

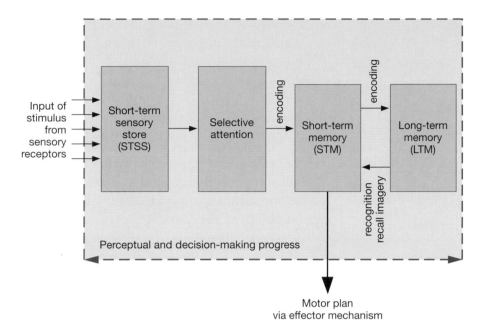

Fig. 8.02 The components of memory

A performer can improve his or her selective attention by:

- using appropriate practice and presentation methods
- highlighting specific cues on which to focus his or her concentration. This can be done by using different guidance methods
- altering the intensity of the stimulus, for example colour and speed of the object, loudness of the sound, and so on
- referring to past experiences
- making the stimuli meaningful or unique, for example make the performer think about the action in a different way. A basketball player snapping his or her wrist when taking a free throw may be told to think of 'waving the ball goodbye'
- reaching the correct level of arousal and maintaining motivation.

Short-term memory (STM)/working memory

The **short-term memory**, or **working memory**, receives the filtered information and compares it to stored information from past experiences before the final decision is made. It has a limited capacity of five to nine pieces of information, which can be retained for approximately 30 seconds. If the information is practised and learned, it is transferred to the long-term memory for future reference or it is released. As outlined previously, this has implications for a coach when discussing guidance. If the coach overloads the performer with information, the performer will not be able to process all of it at once and their learning will be less effective.

A performer can improve his or her short-term memory by:

- **chunking** – the information is arranged into larger units or 'chunks', allowing more pieces of information to be stored. For example, a set play in a game situation will be remembered by a single call, as in a rugby line-out
- **chaining** – the linking together of pieces of information, as used in the progressive part method of practice (see page 203), for example, when a gymnast is developing a sequence
- **using selective attention** – limiting the amount of irrelevant information passing into the short-term memory.

Long-term memory (LTM)

Long-term memory is the permanent retention of information through repetition or rehearsal. It has the capacity to store vast amounts of information for an unlimited period of time. When the performer is faced with a new situation, the relevant stimuli are passed on from the short-term memory, where a comparison is made with any similar experiences. If any recognition does occur, the similarities are noted and a decision is made quickly. If the situation is new, a motor programme will be formed based on available knowledge, but this may take slightly longer and delay the decision-making process.

A performer can improve his or her long-term memory by:

- improving the capability of the short-term memory
- practising and repeating movements, causing 'over-learning' of motor programmes

- developing a range of past experiences, for example modified games and realistic practice situations
- using mental rehearsal
- making the information meaningful, relevant and interesting to the performer.

Table 8.01 compares the possible memory process of both a novice and an experienced performer when confronted with the same situation. Both are playing in a rugby match, in possession of the ball, with support players on either side. They are confronted with a defender attempting to make a tackle.

Decision making and reaction time (RT)

Another key element in the decision-making process is the amount of time the performer takes to receive, interpret, analyse stimuli and formulate an appropriate response. The faster this can be achieved, the more time the performer is likely to have in order to complete the selected skill successfully.

We often attempt to confuse our opponents by giving them false cues, e.g. a dummy, feint or change of tactics, to keep them guessing and ultimately slow his or her reaction time. A performer with a faster reaction time can delay the start of his or her movement, giving him or her a greater opportunity to fully assess the situation and eliminating the need to guess what may happen. For example, a hockey defender may wait until an attacker is closer before

	Novice performer	Experienced performer
STSS	Gathers information about some of his or her own team, opponents, own position; aware of crowd and coach calling instructions	Gathers information about his or her own team, opponents, personal position
STM	Some relevant stimuli collected, for example location of defender and position of one support player plus some irrelevant cues, for example shouts from the crowd about what to do	Eliminates some stimuli, for example crowd noise and location of players who would not be an option to involve, but retains information about several possible teammates' and defenders' positions
LTM	Limited reference data available, distracted by the crowd and either makes the pass to the closest support player or runs into the defender	Large amount of previous experience allows the player to select from a range of options, to pass to the support player in the best position or to kick the ball into a suitable space or to another player

Table 8.01 Memory processes in novice and experienced performers

committing themselves to the tackle and risk either giving away a foul or being beaten by a dummy movement.

There are three key terms that need to be understood when discussing this section:

- **reaction time** – the time between the onset of a stimulus and the initiation of the response. It is the time the information processing system takes to interpret the situation, formulate a motor programme and transmit the information to the muscular system. An example is the time taken when a striker thinks he has the opportunity to score a goal and the start of the shooting action
- **movement time** – the time between the start of the movement and its completion. It is the time the performer takes to physically complete the movement when the muscular system has received the message from the brain via the effector system, for example, the time it takes the striker to move his limbs to strike the ball
- **response time** – the time from the onset of the stimulus to the completion of the movement. It is the combination of the reaction time and the movement time, for example, the overall time the

striker takes to complete the shot from first seeing the ball, his position and the goal.

Many factors affect the speed of a performer's reaction time including:

- **age** – reaction times improve until the early twenties but then become slower
- **gender** – males generally have faster reaction times but as we become older, the difference becomes less
- **fatigue** – tired performers tend to have slower reaction times
- **intensity of the stimulus** – the more intense, the faster the time, for example brighter and louder stimulus help increase reaction time
- **probability of the stimulus occurring** – if the stimulus is expected, there is a reduced element of doubt and anticipation, for example an opponent always plays the same shot in a particular situation
- **presence of a warning signal** – this may be a call or gesture, for example the starter at the beginning of a race issuing commands or coloured lights to begin a grand prix race

Fig. 8.03 Components of response time – reaction time (starting pistol), movement time (sprint start) and response time (sprint finish)

- **personality** – introverts tend to have slower reaction times than extroverts
- **sense used to detect the stimulus** – sight, sound, touch and kinaesthetic awareness all produce differing reaction times
- **previous experience** – the greater the experience, the faster the recall from the long-term memory
- **arousal level** – optimum arousal will cause heightened concentration levels and allow the performer to only focus on key stimuli
- **stimulus-response compatibility** – the reaction time is faster if the required action is normally linked to the stimulus, for example a batsman facing a bowler will select a shot based on how they think the ball usually bounces, depending on the bowler's action and where it pitches on the wicket. If the ball bounces differently, the batsman's reaction time may be slower as an adjustment is required
- **body temperature** – reaction time is slower if the body is cold
- **limbs used** – the further the nerve impulse has to travel, the slower the reaction time, for example hand movements tend to be completed faster than foot movements.

Performers use two forms of reaction time and these forms are dependent on the number of stimuli present and the number of possible responses available. They are:

- **simple reaction time** – involves one stimulus and one possible response. One example is the time a sprinter takes to start moving off the blocks when the gun has been fired
- **choice reaction time** – involves the performer being presented with numerous stimuli, each with a different response. This situation occurs in all open skills, causing the performer to make decisions largely based on past experiences. For example, a water polo player in possession of the ball has to decide whether to pass, move with the ball or shoot, and his or her situation will constantly alter, requiring another decision to be made.

TASK 8.05

For this task you will need playing cards and a stopwatch. In pairs, one times and the other performs; then swap roles. The performer has to complete each of the tasks below.
1. Divide the cards into two piles either red or black.
2. Divide the cards into four piles, one of each suit.
3. Divide the cards into eight piles, each suit with picture cards and numbers separately.
Plot a graph and discuss the results.

Hick's Law

Hick's Law suggests that reaction time will increase in a linear fashion as the amount of information to be processed increases. Based on your results from the Task 8.05, you should observe that your choice reaction time gets slower as the number of options increases, and your graph will probably look similar to Figure 8.04.

This knowledge, when applied to sporting situations, has great implications for the quality of performance. If a performer can develop a range of skills and employ them effectively when faced with a number of different situations, his or her opponent will not know what is going to happen and, as a result, will have to delay the decision-making process until the last moment, which may be too late to be able to respond correctly. For example, a squash player who is able to play a variety of shots from differing positions will find it easier to outwit and deceive an opponent.

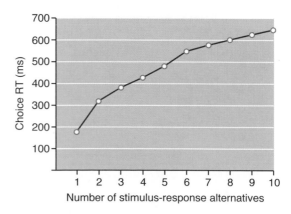

Fig. 8.04 Reaction time curve (Hick's Law)

If, on the other hand, the player is facing a skilled performer, specific cues must be identified in an attempt to limit the number of options and reduce the choice reaction time. For example, the performer may always have a particular mannerism just before executing a shot, or by observing previous performances it may be possible to identify particular shots that are more commonly used in specific areas of the court.

The increase in reaction time can be explained using the **psychological refractory period (PRP)** (Fig. 8.05). The delay is caused by an increase in the information processing time when the initial stimulus is closely followed by a second stimulus. The reaction time is slowed because the first piece of information must be cleared before the second can be processed, as explained by the **single channel hypothesis** (see Fig. 8.06 below).

The practical implications of this to a performer are considerable. If the performer can fake or dummy a movement successfully, often the opponent will be unable to clear the first stimulus in time, causing a delay in the overall response time, thus creating a clear advantage, allowing the move to be completed with slightly less pressure. For example, a badminton player may look as if he is about

APPLY IT!

Practise drawing the relevant diagrams relating to Hick's Law, single channel hypothesis and PRP.

to execute a smash shot, but at the last moment actually plays a drop shot. His opponent will find it difficult to react to the rapid change of shot and direction of the shuttle.

TASK 8.06

Complete the diagram of the PRP with a practical example you have experienced.

The single channel hypothesis (Fig. 8.06) suggests that the brain can only deal with one piece of information at a time. When it receives several pieces in rapid succession, a 'bottleneck' is formed, causing a slowing of the decision making process.

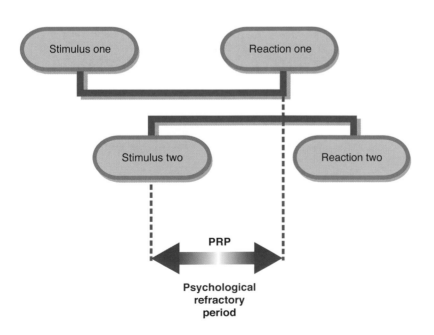

Fig. 8.05 The psychological refractory period

Input   Input

Central processing

Output/ response

Fig. 8.06 The single channel hypothesis

Improving response time

If a performer can improve his or her response time, his or her performance can improve significantly as he or she will have more time to assess the situation and complete the task. One of the most effective methods can be the use of **anticipation**.

Anticipation depends on past experience and involves the recognition of specific cues. The performer attempts to predict the actions of the opponent. This may prove to be effective if the correct choice is selected, but disastrous if incorrect, as there would be insufficient time to recover (as explained by the psychological refractory period). It can mean the performer appears to be highly skilled, executing the skill with plenty of time to spare. The two forms of anticipation are:

- **spatial anticipation** – involves the performer predicting what will happen. For example, the badminton player detects the slight difference in the shot action and is expecting the drop shot
- **temporal anticipation** – involves the performer predicting when the action will happen. For example, a football defender tries to guess when the attacker will actually pass the ball.

Other methods used to improve response time include:

- relevant practice responding to specific cues or stimulus
- mental rehearsal
- concentration on early warning signals
- improvement of selective attention
- control of arousal levels
- improvement of physical fitness
- altering the intensity of the stimulus
- identification of specific actions/cues used by opponents (studying their game).

APPLY IT!

Make sure you are able to outline the positive and negative effects of anticipation on performance.

Motor programmes and subroutines

The third phase of the information processing model involves the actual movement phase of the skill action. It is the 'output' phase. You will need to understand how movement patterns are constructed and how this information can be utilised when designing the most appropriate form of training session, allowing the learner to achieve more effectively.

Several theories attempt to explain how movement actually occurs and is modified. You must be able to outline and evaluate each one, as well as discuss the practical implications this may have on learning and performance.

Some performers appear to have the ability to participate successfully in an activity in which they have little experience. How is this achieved? The performer may have little time to actually learn all the new skills involved, but seems to be able to adapt existing skills to a new situation and refine them as the game progresses. This section will attempt to explain why this may occur and outline the implications for a successful training regime.

APPLY IT!

You will be expected to explain the characteristics of each of the areas outlined in the learning objectives, give practical applications of their use and discuss the various advantages and disadvantages. As discussed in previous chapters, often the best way to gain a fuller understanding of each topic may be to refer back to personal experience and then apply some of the acquired knowledge to your current performances.

When we develop a new skill, during the cognitive and associative phases of learning, the new information is transferred into the long-term memory (see page 177). When a specific action is required, the memory process retrieves the stored programme and transmits the motor commands via nerve impulses to the relevant muscles, allowing movement to occur. This is known as the '**executive motor programme**' (EMP). This programme is

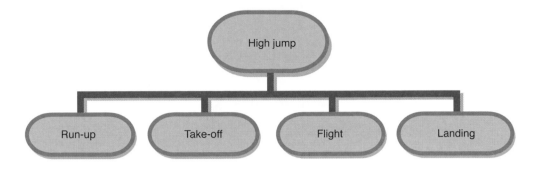

Fig. 8.07 Subroutines of a high jump

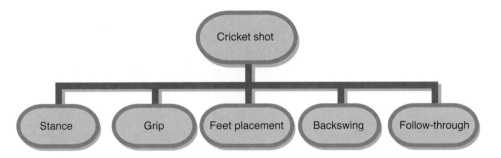

Fig. 8.08 Subroutines of a cricket shot

recalled when needed, modified after execution and stored for future reference. If the skill is well learned or autonomous, the recall process (reaction time) is very short, but during the early stages of learning this may take some time or the movement patterns may not be completed correctly.

Each executive motor programme has an organised series of subroutines, which must be completed in the correct sequence and adapted to the changing environment. For example, Figures 8.07 and 8.08 illustrate the subroutines of a high jump and a cricket shot.

Motor programmes are based on a hierarchical structure involving movements that are autonomous at the lower levels, with more complex subroutines at the peak. As the performer becomes more skilled, the existing executive motor programme is relegated and superseded by a new programme. It becomes autonomous and over-learned. For example, the cricketer, after mastering the subroutines as shown in Figure 8.08 of how to make contact with the ball correctly, will then develop more specific shots depending on the line of the ball, where it pitches and how it moves after bouncing.

Identification of subroutines may help the coach pinpoint specific weaknesses and incorporate a particular type of practice into the training session, for example, whole-part-whole or progressive part practice (see page 202). Some skills may not be broken down so easily, such as running or dribbling skills, and another form of practice may be more appropriate.

TASK 8.07

Identify the core skills required in your chosen coursework activity.
For each core skill, identify the subroutines and highlight two key points of technique for each.

Open and closed loop control theory

Once the executive motor programme has been selected, the movement has to be regulated and adapted. It has been suggested that performers achieve this on three different levels, depending on the extent to which the central nervous system is involved.

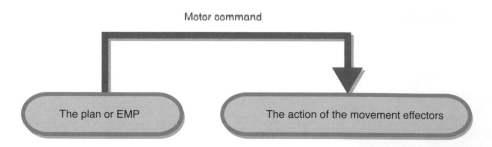

Fig. 8.09 Level 1 or open loop control

Level 1 or open loop control

This level involves the completion of the movement automatically, with no conscious control (Fig. 8.09). These movements are well learned, stored in the long-term memory and retrieved very quickly when required. They are autonomous and can be completed without the need for feedback and adjustment during the execution of the task. It is also known as the '**memory trace**', allowing selection and initiation of the movement, but it has no influence over the control after the action has started.

This process usually occurs during the execution of a closed skill, such as skipping, basketball free throw (Fig. 8.10) or a golf swing, but may also occur during open skills such as catching or kicking a ball.

Fig. 8.10 A basketball free throw is an example of open loop control

Level 2 or closed loop control

This level involves some feedback, which is received via kinaesthetic awareness and the **muscle spindles**. Errors are detected and adjustments are made at a subconscious level, with little direct attention from the performer, for example maintaining a static balance, such as a handstand, or dynamic balance, such as sidestepping an opponent in a rugby match (Fig 8.11).

Fig. 8.11 Sidestepping an opponent in rugby is an example of closed loop control

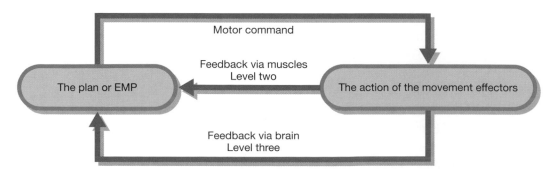

Fig. 8.12 Level 2 or closed loop control

Level 3

This is also closed loop control but this involves a conscious decision by the performer based on feedback received (see Fig. 8.12). The performer pays attention to specific details and has to concentrate and make a deliberate attempt to alter the movement pattern. Often performers in the associative phase of learning will rely on level 3 control to develop his or her skill level. For example, a novice basketball player may have to think about changing hands and the force used when dribbling the ball.

Levels 2 and 3 are also known as the '**perceptual trace**', allowing comparison and modification of movements when compared to a stored model. This is developed through practice and feedback, either received during or after completion, allowing errors to be detected, corrected and updated for future reference. For example, a gymnast completing a routine will constantly evaluate the movements being performed during the sequence and make adjustments as required to maintain balance, speed and control based on his or her knowledge of how each component should feel.

Most performers will experience both open and closed loop control during their performance, depending on their skill level and the task difficulty.

However, there are some criticisms of the theory.

- It assumes that there is a separate memory trace for each movement pattern, which has to be accommodated and recalled from the long-term memory.
- It also suggests practice should be accurate and variance would hinder learning, which recent research has refuted.

- Performers sometimes produce movements that are spontaneous and unusual, for which a memory trace could not be stored.

Feedback

The final stage of information processing is feedback, which is vital to the learning process. It links the output and input phases, effectively 'closing the loop'. We learn from experience either to modify our movements at the time, or store the information in our long-term memory for future reference. Feedback has several purposes including:

- detection and correction of errors causing a change in performance
- motivation – incentive to continue and increase effort
- reinforcement of learning – Thorndike's law of effect (see page 185).

There are different types of feedback which must be subdivided as outlined on pages 210–211.

Improving the information processing system

The information processing system of every performer can be improved to some degree. Throughout this chapter there are specific sections suggesting how this can achieved. Often it is a combination of several methods, which create an overall improvement, and one area links to the next. The skill of the coach/leader is to identify the potential weakness and implement the correct method to facilitate an increase in stimulus dectection, decision making or output.

APPLY IT!

1. Select a skill from your chosen activity and analyse its effectivness in a game situation. Highlight times when the skill is not as effective as it could be, and causes a decline in your performance.
2. Identify potential reasons for the breakdown of the skill, possibly one from each stage of the information processing model.
3. Suggest strategies you could employ to minimise the chance of poor performances in the future.
4. Discuss your ideas with a partner.

ATHLETE PROFILE

The game of real tennis is played on an indoor court with many angled walls to play the ball off and several areas into which the ball can be hit to win the point, making it different from the games of lawn tennis and squash. However, some of the skills required are similar, such as outwitting and deceiving an opponent.

During many hours of practice and competitive games, Claire Vigrass has improved her **information processing system** allowing her to execute her skills to a high level and detect the movements of her opponents. Before a match, in discussion with her coach, she assesses the strengths and weaknesses of her opponent, attempting to highlight specific cues which may indicate particular shots that may follow. This allows her to use her **selective attention** mechanism, not only to ignore the crowd but to watch certain movements that allow her to **anticipate** what may happen, either from a serve or open play. Claire has also developed a wide range of shots which can be played either as a forehand or backhand stroke from all areas of the court. These have been stored in her **long-term memory** and can be recalled quickly (**reaction time**) when required, and cause her opponent to be unsure of what shot she may play (**Hick's Law**). During rallies she is particularly skilled at playing drop shots, often causing players to be caught out of position and allowing her to win the point (**psychological refractory period**).

Refresh your memory

Revision checklist

Make sure you know the following:

▷ The human motor system can be viewed as a processor of information, with sensory information passing through various stages

▷ Information processing involves gathering data, processing the relevant stimuli to form a decision, which is then executed by the muscular system

▷ The process consists of three basic stages:

- Stimulus identification (input)
- Response selection (decision making)
- Response programming (output).

▷ Information gathered is detected via exteroceptors, proprioceptors and interoceptors

▷ The effectiveness with which a performer processes various forms of sensory information often affects overall performance

▷ The memory process consists of the short-term sensory store, short term/working memory and the long-term memory

▷ The better the memory process, the faster the performer's Reaction Time

▷ Reaction Time is affected by many different factors

▷ There are two types of Reaction Time: Simple RT and Choice RT

▷ Response Time = Reaction Time + Movement Time

▷ Hick's Law suggests that there is a linear relationship between the number of stimuli and Reaction Time. The more choices which need to be processed, the slower the Reaction Time

▷ One stimulus, closely followed by a second stimulus, causes the Psychological Refractory Period

▷ The PRP can be explained using the single channel hypothesis, as the brain can only process one piece of information at a time

▷ Anticipation can reduce Reaction Time and can be either Spatial Anticipation or Temporal Anticipation. However it can also cause performance to deteriorate if you make the wrong decision, as adjustments cannot be made in time

▷ Motor Programmes are pre-planned sets of muscular movements, stored in the memory, which can be used without feedback

▷ Motor Programmes are organised in a hierarchical structure, with subroutines making up executive programmes

▷ Subroutines are short fixed sequences which when fully learned, can be completed automatically without conscious control

▷ 'Open loop' explains how we perform fast movements without having to think about them (subconsciously)

▷ Pre-learned mastery of Motor Programmes is essential for open loop control. Feedback is not integral in motor control

▷ The Memory Trace starts the movement and the Perceptual Trace detects and corrects any errors by comparing what is happening to the memory stores

▷ Feedback and kinaesthesis are imperative in closed loop control

Revise as you go

1. Explain the term 'display'.

2. What is the role of the sensory system during information processing?

3. Name in order the four basic stages of information processing.

4. Explain the term 'perception'.

5. What is the function of the 'translatory mechanism'?

6. Outline the 'stimulus identification stage'.

7. Explain the role of 'memory' during information processing.

8. Outline the 'response programming stage'.

9. Name in order the four main stages of the 'memory' process used during information processing.

10. State another term often used for the short-term memory.

11. Outline the capacity, duration and function of the long-term memory.

12. What is simple reaction time?

13. What is the psychological refractory period?

14. Explain the term 'subroutine'.

15. What does the term 'open loop control' mean when discussing motor control?

16. Outline the main difference between 'open loop' and 'closed loop' control of motor programmes.

17. What is the role of 'feedback' during 'open loop' controlled motor programmes.

18. Explain the function of the 'memory trace' during closed loop control.

19. Explain the function of the 'perceptual trace' during closed loop control.

20. What is the function of 'feedback' during information processing?

CHAPTER 9

Learning and performance

LEARNING OBJECTIVES:

By the end of this chapter you should be able to:

▶ identify the difference between learning and performance

▶ outline the stages and characteristics of each phase of learning

▶ explain and interpret learning/performance curves

▶ identify possible causes and remedies for a learning plateau

▶ outline different forms of motivation and the impact they have on learning

▶ understand the theories of learning including cognitive/insight learning, Bandura's observational model and operant conditioning

▶ explain Schmidt's Schema theory

▶ suggest how transfer of learning impacts upon skill development

▶ outline the principles of goal setting and the different types of goal which can be used.

Introduction

As performers, we need to be able to understand how we actually learn skills, which will in turn allow us to develop and refine them further. We also need to be able to analyse our own performance and recognise the progress being made, if any! By developing knowledge of how we learn skills, we can adapt and modify practice situations to elicit the most favourable response, which in turn can become a skill and performed effectively within a competitive environment.

During this chapter you will develop an understanding of the difference between 'learning' and 'performance'. How many times have you completed a skill once but never actually been able to repeat it? Why not? We will try to find an explanation. Also, you will discover why, on occasions, there may be no improvement for some time in your skill level: more importantly, you will be able to outline strategies to rectify this problem. By developing an understanding the theories of learning, you will appreciate the advantages and disadvantages of each method in various practical

situations, allowing for the optimum use of practice time. Other key areas to be studied include the appropriate use of motivation to enhance learning, the use of the concepts of 'transfer of learning' and 'goal setting'.

As with the previous chapter, the key to successfully understanding the theoretical aspects is refining the ability to apply them to actual sporting situations. The easiest way to do this is to refer to your own experiences, both positive and negative, and attempt to explain the consequences. Did your skill levels improve or not? If 'no', what could you do in an attempt to develop your performance?

Learning and performance

The terms 'learning' and 'performance' have very different meanings. For example, how often have you revised for a test or exam, passed with flying colours, but when questioned on the same topic several months later cannot remember all the facts? A similar scenario can be applied to sporting performance: how often have you trained hard for a particular event, performed successfully then rested for a period of time and on returning to compete not been as competent? Have you on one memorable day performed like never before and since then been unable to repeat a similar feat?

There is clearly a difference between 'learning' and 'performance'. Below are several definitions to highlight those differences.

Learning

'Motor learning is a set of processes associated with practice or experience, leading to relatively permanent changes in the capability for skilled performance.'

Schmidt

'A person has learned something if their performance shows improvement from one occasion to the next. Such an improvement must be stable and relatively permanent, and not just a transient increase caused, for example, by a change in fitness level or improvement in health.'

Sharp

'The more or less permanent change in behaviour that is reflected in a change in performance.'

Knapp

The key characteristics of 'learning' are:

*   linked to practice or experience
*   relatively permanent
*   not a fluke or one-off occurrence.

Performance

'Performance may change because of fatigue or emotion, or alcohol, or the surrounding conditions, but in so far as any change is temporary, it is not learning.'

Knapp

'Performance may be thought of as a temporary occurrence ... fluctuating from time to time because of many potentially operating variables.'

Singer

The key characteristics of 'performance' are:

*   temporary
*   not necessarily repeated.

Stages of learning

In order to develop new skills, we must progress through a series of stages so that when one aspect is refined, another can be added, allowing the skill to become more complex. Fitts and Posner (1967) suggested that when you learn a new skill, there are three stages of learning that must be completed:

*   cognitive stage
*   associative stage
*   autonomous stage.

Some performers may progress through each stage quickly or the skill may be simple, allowing it to be mastered easily, for example the basic action of catching and throwing a ball. However, some may be more difficult and may never be reached due to a variety of factors, for example the skill of juggling.

Cognitive stage

The initial stage of learning involves the performer observing a demonstration and/or being given verbal instructions (Fig 9.01). The aim is to create a mental picture, which allows for the development of an understanding of the movement requirements. During this time, the performer is attempting to find the answer to all the basic questions concerning the particular skill and its execution. There may be some initial trial and error attempts to complete the movement pattern, often with limited success.

The majority of the feedback is from an external source as the performer has yet to establish a clear understanding of the motor programme and has limited kinaesthetic awareness allowing them to correct any mistakes. However, this stage is usually short in duration.

The role of the coach or teacher is vital during this stage, allowing a clear mental picture to be created. This must be done by maximising the use of accurate demonstrations, highlighting specific cues, providing time for mental rehearsal, ensuring the learner is paying full attention, avoiding an overload of new information, use of appropriate language and giving reinforcement as required.

Therefore the ideal methods of guidance (see pages 206–209) to use during this stage would be visual and verbal guidance.

Associative stage

The second stage of learning is often referred to as the 'practice' stage. It involves the performer developing and refining the movement patterns of the skill via a combination of practice and feedback (Fig. 9.03). Initially, gross errors are common, which are gradually eliminated until the recognised and consistent skill emerges.

This stage is often longer than the cognitive stage and may vary in length depending on the ability of the performer, the complexity of the skill, the amount and type of practice completed, and the quality of the feedback.

APPLY IT!

A novice performer is attempting to learn the Fosbury flop high jump technique. The coach will explain the technique and either demonstrate themselves or show a video highlighting the specific phases and several key points. The performer will try to create a mental image of what they have to do when it is their turn.

Fig. 9.01 The cognitive stage of learning: instruction

Initially, the majority of the feedback is still from an external source, which concentrates on gross errors. However, as the performer becomes more accomplished and develops a greater kinaesthetic awareness, they are able to identify errors themselves (internal feedback) and implement external feedback, which focuses on more detailed adjustments.

During this phase different forms of guidance can be used to maximise learning. If the performer is unable to execute the skill correctly or may have a concern about their own safety a coach/ teacher can utilise manual or mechanical guidance. This will allow the performer to be supported or forced into the correct position, allowing kinaesthetic awareness to develop. Additionally as the performer develops the use of visual guidance may decline while the use of verbal guidance will still prove useful. However the nature of the verbal guidance will alter as the performer becomes more skilled. Any feedback will become more detailed, aimed at eliminating minor errors rather than basic mistakes.

Fig. 9.02 The cognitive stage of learning: demonstration

Fig. 9.03 The associative stage of learning: practice allows gross errors to be corrected

The performer attempts the Fosbury flop and shows obvious weaknesses in technique. The coach will highlight key points to practise and gradually the weaknesses will be eliminated. As the technique improves, the feedback will become more specific, for example the drive of the take-off knee or the position over the bar. Gradually, the performer will recognise their own mistakes and rectify them as required.

Autonomous stage

The final stage of learning involves the performer becoming highly proficient at executing the skill to the point where it is completed almost without conscious thought (Fig 9.04). Reaching this stage gives many advantages:

- the performer is able to focus on other factors happening during the event, such as other players, tactics or stress management techniques, rather than the execution of the skill
- the reaction time and decision making process are improved

- the particular skill can be used as a basis to develop a more advanced skill – it is in effect relegated to a subroutine (see page 168).

The performer is now able to detect and correct the majority of his or her own errors (internal feedback) and any input from the coach can focus on minor alterations to technique to improve performance.

Once this stage has been reached, it is important for the performer to maintain his level of practice in order to reinforce the movement patterns and ensure the skill can be repeated consistently.

Any form of guidance can be used but the main form would be verbal, as the performer has a good understanding of the movement requirements and can detect any errors. However the increasing use of visual guidance via video analysis can also be useful in highlighting minor faults which need correcting.

The high jumper can now make minor adjustments to his technique during competition, such as altering the run-up, take-off position and timing over the bar. During training, the coach and the performer work together to discuss minor adjustments that may be required to facilitate an improvement.

Fig. 9.04 The autonomous stage of learning

Measuring changes in learning – performance curves

How do we know if we are learning and making progress? Just because time is spent practising a skill, it does not mean there will automatically be an improvement. There may be times when no improvement takes place, which may be demotivating for the performer. It is therefore important to understand how, when and why performance is changing. Each individual progresses at a different rate and the use of a graph is an easy way to interpret such changes. If the results are analysed correctly, training sessions can be modified to achieve a positive outcome and the motivation levels of the performer can be enhanced if they are able to understand the factors influencing their development.

Figures 9.05 to 9.09 show several curves that indicate how an athlete's performance varied during the course of trials or during the time of a test/event. It is important you are able to explain how the performance altered during these times and suggest reasons why it may have happened.

Linear curve

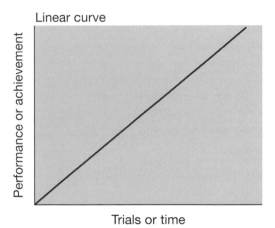

Fig. 9.05 The performance improves in direct proportion to the number of trials or time

Positive acceleration curve

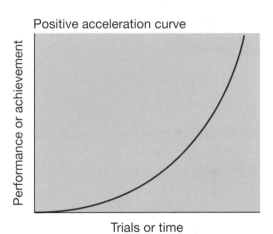

Fig. 9.06 The performance improves slowly during the initial trials but speeds up later

Negative acceleration curve

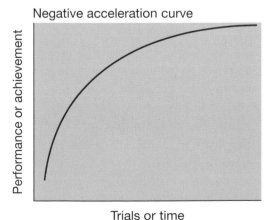

Fig. 9.07 The performance improves quickly during the initial trials but slows down later

S-shaped curve

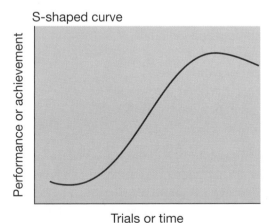

Fig. 9.08 The performance is indicated by a combination of the curves outlined above

Plateau in performance

It is important that both the performer and the coach understand the concept of a plateau during the development of performance for a variety of reasons:

- to maintain the motivation levels
- to modify the training regime to minimise the time spent with no improvement
- to allow the next stage of development to occur if the autonomous stage of learning has been reached.

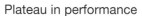

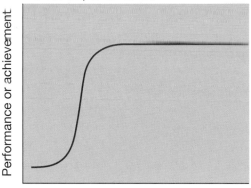

Fig. 9.09 The performance improves but reaches a point at which no further improvement occurs. This may be the final plateau or the first in a series of plateaus

Many factors may cause a plateau including:

- boredom/lack of motivation
- fatigue
- lack of fitness
- inappropriate practice methods
- poor coaching and guidance
- personal ability
- injury/overtraining
- subroutine mastered/transitional period before development of a more complex skill
- task is too complex.

If a plateau does occur (the majority of performers will experience this many times during their careers), appropriate strategies to minimise the time must be implemented. Some strategies are outlined below:

- vary type and content of practice sessions
- set realistic short- and long-term goals

- offer extrinsic rewards
- give new responsibility/role
- give recovery periods
- encourage mental rehearsal
- improve physical conditioning/fitness
- improve coaching knowledge
- provide appropriate feedback
- use whole-part-whole practice (see page 202)
- explain the concept of plateau to performer.

TASK 9.03

1. You are the coach of a novice hockey team which is failing to make progress. Using practical examples to illustrate your answer, outline three possible causes for this lack of development and suggest three strategies to overcome this plateau.
2. Suggest three alternative factors that may be more relevant to an elite-level performer who may be experiencing a plateau in their performance.
3. Attempt a new skill, for example throwing at a target with your non-dominant hand or something similar in nature. With a partner attempt the skill five times and have a rest while your partner has their five attempts. Repeat the process a number of times and record your sucess rate each time. Draw a graph to illustrate your results and compare your graph to others in your group. Discuss your findings.

EXAM TIP:

When asked to interpret a graph, give an explanation of what is happening to the performance and suggest reasons why.

Motivation

Motivation is a key factor when developing the knowledge and understanding of a learner. If a performer wishes to improve their skills, tactics, awareness or any other aspect of their performance, he or she is more likely to remain focused and possess a desire to succeed if they are motivated. Think about the times you have really pushed yourself to master a skill or understand the strategies involved in a game and compare those feelings to a situation where you were not overly concerned about the outcome. What caused those differences?

Motivation can influence your:

- selection and preference for an activity
- persistence
- effort levels
- performance levels relative to your ability level.

There are two broad categories of motivation: intrinsic and extrinsic.

Intrinsic motivation involves gaining self-satisfaction, pride and a feeling of achievement. It often involves overcoming a particular challenge or simply gaining enjoyment from participating. For example, a skydiver will often gain more pleasure from the feelings they experience during the free-fall than from the praise afterwards from well-wishers. The scoring of a goal, winning a competition or achieving a personal best may all create similar feelings and are often sufficient to ensure the performer perseveres with the activity.

Extrinsic motivation, by comparison, involves the performer receiving some form of reward from others, often as a form of reinforcement. These rewards can be subdivided into two categories: tangible and intangible rewards, as illustrated in Table 9.01.

Tangible rewards	Intangible rewards
Cups	Praise
Medals	Fame/publicity/social status
Trophies	Records
Money	Applause
Certificates	

Table 9.01 Tangible and intangible rewards

While the use of motivation is highly desirable, the use of extrinsic motivation must be monitored carefully or it may have an adverse effect. If overused, it may lead to the performer only participating if they will be externally rewarded in some way and the intrinsic motivation will be undermined. If this happens, it may affect their long-term participation in the activity.

The use of national governing body (NGB) award schemes to encourage beginners to participate and strive for improvement is common in many

sports. However, they should not be seen as the only factor to encourage participation. Self-esteem, self-fulfilment, success and personal satisfaction are often more powerful to reinforce and direct behaviour in the long term.

To maximise the effectiveness of motivation, the coach should use the appropriate type of reward:

- depending on the nature of the individual, e.g. one performer may enjoy public praise, while another may simply prefer a private feedback session
- as a result of specific behaviour, e.g. when the correct technique has been achieved
- as soon as possible after the performance, e.g. give verbal encouragement, highlight that the correct technique has been used, issue the achieved time, and so on. If this happens, the action is more likely to be repeated
- to motivate the performer. Reward the performer occasionally and then gradually reduce it. The performer should not become over-reliant on extrinsic motivation and not expect it on every occasion.

Ideally, the performer should be motivated by a combination of intrinsic and extrinsic motivational factors, with the former being viewed as the most important.

TASK 9.04

For each of the examples below, indicate if they are intrinsic or extrinsic. If they are extrinsic, decide if they are tangible or intangible.
- personal swimming survival badge
- gold medal
- monetary bonus for winning a match
- congratulations from another player
- the coach saying 'well done'
- being asked for a TV interview after the game
- election to be team captain.

Theories of learning

Now that you know what the term 'learning' means, you need to understand how we actually learn skills. If you can identify the best method to develop a skill, the learning time can be reduced and the result effectively transferred to a competitive situation. There are three theories that need to be understood:

- operant conditioning theory
- cognitive theory/insight learning
- observational learning.

Conditioning theories of learning

These are also known as 'connectionist' or 'associationist' theories and are based on the 'behaviourist' approach. The basic notion of the theories involves the performer developing a specific link with a certain cue, which is known as the 'stimulus-response bond' or 'S-R bond'. The response is stored in the long-term memory (see page 164) and when the specific

TASK 9.05

List five examples of an S-R bond you experience during your major sport.

stimulus is detected, the appropriate movement is triggered. For example, a cricket batsman will attempt to play a certain type of shot each time the bowler pitches the ball in a particular area, or a netball centre will pass the ball to a specific teammate depending on the agreed call being made.

Operant conditioning

This theory was developed by Skinner, who modified the behaviour of rats in a maze. He altered their environment and depending on their response they received some form of reward or punishment, causing their behaviour to either be repeated or not. He tried to shape their behaviour. If the consequences of their actions were pleasurable, the behaviour was more likely to be repeated. However, if the consequences were unpleasant, they were less likely to be repeated. In other words, the S-R bond will either be strengthened or weakened depending on what happens after the action has taken place. Often the learner will experience 'trial and error' and through a gradual process of elimination will develop the appropriate response with the correct use of reinforcement.

In order for this to occur, the learner may experience either reinforcement or punishment. The former strengthens the S-R bond, while the latter weakens the bond.

Reinforcement may take two forms:

- **positive reinforcement** – this involves the use of a stimulus to create feelings of satisfaction to encourage the repetition of the action, for example praise from a coach, personal satisfaction from completion of the movement, visual feedback such as seeing the target being hit or the ball landing in court, applause from the crowd or any other form of reward
- **negative reinforcement** – this involves the withdrawal of an unpleasant stimulus when the desired response occurs, for example the coach will stop shouting at the team if their actions are correct.

EXAM TIP:

Do not confuse negative reinforcement with negative feedback or punishment. For, example the former would be a coach calling out a key point of technique during practice and, when performed correctly, they stop reminding the performer. The latter would involve the coach criticising the performer.

Punishment may also be used effectively to reduce the likelihood of the actions being repeated. Common forms may include being dropped from the team, penalised for foul play, booked by the referee or fined. However, the continual use of punishment may cause some resentment and have an adverse effect and punishment should be used carefully.

Numerous sports skills are developed using operant conditioning, via the use of drills and conditioned practices. While their use does facilitate the learning and refining of skills, a disadvantage may be a lack of understanding as to why the skill is being executed in a particular manner. As a result, when the performer enters a competitive situation, they may not be able to adapt their 'conditioned' skill to a new environment easily and their performance level may drop. An example of operant conditioning when applied to tennis is outlined on the next page.

1. The coach 'feeds' balls to the player from a specific position in a consistent manner (modifying the environment).
2. The player stands in a certain position and attempts to play the shot repeatedly to a marked area on the opposite side of the court (shaping behaviour).

APPLY IT!

Design a series of three progressive practices using operant conditioning for a sport of your choice.

3. Reinforcement from the coach is provided about the technique in the form of verbal feedback.
4. Reinforcement is obtained by the player via observation of the ball hitting the marked target area.
5. If successful, the player will attempt to re-create the shot and remember the feeling of the movement (kinaesthetic awareness).
6. If unsuccessful, the player will attempt to modify the shot until the correct response is achieved (trial and error).

Fig. 9.10 Operant conditioning used to developed a tennis shot

Thorndike's laws of learning

In order to make the strengthening of the S-R bond more effective, Thorndike suggested that three 'laws' should be implemented:

1. **law of exercise** – the performer must practise the task regularly in favourable conditions, for example when reinforcement is used
2. **law of effect** – the performer is more likely to repeat the task if their behaviour is followed by experiences of satisfaction, for example positive reinforcement
3. **law of readiness** – the performer is physically and mentally able to complete the task, for example has the appropriate motivation and physiological development.

APPLY IT!

Apply Thorndike's laws to a practical situation you have experienced and evaluate their effectiveness.

Drive reduction theory

Hull suggested that learning will occur due to the performer's desire to complete the task and only by achieving their 'drive' will they be satisfied (Fig 9.11). Too much repetition of a skill during the learning phase may actually demotivate the performer and cause 'inhibition'. As a result, Hull proposed that an effective way to strengthen the S-R bond is to ensure the 'drive' or motivation of the performer is always maintained. This will involve the teacher or coach setting new, challenging goals allowing continued development to occur.

APPLY IT!

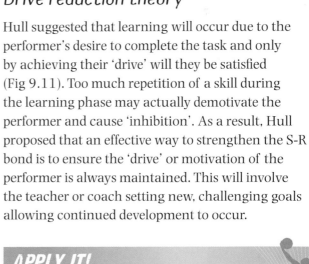

A coach will initially set a novice tennis player the target of learning to play a basic forehand shot. When this has been mastered, a new goal has to be set to maintain the performer's interest and strengthen the S-R bond, such as the top spin forehand shot. The process continues once this skill has been developed.

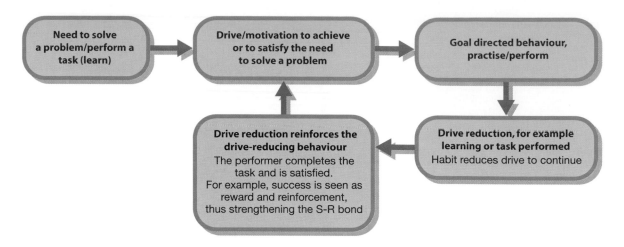

Fig. 9.11 Drive reduction theory

Cognitive theories of learning/insight learning

One of the weaknesses of the conditioning theories is that performers may not fully understand the relationship between the stimulus and response, as they have been more concerned with the consequences of the action. Therefore their performance may be hindered, as they may be unable to modify their actions accordingly. This occurs because the new situation differs from their established pattern of movement and set environmental conditions.

The cognitive, or Gestalt theory allows for this deficiency by proposing that performers learn by thinking about the whole problem. They understand what is required and formulate a response based on previous experiences and the current situation rather than a series of specific responses to various stimuli. They use their perceptual skills to formulate a motor programme suited to the current situation and their own abilities. This form of learning is also known as 'insight' learning, as there is a clear discovery of the relationship between the stimulus and the response. The 'trial and error' learning is not involved in this process.

The coach would ask the performer to complete the whole movement in order to develop an appreciation of how the timing and subroutines of the movement are interrelated rather than break the skill down into its component parts (as in the

conditioning theory). This then allows the performer to adapt their movements more easily to a new situation, for example whether or not to execute a dummy pass/shot during a game depending on the situation at a given moment.

APPLY IT!

A novice high jumper would be asked to complete the entire sequence rather than be taught in stages, giving them the opportunity to 'work out' the most effective movement for them.

A basketball player possesses the required skills to play the game but is not as effective as he could be in the game situation. The coach explains the concepts of offence and defence clearly to the player who then understands his role within the game and how to deploy his skills for the benefit of the team rather than just for himself. If the player is presented with a variety of situations in training, this knowledge can be used later in the game to overcome any new problems that they may encounter.

KEY TERM

Significant other:
a person that is held in high esteem by the individual, e.g. a member of their family, peer group, teacher, coach and role model

Observational learning

Many people learn most effectively by watching others and copying their actions. This is known as a 'vicarious experience'. It is often more productive than merely giving instructions, as a mental picture is formed allowing the individual to create movement patterns more easily. The use of demonstrations can also be made more effective if reinforcement is used and the model (person demonstrating) is either a **significant other** or a competent performer from their own peer group. Bandura suggested there should be four key elements in place to allow this process to occur.

1. **Attention** – the amount of notice taken by the learner while observing the model. The coach can aid this process by identifying a small number of specific cues on which to concentrate, ensuring the demonstration is correct and accurate, not too long, the model is attractive to the observer and the skill being observed can be clearly seen.
2. **Retention** – the creation of a mental picture for future reference. The coach should not overload the learner with verbal information but allow him to observe the demonstration several times to create a clear image. Learners may also be encouraged to picture the movement, a technique known as 'mental rehearsal'. Sometimes a second image may be used to help this image stick in the mind. For example, when learning the techniques of a basketball free throw, to help learners remember to flick the wrist when releasing the ball, they may be told to 'take a cookie out of the jar'.
3. **Motor reproduction** – the learner must have the physical ability and confidence to copy, attempt and complete the skill either immediately or after a series of progressive practice sessions.
4. **Motivation** – the learner must have the drive and desire to copy the actions of the model. This is often based on the successful completion of the observed skill, its importance, the reinforcement received from others and the perceived status of the model.

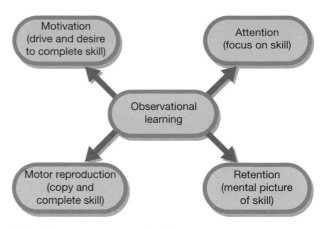

Fig. 9.12 Stages in observational learning

APPLY IT!

The coach of a trampolinist wishes to introduce a new, more advanced move into the routine. Rather than attempt the complex move, another member of the training group is asked to demonstrate the move several times. The coach will highlight several key points of technique to remember and possibly relate the feeling/kinaesthetic awareness to a previously learned skill to make it easier to understand. The coach will also ensure there are no other distractions, allowing the learner to focus entirely on the demonstration, and provide verbal encouragement to boost the performer's motivation level.

TASK 9.06

1. Select a skill, for example dribbling, and devise suitable practices, each based on one of the theories of learning, to introduce it to a group of novice performers.
2. Complete each practice with other students and evaluate its effectiveness.

Each theory has its advantages and disadvantages, and the teacher/coach may find it most effective to evaluate each situation before deciding on the most appropriate to use. Often, within a lesson or training session, a combination may be most suitable depending on the ability and motivation of the participants, the situational factors and the nature of the task.

Schema theory

When a coach/teacher/leader is considering how to develop a skill an understanding of the Schema theory can help to minimise the time taken and reinforce learning. You have previously studied motor-programme theory but one of the major criticisms of this theory is the suggestion that all movements are pre-planned and stored in the long-term memory. The Schema theory, proposed by Schmidt, argues that rather than using memory and perceptual traces to initiate movement, we store in our memory a generalised series of movement patterns that we modify to adapt to the current environment.

When we learn new skills or are playing a game, we recall and alter stored motor programmes to complete the task successfully. For example, when learning a new skill, the performer will draw upon existing skills and modify them where possible to execute the new task. For instance, a student learning the volleyball overarm serve may have previously played tennis and will be able to relate the serving action to the new situation.

We modify many different basic schemas such as running, jumping, throwing and catching, allowing us to develop more specific sport-related skills.

The schemas are initiated, evaluated and updated by two processes:

- **recall schema –** which actually start the movement
- **recognition schema –** which control and evaluate the movement.

Fig. 9.13 A volleyball overarm serve and a tennis serve are similar skills which are modified from the same overarm pattern

Recall schema has two sources of information:

1. **Knowledge of initial conditions** – refers to information about the location of the performer, their environment and limb position. This information is compared to previous experiences. Performers ask themselves, 'Where am I?'

2. **Knowledge of response specifications** – refers to information about the task to be completed, the speed, force, options available and the formulation of a suitable movement. Performers ask themselves, 'What have I got to do?'

Recognition schema also has two sources of information:

1. **Sensory consequences** – refers to the feelings experienced during and after the movement, the kinaesthetic feeling, the sound and any other information gathered via the sensory system, allowing suitable adjustments to be made. Performers ask themselves, 'What does the movement feel like?'
2. **Response outcome** – refers to the end result and a comparison being made with the intended outcome. This information is vital for updating the memory store for future reference when confronted with a similar situation in the future. Performers ask themselves, 'What happened as a result of the movement?'

These sources of information are called **parameters** and are taken into account the next time the skill has to be completed. The parameter is stored within the schema and is used to initiate a response with the correct speed, force and direction required. A performer who develops a wide range of parameters will have a better chance of successfully executing the skill, as they will be more familiar with the specific requirements when faced with the situation during a game. For example, a basketball player who shoots from different places on court will develop a slightly different action for each. However, a player who only practises from the free throw line will find it more difficult to adjust during a game when having to shoot from a variety of locations, as they will find it more difficult to select the exact response required.

Fig. 9.14 David Beckham varies his shot depending on where the free kick is taken from

Implications for training and development of schema

The coach can use this knowledge and develop a range of schema and parameters. This can be achieved in a variety of ways including:

- variation of practice
- avoiding blocked practices (repeated practice of the same skill)
- setting small parameters to facilitate fine adjustments of technique
- ensuring practice is relevant to the competitive situation
- provision of accurate knowledge of results and feedback
- challenging and progressive tasks
- developing as many schema as possible.

APPLY IT!

Transfer of learning

In order to make the learning of skills more effective, the concept of 'transfer' must be understood. Transfer is the effect that the learning or performance of one skill has on the learning or performance of another skill. If the teacher/coach can apply this knowledge correctly, they can decrease the learning time, maximise the use of the time available, develop relevant conditioned practices associated with the full competitive situation and identify areas that may hinder learning.

Transfer of learning

The notion of transfer is likened to the schema theory, allowing us to modify movement patterns to suit new situations. For example, a basketball player would be encouraged to use the skills of movement, spatial awareness and ball handling when being introduced to the game of netball. However, some skills that are well learned may be more difficult to eliminate and hinder the performance, such as dribbling with the ball and shooting with the aid of a backboard.

TASK 9.07

1. Select a skill from your chosen sport.
2. Devise a practice session to develop the schema of the selected skill.
3. Deliver the practice session to a small group and evalute the progress made by the participants.

Fig. 9.15 Example of positive transfer

The different forms of transfer include:

- **positive transfer** involves previously learned skills helping the development of new skills. Various movement patterns may be adjusted to suit the new situation, for example, throwing a javeline develops from experiences of throwing a ball as a child, see Figure 9.15. The coach is able to identify similarities and make comparisons, illustrating to the learner how the movement should basically feel. Other examples include a springboard diver using a trampoline and harness to practise complex moves, and team games often use modified practices such as 3 v 2 or 2 v 1 to develop an understanding of spatial awareness and timing

- **negative transfer** involves previously learned skills hindering the development of new skills. Usually this is temporary and can be eliminated with relevant practices and the coach highlighting the potential difficulties immediately. For example, a tennis player, when playing badminton, may not be able to generate the power needed to hit the shuttlecock effectively because he or she is used to playing with a firm wrist rather than the flexible wrist action required

- **bilateral transfer** involves the transfer of learning from one limb to another, rather than from skill to skill. Often the kinaesthetic awareness from the dominant limb when applied to the other limb can improve performance and allow the performer to develop a wider range of skills and be able to apply them in a greater range of situations. Think back to the section on reaction time and the psychological refractory period in Chapter 8 and how such an advantage could slow an opponent's response time significantly. For example, a games player who can use both feet and hands equally well has a distinct advantage over one who is only comfortable using his or her dominant limb

- **proactive transfer** occurs when the skill being learned has an effect on skills developed in the future. A coach may gradually increase the level of difficulty, develop specific subroutines or employ the progressive part method of practice to ensure the skill is fully understood and mastered. For example, a young tennis player will learn the basic forehand and backhand ground strokes before developing top spin and more advanced shots, but the fundamental movement patterns are the same

- **retroactive transfer** occurs when the skill being developed has an effect on one that has been previously learned. For example, an experienced tennis player may have to alter his or her basic technique as more advanced shots are developed. When developing the forehand stroke, he or she is taught to move into a side-on position, but as his or her skill levels progress, he or she often has a more open stance and alters the basic movement pattern.

- **zero transfer** occurs when one skill has no impact on the learning or development of another skill. For example, the a badminton smash has no influence on the performer when learning the swimming breast stroke.

TASK 9.08

Select a skill, for example a badminton serve or basketball lay-up, and attempt to execute the skill with your non-dominant hand. Discuss with a partner your experiences and explain how you modified your technique in an attempt to improve.

Implications for training

The coach must use this information to structure the training session to maximise the learning opportunity. This can be achieved by:

- identifying elements of the skill that are transferable, improving and hindering learning
- developing good basic movement patterns initially and then progressing to more complex skills

- making practice situations relevant and realistic to the competitive environment, for example swimmers need to spend more of their practice time in the water, rather than on land-based activities; team players need to practise against opposition, not simply unopposed
- eliminating the opportunity for bad habits to develop – negative transfer.

APPLY IT!

Compare the activities listed below and identify examples of positive, negative and bilateral transfer that may occur between each. There may be more than one form present.

- netball
- rugby
- basketball
- gymnastics
- high jump

Goal setting

Another effective method used to control anxiety levels is goal setting. Often this method allows the performer to direct his or her attention away from the source of stress and focus on an achievable target. If goals are set correctly they can have several effects, including:

- development of self-confidence and **self-efficacy**
- increased motivation levels
- improved selective attention
- approach behaviour
- persistence
- a reduction in anxiety.

The coach must take care when setting goals to ensure the performer's motivation is maintained while simultaneously not pushing the performer too far. The type of goal set will depend on the nature of the task, the level of ability of the performer and his or her anxiety levels. There are two types of goal which should be considered:

- outcome goal
- performance goal.

KEY TERM

Self-efficacy:
the level of self-confidence to complete a specific task

Outcome goal

An **outcome goal** judges the performance of the individual against others and the end result. The performer is being compared to others and a social comparison is being made. For example, a swimmer may be set the goal of either winning the race or finishing in the top three places to qualify for the next round. The efficiency and manner of his or her performance is not relevant – only the final result. If the goal setting is realistic and within the performer's capability, and if he or she achieves the aim, his or her motivation is increased. Performers of this nature are said to be 'outcome goal orientated.' However, it can be demotivating if the performer is unsuccessful, especially after repeated attempts, and this can lead to an increase in anxiety levels. Therefore, with novice performers or those who tend to have avoidance behaviour, **performance goals** are more appropriate.

Performance goal

This type of goal judges the performance of the athlete against his or her own standards, rather than making a social comparison with his or her competitors. For example, the swimmer may be set a number of goals for a race, including a good reaction to the starter's gun and effective breathing action, and his or her performance may be evaluated with reference to his or her personal best time rather than their finishing position. If the goals that are set are realistic the performer can evaluate his or her own actions and not worry about comparison with others. This helps to reduce anxiety, allowing the swimmer to remain motivated irrespective of their finishing position.

TASK 9.09

You are the coach of a team. During the pre-season you decide to set both outcome and performance goals. For a sport of your choice, give examples of each type of goal which may be set for the team and individual performers.

The coach may also set specific process-orientated goals which relate to the development of the tactics or technique of the performer and contribute to the overall performance goal. For example, the swimmer may set the goal of a tighter tumble turn with greater leg drive off the wall in order to improve overall performance.

Another factor which needs to be considered is the time span of the goal. It is generally accepted that both long-term goals and short-term goals should be set to maximise their use. Many performers will use major competitions as their focus for long-term goals and sub-divide their preparation into short-term goals. For example, an international performer may base his or her preparation on the timing of the Olympic Games or World Championships and set his or her outcome goals in relation to these events. Throughout the season intermediate goals are set (which may be performance goals) allowing the performer to monitor and evaluate progress. This not only maintains the performer's motivation levels but ensures the performer does not become anxious unnecessarily if his or her ultimate target appears to be beyond reach. If the performer achieves their short-term goal, positive feelings are generated, contributing to an increased level of self-efficacy. Goals should even be set for individual training sessions and evaluated afterwards.

Method and principles of goal setting

In order for goal setting to be effective, in addition to the points outlined previously, many performers ensure their goals fulfil the following criteria, as proposed by Sportscoach UK, and referred to as the 'SMARTER' principle.

- **Specific** – the goal must be related to the individual performer and include precise aims, rather than simple statements such as 'you must put more effort into the race'. Ideally the goals should be clear and unambiguous, with a clear relevance to the ultimate outcome goal.
- **Measurable** – the goal must be able to be assessed and recorded to allow the performer to see his or her progress. Ideally this should be a relatively quick process. It may not always be possible to use objective evidence such as times or passes completed, but any subjective feedback must be as precise as possible.
- **Accepted** – the goal must be agreed between the performer and the coach. Ideally the athlete should be part of the discussion process to establish the goal, which will increase motivation levels and he or she will be more likely to commit him or herself to achieving the end result.
- **Realistic** – any goal must be within the performer's capabilities otherwise his or her anxiety will actually increase because of worry about not meeting expectations.
- **Time-phased** – each goal must have a fixed deadline for evaluation, otherwise the performer may lose motivation. The length of time allowed to achieve the goal will depend on the difficulty of the task.

- **Exciting** – the goal must be viewed as a challenge to the athlete and he or she must be motivated to achieve success and to gain intrinsic satisfaction. This aspect of goal setting must be considered carefully because a target that may seem exciting initially may then lose its impact if success is not achieved; it may then appear unobtainable thus causing anxiety.
- **Recorded** – all goals should be recorded for evaluation. If a goal has been set several months before and there is no fixed record of the agreed target, disputes may arise and again there will be a negative effect on the performer's anxiety level.

If these guidelines are followed, goal setting can be highly effective in the development of a sport performer's career. It allows the performer to remain focused but be constantly challenged, always believing that he or she can improve his or her performance.

APPLY IT!

Before your next competitive event set yourself either an outcome goal or a performance goal. The goal must be SMARTER. For the next event set the other type of goal. Discuss your results with a partner and evaluate which type of goal was the most effective for you.

ATHLETE PROFILE

At the current time Claire Vigrass competes in a range of competitions, some of which offer prize money. However, she is an amateur performer and not eligible to collect any prize money. Despite this fact Claire possesses a clear desire to win and fulfil her dream of becoming the best player in the world. At the moment her **intrinsic motivation** is sufficient to give her the incentive to keep bettering herself. When she won the 2008 US Real Tennis Ladies Open she received the glory and the trophy but if she were a professional performer she would have been able to claim the **extrinsic reward** of £5,000. She knew this before entering but the competition formed part of her **long-term targets**. She set herself the **outcome goal** of reaching the last four in the tournament, and the **performance goal** of improving the accuracy of her serve. She achieved both.

During her training Claire's coach has used a variety of **theories of learning** to develop her skills. She experiences **operant conditioning** when developing a specific serve or return shot to a certain area of the court. The strategies and tactics required in the complex game of real tennis require **cognitive or insight learning** to allow Claire to gain an understanding of how to outwit an opponent and vary her shots depending on the situation. This involves analysing her performance (and that of others) to discuss and develop an understanding of the consequences of their play and the alternative options that could have been used. Finally, Claire uses the opportunity when attending tournaments to observe other players (**social learning**) who are currently better than her. This was the case in the 2008 British Ladies Open Championship where she paid particular attention to how the world's number one player returned service. Claire subsequently devoted time in training to copying her actions.

Refresh your memory

Revision checklist

Make sure you know the following:

▷ Learning involves a permanent change in behaviour developed via practice

▷ Performance is a temporary occurrence

▷ There are three stages of learning; cognitive, associative and autonomous

▷ As you progress through the stages of learning, the main type of feedback used changes from external to internal feedback

▷ Performance curves are a useful indictor to monitor progress

▷ A plateau indicates a period of no development and should be avoided if possible

▷ Motivation helps to maintain task persistence, effort levels and performance levels

▷ Intrinsic motivation involves feelings of pride and self-satisfaction

▷ Extrinsic motivation involves both tangible and intangible rewards

▷ Performers should develop a greater level of intrinsic motivation rather than extrinsic motivation if they are to be most successful

▷ Conditioning theories are based on developing a stimulus-response bond

▷ Operant conditioning involves shaping behaviour and manipulating the environment, followed by reinforcement or punishment

▷ If the required skill/performance is produced it can be strengthened by using positive and negative reinforcement

▷ If the required skill/performance is not produced the teacher can weaken the bond between the stimulus and the inappropriate response (S–R) by:

- giving negative feedback
- using punishment

- ▷ The teacher or coach must try to produce feelings of satisfaction to give strong reinforcements (law of effect)
- ▷ Hull's Drive Reduction theory links motivation to the strengthening of the S–R bond.
- ▷ Cognitive/Insight theories suggest that performers must be able to understand events and the relationship between the various subroutines
- ▷ Observational Learning involves the performer paying attention to the model, remembering the movement, having the ability to execute the skill and finally the motivation to reproduce the action
- ▷ Schema theory suggests movements are modified from existing programmes to suit new tasks
- ▷ There are four sources of information in Schema theory:
  - Initial conditions
  - response specifications
  - sensory consequences
  - response outcome
- ▷ Transfer of learning involves the impact of one skill on the development of another skill. Transfer can be positive, negative, bilateral or zero
- ▷ Goal setting can help self-confidence, increase motivation and reduce anxiety
- ▷ Goals should be SMARTER
- ▷ Outcome goals involve targets linked to the end result
- ▷ Performance goals involve targets linked to the performer's technique and personal standard

Revise as you go

1. Name the three stages of learning.

2. What is the aim of a coach during the first stage of learning? Suggest three methods that may be employed to develop this stage successfully.

3. How does the nature of feedback change as the performer progresses through the various stages?

4. Which stage of learning is usually the quickest?

5. Outline the characteristics of the associative stage of learning.

6. Explain the 'S-R bond'.

7. 'Insight' or 'Gestalt' theories are examples of which theories of learning?

8. What can operant conditioning also be referred to as?

9. Explain the term 'associationist learning theory'.

10. Models are often used to aid learning. Give three factors that may enhance their effectiveness.

11. What does the term 'vicarious experience' mean?

12. List the four elements of Bandura's observational learning.

13. Explain why the cognitive approach to learning may be beneficial to the performer during a competitive situation.

14. Explain Thorndike's three Laws of Learning.

15. Suggest two ways a teacher/coach may manipulate the environment to develop a specific action or behaviour pattern.

16. What is a 'plateau'?

17. Which theory suggests that people learn by observing others and then copying their actions?

18. Suggest two factors that may inhibit the performer reaching the autonomous stage.

19. Name two ways to make learning during the cognitive stage easier for the performer.

20. Which schemas are responsible for starting the movement?

21. Which schemas are responsible for controlling and evaluating the movement?

22. Explain the term 'sensory consequences' when referring to recognition schema.

23. Explain the term 'response outcomes' when referring to recognition schema.

24. Which form of transfer occurs when a skill currently being learned has an effect on a skill in the future?

25. Explain the term 'bilateral transfer' and give an example to illustrate your answer.

26. What do the letters SMARTER represent?

27. Explain the difference between an outcome and a performance goal.

28. Why is it important to set short and long-term goals?

CHAPTER 10

Skill acquisition in practical situations

LEARNING OBJECTIVES:

By the end of this chapter you should be able to:

▶ *outline the factors to consider when organising a training session*

▶ *describe Mosston and Ashworth's teaching styles and outline when to use each effectively*

▶ *understand the various ways of presenting practices*

▶ *explain the different types of practices and when to use each one*

▶ *outline various forms of guidance and how to optimise their use*

▶ *explain the importance of feedback and outline the different types of feedback that can be used.*

Introduction

The contents of this chapter will be examined in a written examination but in the form of an extended question. You may have experienced many of the theoretical areas discussed in this chapter in a practical setting and it is from this viewpoint that the question will be directed. The examiner will be testing your knowledge and understanding by asking a question relating to the use of the theory areas to improve skill. For example, a question may focus on explaining a term and then require you to explain how it can be applied in a practical situation.

Now that you understand what 'learning' actually involves and how it can be achieved, the next stage is to investigate how the process can be made more effective. There are many ways to teach new skills and strategies, some of which are more effective than others. If you can select the most appropriate method for a particular individual or group of performers, not only will the time to learn the skill be reduced, but their motivation levels will remain high and they will retain the information allowing progression to take place.

For each of the areas outlined in the learning objectives above, you will be expected to explain its characteristics, give practical applications of its use and discuss its various advantages and limitations.

Many of the areas will be familiar, as you will have experienced them yourself during numerous physical education lessons and sports practices. However, you may not have previously considered the theoretical basis behind their use and evaluated their effectiveness. Throughout this chapter, it may be advisable to reflect on your past experiences to help you gain a better understanding of each topic and attempt to implement some of the methods into your current training and evaluate their use.

Factors to consider when planning a training session

If the often limited time available during a training session is to be optimised, numerous factors must be considered. A lack of thought and pre-planning can limit the amount of learning that occurs.

Factors in training	
Nature of the performer/learner/participants	
• previous experience • stage of learning • physical and mental abilities • age	• gender • motivation • size of the group
Nature of the task	
• open or closed skill • gross or fine skill • discrete, serial or continuous skill	• self-paced or externally paced skill
Experience of teacher/coach	
• amount of knowledge relating to activity • personality	• relationship with the learner or group
Environmental conditions	
• facilities and equipment • time available	• purpose of the session

Table 10.01 Key factors to consider when planning a training session

An awareness of all of the factors outlined in Table 10.01 will allow the situation to be evaluated, and the most appropriate methods can be utilised.

- A – *command style* – all decisions made by the teacher, no performer input
- C/D – *reciprocal style* – decisions made predominantly by the teacher with some input from the performer
- F – *discovery style* – decisions made by the performers with some guidance and input from the teacher
- I/J – *problem-solving style* – all decisions made by the performer, no teacher input

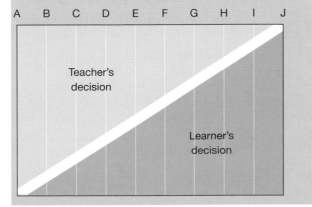

Fig. 10.01 Types of teaching style can be placed on a continuum

1. Observe a lesson or practice session. List all the variable factors and methods used to make learning more effective.
2. Discuss with the coach or teacher the factors they considered to be most important and ask them to justify their reasons.
3. Record the information and at the end of the chapter refer back to your notes and analyse their choice of actions. Would you do anything different? If 'yes', why?

Teaching styles

The teaching style used can have a huge impact on the development of learning. If the appropriate style is used, the learner feels engaged, motivated and secure, which in turn will allow them to develop both the physical capability to perform the skill and understanding of the actions taking place. When considering which style to use, all of the variable factors discussed at the start of this chapter must be considered.

Mosston and Ashworth (1986) suggested a continuum of teaching styles could be used based on who makes the decision about the learning environment and the actions that occur within it. Fig 10.01 illustrates the various styles and how the input varies between the teacher and the learner. Not all the styles have to be remembered. The key styles that need to be learned are:

- **command style** (A)
- **reciprocal style** (C/D)
- **discovery style** (F)
- **problem-solving style** (I/J)

Command style

Command style involves the teacher making all the decisions with no input from the learners. The teacher adopts an authoritarian manner and all the performers complete the same actions.

Advantages	Disadvantages
• Instructions and objectives are clear	• No decision making or input from the learner
• Control and discipline are maintained	• Possible lack of understanding
• Information can be given quickly if time is limited	• Little social interaction with teacher or other learners
• Large groups can be catered for easily	• Limited individual feedback is given
	• Little allowance for individual creativity and responsibility
	• Demotivation as learner becomes disengaged

Table 10.02 The advantages and disadvantages of the command style of teaching

The ideal situations for the command style would be when:

- groups are large, e.g. an aerobics class, or undisciplined groups
- novice performers need to be taught recognised technique
- the situation is dangerous, e.g. rock climbing and athletics throwing events
- tasks are complex, e.g. serial skills such as triple jump
- environmental distractions may require issuing of instructions quickly, e.g. bad weather or 'time-outs' during a game.

Reciprocal style

Reciprocal style involves most of the decisions being made by the teacher with some learner input. The task may be set by the teacher and be completed by the learners working in pairs, alternating the roles of performer and observer/coach.

Advantages	Disadvantages
• Instructions and objectives are clear	• May be difficult with beginners
• Social interaction and communication skills are developed	• Learners may lack sufficient communication skills to be effective
• Learners develop some responsibility for their own learning	• Learners may not be able to analyse movement and therefore provide incorrect feedback
• Some individual feedback is received via teacher and partner	• Difficulty in monitoring large groups to ensure they are all on-task
• Learners develop self-confidence and motivation levels may increase	
• Teacher can still maintain overall control	

Table 10.03 The advantages and disadvantages of the reciprocal style of teaching

The ideal situations for the reciprocal style would be when:

- learners are more experienced
- simple skills are involved, e.g. passing and dribbling
- there is limited danger present
- time is available.

Discovery style

Discovery style involves the teacher guiding the learner to find the correct movement pattern by providing information, giving specific clues or asking questions when appropriate. The teacher acts as a facilitator. There may be one or more solutions to the problem and often the performer may have to adapt the response to suit his or her own abilities.

Advantages	Disadvantages
• Encourages creativity and decision making skills	• Time-consuming
• Development of the learner's responsibility for their own learning	• Difficult with beginners or those who lack creativity
• Learners permitted to work at their own pace	• Limited development if learners have poor communication skills
• Development of a greater understanding of the task	• Progress of large groups is difficult to monitor
• Increased motivation and self-confidence	• Learning is not uniform with all learners
• Improves communication skills and promotes groups interaction	

Table 10.04 The advantages and disadvantages of the discovery style of teaching

The ideal situations for the discovery style would be when:

- creativity is required, e.g. gymnastic routines or devising tactics
- there is no right or wrong outcome, e.g. a dance sequence
- performers have good communication and interactive skills or when one of the primary aims is to develop them
- more experienced performers are involved.

EXAM TIP:

Make sure you learn the characteristics of each style and the situations in which they are most useful.

Problem-solving style

The problem-solving style involves the teacher setting a problem and the learner devising a suitable solution. It is an open-ended approach, encouraging creativity while developing the cognitive and performance elements of the learner.

The advantages and disadvantages are similar to those outlined for the discovery style of teaching. The ideal situations in which to use this teaching style would be when there is no correct outcome, time is not a restriction and the performers are experienced, allowing them to draw on their acquired knowledge.

Generally, as the emphasis on learning moves away from the teacher to the performer, the performer is more likely to be engaged by their learning: motivation and self-confidence will increase and a greater understanding of the task will develop. However, do not presume that the more direct teaching styles do not have a place in learning. Before deciding on the teaching style, all the variable factors have to be considered and the most successful teacher will usually be the one who allows flexibility, utilising a variety of styles depending on the situation. Often within one session several styles may be used to achieve the desired outcome.

EXAM TIP:

You should be able to explain the variables affecting the choice of style: teacher, activity, learner and situation.

TASK 10.02

Outline the teaching style you would adopt in the following situations and justify your reasons.
- Novice performers throwing the javelin
- Novice performers developing gymnastic sequences
- Experienced basketball players during a team practice developing their free throw technique
- Sixth form students rock climbing for the first time.

In pairs, select 10 skills from a variety of sports and suggest the best teaching style to adopt.

Discuss your answers with another pair and justify your reasons.

Fig. 10.02 Long jump is ideal for whole learning

Fig. 10.03 Gymnastics routines are best taught by part learning

Presentation of practices

When introducing a new skill or sequence of movements, the coach has to decide upon the best option that allows the performer to create a clear mental picture and allows for the development of a sound kinaesthetic awareness. This decision often depends on the experience of the performer, the nature of the skill in terms of complexity, ease of breaking it down into subroutines and the ease of transferring subroutines back into the whole sequence.

There are two basic methods that the teacher/coach can use:

- **whole learning**
- **part learning.**

Variations of these methods will be discussed in detail later.

Whole learning

As the name suggests, whole learning involves the performer attempting the whole movement pattern after observing a demonstration or being given verbal instructions (Table 10.05). Many people feel this is an ideal method.

The ideal conditions for using this method are when:

- the skill is simple, discrete or **ballistic**, e.g. golf swing or throwing a javelin
- the subroutines lack meaning if performed in isolation
- the performer is motivated and pays attention
- the performer is experienced or approaching the autonomous stage of learning.

Advantages	Disadvantages
The performer can:	• It is difficult to use with complex skills
• develop an awareness of the entire movement (kinaesthetic awareness)	• It may be difficult for novice performers to execute initially
• understand the relationship between different subroutines immediately	• It is not ideal for dangerous skills
• experience the timing needed to execute the skill successfully	
• develop his own schema (see Chapter 9).	

Table 10.05 Advantages and disadvantages of whole learning

Part learning

In comparison to whole learning, part learning involves the performer completing subroutines of the overall movement in isolation before attempting the overall motor programme or skill. This method can have distinct advantages compared to the whole method (Table 10.06).

Advantages	Disadvantages
• Complex skills can be broken down into different subroutines and learned in stages	• It hinders the development of continuity and timing of the complete skill
• Specific aspects of the technique can be modified	• It reduces overall kinaesthetic awareness
• It allows the performer to develop confidence when practising the skill	• The transfer from part to whole may not be effective
• It reduces the element of risk in potentially dangerous situations, e.g. gymnastic vaulting	• The highly organised skills are difficult to break down
• It allows the performer periods of recovery during physically demanding skills	• It is time-consuming
• It maintains motivation levels as success can be achieved relatively quickly	

Table 10.06 The advantages and disadvantages of part learning

The ideal conditions for using this method are when:

- the skill is complex, e.g. hurdling
- the skill involves long sequences, e.g. gymnastic routines
- there are low levels of organisation, e.g. swimming
- the performer has limited motivation and attention span
- the performer is inexperienced.

Progressive part method

The progressive part method of presentation is a variation on the former method. It involves the performer attempting the skill in stages and linking the phases together after each has been learned. This method is also referred to as '**chaining**'. It is useful when developing gymnastic sequences and set tactical plays such as those used during a rugby match.

Advantages	Disadvantages
• Complex skills can be broken down and introduced gradually	• It is time-consuming
• Novice performers can achieve success	• The performer may become too focused on one particular subroutine
• Performers with limited attention span can remain focused	
• Development of an understanding of the relationships between the subroutines	
• Minimises the risk involved with potentially dangerous skills	
• Transfer to the whole skill can be made easier	

Table 10.07 The advantages and disadvantages of the progressive part method

The ideal conditions for using this method are when:

- the skill is complex
- the skill is serial
- the skill is dangerous
- time is not a constraint
- the performer has limited motivation and attention span
- the performer is inexperienced.

KEY TERM

Ballistic:
a skill that is performed in a short period of time, usually with maximum power

Advantages	Disadvantages
• An overall feel for the movement is developed initially	• Transfer from the part to the whole skill may be difficult
• Success is continuous by developing the weaker subroutines	• Some skills are difficult to break down as the overall timing may be affected

Table 10.08 The advantages and disadvantages of whole-part-whole method

TASK 10.03

Explain how you would present the following skills to a group of novice performers. Justify your answer.

• triple jump	• gymnastic floor routine
• football header	• golf shot
• basketball lay-up	• hurdling
• cricket bowling action	• hockey flick
• sprint start	• volleyball spike

Fig. 10.04 Set tactical plays are often taught via the progressive part method

Whole-part-whole method

Whole-part-whole presentation involves a combination of the major two methods previously outlined. The performer attempts the whole movement after observing a demonstration or being given verbal instructions then develops specific subroutines before completing the whole skill again. There are numerous examples that you may have experienced, such as the long jump, in which the take-off is isolated or the flight phase is practised via drills before transferring the new movement into the entire skill. Similarly, a swimming stroke may be developed in this fashion, or the understanding of tactics via a mini-game or restricted practice. The ideal conditions for using this method are when the skill can be broken down easily.

Types of practice

After the learner has attempted the skill after the initial instruction (presentation of practice), he or she now has to spend time developing and refining the movement patterns. The coach must now decide on the most appropriate type of practice to use, ensuring learning actually occurs, motivation is maintained and fatigue does not limit performance. The variable factors are the periods of active work and recovery time.

There are four main types of practice:

- massed practice
- distributed practice
- variable practice
- mental practice.

Massed practice

Massed practice involves the repeated practice of skills with little or no recovery periods between blocks of trials. This would be used effectively for skills such as shooting at goal/basket or racket strokes.
It would be ideally used when:

- skills are discrete
- the performer is well motivated
- the performer is experienced
- the performer has a high level of fitness
- replication of fatigue within a game situation is required.

However, care must be taken to avoid:

- boredom
- fatigue
- overtraining.

Distributed practice

Distributed practice involves the repeated practice of skills with a recovery period before repetition of the skill or the development of a new task. The recovery period may involve some other form of activity other than just rest or it may include the use of mental practice (see below), feedback or simply time to refocus and re-motivate the performer.
It would be ideally used when:

- the skill is new and complex
- there is repetition of gross skills or those that are physically demanding
- the skill is dangerous
- the performer is a novice
- the performer has low levels of motivation
- the performer has low levels of fitness
- the performer has a short attention span
- a recovery period is needed to receive feedback and evaluate performance.

However, care must be taken to avoid excessive periods of recovery as this may lead to:

- demotivation
- loss of concentration
- ill-discipline within groups.

Variable practice

Variable practice involves the coach using a mixture of both massed and distributed practice within one session. It will help to maintain the interest and motivation levels of the performer and limit the effects of fatigue when required.

Mental practice

Mental practice involves the cognitive rehearsal of a skill without physical movement. This method is particularly useful as it may be utilised before, during and after practice or competition. It is also referred to as 'mental rehearsal' or 'imagery'. The performer will attempt to create a picture in their mind of themselves completing the skill. They can do this in two ways:

- **internal** – involves the performer seeing themselves from within completing the action or in the situation and consequently creating a kinaesthetic feel of the actual movement
- **external** – involves the performer seeing themselves as if they were a spectator or on film. They actually imagine watching themselves performing the skill.

Often, sportspeople can be seen completing such a process immediately prior to competing, for example a high jumper about to jump or a rugby player waiting to attempt a conversion kick. This not only creates a positive mental image, but can also help reduce reaction time, or improve anticipation and control levels of arousal.
It would be ideally used when:

- learning time needs to be reduced, especially for novices
- experienced performers need to prepare for alternative options to situations prior to competition
- the performer needs to concentrate on developing specific aspects or the overall skill
- arousal levels need to be controlled
- confidence needs to be developed
- the performer is injured and some form of practice must be maintained.

Its use may be optimised by:

- finding a quiet location
- focusing on the task and creating a clear picture
- encouraging successful outcomes, not failures
- regular practice
- use during recovery periods.

There is evidence to support the theory that by using mental practice the performer can stimulate the neuromuscular systems involved in creating the movement patterns. While the level of nerve stimulation is insufficient to cause actual movement, it does stimulate minor muscular contractions, thus creating a practice situation. The graph in Figure 10.05 compares the effects of different forms of practice on performance.

Methods of guidance

In order to help the learner gain a clear understanding of the skill to be attempted and then actually improve their performance, guidance is

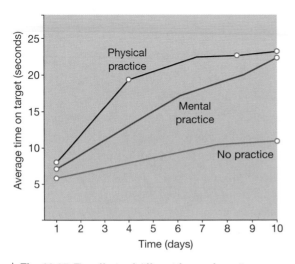

Fig. 10.05 The effects of different forms of practice

TASK 10.04

1. Subdivide a group of performers into three and record the results of ten attempts. The skill can be anything you choose, e.g. basketball shot, volleyball serve, badminton serve and so on.
2. After the initial trials, each group experiences a different form of practice:
   - Group A – practise the same skill for five minutes
   - Group B – no practice, actually perform a totally different skill
   - Group C – mentally practise the skill for five minutes.
3. Complete a second set of trials and record the results.
4. Calculate the average scores for each set of trials, sketch a graph and discuss the results.

used to develop movement patterns and reduce the number of errors made. The form of guidance depends on the situation, the nature of the task and the ability of the performer.

The four main types of guidance are:

- visual
- verbal
- manual
- mechanical.

Visual guidance

Visual guidance involves the performer attempting to create a mental picture of the skill by observing a demonstration, video, pictures, slides or overhead transparencies. The area can also be modified to provide guidance with the use of cones, markings on the floor, hoops or defined target areas.

To optimise the use of visual guidance, the following factors should be considered:

- demonstrations must be accurate
- all information must be relevant to the age and ability of the performer
- use appropriate verbal guidance to focus on key points
- model/demonstrator must be attractive to the performer
- stimuli must be clear and realistic
- modification of the display to enhance information, e.g. bright, colourful markers.

Fig. 10.06 A coach will use a demonstration to help the performer create a mental picture

Advantages	Disadvantages
• Good for performers in the cognitive and associative stages of learning	• Demotivation if the performer is unable to replicate the skill
• Provides a clear idea of the movement pattern to be performed	• Can provide too much information to a novice performer
• Specific cues can be highlighted, which helps to focus the performer's attention	• Poor replication if the skill is inaccurate
	• Static forms of guidance soon lose their impact

Table 10.09 The advantages and disadvantages of visual guidance

Verbal guidance

Verbal guidance involves explaining the motor skill to be performed, either to understand the requirements or to provide feedback. The information may be *general or specific* in nature depending on the ability level of the performer. The information may be used to outline the technique of a specific skill or the strategy for a particular game. To optimise the use of verbal guidance, the following factors should be considered:

- information must be clear and accurate with everyone able to hear the instructions
- limiting the amount of information provided
- language and terminology must be relevant to the age group
- use in conjunction with visual guidance to highlight key points
- use immediately after performance (unless combined with video footage).

Fig. 10.07 Verbal guidance is used to highlight important information and give feedback

Advantages	Disadvantages
• Good for all stages of learning if combined with other forms of guidance	• Demotivation if the performer is unable to replicate the skill
• Very useful for those in the autonomous stage of learning, who may be able to translate the information more easily and correct their faults	• Overload of information – key points should be limited to two or three at most
• Feedback can be given immediately, both during and after the performance	• Difficulty in understanding, especially for novice performers
• Focuses the performer's attention on specific cues when observing a demonstration	• Some movements may be difficult to explain
	• Difficult with large groups and may become boring
	• Over-reliance on feedback during and after performance

Table 10.10 The advantages and disadvantages of verbal guidance

Manual guidance

Manual guidance involves the performer being physically placed, forced or supported into the correct positions. Examples include a gymnast being supported (Fig 10.08) or a coach holding the batsman's arm and guiding them through a cricket shot.

To optimise the use of manual guidance, these factors should be considered:

- avoid overuse; allow the performer to develop their own kinaesthetic awareness
- combine with verbal guidance to focus on key points
- ensure movement pattern is correct.

Advantages	Disadvantages
• Good for all stages of learning, especially novice performers	• Performer becoming over-reliant on help and support
• Reduces fear and builds confidence	• Lack of intrinsic feedback may not help develop true awareness of the movement pattern
• Helps to reduce the risk in some potentially dangerous situations	• Performer does not learn from their own mistakes and may find it difficult to correct them independently
• Development of the correct kinaesthetic awareness of the movement pattern	• Difficult in large group situations
	• Limited use in ballistic/complex movements

Table 10.11 The advantages and disadvantages of manual guidance

Mechanical guidance

Mechanical guidance is similar in nature to manual guidance but involves the use of some form of device for support. Examples include swimming floats, a trampolining belt harness or any form of apparatus that restricts movement to ensure the correct pattern is followed.

The advantages, disadvantages and methods to optimise its use are similar to those outlined above for manual guidance.

Fig. 10.08 Manual guidance is used to develop confidence and ensure the correct movement pattern is completed

EXAM TIP:

You should be able to explain which form of guidance is most appropriate in different situations and justify your reasons.

TASK 10.05

Outline the forms of guidance you would use to introduce the skills listed below to a group of novice performers. Justify your reasons and give practical examples to illustrate your answer.
• gymnastic vault
• set plays in a basketball game
• swimming – front crawl
• torehand tennis shot
• high jump

Fig. 10.09 Mechanical guidance is used to develop confidence and ensure the correct movement pattern is completed

Feedback

The final stage of information processing is **feedback** (see Chapter 8). This is vital to the learning process. It links the output and input phases, effectively 'closing the loop'. We learn from experience either to modify our movements at the time or store the information in our long-term memory for future reference. Feedback has several purposes including:

- detection and correction of errors causing a change in performance
- motivation – incentive to continue and increase effort
- reinforcement of learning – Thorndike's law of effect (see page 185).

The different types of feedback are subdivided and are outlined below.

The two major categories are:

- **intrinsic or internal feedback** – this is received from within the performer via proprioceptors and is known as **kinaesthetic feedback**. As performers become more skilled, they are able to detect and correct their own errors more easily. For example, an experienced trampolinist will be able to make minor adjustments during his or her routine, whereas a novice will not be able to do so without the help of their coach
- **extrinsic or external feedback** – this is received from outside the performer, usually via sound or vision, via their exteroceptors. It may also be known as **augmented feedback**. The information is given by a coach, teacher, supporters, teammates, video or photographs. It is particularly useful in the cognitive and associative stages of learning, as the performer has yet to develop their kinaesthetic awareness, which allows them to correct their errors via intrinsic feedback.

In addition to these two broad categories, there are other forms of feedback.

- **Continuous feedback** – this is received during the performance via the proprioceptors and kinaesthesis, e.g. the feel of the shot when playing badminton, or via the coach issuing instructions.

- **Terminal feedback** – this is received after the performance. It may be issued immediately by the coach or given later, e.g. when observing a video recording of the event.
- **Positive feedback** – this is used as a form of reinforcement, encouraging the performer to repeat the action. For example, the coach praises a shot or the performer sees that the result is effective.
- **Negative feedback** – this is used to discourage a repetition of the action if the technique was incorrect. For example, the coach would highlight incorrect points of technique or the performer may correct the error themselves if the shot was out.
- **Knowledge of results (KR)** – feedback that the performer receives concerning the outcome of the action. It may be the number of goals scored, recorded times and distances, or the statistics collected concerning accuracy and completed shots or passes. It is a form of external feedback and is particularly useful in the early stages of learning.
- **Knowledge of performance (KP)** – this is information that the performer receives about the quality of his or her technique or performance. It can be internal or external feedback, depending on the stage of learning. For example, a swimmer's coach may analyse his or her techniques with the use of video and adjust the training programme accordingly.

Table 10.12 compares knowledge of results and knowledge of performance for two activities.

	Knowledge of results	Knowledge of performance
Long jump	7.24 metres	More drive needed from the knee during take-off
Tennis shot	Ball was wide of the tram line	Racket face was too open

Table 10.12 Knowledge of results and knowledge of performance for tennis and long jump

Making feedback effective

If feedback is used correctly, it can accelerate the learning process and boost motivation. If used incorrectly, it can confuse and discourage a performer. The coach should consider the ability level of the performer and the nature of the task when deciding on the most appropriate form to use.

Here are some key points to using feedback successfully.

- It must be relevant and modifications made according to the ability range of the performer.
- It should be limited – no more than three points of information or the performer will be overloaded with information.
- It must be accurate and specific – give parameters, e.g. direction and speed.
- Ideally, it should be issued immediately when the action is fresh in the performer's mind.
- Allow time to digest the information and to make modifications, possibly combined with mental rehearsal.

- Keep it brief – do not get bogged down with long, detailed instructions.
- Do not overuse – the performer may become over-reliant on feedback and fail to develop their own understanding.
- Set appropriate goals or targets to improve motivation.

TASK 10.06

1. In pairs, select any aiming skill to be completed blindfolded, for example badminton serves into a hoop. The performer completes five attempts under each of the following conditions:
   - no feedback
   - limited feedback – simply 'yes' or 'no'
   - detailed feedback – direction, force, and so on.
2. Record the results and discuss the implications of feedback on performance.

ATHLETE PROFILE

Depending on the time of year and her competitive commitments, Claire Vigrass usually devotes three or four training sessions per week to developing her stroke play and tactical awareness. In consultation with her coach, they decide on the focus of the session and how it will be structured.

In many sessions Claire focuses on specific areas of weakness and, as a result, often experiences **massed practice**. For example, prior to the 2008 US Ladies Open, she spent considerable time developing her service, both in terms of accuracy and increasing the variety of shots played. At other times of the year she undertakes more **variable practice**, where numerous aspects of the game are developed. Claire has also been using **mental practice** away from the practice court to complement the physical training. The particular focus has been on visualising both playing and receiving the serve.

Throughout her development as a real tennis player, Claire has received a considerable amount of **guidance** from a variety of sources. She often partners her sister in doubles tournaments, who offers **verbal guidance** and **feedback** during the matches. However, the main source of guidance is from her coach, who in addition to verbal guidance often uses **visual guidance** in the form of video recordings of her matches and practice sessions. Weaknesses in the execution of particular strokes are identified and suitable practices developed. This was the case when Claire had to understand how to correct a weak backhand stroke when forced into the back corner of the court. Video playback has also helped her to improve her tactical play by analysing the outcome of good and poor shots.

Refresh your memory

Revision checklist

Make sure you know the following:

▷ Before taking a training session you need to consider the nature of the performers, the nature of the task, the experience of the coach and the environmental conditions

▷ Various teaching styles can be used depending on the situation

▷ Command style involves the teacher making all the decisions

▷ Reciprocal style involves setting a task and the learners helping each other

▷ Discovery style involves setting a task and helping the learners find a solution when they need help

▷ Problem-solving style involves letting the learners devise the solution to the task on their own

▷ When deciding on whole or part practice the complexity and organisation of a skill/task needs to be analysed in relation to the individual needs of the learner and the situation

- Whole practice involves experiencing the entire skill

- Part practice involves developing one or more parts of the skill in isolation

- Progressive part and whole-part-whole practice involve manipulating the subroutines to develop weaknesses before attempting the whole skill

▷ When time is devoted to developing and refining a skill, the practice time can be either massed, distributed, variable or mental practice

▷ Massed practice involves the repeated practise of skills with little or no recovery periods between blocks of trials

▷ Distributed practice involves the repeated practise of skills with a recovery period before repetition of the skill or the development of a new task

▷ Variable practice involves the coach using a mixture of both massed and distributed practise within one session

- ▷ Mental practice involves the cognitive rehearsal of a skill without physical movement
- ▷ There are four types of guidance:
  - Visual guidance involves watching a demonstration, video, etc.
  - Verbal guidance involves giving instructions and advice on what to do
  - Manual guidance involves physically moving someone into the correct position
  - Mechanical guidance involves the use of some form of support to aid the correct movement
- ▷ Feedback helps to detect and change errors, provide motivation and reinforce learning
- ▷ Internal feedback comes from within the performer via proprioceptors and is known as kinaesthetic feedback

Revise as you go

1. Explain the term 'whole learning'.

2. Which practice method involves the performer attempting to develop specific subroutines of a skill in isolation before putting them into the correct sequence?

3. Suggest three factors a coach should consider when deciding which form of practice would be most suitable.

4. Explain the term 'massed practice'.

5. Which type of practice involves the performer completing a set of tasks and taking a recovery period before progressing to the next set of tasks?

6. Suggest three ways in which the recovery period during distributed practice can be used effectively.

7. Explain three ways of how mental practice can help the performer.

8. What form of guidance is the most effective to help the performer create a mental picture of the action?

9. Give three examples of how a coach may use visual guidance.

10. Suggest two advantages of mechanical and manual guidance.

11. Suggest three factors that need to be considered before deciding on the most appropriate teaching style.

12. Explain what is meant by the 'command style' of teaching.

13. Give two disadvantages of the command style of teaching.

14. Which form of motivation involves gaining self-satisfaction or pride from achievements, challenging yourself, or just taking part for enjoyment?

15. Which form of motivation involves receiving some form of reward for participation from others?

16. Give two examples of a tangible reward.

17. Give two examples of an intangible reward.

18. Explain why coaches should be careful in their use of extrinsic motivation.

19. Explain two advantages of the reciprocal style of teaching.

20. Why might the discovery style of teaching be inadvisable in some situations?

21. Name the most appropriate style of teaching when developing the basketball lay-up skill with a group of Year 11 GCSE students.

22. Suggest two advantages of the problem-solving style of teaching.

23. Why should a variety of teaching styles be used?

24. Suggest two reasons why feedback is used.

25. What kind of feedback is received via the proprioceptors, developing a performer's kinaesthetic awareness?

26. What is the term given to feedback that is given after the activity?

27. Explain the term 'knowledge of results'.

28. Explain the term 'extrinsic feedback' and give two examples of how a performer may receive this form of feedback.

29. Why is continuous feedback useful to a performer?

30. Suggest two ways in which the coach can use feedback most effectively.

Get the result !

To produce an effective triple jump, an athlete has to use their muscles and joints correctly and demonstrate a high skill level.

a) Successful triple jumpers will use their abilities to improve their level of skill.

Briefly explain the terms *skill* and *ability*.   (2 marks)

b) What are the characteristics of a *skilled* performance?   (3 marks)

c) The skill of triple jumping can be classified according to various continua.

Classify the triple jump according to the following **four** continua **and** justify each of your choices.

- Open to closed

- Self-paced to externally paced

- Discrete to continuous

- Gross to fine   (4 marks)

d) To develop skills practice is essential. What factors should a coach consider when deciding whether to use *massed* or *distributed* practice?   (3 marks)

Model answer

Examiner says:

erall this is a very good
swer, which is well written
d concise. The student has
luded several additional
nts in some of the answers
ensure they achieve as
ny marks as possible.
two marks, the answer
hlights two key differences
ween 'skill' and 'ability'. Skill
earned and ability is innate.
is sufficient to gain the
rks, but they demonstrate
ditional knowledge
laining the relationship
ween the two terms, which
ood but not specifically
uired on this occasion.

Student answer

a) Skill is an action that has been learned, which can be repeated again and again. Ability underpins skill, they are inherited and innate traits that determine how well a performer is able to carry out an act, e.g. strength and balance.

b) Characteristics of skilled performance are that the performance will be perfect, consistent, and efficient, seem effortless as well as being fluent and aesthetically pleasing.

Examiner says:

As with the previous answer the student has given plenty of detail and achieved maximum marks for stating three characteristics; *consistent, efficient* and *effortless*. Again they have provided extra characteristics in case any of the first answers may be classed as repeat answers in the mark-scheme.

This is a well structured answer because they have stated where they would place the triple jump and justified their reasons for doing so. This would achieve three out of four marks because in the final point relating to the gross – fine continuum the answer is a bit vague and makes no reference to 'large muscles' being involved.

c) Open – closed. More towards the closed than the open because the skill has been learned beforehand to be repeated the same each time. It is not affected by the environment, for example, there are no opponents.

Self-paced – externally paced. More towards self-paced because you are able to take your time when deciding to start (within reason) and it is not affected by other people.

Discrete – continuous. It is a serial skill because there are a number of subroutines which have to be performed in the correct order to complete the skill.

Gross – fine. More towards gross than fine because it is a relatively large action unlike a fine skill e.g. darts.

d) When a coach/leader is deciding when to use massed or distributed practice, they must take into account the age of the people and maturity levels, fitness levels and their levels of motivation/interest in the sport or activity.

In this final section with the focus now on factors to take into account when planning a training session, the answer is again concise and contains enough detail for full marks. They have highlighted age, fitness and motivation, but could also have received marks for complexity of the skill, ability of the learner and the time available.

Examiner's tip

If the question asks you to name, list or state the examiner will only take the first specified number of points. For example, 'name three abilities required to perform a triple jump.' However if you are asked to 'explain' or 'outline' usually all your answers will be marked and those that are wrong will be ignored.

When asked to 'briefly explain' think of the definitions of the terms in the question and write about them in your own words. A tip for revision is to learn definitions but don't worry if you can't remember them word for word.

Check how many parts are required to answer the question fully. Look for the words in bold letters. If there is an 'and' make sure you answer the second part or you will not be able to get full marks.

Games players will take part in regular training and practice to improve the execution of their skills.

a) Name the **three** stages of learning.

(2 marks)

b) Describe the characteristics of the level of performance associated with each stage.

(3 marks)

c) Schmidt's Schema theory suggests performers use **four** sources of information to modify their motor programmes. Briefly explain each source of information.

(4 marks)

d) Outline how a coach can enable schema to develop.

(3 marks)

Model answer

Examiner says:

The answer is well written and shows plenty of knowledge. Two marks are awarded as all three stages of learning are named. If only two were named correctly only one mark would have been achieved.

Student Answer

a) The three stages of learning are the cognitive, associative and autonomous stages.

b) The Cognitive stage means that the skill is new so not executed very well. The performer relies on external feedback more than intrinsic.

The Associative stage means that the skill has now been learned but still is not perfected. The performer begins to develop intrinsic feedback and correct some of their mistakes.

The Autonomous stages means the skill is now perfected and can be repeated. They can use internal feedback to correct any errors.

Examiner says:

A good answer gaining three marks. Each of the stages has been clearly identified with the characteristics of each provided. Additional details about the type of feedback used in each stage have been provided but on this occasion would not be worth any marks. However this is good examination technique to provide extra information which may possibly be worth marks and shows the examiner you have a good understanding of the topic.

c) The four sources of information are subdivided into two main areas. The first is Recall Schema, which involves 'Initial Conditions', where you are when the action takes place.

'Response Specifications' or what you have to do to complete the skill.

The second group are called Recognition Schema, which control and evaluate the movement and include Sensory consequences and Response outcome.

d) A coach can enable schema to develop by encouragement given to the performer, feedback straight after the practice and varying the practice so that they do the skill in lots of different situations.

Examiner's tip

The questions will often require not only theoretical knowledge but an understanding of how that knowledge can be transferred to a practical situation. For each of the topics covered make sure you can explain how training sessions can be improved using this information. It may help to relate it to your own experiences.

When possible link your answers to practical examples. This helps to show the examiner you fully understand the concept of the topic being discussed and may be enough to give you the mark. However, when using an example make it specific. Don't simply state the name of a sport, think of a specific skill to illustrate your point. For example, if asked about stages of learning, select a sport, such as trampolining and explain how the performer progresses through each stage when learning a new skill such as a somersault.

UNIT 1

Opportunities for and the effects of leading a healthy and active lifestyle

Section 3: *Opportunities for participation*

Concepts of physical activity

Introduction

In everyday life, we use terms such as play, leisure, recreation, sport, **physical education** and so on, often interchangeably. At this stage in your learning, it is necessary to adopt a more analytical approach and to try to tease out the characteristics that make each concept unique, and yet also appreciate the interrelationship existing between them. You are not required to learn specific definitions or theories but you need to be able to explain them using your own words.

For each concept, we need to clarify the following points:

• the structure of the activity: the level or sophistication of its organisation
• the motivation: the reasons people engage in the activity
• the benefits: what people gain from participating in the activity.

Many students find this part of the specification difficult to grasp, so we are going to try and begin at the start of it all – **play**. Play is the first experience we have as young children learning basic physical skills. We will then move on to recreation, which is slightly more organised than play but not as organised as sport, which will be the third concept we will examine (see Figure 11.01). For each concept, you will be asked to draw from your own experiences to help you understand the relevance of this unit.

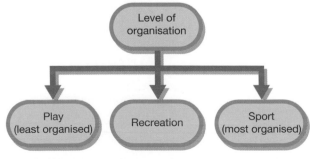

Fig. 11.01 Level of organisation increases from play

Play

Play is one of the first types of activity we engage in as young children. As such, it can be viewed as a natural development of children and may appear a useful and logical starting point in understanding the differing concepts of physical activity.

Many theories have been developed in an attempt to explain the value of play for the individual child and for society. The psychologist Piaget (1962) was very influential in determining how we consider play in the modern era. He proposed that play develops alongside children's cognitive development. He identified:

- **mastery play** – play that allows the child to develop muscle control in order to feel a sense of control over the physical environment. In this context, play can be viewed as helping in the physical development of children. From early on, the child needs to make an impact on its environment and early play is often physical, concerned with sensory or motor coordination

- **symbolic play** – occurs in the second stage, involving the child in make-believe and pretend play. This can also involve mimicry, whereby the child tries to make sense of their world by taking on the role of others. This can be called 'role rehearsal'. Examples of popular games would be 'mummies and daddies' and 'doctors and nurses'. When adults 'play', they tend to want to escape from the real world and forget the stresses of life, but children use play to 'master their world'

- **rule-bound play** – as the child begins to develop cognitively, it engages in activities whereby the child learns to develop structured activities from which they can experience more enjoyment from **competition** and achievement. In children's play there are no pre-set rules. Each play situation starts afresh or spontaneously, with children making up their own rules, modifying them and also officiating themselves. This gives them control over their play group and encourages decision making and independence. It is very important that the play group adhere to the rules agreed by them. Agreement suggests

levels of negotiation and compromise – social skills considered important to society.

Play is also entered into voluntarily, i.e. children choose to play. They are not playing because it is expected of them. The true play experience comes from within the child.

Another important feature of play is that it is intrinsically motivated – this means that there is no ulterior motive for playing other than the wish to play for the enjoyment that comes from the activity. The children are developing many skills, but at a young age, they are not aware of this and this is not why they play. They just want to have fun. There are no leagues, cups or extrinsic rewards. Therefore, can play be serious? Children's play is generally accepted as being 'non-serious'. This means the outcome is not considered serious by society. Play provides a basis for 'reality' but in a safe environment, allowing for exploratory behaviour. The child, in effect, learns 'how to learn' through play, and this knowledge can be used into adulthood.

Although children experience a lot of freedom in play, there are necessarily some restrictions

KEY TERMS

Physical education:
the instilling of skills and values through the medium of physical activity in an educational setting

Play:
when someone 'plays', they engage in an activity for personal amusement

Competition:
the very nature of competition is to aim to achieve what another is aiming to achieve at the same time, before they do

they face, particularly regarding safety. Adults will usually impose defined space boundaries which they must abide by, as well as occasional time limits such as teatime, break-time and so on. Sharing equipment and space, such as a playground or garden, can also be a constraint.

TASK 11.01

Using your own words, explain the following definitions of 'play'.
- 'Play is a voluntary activity, never a physical necessity or moral obligation.'
- 'Play is an activity from which you get immediate pleasure without ulterior motive.'

KEY TERMS

Play:

other useful definitions to be aware of are:

'Play is a voluntary activity or occupation exercised within certain fixed rules of time and place according to rules freely accepted and absolutely binding, having its aim in itself and accompanied by a feeling of tension, joy and the consciousness that this is different from ordinary life.'

Huizinga (1964)

'Play is activity – mental, passive or active. Play is undertaken freely and is usually spontaneous. It is fun, purposeless, self-initiated and often extremely serious. Play is indulged in for its own sake; it has intrinsic value; there is innate satisfaction in the doing. Play transports the player, as it were, to a world outside his or her normal world. It can heighten arousal. It can be vivid, colourful, creative and innovative. Because the player shrugs off inhibitions and is lost in the play, it seems to be much harder for adults, with social and personal inhibitions, to really play.'

G. Torkildsen (1983)

TASK 11.02

From the information already covered on children's play, explain:
a) its level of organisation
b) the attitudes the children bring to the play world
c) any constraints or restrictions that may occur on children's play.

Play also interrelates with other concepts. For example, there is a relationship between play and physical education, and between play and recreation.

APPLY IT!

The Children's Secretary Ed Balls recently announced 'the largest government investment in children's play in this government's history' in the Children's Plan. The plans include funding for 30 new, supervised adventure playgrounds and £225 million to create and improve thousands of play spaces to allow all children more opportunities to play outdoors.

The **Children's Plan** states:

'Parents and children told us that they wanted safe places to play outside, and we know that play has real benefits for children. We will spend £225 million over the next three years to:
- offer every local authority capital funding that would allow up to 3500 playgrounds nationally to be rebuilt or renewed and made accessible to children with disabilities
- create 30 new adventure playgrounds for 8- to 13-year-olds in disadvantaged areas, supervised by trained staff
- we will publish a play strategy by summer 2008.'

Play and physical education

If a teacher wanted to consider the value play has for children, there are certain aspects they could incorporate into a lesson such as:

- giving children some choice in terms of activity or equipment
- allowing them to make up their own games and routines
- use of mini games or adapted games rather than full-sized games
- instilling an element of fun.

Play and recreation

We tend to use the term 'play' when referring to young children. We do not often use the term in relation to adults. Equally, we do not use the term 'recreation' when referring to young children,

Fig. 11.02 Play is . . .

probably because recreation is connected with a break from the world of work, which does not involve children. However, when adults are at play, we generally use the term 'recreation'. It immediately suggests that recreation and play have shared characteristics, but because adults are involved, there will be some differences. One of the common characteristics would be their primary motive being intrinsic and both would be undertaken voluntarily.

REMEMBER!

The term 'play' refers to young children and is participated in purely for intrinsic reasons.

Recreation

In the modern day, recreation tends to be valued for its own sake and is viewed as an important aspect of life for individuals and society. The following definition attempts to highlight the main features of recreation:

'Recreation consists of activities or experiences carried on in leisure, usually chosen voluntarily by the participant – either because of satisfaction, pleasure or creative enrichment derived, or because he perceives certain personal or social gains to be gained from them. It may also be perceived as the process of participation, or as the emotional state derived from the involvement.'

R. Krauss (1971)

However, in the past, certain religious groups, particularly the Puritans in the sixteenth century, have actively discouraged recreational activities believing them to be a sinful waste of time.

With the advent of industrialisation in the nineteenth century, recreation was seen to have positive qualities. Recreation literally means 'to restore to health', so, by allowing recreation, people's energies for work were restored and they became more productive.

When work patterns became regulated, leisure time became woven into people's lives. There was a need to provide for that time and create opportunities for recreational activities in order to create an orderly society with individuals who could appreciate rule-governed behaviour. The potential for trouble, with hordes of working-class people unoccupied during their leisure time, was something the middle-class authorities needed to be aware of and cater for.

People in positions of power felt that society had an obligation to provide recreational facilities. As it was the middle and upper classes who had the resources to do this, they would be providing for activities they approved of. This could be seen as a form of social control, as people's energies could be controlled through recreational and sporting activities, keeping them content and giving them fewer reasons for becoming rebellious. This also allowed the transmission of middle-class values, such as respect for rules, into wider society.

Recreation must also be seen as a means of **socialisation**. This means citizens are provided with acceptable activities to participate in. They are, therefore, learning behaviour patterns acceptable to society such as adhering to rules, etiquette and so on. People initially learn cultural values through the family (**primary socialisation**) in the early years, and play in very young children would be reflective of their family's values. However, as children move into the wider world, such as nursery, school, libraries, clubs and so on, they may begin to learn other values (**secondary socialisation**), which may or may not coincide with their family values.

KEY TERMS

Socialisation:
the term given to the process of individuals learning the cultural norms and values of their society

Primary socialisation:
occurs through the immediate family group from birth to approximtely three years

Secondary socialisation:
occurs as the child interacts with wider socialising agents such as school

Today, leisure and recreation are now a boom industry and cannot be seen as something unimportant or trivial. The amount of money involved and the political decisions made, the varying opportunities experienced by different social groups, mean we do need to consider them as important parts of our society.

We have already stated that the term 'play' is used when referring to young children. However, when adults are at play, we generally use the term recreation. Earlier in the chapter we suggested that recreation and play have shared characteristics, such as their informal organisation, but because adults are involved, there will be some differences, particularly in the reasons or motives for participation.

APPLY IT!

At what stage in an individual's life would we begin to use the term 'recreation'? Consider your own life. As we move into the teenage years, physical activity takes on different connotations. We have learned more formal types of sporting activities, and work patterns, through school and part-time employment, have begun to take shape. As soon as you feel your motivation for taking part in an activity is for reasons such as to make friends, increase your level of fitness or have a break from work, you are moving into the world of recreation.

Recreation itself could be passive or active. It could involve reading a book or listening to music. For our purposes, we need to concentrate on the more active type of recreation. This is what we will call 'physical recreation'. It will share the same characteristics as recreation but it should have some physical output where energy is expended. Another common term used in this instance is '**active leisure**' or 'active recreation'.

Shared characteristics of play and recreation

- Play and recreation must be entered into freely, of one's own free will. Any sense of obligation to take part means the play and recreational experience will be lessened.
- The primary motive for participating in play and recreation should be for enjoyment.
- Play and recreation are informal in their **structure**.
- Play and recreation provide a sense of well-being.
- Play and recreation develop skills – physical, cognitive, social and emotional.
- The outcome of play and recreation is non-serious.
- A casual **attitude** is adopted, as the outcome or end product is non-serious, compared to participating in sport.

Differences between play and recreation

Although intrinsic motivation is the primary aim for both play and recreation, some other motives may well become involved in the recreation process.

KEY TERMS

Active leisure:
physically energetic recreational activities

Structure:
how something is organised: how formal the structure is or how tightly defined

Attitude:
the opinion or feelings of individuals towards an object. For example, an individual may adopt a casual or serious approach towards an activity

Opportunity:
a chance to experience something beneficial

Individuals may well use recreation to escape from the stresses of their daily lives, or view it as an **opportunity** to improve their social lives, or simply to become healthier. In terms of structure, both play and recreation are loosely organised but recreation is more organised than play. Adults tend to take part in recognised physical activities, though usually with modified rules, e.g. using jumpers for goalposts.

TASK 11.03

1. What personal and social benefits can be gained from participating in recreation?
2. Outline activities in your own life that could be classed as recreation. Justify your choice.
3. What are the shared characteristics of play and recreation?
4. In what ways are play and recreation different?

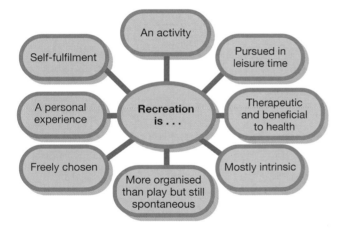

Fig. 11.03 Recreation is . . .

your choice (Figure 11.04). Similarly to play and recreation, leisure serves several functions for the individual and society (Table 11.01)

Individual	Society
• Provides relief from stress – cathartic/relaxing	• Keeps mass of population occupied
• Promotes physical and mental well-being	• Re-creates energies for work
• Active leisure = health and fitness	• Economic benefit – leisure boom industry
• Entertainment	• Maintains cultural traditions (national/regional/class-based and so on)
• Self-fulfilment	• Integrates society
• Acquisition of new skills	
• Social/communication/friendships	

Table 11.01 The functions of leisure

KEY TERMS

Leisure:
leisure is free time to pursue activities of your choice that will enhance the quality of your life

Free time:
surplus time left over after all necessary chores have been completed

Leisure

A common phrase when studying recreation has been 'carried out in **leisure** time'. We now need to consider the concept of leisure. What is leisure? Leisure is **free time** from all other obligations such as work, including school work, domestic chores, eating, sleeping and so on. It is free time to pursue any activity of

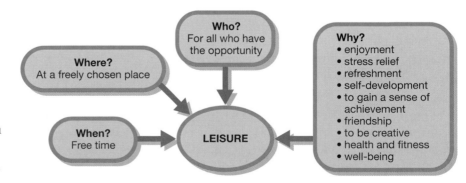

Fig. 11.04 What is leisure?

TAKE IT FURTHER

1. Draw a timetable of your typical week. Try to include everything such as domestic chores, school/college work, part-time jobs, sleeping and so on. Try to work out how much genuine leisure time you have.
2. Then place in regular activities that you would class as leisure or recreation activities.
3. Decide which activities are the most beneficial to you in terms of being life enhancing, self-fulfilling and so on.

In the UK, leisure activities are provided by three main sectors: private, public and voluntary. Each sector makes value judgements about which activities will be made available to the general population. Traditionally, the wealthier sections of society have had more control over their recreational activities, as they are able to provide for themselves. The general public is more dependent on what is provided. Even today, if public tennis courts were not available in leisure centres or schools, many of us would not be able to play tennis. Few of us can afford a tennis court or have a garden large enough to accommodate one.

How much time do we have for leisure?

There is no clear answer to this question. It is dependent on who you are in society and which culture you live in. In this chapter, we will concentrate on the present day and the culture of the UK, recognising that it is a multi-cultural society.

Leisure is free time from work, so the number of hours you work, combined with the nature of your work (is it manual and active or more sedentary?) will directly influence the amount and type of leisure you wish to pursue. Our work patterns have changed since the beginning of the twentieth century, from a heavy manufacturing base to a greater service sector. Hours tend to be more flexible and work tends to be more inactive. An extreme example to illustrate this point may be the decline in industries such as shipbuilding and the increase in service industries, such as call centres! In the latter situation, recreation activities pursued may be more active in order to achieve some balance in life.

Unemployment is usually enforced, so this time would not be classed as true leisure as the individual has not chosen to have that time free. This might be classed as 'enforced leisure'.

Has the status of leisure increased?

Leisure has always occupied a high status in the lives of the wealthier sections of society. They have often been referred to as 'the leisured classes'. They have had the pre-requisites for leisure – free time, opportunity and choice. The lower classes have traditionally been encouraged to work and leisure has been seen as a waste of time. It took many years for the industrial working classes to earn the right to leisure. However, many people today work to enjoy a better quality of leisure time. So we could say that, whereas before leisure was viewed as a tool to re-create people's energies for work, people today use work in order to provide the means for a better quality of leisure activities.

Have the opportunities for leisure increased?

The opportunities for leisure have definitely increased since the nineteenth century, as working hours have reduced and provision for leisure has increased. Other factors have also been significant:

- increased life expectancy/better health allow more energy and time for leisure
- labour-saving gadgets such as washing machines
- increase in disposable incomes
- educating for leisure in schools
- personal mobility such as cars allows more access to facilities
- more facilities
- early retirement.

Leisure time depends on who you are!

Women in our society are known to have the least amount of leisure time due to an increased role in the workplace, as well as remaining the person with the most responsibility for domestic chores. If they do not work, they will often have young children to care for, so pursuing a leisure activity can be awkward if childcare provision is either scarce or costly.

Type of leisure activity depends on who you are!

Social class can still be a significant factor. Traditionally, the terms 'high culture' and 'low culture' have been used to highlight the differences in the type of recreation activities in which different social groups are most likely to be involved (Table 11.02).

High culture, e.g. polo, gymnastics	Low culture, e.g. football, boxing
• Traditionally refers to cultural pursuits of higher social classes	• Traditionally refers to cultural pursuits of lower social classes
• Reflects lifestyle of wealth, free time, privileged education, etiquette	• Reflects lifestyle of popular culture
• Activities tend to require a level of refinement and understanding	• Open to change with trends and social development, e.g. skateboarding
	• Activities tend to be easy to understand, providing entertainment value and quick excitement

Table 11.02 Types of leisure activities

Multicultural societies, such as the UK, also house many different cultures with different religious beliefs, cultural traditions and customs. Different ethnic minority groups will also have varying approaches to how they occupy their leisure time (see Chapter 12).

TASK 11.04

1. Outline as many key words as you can that characterise leisure.
2. How can you distinguish between leisure and recreation?
3. What is meant by the term 'active leisure'?

'Leisure can conceptually embrace the freedom of play, the recreation process and the recreation institution. Leisure can be presented as the opportunity and means for play and recreation to occur.'

Torkildsen (1983)

Choice is a crucial element in all the three concepts covered so far. When the element of choice begins to lessen, the play, recreational and leisure experiences will begin to decline. This can become evident in situations where an individual chooses to participate in an activity and gradually becomes more involved in the organisation of the activity, such as a captain or a coach. Slowly, a sense of obligation to turn up occurs and the activity can begin to feel more like a chore. The true recreational experience can begin to diminish.

REMEMBER!

The three prerequisites of leisure are: free time; opportunity; choice.

At the other end of the spectrum from play is sport. Its level of organisation and the motivations of participants set it apart from the previous two concepts.

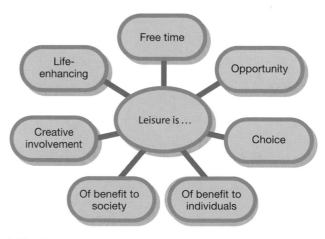

Fig. 11.05 Leisure is …

Sport

> **KEY TERM**
>
> **Sport:**
> sport is a competitive and institutionalised physical activity

'Sport is an institutionalised, competitive activity that involves vigorous physical exertion or the use of relatively complex physical skills by individuals whose participation is motivated by a combination of intrinsic and extrinsic factors.'

Coakley (1993)

'Physical activities with established rules engaged in by individuals attempting to outperform their competitors.'

Wuest, Buscher (1991)

Most of you will belong to or have belonged to sports clubs, either in school or locally. The best way of approaching the concept of sport is to remember your experiences as you became more involved and serious about a particular activity. What changed a recreational activity into becoming a sport?

> **APPLY IT!**
>
> You could be participating in the same activity as someone else, for example football, but they could be participating in sport and you could be participating in recreation. It will depend on the attitude each brings to the activity and the level of structure surrounding the activity.

The participation pyramid (Fig 11.06) shows the four levels of participation in ascending order. The learning of basic motor skills begins at the foundation level and the most advanced sport performers will reach the apex of the pyramid. The majority of people will occupy the middle two sections.

In physical education lessons (**foundation** level), children are introduced to the basic skills and are usually given the opportunity to extend

Fig. 11.06 The participation pyramid

their interest in the activity by opting to participate in extra-curricular activities or to join sports clubs in the community (**participation**). When participants begin to train to develop skills, compete under officially recognised rules, with important outcomes, we could determine they are involved in sport. This could occur at the stage of participation. **Performance** level is usually considered to be of regional standard and **exellence** level can be reached in terms a personal achievement; elite is the level to which only a few aspire.

> **TASK 11.05**
>
> 1. Outline where you think you are in relation to the participation pyramid in a number of sporting activities.
> 2. What factors have been influential in this process? You might like to consider factors such as parental influence, peer group, religious and/or cultural, access to resources, education and so on.

Characteristics of sport

When thinking about play, the first aspect we considered was the level of physical activity. Children learn to control their bodies and produce movements that are effective in helping them control and make an impact on their environment. At the level of sport, specific skills will have been mastered in order to be an effective performer. If we take a simple game involving throwing and catching, by the time a child has transferred this skill into basketball, they will need to practise until they can produce a variety of passes effectively, considering the weight and direction of the pass, dependent on the game situation. The ability to reproduce the same movement consistently and effectively is what we call skill.

Children will have moved on from the situation of making up their own rules to learning formally laid down rules, which are externally enforced by officials. This requires a level of cognitive development as well as a moral code, which allows the individual to accept the need for rules.

The aspect of choice is also important. People do choose to participate in a sport, but often extrinsic reasons can begin to dominate. They may feel an obligation to their teammates or coach; they feel an obligation to themselves to achieve the best they can, and, in the case of a professional sportsperson, the sport becomes their work!

People, other than the performers, are involved in the sport process. We have already mentioned rules. These have to be drawn up by an international sport federation, such as FIFA, and disseminated across the world in order that all clubs adhere to them. Officials, such as referees, linesmen, scorers and coaches, to name but a few, make up the administrative system.

Practice and training become more important as selection is often an aspect of sport. It requires individuals to prove they are better than the next person, and commitment and dedication to training will often separate the highly successful from the mediocre. At the level of recreation, a group of people can participate in a kick about in the park whatever their level of skill. This is because the outcome is not as important as if they were playing in a club match.

Sport is often structured into competitive levels and individuals can move up the levels as they improve.

Fig. 11.07 Sport is …

Benefits and problems of sport

Why do so many of us participate in sport? We must feel there is some benefit to it (Table 11.03). On the other hand, there have been many criticisms of sport (see Table 11.04). George Orwell said it was 'war minus the shooting'.

Individual	Society
• Health and fitness	• Healthy society
• Socialising and making friends	• Integration of society
• Acquiring new skills	• Skills useful in life
• Cathartic/enjoyment	• More relaxed society
• Alleviates boredom	• Social control
• Sense of achievement	• Sport a boom industry
• Pride in self and community	

Table 11.03 Benefits of sport

Individual	Society
• Take it too seriously/ obsessive	• Pride – community and national
• Deviant behaviour in order to win	• Society condones deviant behaviour
• Armchair enthusiasts rather than participants	• Media encourages non-active
• Discriminatory if female, ethnic, disabled	• Popular sports receive most publicity

Table 11.04 Problems of sport

TASK 11.07

What is the opposite of each of the following words?

- Recreation
- Sport
- Intrinsic
- Choice
- Outcome unimportant
- Spontaneous

TAKE IT FURTHER

1. How can an international sport fixture be referred to as 'war minus the shooting'?
2. What counter-arguments would you give to support international sport?
3. Give three benefits of sport for the individual and society.

Positive values of sport	Negative values of sport
Competitive: aiming to achieve what another is aiming to achieve at the same time/learn how to win and lose	Gamesmanship: bend the rules of the sport in order to gain an advantage
Sportsmanship: qualities such as fairness, respect for opponents and playing within the rules	Win at all costs: winning is the primary aim even if it means breaking the rules; it could be an intention, for example 'take him out'
Amateurism: participate in sport for the love of it and without financial gain; it is not just the winning that is important but also how you participate	Cheating: deliberately breaking the rules of the sport, for example professional foul
Assertive: goal-directed, non-aggressive behaviour in a sporting situation	Aggression: the behaviour in a sporting situation which intends to cause harm to an opponent

Table 11.05 Positive and negative values in sport

Values in sport

So far, we have looked at the characteristics and benefits of sport. What about the **values** invested in sport (Table 11.05)?

The way in which we view the world is determined by many factors. One important factor is who we are and the values we have learned from our society (socialisation), and consequently whether we have accepted or rejected them.

It is probably fairly obvious, living in our society, why most of these points are in a particular category. However, why is the term 'amateurism' in a value category at all? Is it not just a sporting term?

The values embodied in amateurism, such as fair play, the idea that taking part in sport is more important than the winning, emerged during the nineteenth century when much of sport was controlled by the upper and middle classes. This section of the population was able to engage in sporting activities for fun and enjoyment. They did not need to earn a living from sport.

Attitudes such as these take many years and sometimes generations to change. Also, it is interesting to realise that not all countries adopted this point of view. Countries such as the USA, a much younger country than the UK and with a less strict social class distinction, found professional sport much more in keeping with its cultural beliefs. So, values are dependent on who you are and what culture you belong to.

When analysing sport, it is also important to consider the attention given to winning.

The value of winning

The amateur code emphasised playing sport for the love of it without monetary gain. It also stressed the importance of how you play becoming almost more important than whether or not you won. Hence the terms 'fair play' and 'sportsmanship', and showing courtesy and respect for your opponent developed.

The nineteenth-century amateurs enjoyed a variety of sports and the all-rounder had great status. There was honour in victory and defeat.

The very nature of professional sport is to earn money from sport and it has become a livelihood for many people. Therefore the outcome is more significant. This results in performers specialising in an activity and training hard in order to secure a victory. It also means that 'win at all costs' has become a sport ethic. Performers may take drugs, may deliberately foul and so on as the rewards for winning become ever greater.

Physical education and school sport

In this section we will concentrate on the concept of physical education. The aims of physical education are to teach:

- activity-specific skills such as throwing: i.e. motor development
- fitness such as endurance: i.e. physical development
- knowledge such as the rules of an activity: i.e. it is cognitive
- values such as sportsmanship: i.e. it is cultural.

Physical education delivers these objectives via many sports. It has become a requirement of the National Curriculum to teach a variety of activities rather than a select few. The more experiences children have, the more likely they are to continue these activities into later life. Therefore activities ranging from team games, individual, competitive and non-competitive should be taught. It aims to offer a balanced physical education programme.

You will have experienced physical education throughout primary and secondary school. You have chosen to study it as an examination subject. Similar to sport, physical education is a highly structured activity: everyone knows beforehand when the lesson will take place, the duration, the nature of the activity and the number of people involved.

However, physical education also has qualities that set it apart from play, recreation and leisure.

- It lacks choice. It is compulsory! This can affect the attitudes of children taking part as it is enforced. It can often create feelings of resentment.
- Learning takes place but the educational aspect has been formalised.
- The purpose of physical education is to teach children activity-specific skills in a range of activities.
- There is a physical education teacher in authority over the children. This is quite different from play and recreation, which is mostly self-initiated and self-officiated.
- In sport, the role of the authority figure is the sports coach. (We will look at the roles of the physical education teacher and the sports coach further on in this chapter.)

Another important remit of physical education is trying to encourage children to appreciate the value of a healthy lifestyle and understanding the important role exercise plays in this. Lifetime activities are becoming central to the choice offered in school physical education programmes.

As well as being able to perform physical activities, children are also expected to be able to analyse and evaluate movement. They need to develop their critical understanding.

It is no coincidence at this stage that the word 'sport' has been used sparingly. The government is investing a lot of money into physical education *and* school sport. In the UK, we have traditionally treated

Physical	Intellectual/cognitive	Social
• Motor development, for example coordination, agility and balance	• Appreciation of movement	• Teamwork and cooperation
• Fitness	• Critical performer	• Leadership
• Skilfulness, e.g. activity-specific skills	• Observation and analysis	• Communication and social skills
	• Learning rules	• Trust in others
	• Learning strategies and tactics	• Pursue recreational activities after leaving school
	• Problem solving	

Table 11.06 Objectives of physical education for the child

TAKE IT FURTHER

1. Conduct a survey of the types of activities your group have experienced in physical education lessons.
2. Categorise the activities under the headings: team, individual, game and movement.
3. Has your group experienced a balanced physical education programme? What might prevent a school offering a balanced programme?

these two concepts differently, believing them to have very different purposes. They merely focus on the same sporting activities.

KEY TERM

School sport:
the competitive, performance-orientated extra-curricular activities offered by schools, for example school netball and football teams

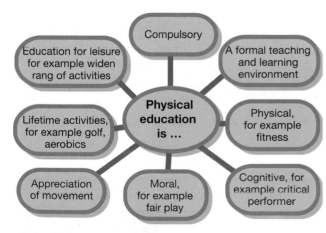

Fig. 11.08 Physical education is …

Physical education is concerned with the needs of the child – their physical, emotional and social development. Physical education teachers use physical activities to develop children's:

- confidence and self-esteem
- aesthetic appreciation
- physical competencies
- social awareness.
- creativity and expressiveness

School sport is more concerned with developing children's ability to perform sporting activities and with results and performance standards. It is extra-curricular and voluntary, and is therefore an expression of children extending their initial interest in the activity. They are given opportunities to be more competitive and experience representative sport. In some instances, its philosophy and objectives may be more similar to club sport in society than physical education. It is interesting to note that in some countries physical education and school sport are both compulsory.

TASK 11.08

1. What are the advantages and disadvantages of keeping physical education and school sport separate?
2. What physical, social and moral values can children gain from school sport?

REMEMBER!

School sport refers to extra-curricular activities and physical education refers to the compulsory core physical education lessons.

Role of a physical education teacher	Role of a sports coach
• Compulsory: this is a National Curriculum subject; children have to attend	• Voluntary: children will have chosen to participate
• Range of activities: the National Curriculum requires a variety of activities to be taught	• Specialism: the sport coach tends to have specialised in their activity and may coach to a higher standard
• Ability level: mixed ability classes are the norm for physical education lessons	• Ability level: performers will normally be taught according to their ability; some selection tends to occur
• Children's needs: physical, psychological and emotional needs are developed and nurtured above their performance results	• Performance: the sports coach is often measured by the progress of their performers and therefore there is a concentration on results
• Values: values such as teamwork, sportsmanship and cooperation are encouraged	• Values: values such as commitment, dedication to training and competitiveness are encouraged

Table 11.07 The roles of a teacher and a coach

Who teaches physical education and school sport?

In the UK, the physical education teacher is usually responsible for both physical education and school sport. This suggests that they have to adopt different roles during the school day. By analysing the role of a teacher and a sports coach, it can further our understanding of these two concepts (Table 11.07). When taking a representative school team, the physical education teacher may tend to adopt the role of a sports coach.

Some schools face problems when they offer school sport:

- it is based on teacher goodwill
- lack of funding for transport and facilities
- pupils having competing leisure interests and part-time jobs
- risk assessment/safety considerations.

However, many people feel the benefits outweigh the disadvantages.

TAKE IT FURTHER

So far, we have contrasted physical education and school sport. What about the relationship between school sport and club sport? Many of you will already have experienced both. Are they similar or different (see Table 11.08)?

Similarities	Differences
• Participate in the same sporting activities	• Teacher in school rather than a sports coach
• Learn skills and tactics	• Conflicts between school and club expectations
• Are formally taught	• 'Win at all costs' may be emphasised more in club sport
• Physical education teacher may adopt role of a coach	
• Still aim to be successful/win	

Table 11.08 Contrasts between school sport and club sport

APPLY IT!

The government says it is committed to increasing the role of physical education and school sport. It is investing millions in trying to improve the infrastructure that will enable this to happen. However, physical educationalists might be suspicious if it appears that the traditional philosophies are being threatened and may feel that they should not be used as a 'nursery' for sporting talent. What do you think?

REMEMBER!

We can conclude by saying that:
- physical education uses sporting activities to achieve its aims
- school sport is offered as an additional experience to most children to develop levels of skill with a more competitive emphasis
- schools try to offer some link between themselves and local sports clubs – an increasingly important government policy (see Chapter 12).

TAKE IT FURTHER

Have you ever been on an activity holiday such as PGL or participated in a school ski trip or done some rock climbing? In pairs, consider how these experiences differed from other types of sporting activity.

TASK 11.09

Place the following activities in their natural environment of land, air or water.

• Rock climbing	• Abseiling
• Skiing	• White water rafting
• Paragliding	• Parachuting
• Scuba diving	• Rambling
• Canoeing	

Outdoor and adventurous activities

The types of activities we will be discussing in this final section are different from 'everyday' sports. They can be called outdoor pursuit activities, outdoor and adventurous activities, extreme sports or outdoor pursuit activities in the natural environment.

Outdoor and adventurous activities became popular with the upper and middle classes in the nineteenth century. They were the group in society who were able to enjoy more leisure time, disposable income and personal transport long before the working classes had access to them. During the nineteenth century, and with the onset of industrialisation, the working classes began to participate. As people began to live in cramped, polluted towns, poets such as Wordsworth provided attractive images of the countryside to which people could escape to restore their energies. This, combined with advances in communications, particularly the railways, made access to the countryside possible for working-class people.

During the twentieth century and to the present day, these activities have continued to grow in their levels of participation. People have enjoyed more leisure time and disposable income, and as work patterns have become more flexible and sedentary (inactive), people may seek more excitement and adrenalin rush in their recreation, as well as needing to escape from stressful jobs and lifestyles.

Traditionally, outdoor and adventurous activities would appeal to more conservative individuals wishing to take part in activities with little need for competition, as these are activities that can be participated in without rules and without opponents. In the latter half of the twentieth century, the media portrayed these activities as fashionable and attractive to the youth culture, particularly as new sports have emerged such as snowboarding and jet-skiing, often due to advances in technology. They are now fashionable pastimes with a whole new leisure industry catering for them.

Access to more isolated environments has been one of the restrictive features of these activities. This has been partly overcome by creating man-made versions, such as climbing walls and dry ski slopes, and there is an increasing number of clubs catering for these sports. This has enabled more people to be introduced to these sports allowing them to practise the basic skills before actually visiting the natural environment. Because more people have access to different modes of transport, including cars, the more remote parts of the country are now becoming accessible.

Management companies are increasingly using these types of activities in testing managers for their personal qualities such as problem-solving, team leading and so on. Apart from taking place in the natural environment, these activities are also characterised by their sense of danger or risk, which are inherent in the activities themselves.

Many of these activities can be adapted for people with special needs and disabilities, such as skiing, canoeing and so on. Society recognises that people with special needs have as much right to enjoy these activities as anyone else and equal rights demand that governing bodies seek to ensure their sport is made more accessible. The benefits listed below are just as applicable to people with special needs.

Fig. 11.09 Outdoor and adventurous activities are . . .

Developments in technology have also enabled adaptations such as specialised equipment for skiing.

Many benefits can be gained from pursuing outdoor and adventurous activities. Some of these are:

- a sense of freedom (some of these sports can be played alone)
- handling risk
- leadership and response to leadership
- crucial decision making
- appreciation of the natural environment and environmental issues
- trust in yourself/self-reliance/knowing, but also challenging your personal limits
- trust in others/teamwork
- escape from pressures of urban lifestyles
- sense of danger/adrenaline rush
- cross-curricular links in schools with geography and fieldwork studies.

KEY TERMS

Adventure:
an undertaking that involves risk and may have an unknown outcome

Objective danger:
danger that is not under the control of the individual, such as an avalanche

Subjective danger:
danger that is under the contorl of the individual, for example the careful planning of a route to avoid hazards

TAKE IT FURTHER

How might an inner-city school help prepare its pupils to develop the necessary skills in a range of outdoor and adventurous activities before embarking on an adventure holiday to the natural environment?

Mortlock (1984) suggests there are four main stages of adventure:

- **play** – little challenge or risk
- **adventure** – individual is placed in challenging situations relative to their skill levels
- **frontier adventure** – individual is experienced and skilful and able to explore wilderness areas
- **misadventure** – something has gone wrong such as an accident.

Adventure and frontier adventure are the most desirable situations to experience.

TASK 11.10

Consider Figure 11.12 and establish the difference between objective danger and subjective danger, and explain how this varies according to the difficulty of the challenge.

Risk is being increasingly analysed in our society. Most people will have heard the term 'risk assessment'. It is a modern social phenomenon that we are trying to eliminate all risk from our lives. It began with the best intentions of trying to avert unnecessary tragedies and protect individuals from institutional negligence. However, combined with the blame culture that is evolving and the risk of huge compensation payouts, many people feel the situation is getting out of control. The effect this is having in schools is worrying. Many teachers are beginning to withdraw their involvement in trips, as risk assessments have to be carried out in great detail and can leave them liable should anything go wrong.

Fig. 11.10 Play is the first experience of learning basic physical skills

Fig. 11.11 Sport involves competitive physical activity with established rules

Many people feel there are benefits to the individuals when learning to handle risk. We do risk assessments every day, for example when we cross a road we make a judgement call. Outdoor and adventurous activities provide a wealth of learning experiences in this area. **Real risk** comes from the environment such as an avalanche, flood or landslide. This should be avoided at all costs as it will most likely result in serious injury or death. With careful planning, it can be avoided to some extent, but the more experienced a performer becomes, the more likely they are to enter 'wilderness' areas where the environment becomes increasingly unpredictable. **Perceived risk** is the sense of danger

or excitement the individual gets from the activity. It can be the experience of abseiling for the first time, with the anxiety and adrenaline rush, but with safety ropes the activity is under control.

Outdoor education v. outdoor recreation

We need to clarify the two terms **outdoor education** and **outdoor recreation**. They both involve the same type of sporting activity, i.e. outdoor and adventurous activities such as canoeing, abseiling and skydiving, but the difference between the two terms is the context in which we may refer to them. If you have been on a school trip to participate in these activities, then the correct term would be 'outdoor education' as it has taken place in an educational setting. However, if you took part in the same activity on a weekend away with friends, then the correct term would be 'outdoor recreation' and the qualities of recreation that we have already studied would still hold true, as they are entered into voluntarily and in an individual's free time. Although learning is still taking place, it

KEY TERMS

Real risk:
risk from the environment such as a rock fall, which is beyond anyone's control

Perceived risk:
potential risk that an individual is aware of; this adds to the sense of danger

Outdoor education:
outdoor and adventurous activities in the natural environment in an educational setting, for example a school ski trip

Outdoor recreation:
outdoor and adventurous activities in the natural environment in an individual's own free time, for example a ski trip with friends

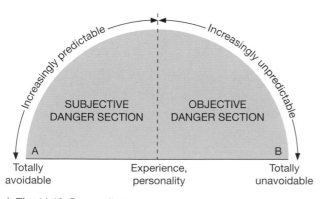

Fig. 11.12 Danger diagram

Educational values	Recreational values
• Appreciation of natural environment	• Free time
• Environmental/ conservation issues	• Choice
• Cross-curricular/map reading	• Opportunity
• Survival skills	• Enhance quality of life/creativity and participation
• Personal limits/ knowledge	• Active leisure
• Teamwork/leadership	• Escape stresses of life
• Appreciation of natural environment	• Health
	• Intrinsic
	• Sense of achievement/ fulfilment

Table 11.09 Values of outdoor education and recreation

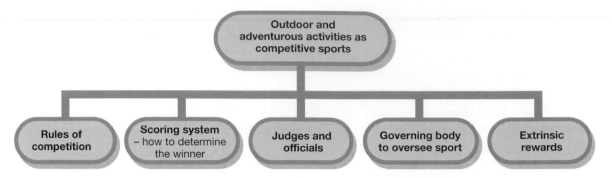

Fig. 11.13 The features of competitive outdoor activities

is not within an educational setting, i.e. under the aegis of a school or education institution.

Outdoor education encompasses activities/sports such as canoeing, climbing, rafting, skiing and so on. The values that individuals derive from them can be very different from those of other sports. They can be competitive or non-competitive; they take place in challenging and exciting environments, which induce fear and exhilaration. They develop interpersonal skills such as self-reliance, leadership, teamwork and critical decision making. There are strong reasons why outdoor education should be on the National Curriculum, and in even greater depth, but schools face many problems in trying to offer a valuable programme:

- an already congested timetable
- lack of teacher specialists
- lack of funds

REMEMBER!

- Outdoor and adventurous activities take place in the natural environment.
- Outdoor education is the participation in outdoor and adventurous activities in an educational setting.
- Outdoor recreation is the participation in outdoor and adventurous activities in an individual's free time.

- accessibility to natural environments
- safety issues in a risk assessment culture.

However, there are cross-curricular links that could be made with subjects such as geography and biology fieldwork, and schools could adapt their own environments to teach the basic skills of many of these activities such as:

- use of dry ski slopes
- swimming pools for canoeing/scuba diving
- parks for orienteering
- climbing walls.

Outdoor and adventurous activities as competitive sports

We have already established that many of these activities can be participated in purely for the personal challenge but as Chris Bonnington in his book *Quest for Adventure* writes:

'*In theory, climbing is a non-competitive sport. In practice, however, there is a very high level of competition. At its simplest level, a group of climbers bouldering almost inevitably start to compete, trying to outdo each other, to solve a climbing problem that has beaten the others ... in any activity competition is a spur to progress.*'

Many outdoor and adventurous activities are now institutionalised competitive activities in their own right. Figure 11.13 suggests what is required for an outdoor activity to become a competitive sport.

ATHLETE PROFILE

Rochelle Plumb is a member of the European Ladies Senior Horseball Team. She has, therefore, reached the highest levels in her sport and can be classed as an elite performer. She has represented Britain at the Junior and Ladies European Cup. She has recently finished studying A Levels at Colchester Sixth Form College with the intention of progressing to Loughborough University to read Human Biology.

Interestingly, horseball is a relatively new sport. The game was created in France in the 1970s as an exercise to improve skill and discipline between horse and rider. It is a mixture of rugby, polo and basketball played on horseback while shooting a ball through a high net (approximately 1.5m x 1.5m) in order to score points. It is one of the ten disciplines officially recognised by the International Equestrian Federation.

It was introduced to Britain at an exhibition tournament at the Horse of the Year Show in 1990. It gained success since and has spread across Europe and overseas. The most important international competition is the European Horseball Championship, but in 2006 the first World Pato-Horseball Championship was organised.

Here Rochelle traces her route through the sport from participating at a recreational level to participating at a high level in the sport. One of the factors that influenced her initial interest in horse riding was the early introduction to the sport by her parents when she was only two years old. Much of her leisure time has spent horse riding for fun and she has benefited from owning her own horse. As she became more skilled she became a member of the Essex Young Farmers Pony Club and began competing in competitions early on. This necessitated a lot of training, coaching and understanding the rules of the various competitions she entered.

Fig.11.14 Rochelle competing in a horseball match

Refresh your memory

Revision checklist

Make sure you know the following:

Concepts

▷ Play is a concept referring to activities engaged in by young children. Its primary purpose is to have fun. Play is spontaneous with rules which are fluid and flexible; children initiate and govern their play world independently of adults. Children can use play to learn about the real world

▷ Adult play is termed 'recreation'. Adults 'play' to escape reality

▷ Recreation is an activity done in leisure time. The primary aim of recreation is intrinsic with some extrinsic motivation, such as getting fit. Recreation should restore an individual's energies and health

▷ Physical recreation is another term for active leisure

▷ The pre-requisites of leisure are free time, opportunity and choice. Leisure serves the interests of the individual, such as self-satisfaction, as well as the needs of society, such as social control

▷ Sport is the most organised and formalised of all the concepts of physical activity. Rules are pre-set and externally enforced. The outcome is serious and therefore training and performance levels are important

▷ Physical education is the instilling of skills, knowledge and values through the medium of physical activity. The physical objectives are aspects such as being able to improve fitness; social objectives are aspects such as learning to work in a team; and the intellectual benefits are aspects such as learning rules and tactics

▷ Outdoor and adventurous activities take place in the natural environment, such as are skiing and canoeing. Characteristics include risk and danger and benefits of participation include handling risk and appreciation of the natural environment. These activities can be competitive or non-competitive. To be competitive they need to be organised as having rules, officials to enforce rules and so on

Revise as you go

1. Why can play be spontaneous?

2. What motivates children to play?

3. What is physical recreation also known as?

4. State three characteristics of physical recreation.

5. What are the three main pre-requisites of leisure?

6. How can work affect leisure?

7. What does the term 'institutionalised' mean when referring to sport?

8. Give three characteristics of sport.

9. What physical objectives does physical education have?

10. What personal qualities does physical education encourage in children's development?

11. What types of activities are included in the terms 'outdoor education', 'outdoor recreation' and 'outdoor and adventurous activities'?

12. What is the difference between outdoor education and outdoor recreation?

13. What are the benefits of play, physical recreation and sport to:

   - the individual

   - society?

CHAPTER 12

Development of physical education and policies to increase participation

LEARNING OBJECTIVES:

By the end of this chapter you should be able to:

▶ understand the development of physical education from the nineteenth century to the present day

▶ appreciate the legacy of the nineteenth-century public schools in their rationalising of mob games and creation of an educational context for team games

▶ know about athleticism and Muscular Christianity with their concepts of character building, loyalty and leadership

▶ trace the development of state school physical activity, from drill to physical training to physical education, and understand the rationale behind the changes

▶ understand how the post-1950 publication of Moving and Growing influenced the present-day scene in terms of child-centred learning through the movement

approach and greater curriculum breadth

▶ use knowledge of the past to help you appreciate the current situation with the National Curriculum – its structure, objectives and reasons for being

▶ understand the role of government through a century of educational changes, particularly the level of government control over education

▶ Identify and appreciate the initiatives such as: Physical Education, School Sport and Club Links Strategy (PESSCLS); Sports College Status as well as School Sports Coordinators; Active sports; TOPS programmes and whole sport plans (WSP)

▶ Identify the relevant organisations with responsibility for increasing participation especially Sport England, Youth Sports Trust and national governing bodies.

Introduction

In this chapter we will begin to study the development of physical education from a chronological viewpoint, which means we will firstly look at the legacy of the nineteenth-century **public schools**. These schools were established well before any state schooling was thought of and is therefore a reasonable place to begin our study of physical education.

KEY TERM

Public school:
a private, independent, fee-paying school

Public schools

Public schools have a long tradition in Britain dating back to the original nine schools of Eton, Harrow, Rugby, Charterhouse, St Paul's, Winchester, Merchant Taylors', Westminster and Shrewsbury. These schools were very prestigious and only catered for the upper classes in Victorian society, i.e. those that could afford to send their sons there and who had a high social standing.

During the nineteenth century, the middle classes emerged with their new found wealth and desire to emulate the lifestyles of the upper classes. They were not welcomed in the established gentry schools and were to build their own copies, which were called proprietary colleges, such as Marlborough and Clifton.

Aims

The nineteenth-century public schools were aiming to educate the future leaders of society in their roles as politicians, lawyers, doctors and so on. Leadership skills, as well as the behaviour befitting a gentleman, were considered vital ingredients in the boys' education. Through education, the boys were taught respect for social order and prepared to serve their country in whatever capacity was required of them.

Characteristics

These schools for the upper and middle classes were very prestigious establishments. They were fee-paying and therefore elitist, as only a small section of society could afford to send their sons to them. They were institutions run on a hierarchical structure with the prefects or sixth form having control over the younger boys. They were single sex, firstly for the sons of the gentry and later, for their daughters. As there were only a few schools, they were often a long way from the boys' homes and the boys had to board. The boys would leave home at an early age and would have been institutionalised for many years during term time. This institutional lifestyle was to have a profound impact on the characters of the boys as they learned their place in the hierarchical structure. The older boys would become prefects in the sixth form and would have younger boys – fags – to serve them. The bullying that arose from this situation could be harsh and frightening.

Physical activities

Originally, the boys had many unsupervised afternoons and often caused problems in local areas as they trespassed on local landowners' property, engaged in poaching and gambling and were generally out of the control of the masters/teachers. The authorities disapproved of many of the boys' activities, as they took place off school grounds, had no moral qualities and brought the school's reputation into disrepute. The boys participated in many types of physical activities such as 'mob' style games such as football, swimming, cross-country running, fighting, racket games and so on. However, team games would become their dominant recreational activity for a number of reasons, not least because the schools were under pressure from the government to control the behaviour of the boys. A government report in 1864, the Clarendon Commission, recognised the educational value of team games.

> **REMEMBER!**
>
> It is important to understand who the schools were catered for, their characteristics and overall purpose. The section on the development of football (below), will give you some knowledge of the nineteenth-century public schools.

Technical development of games

The boys arriving from their villages would bring versions of mob games and country pursuits, such as coursing and fishing, with them and would participate regularly in their spare time. The mob games were often violent and disorderly; they had few rules as they were played by the working classes in society. The masters realised the potential of these games in channelling the boys' energies and in keeping them on the school grounds. The schools would only allow the mob versions to be played if they were given rules. Mob football, played by the working classes in their villages, was now to change forever:

- it was played regularly
- it was given rules
- boundaries were reduced
- the number of players was restricted
- the equipment and facilities became more sophisticated
- a division of labour was introduced with positional roles
- tactical and strategic play evolved
- leadership roles, in the form of captain and so they were highly respected

- a competition structure was devised, initially through the house system
- individual school rules gave way to nationally recognised rules (codification).

Many of the schools developed their own unique games, mostly as a result of the architectural features of their own schools and, for many, the traditions are retained as a testament to their heritage.

APPLY IT!

Account of the Eton wall game
It is not known exactly when the Eton wall game was first played, but the first recorded game was in 1766. The first of the big St Andrew's Day matches – between the Collegers and the Oppidans – was probably in 1844. The rules must obviously have been more or less agreed by then, but they were not actually printed and published until five years later.

The rules have been revised from time to time since 1849, but the game has remained essentially the same. The field of play is a fairly narrow strip, about five metres wide, running alongside a not quite straight brick wall, built in 1717, and about 110 metres from end to end. As in all forms of football, each side tries to get the ball down to the far end and then score. Players are not allowed to handle the ball, not allowed to let any part of their bodies except feet and hands touch the ground, not allowed to strike or hold their opponents, and there are also exceedingly strict 'offside' rules (no passing back and no playing in front); apart from that, almost anything goes.

A striking feature of the early organisation of the games in public schools was that the boys organised the activities themselves. This was called 'self-government' and gave the boys many organisational skills, which they would use later on in life. Games committees were set up by the boys. The hierarchical structure amongst the boys also allowed the prefects to organise the younger boys and could be seen as a form of **social control**. Initially, the masters had little to do with the organisation and it was only later that **Blues** would be recruited as valuable members of staff in helping the school achieve notable victories on the field of play. By this time, the games cult had taken over and success on the sports field would be used by headmasters in order to impress future parents. Fixtures were reported in

the press and the 'sports day' became a public relations exercise to the 'old boys', parents and governors. The headmasters began to support the increasing use of sport by employing blues from universities who could help coach the teams as well as providing facilities, time and funds, in fact very similar to a headteacher today.

KEY TERMS

Social control:
process whereby society seeks to ensure conformity to the dominant norms and values of that society

Blues:
term used at Oxford and Cambridge universities where sport performers were awarded a 'colour' for playing in the university team. In the nineteenth century, 'blues' often returned to their old schools to assist in the coaching of sporting activities

Moral qualities began to be assigned to team games in the nineteenth-century public schools. We have already seen how the government wanted the boys' activities to be more closely supervised and orderly. At the same time, in society, many changes were taking place, especially the civilising and disciplining of the working classes. The middle and upper classes were also needed to be seen to display higher moral qualities.

TASK 12.01

Make a list of moral qualities we believe are learned through team games.

APPLY IT!

Thomas Arnold, the head of Rugby School, only encouraged team games for the moral qualities he thought the boys could gain from participating in the activities. He did not revere games for their own sake, only for the purpose they could serve. He believed the moral qualities of teamwork, loyalty, bravery, courage, decision making and gentlemanly conduct could be acquired through team games. The individual was not as important as the team and winning should be sought in a sporting manner. Winning was to become more important later on and many people began to feel that the cult of athleticism had gone too far.

Physical endeavour	Activities	Moral integrity
• Appreciation of health and fitness	• Rugby	• Sportsmanship
• Toughen up an indulgent society	• Football	• Teamwork
• Competitive in a competitive society	• Cricket	• Honour/loyalty
• Combat tendency to over-study	• Racquets	• Leadership/response to leadership
		• The high status held by the elite games players

Table 12.01 Athleticism

Athleticism (see Table 12.01) was a movement that began in the public schools that was devoted to the combination of physical endeavour with moral integrity. This movement ran parallel to the Muscular Christianity movement, amateurism and Olympism. All these concepts embraced the physical and moral benefits of participation in rational sporting activities. They have been the legacy of British sport in which we play down the importance of winning and instead stress that how you take part is more important. These were very much the values of the middle and upper classes in the nineteenth century and reflected a lifestyle of ease and few monetary worries.

Athleticism	Muscular Christianity
• Manliness/physical robustness	• Working for a team/ loyalty to the cause
• Pursuit of physical endeavour/effort/ striving	• Conforming to the rules/ principle of fair play
• Appreciating the value of healthy exercise/fitness	• Playing honourably more important than winning
• Accepting the discipline of rule-regulated activity	• Use of 'God-given' abilities
• Moral integrity	• Performance dedicated to God

Table 12.02 Comparison of athleticism and Muscular Christianity

REMEMBER!

In the nineteenth century, the appreciation of a healthy lifestyle was more important than the homage to fitness that we pay today.

TASK 12.02

How would the nineteenth-century rational game of rugby football match the concept of athleticism?

Muscular Christianity (see Table 12.02) was a movement begun by Charles Kingsley in the nineteenth century. It was an evangelical movement combining the Christian and chivalric ideals of manliness. It included the belief that healthy bodies were needed alongside healthy minds in order to serve God. The muscular Christians only supported rational activities, i.e. those activities that were governed by rules and codes of behaviour.

EXAM TIP:

If you are asked to match the concept of athleticism to a specific activity, you need to say what the similarities are; for example, teamwork. The converse could be required, for example, how would gymnastics not reflect the values of athleticism?

What has been the legacy of the nineteenth-century public schools? We still believe today in teaching team games for their character-building qualities and believe learning how to be competitive is still an important part of modern life. Many schools adopt a competitive fixtures afternoon as well as house systems, and many have established their own traditions of excellence.

REMEMBER!

In the nineteenth century, the combination of the physical and moral was of paramount importance.

Public schools	Spread of athleticism into society	Universities
• Village games brought to schools	'Old boys' as they left school took on various positions as:	• A **melting pot** for the individual school rules
• Played regularly in free time	• officers in the military – spread games to the troops	• Rules codified
• Individual school rules linked to unique architectural features of the schools	• employers – spread games to their employees via factory teams and provision of time and facilities	• Technical developments made to sports
• House competitions	• clergy – spread games to their parishioners such as Sunday school teams	• Improved standards of performance
• Codified rules	• teachers to the pupils	• New activities developed
• Inter-school fixtures	• engineers/diplomats and so on across the British Empire	
• Blues as teachers		

Table 12.03 Effects of the public schools and universities on the development of sports

TAKE IT FURTHER

Research a well-known public school in relation to the type of activities that were popular in the nineteenth century.

KEY TERM

Melting pot:
a place where different peoples, styles, etc. are mixed together. The different public school versions of the games came together at the universities where a national interpretation of rules was produced

State school education

Dates	Developments in state schooling	Physical activities
Pre 1870	No formal state education – some public provision	
1870	Forster Education Act – foundations of state education laid	Drill training linked to Swedish gymnastics
1899–1902	Boer War	Military drill to be introduced via the Model Course
1902–04	War Office exercises	The Model Course
1904/1909/1919	**Centralised** government control of physical activity in state schools	Early Syllabuses of Physical Training
1933	Last centralised Syllabus of Physical Training	Content more varied
1944	Butler Education Act	More of a recreational focus for schools
1952	Influence of **child-centred** learning in primary schools	*Moving and Growing* – publication for primary schools
1988	Education Reform Act National Curriculum introduced	Wider range of activities to be taught with attainment levels

Table 12.04 Development of state school education and physical activities

Era	Terminology	Developments	Government control
late 20th century		1988 National Curriculum for Physical Education	growing centralisation
mid 20th century	Physical Education	planning the programme and moving and growing 1950's	decentralised
		later syllabuses of Physical Training 1919 and 1933	centralised
	Physical Training	early syllabuses of Physical Training 1904 and 1909	
early 20th century		Swedish gymnastics – competed with military drill via model course 1902–1904	
	Drill – therapeutic and military	fitness and health of working classes primary concern	
late 19th century		state school education following Forster Education Act 1870	

Table 12.05 Nineteenth to twentieth-century development of physical activities in state schools

KEY TERMS

Centralised:
to draw under central control – the government directs policy across a country to seek some uniformity

Child-centred:
basing a programme of study around a child's physical, cognitive, social and emotional needs

Prior to 1870, the working classes had no formal education other than that provided by some parishes. With the introduction of the Education Act 1870, it was soon to become compulsory for all children to attend a state school. This was met with mixed feelings – it was not immediately popular with the working classes as the children would no longer be working and they would lose vital income.

Aims

The purpose of the state schools was to provide an education for the working classes. There were various reasons for this. Many social reformers and philanthropists had worked hard to secure a better lifestyle for the working classes and keep young children away from unsafe factory work, and employers were increasingly needing a more disciplined and educated workforce. However, the working classes needed to acquire basic skills – the three Rs (reading, writing and arithmetic). The fourth R would be religious education, which was an important part of state education for many years. It was a way of instilling moral values, espoused by the middle classes, as church attendances were falling. The working classes were going to be the workers, obeying commands from their employers, therefore discipline and obedience were important values for them to learn rather than the leadership and decision-making skills that were being promoted in the public schools for the middle and upper classes.

Characteristics

Experiences for the working-class children in state schools were very different to those of the sons of the gentry in their public schools. Small, cramped spaces with no recreational facilities imposed restrictions on the activities they could offer. This was combined with the philosophy that the working classes at the latter end of the nineteenth century would have no need of recreation. These schools were built in local areas, were day schools and catered for both sexes. Most age groups were taught together. These schools were also to be free of charge, in stark contrast to the public schools.

Physical activities

Swedish gymnastics formed the basis of early state school physical activity. The Board of Education favoured the Swedish variety over the German style, which required gymnastic equipment. The Swedish system was based on **therapeutic** principles and on the scientific knowledge of the body at the time. The exercises were free standing and free flowing and taught in an instructional style.

Following the Boer War (1899–1902), the heavy losses suffered by Britain were blamed on Swedish gymnastics for not being rigorous enough – physically or mentally. There was a need to increase the health and fitness of the working classes and impose strict discipline.

Swedish gymnastics was therefore replaced by the Model Course in 1902, which were military drill-style exercises taken directly from the War Office. However, they took no account of the children's needs and were also taught by non-commissioned officers (NCOs). These were low-ranking officers who were unpopular with the teachers. The children were taught in a **command-obey style** and the exercises were mainly free standing, static, and the only equipment required were sticks or staves as dummy weapons in order to teach weapon familiarity.

KEY TERMS

Therapeutic:
a term relating to curative practices to maintain health. This was a popular term in the nineteenth century when linked to exercise and the poor health of the working classes

Command-obey style:
teaching style in which the teacher adopts an authoritarian manner, making all the decisions with no input from the group

TASK 12.03

Why would the command-obey style of teaching be considered suitable for state school children?

From Table 12.04, you will see that the Model Course only lasted two years (1902–04). This was because it had no educational focus, did not cater for children's needs and was questionable in its intention of improving the health and fitness of the children. The exercises were mainly static and dull.

Syllabuses of Physical Training

The Model Course was to be replaced by the Syllabuses of Physical Training in 1904, 1909, 1919 and 1933. They sought to stress the physical and educative effects of sporting activities. However, who was going to teach physical training? The non-commissioned officers were no longer being used in the schools and the basic class teacher had no experience in teaching physical training. The government therefore needed to produce a prescriptive syllabus that a teacher could follow quite easily. Also, radical changes to the content and teaching style would not occur overnight. Schools still had limited facilities and the working classes

EXAM TIP:

You will not need to know details of the syllabuses but be prepared to outline the main differences between the early syllabuses and the last one in 1933.

were still required to be obedient. Changes would happen gradually over a number of years. Therefore the style of teaching was still similar to drill but without the military content.

Last Syllabus, 1933

By now, there was more free movement, creativity and group work. Children were increasingly encouraged to use their imagination and there was a greater focus on the development of skills. There was growing interaction between the teachers and pupils and the influence of specialist teachers trained in the techniques of Rudolf Laban was being felt.

TASK 12.04

1. Give three differences between the lesson objectives of a physical training class in 1906 and a physical education lesson in 1953.
2. Give three differences between the content of a physical training class in 1906 and a physical education lesson in 1953.

Influence of the First and Second World Wars

The First World War made an impact with growing appreciation of the value of recreational activities in boosting the morale of the troops, and there was a widespread belief that the country should not become involved in any more wars.

The Second World War saw the destruction of some schools and the growing influence of female teachers as many male teachers enlisted. The apparatus that was brought into schools following the war was a direct result of the commando training that had taken place during the war. Troops needed to engage in a more mobile style of fighting and to be able to solve problems. The educational value of this type of activity was recognised and different styles of teaching were to emerge in order to develop children in a more positive way, with a recognition of their physical, mental, social and emotional needs. This was reflected in the publication *Moving and Growing*.

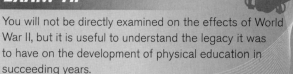

EXAM TIP:

You will not be directly examined on the effects of World War II, but it is useful to understand the legacy it was to have on the development of physical education in succeeding years.

The publication *Moving and Growing* in 1952 was produced by the Education Department as a guideline for primary schools. Primary school teachers were not trained specifically in physical education. The apparatus was brought in following the Second World War to encourage a problem-solving approach to physical activity. The term 'physical education' had now evolved, giving it a very different emphasis from the earlier term 'physical training'. Immediately, it suggests that there was now a belief that the mind needed to be involved as well as the body. This was combined with the movement approach from the Centres of Dance to develop:

- exploratory work
- problem-solving
- creativity
- skill-based work
- other activities such as dance, movement, swimming and national dances.

These developments reflected changes in educational thinking. There was now a more child-centred approach, with teachers being able to show initiative and autonomy. The teaching style had changed from a command-obey style to a more **heuristic**

KEY TERMS

Heuristic:
serves to discover or reach an understanding of something through exploratory work or trial and error. The problem has open-ended possibilities rather than pre-determined goals set by adults; therefore a sense of success is more likely to occur

Educational gymnastics:
children given a stimulus use gymnastic skills to answer a task according to their own ability

or guidance style of teaching whereby the children are given a stimulus and they respond through movement within their own capabilities. This was particularly true in **educational gymnastics** and dance. In the early 1980s, there was also a similar movement in the teaching of games, where children were encouraged to make up their own games, devise their own rules and so on.

TASK 12.05

Describe the changing roles of the child and the teacher from 1900 to 1950.

Recreative focus

For the last decades of the twentieth century radical changes were made to the physical activities the children at state schools experienced. The Butler Education Act 1944 required local authorities to provide for recreational sporting facilities within their schools. This was a very different philosophy to the one held at the beginning of the twentieth century, which believed the working classes had no need for recreation. The secondary school teacher was now fully trained and was therefore no longer dependent on following a syllabus drawn up centrally. Physical education teachers were to experience about 40 years of a **decentralised** system where they had their own autonomy and could choose their own physical education programme.

TASK 12.06

What are the advantages and disadvantages of a decentralised system of physical education? List two of each.

KEY TERMS

Decentralised:
the dispersal of power away from the centre towards outlying areas. It is a system of government that is organised into smaller units with more autonomy

Critical performer:
children should be encouraged to observe and be able to analyse physical activities in a knowledgeable way

Present-day physical education

Towards the end of the 1980s, the government of the time introduced the National Curriculum. This was because the government wanted:

- more control of education
- more teacher accountability
- national standards set for education
- a wider range of activities to be taught.

This represented a return to a centralised approach towards education. All state schools now follow set guidelines about set subjects to teach, which are inspected by OFSTED.

TASK 12.07

What are the advantages and disadvantages of a centralised approach towards education?

Physical education continues to be a compulsory subject that pupils must follow from the ages of five to sixteen. The government must consider physical education to be an important subject, so what are the aims of physical education? Through physical education, children should be able to:

- achieve physical competence and confidence
- perform in a range of activities
- achieve physical skilfulness
- gain knowledge of the body in action
- become a 'critical performer'
- learn competitiveness, creativity; face up to challenges
- learn how to plan, perform and evaluate
- discover their abilities, aptitudes and make choices for lifelong learning.

TASK 12.08

1. Consider the aims above against the Model Course (1902–04) and the early Syllabuses of Physical Training (1904, 1909).
2. Explain, using examples, how you have acquired these qualities through your physical education experiences. An example might be, 'I have learned to plan and perform a ten-bounce trampoline routine.'

Key concepts of the National Curriculum

- Therapeutic functions
  One of the main aims of the National Curriculum for physical education is to raise awareness in children of the need for a healthy lifestyle. Modern life tends to encourage children to be more sedentary; active play has been reduced in favour of the television and computer games. Increased safety concerns have led to children not walking to school as much as earlier generations and the fast food culture is leading to an increasing problem of obesity.

- Creativity
  Since the middle of the twentieth century, children have been required by educationalists to be more creative and imaginative in their physical education lessons. With the advent of the National Curriculum, this has been given even more importance as it is also assessed more formally.

- Recreational breadth
  During the twentieth century, the range of physical activities taught in schools has gradually increased. The National Curriculum has made this a more formal requirement in trying to combat the potential problem of teachers only teaching a few activities. Schools have developed more facilities, greater use has been made of community facilities and since the 1970s there has been an explicit policy of educating people to use their leisure time effectively. The general idea is that the more activities you experience, the more likely you are to find one you enjoy and carry on into later life.

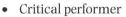

HOT LINKS

www.dfes.gov.uk

- Critical performer
  The National Curriculum aims to provide people with knowledge of other roles in sport other than just the performer. Such roles as officiating, coaching, spectating, leadership roles and so on encourage children to appreciate physical activities in many different ways.

Range of activities

The current aims of physical education can be taught through a range of physical activities. Too much concentration on one activity would not provide a balanced physical development. The National Curriculum classifications are:

- games (invasion, striking and fielding, net/wall)
- athletic activities
- swimming
- gymnastics
- dance
- outdoor and adventurous activities.

What do we mean by a broad and balanced physical education curriculum? A school cannot possibly offer every sport available but there should be a balance of activities that are team and individual, competitive and non-competitive. The activities can be selected from different categories of sports (Table 12.06).

Invasion	Net/wall	Striking/fielding	Target	Movement
Football	Tennis	Cricket	Golf	Gymnastics
Netball	Badminton	Rounders	Bowls	Dance
Basketball	Table tennis	Softball		Trampolining
Hockey	Volleyball			Athletics
				Swimming

Table 12.06 Categories of sport

TAKE IT FURTHER

Fill in a table outlining the activities you have been taught as part of your physical education since the age of five. Discuss as a group the similarities and differences and whether you consider yourself to have received a balanced physical education.

Structure of the National Curriculum

There are four key stages with eight levels of attainment.

Primary school

- Key Stage 1 (5–7 years)
  Pupils are required to study three areas: gymnastics, games and dance. Pupils need to develop simple skills and eventually sequences of movement independently and then with a partner. Pupils should be taught about changes that occur to their bodies as they exercise and to recognise the short-term effects of exercise on the body.
- Key Stage 2 (7–11 years)
  Six areas could be studied: games, gymnastics, dance are compulsory: plus two others from athletic activities, outdoor and adventurous activities, and swimming and water safety. Pupils need to improve motor skills and coordination, develop more complex patterns of movement, sustain energetic activity and understand the effects of exercise.

The class teacher in the primary school is not usually a physical education specialist although specialist help is usually sought for swimming. In recent years, many national governing bodies are beginning to tap into the primary school as a result of lottery funding. Governing bodies, such as the All England Netball Association, have the money to send in coaches to initiate interest within the schools. Governing bodies need to highlight in their policies and plans how they intend to increase participation at the grass roots level of sport if they are to access extra lottery funding. These initiatives are often an option for schools, but, nevertheless, they do

increase the range of activities offered at school and raise the awareness of sport among young children. This is the stage when children are learning the fundamental motor skills they will require in more specific sporting situations and therefore it is vital that they receive the best teaching possible. The TOP programme, run by the Youth Sports Trust, and specialist Sports Colleges, with their school sport coordinators, are contributing to the experiences offered at primary schools.

APPLY IT!

Outline the variety of physical activity experiences available to primary school children today.

Secondary education

- Key Stage 3 (11–14 years)
  Games plus three other areas; one must be gymnastics or dance. Pupils need to refine motor skills, undertake more complex movements, learn rules and tactics and how to recover after activity.
- Key Stage 4 (14–16 years)
  Two out of the six areas need to be studied. Pupils should be prepared to plan, undertake and evaluate a safe health-promoting exercise programme and show understanding of principles involved.

APPLY IT!

Access the DCSF website (www.dfes.gov.uk) and make yourself aware of the general requirements for each key stage of the National Curriculum.

Assessment in physical education

Each key stage has an end of key stage description and eight levels of attainment. When writing a report, teachers need to record pupils' planning, performing and evaluation. The teacher needs to indicate whether the pupil is working beyond, at the level or towards the end of key stage description.

Everyone recognises the need for assessment but some teachers are concerned that the amount of assessment or testing can be overdone (Table 12.06).

Attainment targets are set for the four key stages where children are assessed on their knowledge, skills and understanding involved in the areas of activity experienced. The purpose of attainment targets is to set some general expectations of what children should be able to accomplish by the end of each stage.

Advantages of assessment	Disadvantages of assessment
• Clear objectives and goals to reach	• Too much time on testing and not participating
• Gives incentives/ rewards and motivation to improve	• Tests are mainly subjective
• Improves quality of teaching	• Not every child can achieve the highest levels
• Gives recognition to good teachers	• Can demotivate teachers and children due to unfair comparisons
	• Too much pressure – takes away the fun element

Table 12.07 Arguements for and against assessment

- Level 1
  Pupils copy, repeat and explore simple skills and actions with basic control and coordination. They start to link these skills and actions in ways that suit the activities. They describe and comment on their own and others' actions. They talk about how to exercise safely and how their bodies feel during an activity.

- Level 4
  Pupils link skills, techniques and ideas and apply them accurately and appropriately. Their performance shows precision, control and fluency, and that they understand tactics and composition. They compare and comment on skills, techniques and ideas used in their own and others' work, and use this understanding to improve their performance. They explain and apply basic safety principles in preparing for exercise. They describe what effects exercise has on their bodies and how it is valuable to their fitness and health.

- Level 8
  Pupils consistently distinguish and apply advanced skills, techniques and ideas, showing high standards of precision, control, fluency and originality. Drawing on what they know of the principles of advanced tactics or composition, they apply these principles with proficiency and flair in their own and others' work. They adapt it appropriately in response to changing circumstances and other performers. They evaluate their own and others' work, showing that they understand the impact of skills, strategy and tactics or composition, and fitness on the quality and effectiveness of performance. They plan ways in which their own and others' performance could be improved. They create action plans and ways of monitoring improvement. They use their knowledge of health and fitness to plan and evaluate their own and others' exercise and activity programme.

As well as the core curriculum lessons, children are also offered many other sporting experiences while at school.

'**Extra-curricular activities**' is the term given to the optional activities offered in schools during lunchtime and after school. They offer purely recreational experiences as well as competitive fixtures. Another term for this is '**school sport**' and this should be viewed differently to physical education, which refers to the compulsory core lessons. There is an overlap between them but their central focus is different. The hope is that physical education will provide the building blocks that the extra-curricular programmes can enhance and extend a child's interest and aptitude. One problem is that extra-curricular activities rely on the goodwill of teachers.

In the 1980s, there was a decline in the extra-curricular opportunities offered to children in the state school sector. Many factors affected the drop in competitive school sport such as:

- teacher strikes based on contractual hours reduced teachers' goodwill
- financial pressures of running fixtures
- the competing leisure and employment options of teenagers
- the anti-competitive lobby.

TASK 12.09

1. Consider activities that you have taken part in competitively and decide what benefits you have gained from them.
2. What problems can competitive sport produce for some people?

Current government policies
The 'age' issue

The fall in sports participation with age is worrying because individuals reduce their chances of maintaining health and agility and being able to live independently into their old age. Research shows that people who are exposed to a wide range of sporting activities in their youth are more likely to continue to participate throughout their lives – the 'sports literacy' effect. People who are in the older age groups in the 1990s were more likely to be 'sports literate' than those who were in the equivalent age groups in the 1970s.

There is a dramatic drop in participation once young people leave school. This drop is higher in the UK than in a number of other European countries. This drop in participation can be called 'the **post-school gap**' (see Table 12.08) and has concerned the government and sporting institutions for many decades.

There have been calls for more lifelong activities to be encouraged at schools, as these appear to be the activities that this age group are attracted to. Sustaining a broader choice at school is likely to support lifelong learning.

Reasons for the post-school gap	Solutions to the post-school gap
Physical education is no longer compulsory	Improve links between schools and clubs
Young adults have many competing leisure interests	Instil knowledge of the need for a healthy lifestyle
Facilities are no longer as accessible or free to use	Concessionary rates
Traditionally poor links between schools and clubs	Youth sections at clubs
Less leisure time as full-time work and increasing domestic responsibilities take hold	Promote recreational sports as well as the competitive element

Table 12.08 The post-school gap

KEY TERM

Post-school gap:
the drop in sport participation when young adults leave full time education

Lifelong learning is a government policy that aims to enable people to be occupied in activities that will enrich their lives, as well as that of the community, for a very long time. Activities such as golf, bowls, swimming and so on are sporting activities that people can continue with for the rest of their lives. Traditionally, the British physical education programme has consisted of a diet of team games, and yet research suggests these activities are not successful in retaining people's interest at a participation level as they get older. Is there a point to be made for encouraging other sporting activities in schools that people could continue with for longer? Since the 1970s, schools did begin to branch out and offer other activities, sometimes using community facilities in an attempt to foster in young people the opportunities available in their wider community.

If this youth section drops out of society the social consequences are costly. Sport is seen as one way of including them in positive activities, channelling their energies, making them less likely to resort to drugs, alcohol and so on. Sport can help them acquire new skills and help integrate them into wider society.

Schools have been challenging the idea of only teaching the traditional activities and with the help of national governing bodies they are trying to introduce different sports into their curriculum. Adaptations in equipment and the development of mini games have meant more activities are suitable to be taught in schools.

In the UK, we have traditionally kept physical education and school sport separate, believing them to serve different aims. There is a growing belief today that these two strands should be brought closer together and many initiatives are taking place to try to achieve this such as the Physical Education, School Sport and Club Links Strategy (PESSCLS) and Sports College status being given to some schools. Many of these initiatives begin at government level and are implemented by organisations such as Sport England, Youth Sports Trust and National Governing Bodies.

Sport England

Sport England has a Royal Charter, which means it should be free from political control but still accountable for its actions. It is the government-funded agency responsible for providing the strategic lead for sport in England in order to deliver the government's objectives. It is also a distributor of the Lottery Sports Fund. The Sport England mission is to make England an active and successful sporting nation.

Its role is to:

- be the strategic lead for sport in England
- make focused investments through partners
- provide advice, support and knowledge to partners and customers
- influence the decision makers and public opinion on sport.

Its objectives are to:

- start – increase participation in sport in order to improve the health of the nation, with a focus on priority groups
- stay – retain people in sport and active recreation through an effective network of clubs, sports facilities and coaches, volunteers and competitive opportunities
- succeed – achieve sporting success at every level
- ensure internal efficiency – that we operate and allocate our resources with maximum effectiveness.

These objectives are central to many of the sports policies currently operating in the UK among organisations such as schools, clubs, national governing bodies and their whole sport plans (WSP), the Youth Sports Trust with its TOPS programmes and the Physical Education, School Sport and Club Links Strategy (PESSCLS).

HOT LINKS

www.sportengland.org

Sports Colleges

Sports Colleges are part of the specialist schools programme run by the Department for Children Schools and Families. In September 2003, there were 228 designated Sports Colleges and by February 2008 the total exceeded 440. They will have an important role in helping to deliver the government's 'Plan for Sport' (Figure 12.01):

'They will become important hub sites for school and community sport, providing high-quality opportunities for all young people in their neighbourhood.'

Richard Caborn – Minister for Sport

School sport coordinators

By February 2008 there were 3200 school sport coordinators working across families of schools with 18,000 primary link teachers. Figure 12.08 illustrates the way a typical school sport coordinator (SSCo) partnership might work.

Fig 12.01 Ethos and key characteristics of Sports Colleges

APPLY IT!

Specialist Sports Colleges – a runaway success

'Putting sport into the curriculum'

The Youth Sport Trust, the national charity underwritten by government funding to implement school sports strategy, released its report in February 2008 on the impact of specialist secondary schools and special schools and academies. It was in September 1997 that the first 11 sports colleges came into existence. Just 10 years on and the figure is 448.

Specialist Sports Colleges	448
School Sport Partnerships (groups of six schools)	450
School Sports Coordinators	3,200
Competition managers (by Sept 2008)	225

The sports colleges have gone from strength to strength. For instance, 96 per cent (over 373,000) of pupils at sports colleges are meeting the government's target of taking part in 2 hours of high-quality PE and school sport per week compared to the national average of 86 per cent. This is an encouraging move in the right direction but some would argue that more hours on the curriculum are still needed.

There are 25 per cent of pupils actively involved in sports leadership and volunteering in the sports colleges compared to the national average of 14 per cent for all schools in 2007. This represents a 9 per cent rise in the last year alone.

Of the sports colleges surveyed, 33 per cent had at least one pupil who was an athlete performing at international level, and almost 00 per cent of sports colleges run an education, mentoring and support services programme to support their gifted and talented pupils. More than 38 per cent (one in three) of sports colleges also operate a sports performance academy on site.

It has also been shown in several studies that sports colleges develop improvements in pupil motivation, attendance, understanding, behaviour and concentration. There is strong evidence that they also have an influence on overall school improvement.

The Secretary of State for Children, Schools and Families comments that the Specialist Sports Colleges 'are leading the way in using sport as a way of engaging young people in wider education'.

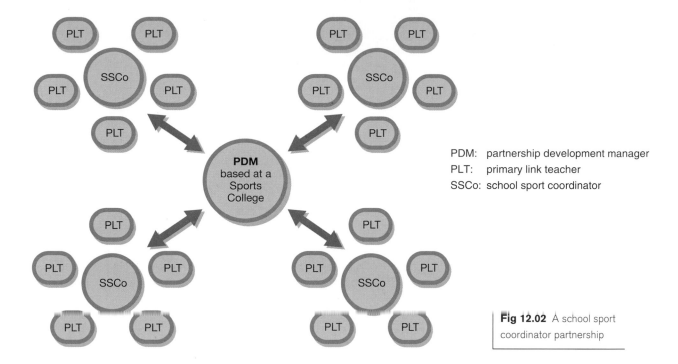

PDM: partnership development manager
PLT: primary link teacher
SSCo: school sport coordinator

Fig 12.02 A school sport coordinator partnership

The partnership around a Sports College starts with an average of four schools, ultimately growing to eight schools. Each partnership receives a grant of up to £270,000 a year. This helps pay for the full-time partnership development manager (PDM).

The primary link teacher (PLT) is located within each of the primary/specialist schools within the partnership with a remit to improve PE and school sport within the primary school. They have 12 days a year to act as link teachers.

The school sport coordinator partnership is based around families of schools with a team made up of a partnership development manager (PDM), SSCo and PLT. Their role is to enhance opportunities for young people to experience different sports, access high-quality coaching and engage in competition. They are released two days a week.

The partnership development manager is usually located within a Sports College and manages the development of the partnership and the links with other PE and sport organisations.

The overall aim of the partnership is to ensure children spend a minimum of two hours a week on high-quality PE and school sport. Six strategic objectives have been set:

- strategic planning – develop and implement a PE/sport strategy
- primary liaison – develop links particularly between Key Stages 2 and 3
- out of school hours – provide enhanced opportunities for all pupils
- school to community – increase participation in community sport
- coaching and leadership – provide opportunities in leadership, coaching and officiating for senior pupils, teachers and other adults
- raising standards – raise standards of pupil achievement.

TASK 12.10

What would be the advantages of attending a school that has been granted Sport College status?

The Physical Education, School Sport and Club Links Strategy (PESSCLS)

This is a current government policy aiming for 'high-quality physical education and sport'. Above all, it demonstrates the increasing trend towards developing strong links between schools and local clubs (Table 12.09). It is part of the school sport

Opportunities	Description
FA Charter Standard Schools Programme	Involves primary, middle, secondary and special schools, independent and state, required as part of the criteria for all schools to form a partnership with a local charter standard club for boys and girls
FA Charter Standard Development Club	Requires clubs who have met the development criteria (minimum of five teams) to create a partnership with a local school or schools as part of their football development plan
FA Charter Standard Community Clubs	Requires clubs (minimum ten teams, male and female) to form schools to club links and appoint a voluntary schools liaison officer
FA TOP Sport Football Community Programme	Targets young people aged 7–11 who are less likely to be participating in football for their school due to more limited opportunities and helps them move onto Charter Standard Club
Active Sports Girls Football Programme	The Active Sports Programme is a fundamental part of the FA's strategy for the development of girls' football. The framework includes a school-to-club link scheme for 10–16 year-olds called 'Kick Start'
FA Spoonbility Community Programme	This is an educational programme designed as part of the FA TOP Sport Football Programme to assist young people with disabilities to participate in football

Table 12.09 The Football Association (FA) school-to-club links programme

coordinators partnership, and the overriding aim is to give all children in school the minimum of two hours high-quality sport and physical education a week.

The project has eight sub-delivery programmes (see Table 12.10) and is closely linked with a separate project to implement the recommendations of the Coaching Task Force.

What does the government think high-quality sport and physical education can contribute to individual children and society? The following points are summarised from the government's document 'Learning through Physical Education and Sport'.

Characteristics of high-quality physical education and sport:

- pupils who show a strong commitment to making PE and sport an important and valuable part of their lives
- know and understand what they are trying to achieve
- understand how PE and sport contribute to a healthy lifestyle
- have the confidence to get involved

- develop the necessary skills and be in control of their movements
- respond effectively to a range of different competitive, creative and challenging type activities, as individuals and in groups
- think clearly and make appropriate decisions
- show a desire to improve and achieve
- have the stamina, suppleness and strength to keep going
- enjoy physical education and school and community sport.

Why is the government so keen to promote high-quality physical education and sport?

HOT LINKS

www.thefa.com for the Football Association

TASK 12.11

Research another national governing body and its response to the government's strategy of developing school and club links.

Component	Description and aims
Specialist Sports Colleges	A specialist system is being created in which every secondary school has its own special ethos and works with others to spread best practice and raise standards
School sport partnerships	Families of schools that come together to enhance sporting opportunities for all. They are made up of one specialist Sports College, eight secondary schools and approximately 45 primary or specialist schools
Gifted and talented	Part of a wider strategy to improve gifted and talented education. Aims to improve quality of teaching, coaching and learning, and raise aspirations, which will improve performance, motivation and self-esteem. Young people with potential will be encouraged to join junior sports clubs and develop links between NGBs and school
QCA investigation	The Qualifications and Curriculum Authority is investigating the impact of 'high-quality sport and PE' on schools that have undertaken the project. Many schools have seen wider benefits to the school including better standards, better behaviour, positive attitudes and higher self-esteem
Step into Sport	Sport relies on 1.5 million volunteer officials, coaches, administrators and managers. Step into Sport encourages children and young people to lead and volunteer
Professional development	In order to deliver high-quality PE and sport, teachers and other professionals need training and to be able to draw on resources
Club links	To increase the proportion of children guided into affiliated clubs from the school sport coordinator partnerships
Swimming	It is a statutory requirement that 80 per cent of children should be able to swim 25 metres by the end of Key Stage 2

Table 12.10 The eight components of the PESSCLS

Active Sports programme

This is a scheme coordinated by Sport England based on four policy headings:

- active schools – forms the foundation
- active communities – looks at breaking down the barriers to participation and considers equity issues
- active sports – links participation to excellence such as participation in the Millennium Youth Games
- World Class England – operates four programmes of 'World Class Start', 'World Class Potential', 'World Class Performance' and 'World Class Events'.

They are meant to act as building blocks and are not necessarily linear, as shown in Figure 12.03. They also complement the participation pyramid of foundation, participation, performance and excellence (see Fig. 11.06). The majority of the funding will come from the National Lottery and there will be a strengthening of the regional set-up via local authorities. There will be a framework around all experiences available to potential participants such as the National Junior Sports Programme, Sportsmark and Coaching for Teachers.

Sportsmark and Activemark

These awards are given to schools, secondary schools and primary schools respectively, for showing good provision for sport and physical education. Sportsmark and Activemark are currently being revamped and a new Sports Partnership Mark is to be introduced because:

- the awards were developed some time ago when little other investment was being made into school sport. Today the kitemark has superseded these awards
- the government is now making investment into PE and school sport, and is delivering the national school sport strategy.

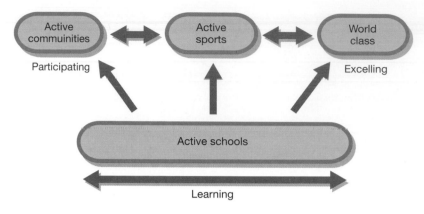

Fig 12.03 The Active Sports programme

National governing bodies (NGBs)

A national governing body is responsible for its own sport, overseeing competitions and ensuring internationally agreed rules are adhered to. The NGB then affiliates to the International Sport Federation (ISF). An example would be the FA and FIFA. In the past, NGBs in the UK have been very independent, but nowadays, as they become more dependent on lottery funding, they have to demonstrate that they are meeting some of the core objectives of the government.

There are approximately 300 governing bodies in the UK. Many are run by unpaid volunteers, though depending on the size of the organisation this has in many cases become the responsibility of paid administrators. They are largely autonomous from the government and are represented by the Central Council of Physical Recreation (CCPR).

Despite the considerable differences between the different governing bodies there are some common aims including:

- establish rules and regulations in accordance with the International Sport Federation (ISF)
- increase participation at the grass roots level
- talent identification and talent development
- organise competitions
- develop coaching awards and leadership schemes
- select teams for country or UK at international events

- liaise with relevant organisations such as the CCPR, Sport England, local clubs, British Olympic Association and International Sport Federations.

Challenges for national governing bodies

- New sports are attracting participants and providing competition for the older, more established sports.
- The decline in school sport has led to governing bodies having to consider how best to develop talent.
- There has been a blurring of amateur and professional sport.
- The need to compete internationally with countries who have developed systematic forms of training has made the governing bodies develop the coaching and structuring of competitions.
- Funding has become a key issue. National governing bodies receive money from their member clubs but elite sport requires huge sums of money. For this governing bodies have had to market themselves in the modern world, especially in trying to attract television coverage which in turn brings in sponsorship deals.
- Lottery funding often brings with it certain requirements such as meeting government targets for participation and developing talent.
- NGBs must produce Whole Sport Plans (WSP).

What are WSPs?

- A **whole sport plan (WSP)** is a plan for the whole of a sport from grass roots right through to the elite level, that identifies how it will achieve its vision and how it will contribute to Sport England's 'start, stay and succeed' objectives
- WSPs are Sport England's new way of directing funding and resources to NGBs.
- WSPs will identify the help and resources NGBs need to deliver their whole sport plans, e.g., via partners such as county sport partnerships and programmes (e.g. the Physical Education, School Sport and Club Links Strategy (**PESSCLS**)). They will provide the opportunity to measure how the NGBs are delivering their sports.

Key performance indicators

Seven key performance indicators (KPIs) have been agreed that reflect proposals and feedback from Sport England, UK Sport, NGBs and other partners. Sport England will use these high-level KPIs to measure the achievements delivered by the whole sport plans.

The seven KPIs that should be addressed in each plan are:

Start and stay
1. Participation – an increase in participation through NGB-driven activity
2. Clubs – the number of accredited clubs within the sport
3. Membership – the number of active members of clubs within the sport
4. Coaches – the number of qualified coaches and instructors delivering instruction in the sport
5. Volunteers – the number of active volunteers supporting the sport

Succeed
6. International success – performance by teams and/or individuals in significant international championships and world rankings
7. English athletes representing GB – the percentage of English athletes in GB teams in sports competing as GB.

What will WSPs achieve?

- In short, 'start, stay and succeed' (Sport England's objectives).
- The WSPs will allow Sport England to give focused investments to NGBs against the resources they need to achieve their objectives.
- Measurable results will give us an indication of how well NGBs are performing and whether Sport England is getting value for money from our investment.
- Whole sport plans will help create more links with regions and partners in all aspects of sport, benefiting us all through shared best practice.

APPLY IT!

The English Volleyball Association – Whole Sport Plan

'Putting Volleyball at the Heart of your Community'

In November 2003 Sport England brought all the national governing bodies (NGBs) of sport together to talk about a COMMON VISION FOR SPORT IN ENGLAND. This meeting mapped out what Sport England expected a 'Whole Sport Plan' to look like. The plan would address three main issues – how NGBs would encourage people to START, STAY and SUCCEED in sport.

Start – increase participation in sport in order to improve the health of the nation

Stay – retain people in sport and active recreation through an effective network of clubs, sports facilities, coaches, volunteers and competitive opportunities

Succeed – achieve sporting success at every level

To support the EVA, during this time, Sport England provided interim funding of £125,000. This funding was to carry out a number of pieces of work, a participation audit, a marketing audit and a modernisation review of the use of human resources and roles and responsibilities. The funding also provided the association with two new staff members, one to develop the Whole Sport Plan application and the other to start work on resources to support the Volleyball workforce, the volunteers.

The main objectives for the EVA Whole Sport Plan are:

- To increase participation in a thriving network of expanding clubs that provide enjoyment and access, irrespective of age or ability
- To develop a strong sustainable club structure and widen access

- To develop an extensive programme of volunteer recruitment, training and retention
- To develop an integrated programme of competition at all levels and their promotion
- To identify and work with key agencies and develop a network of strategic partnerships to deliver a quality Volleyball experience such as the County Sports Partnerships and School Sports Colleges
- To be flexible and respond to new ideas and opportunities
- To expand the staffing structure at the National Office. The main focus of the office-based staff will be to support the workforce – the volunteers.
- To develop a robust data collection and IT system that will allow the National Office to collect, collate, analyse, and share up-to-date information with the membership and other agencies.

The plan was agreed by Sport England in March 2005 and the annual grant received from Sport England has increased from £208,000 to £350,000 per year for the 4 years of the plan 2005/2009.

The implementation of the plan has just started, the roll out will be gradual, through the EVA strategies and the Commission plans which are being developed and reviewed. The biggest change, that will be obvious to the majority of membership, will be the new website, with online registration, shopping, better navigation, many new areas and downloads.

For more information about the EVA WSP
www.volleyballengland.org/clubs/index.php.

Sports Leaders UK (new operating name of the British Sports Trust)

Sports Leaders UK believes it needs to provide the opportunity and motivation for anyone to make a meaningful contribution to their local community. It aims to achieve this through the nationally recognised qualification of the Sports Leader Awards, whereby people can learn essential skills, such as working with and organising others, as well as motivational, communication and teamwork skills.

HOT LINKS

www.sportsleaders.org

Following a recent two-year £2.38 million government grant to encourage further participation in volunteering, particularly among young people, the British Sports Trust, organisers of the Sports Leader Awards Scheme, is now keen to further develop its partnerships with organisations and groups working with young people aged 14–19. The grant is part of the £7 million Step into Sport initiative, which will see the British Sports Trust, the Youth Sport Trust (YST) and Sport England teaming up to help train a new generation of volunteer coaches, mainly aged 14 to 19. The project aims to create around 60,000 young coaches and a further 8000 adult coaches and officials.

- The Junior Sports Leader Award: for 14- to 16-year-olds, this award is taught mainly in schools within the National Curriculum for physical education at Key Stage 4. The award develops a young person's skills in organising activities, planning, communicating and motivating.
- The Community Sports Leader Award: for those aged 16 years and over, this popular award is taught in schools, colleges, youth clubs, prisons, and sports and leisure centres nationwide.
- The Higher Sports Leader Award: builds on the skills gained through the Community Sports Leader Award to equip people to lead specific community groups such as older people, people with disabilities and primary school children. The award includes units in event management, first aid, sports development and obtaining a coaching award.
- Basic Expedition Leader Award: for those interested in the outdoors and builds the ability to organise safe expeditions and overnight camps.

Core values include:

- Developing leadership – teaching people the ability to organise activities, to lead, motivate and communicate with groups.
- Developing skills for life – helping people reach their true potential.
- Providing a stepping-stone to employment – offering a qualification to get started.
- Encouraging volunteering in communities – motivating others to organise safe sporting activities in their communities.
- Reducing youth crime – young people engaging in positive activities.
- Supporting more active, healthier communities – by providing sports leaders to organise a range of physical activity sessions.

Youth Sport Trust

HOT LINKS

www.youthsporttrust.org

This organisation is becoming a key player in all the government's strategies for grass roots sport. Its mission is to support the education and development of all young people through physical education and sport in order that they can experience and enjoy PE and sport through a quality introduction at their own level of development. The teaching, coaching and resources should be of the best quality possible and healthy competition should help develop a healthy lifestyle so everyone can achieve their potential. The YST is also involved in supporting and developing the specialist Sports Colleges and school sport coordinators initiatives.

The Youth Sport Trust plays a central role in supporting the Department for Children, Schools and Families (DCSF) and the Department for Culture, Media and Sport (DCMS) in the delivery of the national strategy for PE, School Sport and Club Links Strategy (PESSCL).

By 2008 the aim is to increase the percentage of school children who spend a minimum of two hours per week on high-quality PE and school sport within and beyond the curriculum to be 85 per cent. A further challenge came in December 2004 when the Prime Minister announced a new initiative to offer all children at least four hours of sport every week – at least two hours curriculum PE and an additional two to three hours beyond the school day.

PESSCL in action

The PESSCL strategy has key strands, each designed to maximise opportunities for young people to access high-quality PE and school sport.

As part of the strategy, the YST works in partnership with the DCSF and DCMS to support the development of Specialist Sports Colleges and School Sport Partnerships. In addition, support is provided for the following strands:

- Step into Sport – a programme which focuses on young people aged 14 to 19, giving them a chance to become involved in sports leadership and volunteering.
- Gifted and Talented – a programme designed to help elite young athletes realise their potential.
- The National Competition Framework – which aims to build a world-class system of competitive sport for young people.

TOP Programmes – providing a sporting pathway for all young people

The YST has developed a series of linked and progressive schemes – the TOP programmes, for those aged from 18 months to 18 years. Key features of the programme are:

- resource cards
- child-friendly equipment
- quality training for teachers and deliverers.

They encourage all young people, including those with disabilities, teenage girls and gifted and talented athletes to thrive, as well as providing ongoing support to teachers and others working with young children.

Other projects the YST is involved with are:

- inclusion of young disabled people
- encouraging more teenage girls to take part
- tackling social exclusion within primary schools through playground development
- supporting gifted and talented young sports people.

TAKE IT FURTHER

Discuss the suggestion that 'schools should become the nursery of sporting talent'.
NB: Remember to give both sides of the argument.

Programme	Description
TOP Tots (18 months to 3 years)	TOP Tots uses physical activity to develop communication and language techniques, coordination, cooperation and social skills.
TOP Start (3 to 5 years)	TOP Start is focused on developing basic movement and ball skills. It is designed to encourage the full integration of children with disabilities.
TOP Play (4 to 9 years)	TOP Play offers this age group the chance to develop their core physical and movement skills.
Primary TOP Programmes supported by Sainsbury's Active Kids (7 to 11 years)	As well as developing skills in a range of sports for young people, the Primary TOP programmes provide an enhanced set of resources and training for teachers.
TOP Link (14 to 16 years)	TOP Link encourages 14- to 16-year-old secondary school students to organise and manage sport or dance festivals in local primary schools.
TOP Sportsability (all age groups)	TOP Sportsability focuses on the integration of disabled and non-disabled young people through a variety of sporting challenges.

Table 12.11 TOP programmes for performers aged 18 months to 18 years

Definition:
The inculcation of skills and values through the the medium of physical activity

Historical developments and government involvement:
- 1870 - introduction of State Education (centralised)
- 1902-1904 -Model Course/ Drill (centralised)
- 1904-1933 - Syllabuses of PT (centralised)
- 1950-1952 -'Moving & Growing' and 'Planning the Programme' (decentralised)
- 1988 - National Curriculum

National Curriculum:
- 1988 Education Reform Acts
- Foundation and whole school subject
- Key stages with Programmes of study
- Attainment targets
- Centralised policy
- Wider range of activities
- Not just performance based, also planning and evaluation
- Experience of coaching and officiating

Objectives:
- Skill development
- Technical development
- Strategies and tactics
- Rules and their application
- Fitness and health
- Safety
- Decision making
- Preparation for active leisure

PHYSICAL EDUCATION

Advantages:
- Uniformity of experience
- Coordinated approach
- Guidance with teachers
- Wide range of experience for pupils

Disadvantages:
- No allowance for regional variations
- Can limit choice for teachers
- Traditions of schools lost
- Cost of facilities and resources greater

Values:
Self-worth
Fair play and sportsmanship
Teamwork
Appreciation of others

Closing the post-school gap:
- Club links with school
- Taster days
- Discounts
- Promote recreation and social use
- New activities
- Youth development officers
- Youth secions at clubs

Sport Development Continuum:
- Excellence – national standards and representation
- Performance – improving standard through coaching, competition and training Voluntary and free choice
- Participation – for fun, fitness and improvement in own time in the form of extracurricular activities
- Foundation – curriculum time, compulsory with mixed abilities developing a positive attitude and skills to become movement literate

Assessment and examinations:
- Advantages – clear aims and goals, student progression, teacher accountability, increases the status of the subject
- Disadvantages – loss of practical time, difficult to test objectively, excellence is only for a few, PE should be about release of energy and fun

Sport – raising the game:
- Sportsmark and Sportsmark Gold
- Sports college status
- Challenge funding
- National Junior Sports Programme
- Coaching for Teachers
- Encourage links between club and school

Fig. 12.04 Developments in physical education

ATHLETE PROFILE

Rochelle Plumb attended a local state school where equestrian activities were not part of the curriculum. However, her love for sport and her competitive instincts were enhanced. She was a keen netball player and she says, 'Netball has definitely been an advantage for being able to adapt to horseball, especially in terms of passing, shooting and learning to be a member of a team.' At Sixth Form College she was given the opportunity to study, and successfully completed, the Level 4 Equine Studies in Stable Management.

Her choice of Loughborough University was heavily influenced by the proximity to Nottingham Horseball Centre where she will be able to build on her initial successes and hopefully move on to the World Cup.

Exam**Café**
Relax, refresh, result!

 Refresh your memory

Revision checklist

Make sure you know the following:

▷ Education in the UK began with the nineteenth-century public schools, established to educate the future leaders of society

▷ Team games, in particular, were devised for their positive effect on the health of the boys as well as their moral and character-building qualities

▷ Games developed from their 'mob' origins, characterised by being violent with few rules and only played occasionally. Activities, such as mob football, developed technically, with written rules, tactical play and set boundaries, as well as morally through values such as sportsmanship and loyalty to one's team. Two terms encompassed these qualities:

- Athleticism, defined as 'physical endeavour with moral integrity'

- Muscular Christianity, the recognition by the church of the benefits of rational sport in improving the health and moral values of the population

▷ Within state schools, physical activity was treated very differently. These schools were established to educate the working classes who initially were not deemed worthy of recreational pursuits

Terminology:

▷ Drill, sometimes military in its content, was popular at the end of the nineteenth century and beginning of the twentieth century

▷ Physical Training became the focus from 1904–1933 whereby the emphasis was still on training the body to improve health, via the Syllabuses of Physical Training

▷ Physical Education emerged by the 1950s, whereby cognitive development was encouraged alongside the physical development of children. The programme *Moving & Growing* gave teachers guidelines on how to develop children by using a stimulus and guiding them to discover and problem solve within their capabilities. This was a child-centered approach.

- The National Curriculum was established in 1988. It has four key stages with levels of assessment suggesting some accountability of teachers and setting national standards of achievement

- Government control of education has changed over the last two centuries
  - 1900–1933   centralised
  - 1934–1987   decentralised
  - 1988 to present day   centralised

- Over the last two decades the number of government-initiated policies for physical education and school sport has risen, examples being Physical Education, School Sport and Club Links Strategy and specialist sports colleges

Revise as you go

1. What were the characteristics of sport in the nineteenth-century English public schools?

2. How did the technical development of games occur in the public schools?

3. What moral elements were developed through sporting activities? Use examples.

4. What has been the legacy of nineteenth-century public schools on current-day physical education programmes?

5. Name three characteristics of physical education in the early state schools.

6. What were the three main aims of the Model Course? Give three main aims of physical education today.

7. How many key stages are there in the National Curriculum?

8. What roles, other than as a performer, does the National Curriculum require pupils to perform?

9. What is meant by 'high-quality physical education?'

10. The British Sports Trust delivers four Sport Leader Awards. What are they? What are the core elements of the active sports programme run by Sport England?

11. Describe what is meant by a 'whole sport plan'.

12. What is incorporated within the PESSCLS programme?

13. Explain what the following term signifies: 'active schools'.

LEARNING OBJECTIVES:

By the end of this chapter you should be able to:

▶ understand the tradition of local authority provision for sport and physical recreation as a public service

▶ understand the central government policies of 'best value' and their impact on local authority provision for sport and physical activity

▶ understand the comparison of provision for sport and physical recreation between the public, private and voluntary sectors.

Introduction

For this specification, you need to focus on the **administration** of physical recreation and sport at the participation or **grass roots** level. It is the A2 specification that concentrates on high-performance sport. Refer back to Figure 11.06 for details of the participation pyramid.

For most of the twentieth century, there was very little legislation covering sport and this was some indication of the low priority given to sport by consecutive UK governments. This is because sport developed in the UK from the grass roots level upwards, rather than as part of a government's **policy**. However, there was a shift in government thinking in the latter decades of the twentieth century, showing the UK government beginning to take more notice of sport, its function within society and the benefits it could have for local communities and the nation as a whole.

The structures for administering and delivering sport in the UK are very complex, as they have evolved over a century and a half in an ad hoc fashion. In other countries, where sport developed later and where governments saw its potential, there tended to be more government control from an earlier stage and more uniformity in their structures and policies. We would call this a centralised system. In the UK, we have a more decentralised system, which is good for allowing regions to adapt policies suitable to their own needs but has led to a situation

KEY TERMS

Administration:
the involvement of government at local, regional, national and international levels. Administrative tasks include governing sport, making decisions and creating and distributing finances and resources

Grass roots:
the essential roots of learning sporting skills at the foundation and participation level of sport

Policy:
a course of action or administration recommended or adopted by a party or government. A policy is put in place as an action intending to achieve an aim

where many organisations involved in sport policy tend to have similar and sometimes competing roles. Recently, there has been a trend towards trying to simplify the bureaucracy and delineate the roles of various organisations.

Administration of physical/ active recreation in the UK

Broadly speaking, there are four main sectors responsible for the delivery of physical activity/ recreation:

- local government (public sector provision)
- voluntary sector (clubs and national governing bodies)
- private sector
- education (schools, further education (FE) and higher education (HE).

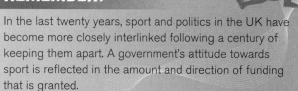

REMEMBER!

In the last twenty years, sport and politics in the UK have become more closely interlinked following a century of keeping them apart. A government's attitude towards sport is reflected in the amount and direction of funding that is granted.

EXAM TIP:

You will not be directly examined on the structure of the organisations but it is advisable to know how they interrelate in order to understand their policies and how they attempt to implement them.

Key organisations involved in sport in England (taken from Game Plan – DCMS, 2002)

National (government):

- *Department of Culture, Media and Sport* (DCMS)
- Other government departments such as DCSF – Department for Children, Schools and Families (responsible for funding physical education and school sport)

National (non-government):

- UK Sport
- UK Sports Institutes
- *Sport England*
- English Institute of Sport (EIS)
- *National governing bodies* (NGBs)
- National sports organisations including Youth Sports Trust (YST) and the British Sports Trust (now known as Sports Leaders UK)

Regional:

- Sport England's Regional Offices (directed by Sport England's central office)
- Regional cultural consortia (bring together the activities of the DCMS in the regions – sport as part of overall culture)
- Nine regional sports boards (RSB) bring together key regional sports stakeholders to provide a voice for sport in the region
- Government offices (each has a DCMS representative with sport included as part of DCMS policies)
- Regional Federations of Sport and Recreation bring together representatives of governing bodies and other national sports organisations at regional and county level
- County partnerships
- National governing bodies (NGBs) at regional and county level

Local:

- *Local authorities*
- NGBs at local level
- *Local sports councils*
- *Local sports clubs and associations*
- *Private health and fitness clubs*
- Further and higher education institutions/ schools (private and state).

EXAM TIP:

While it is important that you have an overall idea of the number and level of organisations involved in sport development, for the purpose of revision you need to focus on those organisations outlined in the learning objectives and italicised in the list of key organisations.

Points for consideration

- Central government, through the Department for Culture, Media and Sport (DCMS), is responsible for the overall development of sports policy in England
- There are four sports councils (Sport England, Sportscotland, the Sports Council for Wales and the Sports Council for Northern Ireland) in the UK, which form the link between government and sports organisations, and they distribute government and lottery funding. The four home countries each have their own remit to set different sport policies.
- National sports organisations are independent of government and represent different interest groups. The most notable for your purpose of study is the Youth Sports Trust.
- Each sport has at least one national governing body, which oversees rules and competitions for their own sport. The NGB also delivers funds with a focus on coaches, officials and administrators. There are over 300 governing bodies for the 112 sports recognised in the UK. Sometimes there are specific subsets within sports (such as women or specialities). This can lead to internal competition for funding and resources.
- Local authorities (public sector) are the biggest key providers for sport and recreation, yet it is not one of their statutory duties. Provision for sport and recreation is permissive rather than mandatory – that means they can choose what level of provision they provide. They work in partnership with the voluntary and private sectors providing opportunities through their sport development officers (SDO) and teams. Recently, sport has been used as a vehicle for delivering wider community development issues, such as health, employment and reduction in

crime. It reflects the government's policy of 'joined-up thinking'. In two-tier areas, the district council is responsible for sport, with the county responsible for education and overall strategic planning.
- Local sports clubs, run by volunteers and affiliated to their own national governing body, provide the most opportunities at participation levels, that is, the non-high performance levels of sport. It is estimated that currently there are some 110,000 voluntary sport clubs in the UK.

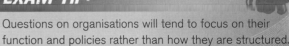

Funding for sport and physical activity

Three important points emerge:

- the local authorities (public sector) bear the brunt of providing for sport and physical activity
- actual public sector spending on sport and physical activity is often higher than quoted
- although very substantial, local authority expenditure has remained relatively stable with a large proportion going to indoor sports.

One fact is undeniable – lottery funding in the last decade has significantly increased the amount of **funding for sport**, combined with increases in exchequer/government funding and television rights. Perhaps an important point to note is that as lottery sales appear to be decreasing (they reached a peak in 1997/8), government funding may prove to be crucial in the next few years.

The voluntary sector holds up the grass roots delivery with a network of 110,000 community amateur sports clubs run by 1.5 million volunteers. The private sector has grown dramatically with almost 3 million people belonging to private fitness clubs, compared to 2.4 million members of public health and fitness centres. Could this provide an alternative to public provision in the future? If so, what about the people who clearly could not afford the high membership fees charged by private clubs?

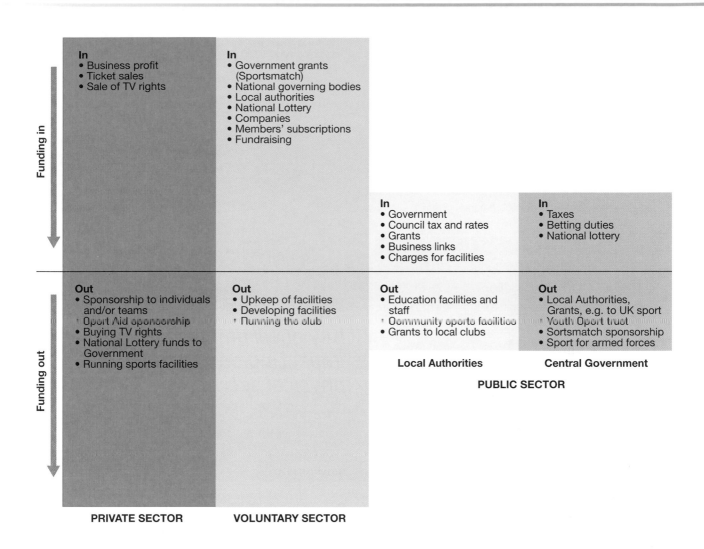

Funding in

In
• Business profit
• Ticket sales
• Sale of TV rights

In
• Government grants (Sportsmatch)
• National governing bodies
• Local authorities
• National Lottery
• Companies
• Members' subscriptions
• Fundraising

In
• Government
• Council tax and rates
• Grants
• Business links
• Charges for facilities

In
• Taxes
• Betting duties
• National lottery

Funding out

Out
• Sponsorship to individuals and/or teams
• Sport Aid sponsorship
• Buying TV rights
• National Lottery funds to Government
• Running sports facilities

Out
• Upkeep of facilities
• Developing facilities
• Running the club

Out
• Education facilities and staff
• Community sports facilities
• Grants to local clubs

Out
• Local Authorities, Grants, e.g. to UK sport
• Youth Sport trust
• Sortsmatch sponsorship
• Sport for armed forces

Local Authorities   **Central Government**

PUBLIC SECTOR

PRIVATE SECTOR   **VOLUNTARY SECTOR**

Fig 13.01 Three sectors fund sport in the UK

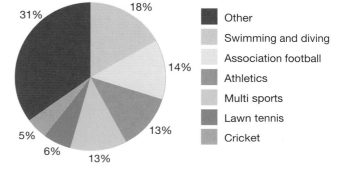

70% of lottery funding has gone to 6 activities since its inception (100 = £1.2bn)

- 31% Other
- 18% Swimming and diving
- 14% Association football
- 13% Athletics
- 13% Multi sports
- 6% Lawn tennis
- 5% Cricket

Legend:
- Other
- Swimming and diving
- Association football
- Athletics
- Multi sports
- Lawn tennis
- Cricket

Fig 13.02 How lottery funding is distributed among sports

Source: DCMS lottery database

KEY TERM

Funding for sport:
sum of money set aside for the purpose of sport; can be obtained from a variety of sources including individuals, commercial organisations such as companies, and national government

APPLY IT!

All England Netball Association
Development programmes
The AENA has a range of development programmes, specifically designed to encourage young people to take part in netball. In addition, a Club Action Planning Scheme has been set up to foster good practice in the development of players, coaches and umpires at all levels of the game. The scheme is directly linked to Sport England's own Clubmark.

Year	National	Community
1995 – 1996	£212,500	£158,544
1996 – 1997	£1,170,750	£2,043,230
1997 – 1998	£1,269,919	£4,077,801
1998 – 1999	£1,748,640	£7,844,923
1999 – 2000	£2,283,171	£7,026,495
2000 – 2001	£1,904,860	£2,132,809
2001 – 2002	£1,982,001	£4,605,322
2002 – 2003	£1,965,376	£2,858,816
2003 – 2004	£1,125,569	£84,482

Table 13.01 Previous funding

Note: National funding is a total of Exchequer funding and the World Class Programme. Community funding is a total of the following programmes: Community Capital, Safer Sports Grounds, Active Communities Development Fund, all Active Sports Programmes, Community Athletics Refurbishment Programme, Football Youth Development, School Sport Coordinators, Sport Action Zones and Awards for All.
The summary is by the financial year, according to the start date of the award period – an award may continue over a number of years.

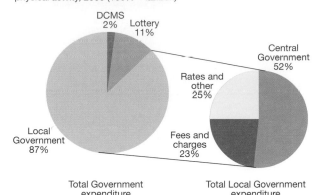

Estimated government and lottery expenditure on sport and physical activty, 2000 (100% = £2.2bn)

DCMS 2% Lottery 11%

Central Government 52%

Rates and other 25%

Local Government 87%

Fees and charges 23%

Total Government expenditure

Total Local Government expenditure

Fig. 13.03 Government and lottery expenditure on sport
Source: Leisure Industries Research Centre

Key government policies impacting on sport and physical activity

Since the last decade of the twentieth century, major policies regarding sport have been implemented by consecutive governments. Game Plan 2002 is the most recent.

Equity in sport: The government wants everybody to have the opportunity to participate in sporting activities, regardless of age, sex, race or disability. The basic principle of equity is being applied to all centrally funded schemes. Social inclusion for under-represented groups is an important part of community sport policy. The groups being prioritised by the government are: children in schools, people with disabilities or special needs, people from ethnic minority groups and women (see Chapter 14).

Facilities: Local authorities are the providers of sport and recreation facilities as they are best placed to make decisions about the direction of taxpayers' money. The government has recently introduced new protection to prevent the unnecessary sale of school playing fields. Local authorities must conduct an assessment of the playing fields and the needs of their communities before considering any application to sell a playing field. It is Sport England's policy to object to proposals by local authorities concerning any

- Target 1 – Enhance the take up of sporting opportunities by 5 to 16-year-olds so that the percentage of school children in England who spend a minimum of two hours each week on high-quality PE and school sport within and beyond the curriculum increases from 25 per cent in 2002 to 85 per cent by 2008, and to at least 75 per cent in each School Sport Partnership by 2008. (Joint target with Department for Children, Schools and Families and Department of Health).
- Target 2 – Halt the year-on-year increase in obesity among children under 11 by 2010, in the context of a broader strategy to tackle obesity in the population as a whole.
  (Joint target with Department for Children, Schools and Families and Department of Health).
- Target 3 – by 2008, increasing the number who participate in active sports at least 12 times a year by 3 per cent, and increasing the number who engage in at least 30 minutes of moderate intensity level sport, at least three times a week by 3 per cent.

planning applications unless there are exceptional circumstances.

Health: The government's overall objective is to increase participation levels of all people to ensure that society generally achieves the minimum levels of physical activity necessary for maintaining health. A key aim is to ensure young people continue to be active beyond the statutory school leaving age.

Local authorities

Although the responsibility to deliver sporting opportunities is a non-statutory requirement, the government is placing a stronger emphasis on the key role that culture, sport and tourism can play in improving people's quality of life, and how it has the potential to impact upon the wider social, economic and environmental agendas. For this reason, it states that investment in sport is a necessity for local authorities. The government has highlighted the need for local authorities (LAs), as the largest providers of sporting opportunities, to encourage people to lead healthy, active lifestyles, particularly young people. Any local authority improvement plan needs to

Write to your local sport development officer (SDO), asking for details of their aims for sporting and recreational provision. SDOs are usually based within the Leisure Services Department of the borough council.

address priorities for their area and **leisure services** will be subject to scrutiny through the government's '**best value**' process. The purpose of such a plan is to provide strategic direction for the provision of sport in the region. It also identifies key issues and sets a framework for managing performance.

Sports development

The sports development process that local authorities are involved in can be defined as enhancing '*opportunities for people of all ages, degrees of interest and levels of ability to take part, get better and excel in their chosen sport*' (Eady, 1993). Sports development is:

- proactive, planned and with achievable outcomes
- concerned with change, expansion and growth
- relevant to local needs
- enables others to provide opportunities
- partnership-based and raises awareness that equal opportunities require an enormous effort if sport opportunities for all are to be realised.

Leisure services:
includes sport, arts, museums, parks and recreation

Best value:
a key government policy (Local Government Act 1999) that requires local authorities and any other related organisations to consider the best value for money they can provide as well as considering the value of the experiences they offer

Regeneration:
the positive transformation of a place, whether residential, commercial or open space, that has previously displayed symptoms of physical, social and/or economic decline

The key organisations that have produced policy documents which will influence the planning process for local authorities are the government, through the Strategy Unit, the Department for Culture, Media and Sport, and Sport England. The key messages from these policies are:

- the important health benefits of active participation in sport
- the strong 'feel good' factor brought about by sporting success
- the importance of young people taking part in sport, in and out of school, and maintaining this participation
- the positive impact sport has on local communities and **regeneration** areas

Best value

'Best value' is a key government policy (Local Government Act 1999) that requires local authorities and any other related organisations to consider the best value for money they can provide as well as considering the value of the experiences they offer. Sport England has worked with local authorities to improve sport through facility development, raising standards of management, sports development initiatives, events and campaigns. Together they balance national objectives and priorities with those at local level. Best value put simply is about:

- finding out what people want and expect
- setting standards that match expectations
- delivering services to these standards
- measuring and demonstrating successful service delivery
- reviewing expectations, standards, delivery and success.

The document *The Value of Sport* (1999) poses the challenge – Why invest in sport? It demonstrates that sport can make a difference to people's lives and to their communities. It emphasises that for every pound spent on sport there are multiple returns in:

- improved health
- economic regeneration

- reduced crime
- improved employment opportunities.

Sport impacts on a whole range of corporate policy issues – local authorities need to highlight this in visible and tangible ways in order to secure funding:

·	sustainable communities	·	job creation
·	anti-poverty	·	environmental protection
·	equity and equality	·	crime prevention
·	community safety	·	healthy lifestyles
·	social and economic regeneration	·	social cohesion
·	inward investment	·	community development
·	lifelong learning		

'Regeneration is not simply about bricks and mortar. It is about the physical, social and economic well-being of an area; it is about the quality of life in our neighbourhoods.'
(Towns and cities: Partners in urban renewal)

What does value mean?

The word 'value' is used a lot in relation to sport, but what does it mean? The value of sport should not be underestimated in terms of the social, economic and environmental benefits to be gained by individuals, communities or even the country. Residents of any local area place a high level of expectation on the availability of a range of good quality, accessible and affordable sporting opportunities. The range of leisure activities and opportunities is increasingly seen as an important indicator of the quality of life in an area. A local population will often judge a council's performance by the leisure facilities they have provided. In particular, sport has the potential to:

- encourage those who feel excluded from society to access a wide range of services and facilities, creating a renewed sense of purpose, helping to bring people together and provide a common identity
- contribute to personal development through the enhancement of new skills, social interaction and well-being

- deter people from anti-social behaviour, allowing them to channel and challenge offending behaviour in a non-threatening environment
- improve health by keeping people physically active and promoting the health benefits associated with exercise
- create employment opportunities, which help to improve the economy
- advance young people's development by instilling self-belief and a sense of achievement.

Development plans

Some factors that influence sports development are:

- economic: the wealth of the community, i.e. the average socio-economic grade of the majority of the population
- cultural: e.g. the local ethnic mix and historical traditions
- geographical: e.g. is it a rural or urban population?
- political influences: the leanings of the elected council/historical investment in sports services

TAKE IT FURTHER

Imagine you work for the local authority and need to prepare a development plan for sport. What factors would you have to consider?

- facilities available: from the education and private sectors and so on
- aims/plans of other groups/work with existing partnerships.

Local provision of leisure

We have stated that local provision for leisure comes from three main areas:

- public (via the local authority)
- private (from businesses aiming to make a profit)
- voluntary (from the grass roots of local clubs).

They each have their different characteristics (see Tables 13.02 and 13.03), but a local community is dependent on all three contributing.

Public, e.g. local leisure centre	Private, e.g. private fitness centre	Voluntary, e.g. local netball club
• Business operations run by local authorities	• Privately owned registered companies	• Business operations owned by members
• Trading on set prices/charges according to a pre-set budget	• Trading on normal profit/loss/self-financed	• Possibly on trust/charity basis: trading on normal profit/loss/breakeven
• Managed by local authority employees	• Managed by owners and their employees	• Managed by members committees/may employ staff
• May involve subsidies as a matter of policy/council tax or equivalent	• Must operate and survive in open market/make a profit/compete	• Financed by members' fees, fundraising, sponsorship
	• Funds from membership fees	

Table 13.02 Characteristics of each sector

Public	Private	Voluntary
• Provides a service for the local community	• Aims to make a profit for the owner	• Provides for grass roots of sport
• Tends to be more affordable than the private sector	• Can cater for a more exclusive and wealthier clientele	• Tries to increase participation in their sport
• Social impact on health, employment and occupying population in positive activities		

Table 13.03 Objectives of each sector

TASK 13.01

Conduct a survey of your local area and try to determine the number and types of leisure facilities available for use by the local community. You might like to visit the Sport England website when researching your answer.

TASK 13.02

Conduct a survey of a private fitness centre and a public sector fitness centre and compare their service in terms of cost, quality of service and facilities.

Private provision of sporting and leisure facilities has increased in the last decade. In your local area you may well find examples of private gyms, golf clubs and so on. The overriding aim of these facilities is to make a profit while providing a service which people may feel cannot be matched by a public sector facility. Clearly this is not always the case! Members have to pay a membership fee and this is what makes it feel like an exclusive and elitist environment.

Some public sector facilities now also offer membership deals in order to attract customers.

The **voluntary sector** is made up of local sports clubs set up be people interested in the sport and wishing to provide opportunities for participation in their sport. Large variations exist in relation to the size of club and the level or standard that the sport may be performed at. Many of you will belong to such clubs.

TAKE IT FURTHER

Discuss among your peer group the type of clubs you belong to: their function; cost; administration.

ATHLETE PROFILE

Rochelle Plumb has moved up through the participation pyramid (see page 228) from the foundation level, where she was introduced to the basic sport skills via her parents, to the participation level where she joined the local pony club, and then on to the performance and excellence levels culminating in representing Britain in the European Cup.
The development of the sport at club level in Britain came about as a result of the establishment of the sport in France and interested individuals then setting it up in the UK. The English League is currently expanding and has over two hundred members. This comprises of a senior and junior league.
Without the existence of an international (International Horseball Federation) and national governing body (British Horseball Association, BHA) for the sport, Rochelle would not have had the opportunity to progress in horseball and pit herself against similarly talented individuals and teams.
The United Kingdom Coaching Certificate Levels 1 and 2 have been endorsed by the British Equestrian Federation and Rochelle has been successful in gaining Level 1.

Refresh your memory

Revision checklist

Make sure you know the following:

▷ The term 'public sector' refers to local authority provision of recreational and sporting activities for a local community. This is not a legal obligation but a service that is expected by the community and provides benefits to the individual and the local population, such as health and reductions in crime rates

▷ The term 'private sector' refers to the provision of recreational and sporting activities by an individual whose motive is primarily motivated by profit and aims to provide an exclusive service to its members

▷ The term 'voluntary sector' refers to those individuals whose passion for a particular recreational and sporting activity has motivated them to continue participating and encouraged others to experience the activity by organising the club and competitive experiences themselves

▷ Levels of participation in recreational and sporting activities can be illustrated by the participation pyramid:

- foundation (introduction to basic sport skills)

- participation (an individual chooses to participate further either through extra curricular activities at school or joining a local sports club)

- performance (where skills are refined and the quality of performance is important, usually at a high club or regional level)

- excellence (at the elite level of performance usually recognised to be at national and international level)

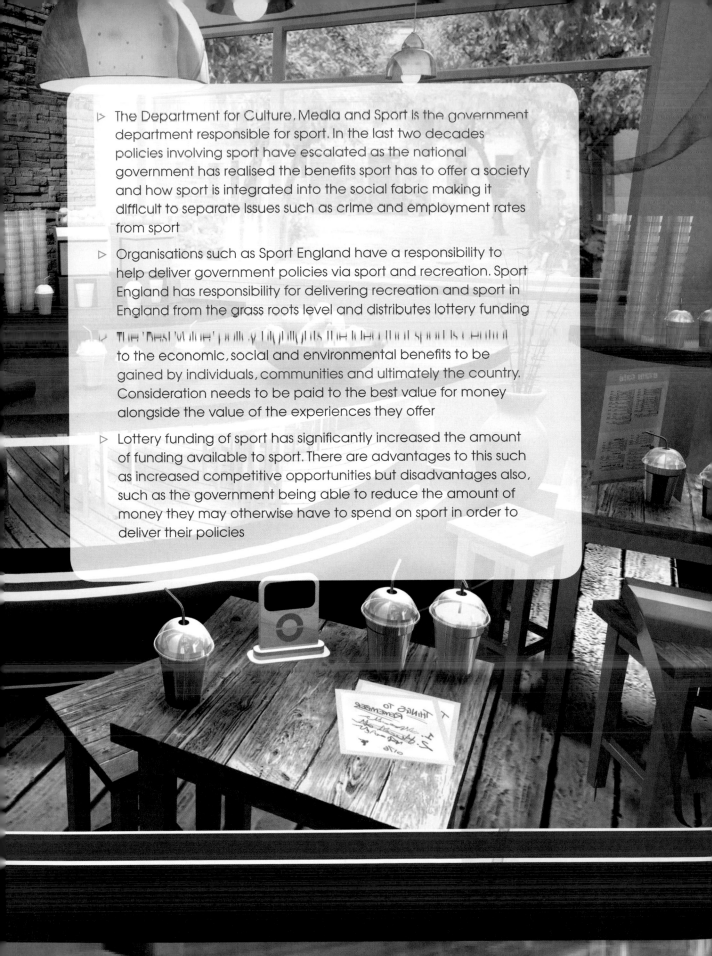

▷ The Department for Culture, Media and Sport is the government department responsible for sport. In the last two decades policies involving sport have escalated as the national government has realised the benefits sport has to offer a society and how sport is integrated into the social fabric making it difficult to separate issues such as crime and employment rates from sport

▷ Organisations such as Sport England have a responsibility to help deliver government policies via sport and recreation. Sport England has responsibility for delivering recreation and sport in England from the grass roots level and distributes lottery funding

▷ The 'Best Value' policy highlights the idea that sport is central to the economic, social and environmental benefits to be gained by individuals, communities and ultimately the country. Consideration needs to be paid to the best value for money alongside the value of the experiences they offer

▷ Lottery funding of sport has significantly increased the amount of funding available to sport. There are advantages to this such as increased competitive opportunities but disadvantages also, such as the government being able to reduce the amount of money they may otherwise have to spend on sport in order to deliver their policies

Revise as you go

1. The voluntary sector is comprised of local clubs set up by people interested in the sport and recreation.

2. What does DCMS stand for and what is its role in relation to sport?

3. What is meant by a decentralised administration and what are the advantages and disadvantages of this set-up?

4. What does 'centralised' mean?

5. Why should the UK government want to spend large sums of money on sport in local communities?

6. What is meant by the public sector?

7. What does 'non-statutory' mean in relation to a local authority's responsibility in delivering sport opportunities?

8. What objectives would a local borough council have in terms of leisure provision in its local area?

9. What advantages are there to a local authority developing a strategic plan for leisure provision?

10. What is the value of sport to local residents in a local community?

11. How could the make-up of a population affect leisure provision?

12. Give two factors that explain what is meant by the voluntary sector.

13. Give two key features of the private sector in relation to leisure provision.

14. State three points to explain 'best value'.

LEARNING OBJECTIVES:

By the end of this chapter you should be able to understand:

▶ the terms equal opportunity; discrimination; stereotyping; inclusiveness and prejudice

▶ the effectiveness of national governing body policies in achieving equal opportunities in active recreation and sport for a variety of social groups

▶ the barriers to participation and possible solutions to overcome them for the following target groups:
  • people with disabilities
  • low socio-economic social class
  • ethnic minority groups
  • gender.

Introduction

PHED 1 of the AS course studies factors that have influenced how certain people have been able to maximise their opportunities for participating in active recreation and how others have experienced many more restrictions on their participation. Although we can safely say that opportunities for the majority of the population have improved over the last century, there are still unacceptable levels of inequalities experienced by certain groups. This chapter is going to explore these issues further, focusing on participation levels in active recreation rather than high level sport.

In the government's mission for sport, *Game Plan*, figures have been produced under the title, 'Where are we now? The state of sport today.' It might be useful to begin with some facts and figures to appreciate the reality of the situation.

• The quality and quantity of participation in sport and physical activity in the UK is lower than it could be, and levels have not changed significantly over recent years.

• For sport, only 47 per cent of the UK population participate in sport more than 12 times a year, compared to 70 per cent in Sweden and almost 80 per cent in Finland.

• For physical activity, only 32 per cent of adults in England take 30 minutes of moderate exercise five times a week, compared to 57 per cent of Australians and 70 per cent of Finns.

• Young white males are most likely to take part in sport and physical activity, and the most disadvantaged groups least likely.

• Participation falls dramatically after leaving school and continues to drop with age.

• The more active in sport and physical activity you are at a young age, the more likely you are to continue to participate throughout your life.

• The levels of participation in the UK are lower than those in Scandinavia, but so is the regularity and quality of that participation.

If we need to increase participation in sport and active recreation across the population, then there is a particular need to target specific groups who are below the national average. These can be called focus, priority or target groups.

It would appear that the group with the highest participation rates come from the white, male, middle-class section of society. This would also be the group we would call the 'dominant group', as they have the most access to employment, decision making and control of the major social institutions such as the law, education, media and so on. This group traditionally could be seen to protect its own position, for example by establishing laws or membership clauses, or having in place discriminatory practices that will limit the opportunities of other groups, usually based on **prejudicial** attitudes.

KEY TERMS

Prejudice:
an opinion or attitude, especially an unfavourable one, based on inadequate facts, often displaying intolerance or dislike of people due to race, religion, gender or culture. If a prejudicial attitude was acted upon it would be called discrimination

Stereotype:
a standardised image or concept shared by members of a social group whereby certain behaviour traits are associated with particular types of individuals or groups. This usually involves negative images/expectations relating to gender, race and people with disabilities

It would appear that groups with the lowest participation rates in active recreation are from the same groups that have been identified as most likely to suffer from social exclusion:

- ethnic background
- females
- disability
- demographics/rural areas/inner cities.
- youth
- age
- low income

The question could be posed – so what? If people prefer not to participate, why should the government and national sport organisations feel any sense of obligation to change their minds and habits?

As a society, there is a definite belief that sport is good for people: it provides enjoyment, contributes

to health. As part of a wider social policy, it can help reduce crime levels and increase educational attainment; it can create a sense of pride in community and country.

It is more likely that some sections of the population do not participate as much as others due to fewer opportunities and traditional **discrimination**, and therefore have not had the same opportunities to make informed decisions as to whether they would like to participate in active recreation or not.

KEY TERMS

Discrimination:
to make a distinction: to give unfair treatment especially because of prejudice

Social exclusion:
a shorthand term for what can happen when people or areas suffer from a combination of linked problems such as unemployment, poor skills, low incomes, unfair discrimination, poor housing, high crime, bad health and family breakdown

Social mobility:
movement of individuals up or down the social class structure

Social exclusion

The **Social Exclusion** Unit was set up by the government in 1997, with a broad remit to 'reduce social exclusion by finding joined-up solutions to interconnected problems'. The government has invested funds in trying to tackle the economic causes of exclusion and attempting to improve people's lifestyles by creating opportunities for them to develop their education and skills.

The term 'joined-up solutions' refers to the government's belief in recent decades that many social policies interrelate and affect each other. It involves developing working partnerships among different organisations. In previous years, there may have been a policy for health and a separate one for employment and reducing crime. Nowadays, the government recognises that these social issues often interrelate and separate policies are a false economy.

Cost to the individual	Cost to the taxpayer	Cost to the economy
• Individuals not realising their educational potential	• Expenditure in 2001–02 totalled £30.7 billion in income support, housing benefit and so on	• A lack of skilled workers, resulting in a productivity gap between the UK and its international competitors
• Higher risk of unemployment	• Cost of school exclusions estimated at £406 million	• Lack of customers – low income reduces the nation's spending power
• Poorer physical health	• A report calculated that if one in ten young offenders received effective early intervention, the annual saving would be in excess of £100 million	
• Crime and fear of crime affect the most deprived communities		

Table 14.01 Cost of social exclusion

Group excluded	Youth			Poor/ unemployed	Women	Older people	Ethnic minority	People (disabilities/ learning difficulties)
Constraint/exclusion factor	Child	Young people	Young (learning difficulties)					
Structural factors Poor physical/social environment	X	X	XX	XX	X	X	XX	X
Poor facilities/community capacity	X	X	XX	XX	X	X	X	XX
Poor support network	X	X	XX	XX	X	X	X	XX
Poor transport	XX	XX	XX	XX	XX	XX	X	XX
Managers' policies and attitudes	X	X	XX	XX	X	X	XX	XX
Labelling by society	X	X	XXX	X	X	X	XX	XX
Lack of time structure	X	X	XX	XX		X		X
Lack of income	X	X	XX	XXX	X	XX	X	XX
Lack of skills/personal and social capital	X	X	XXX	XXX	X	X	XX	XX
Fears for safety	XX	XX	XX	XX	XXX	XXXX	XX	XX
Powerlessness	XX	XX	XXX	XX	XX	XX	XXXX	XX
Poor self/body image	X	X	XX	XX	X	X	XX	XX

Note: The number of x signs shows the severity of particular constraints for particular groups

Table 14.02 Constraints and exclusion in sport and leisure

Source: DCMS

Social mobility

When subordinate groups are discriminated against, their opportunities for **social mobility** and participation in a variety of sports can be limited.

Social mobility has increased throughout the twentieth century. The middle class expanded while the working class declined in size, reflecting structural changes in society and the economy as a result of economic growth. However, in recent decades, the improved opportunities enjoyed by greater numbers of children have begun to slow down and have halted in some cases. This is due to the contraction in skilled manual work in the early 1980s and a slower growth in the number of professional and managerial jobs.

Any sporting policies will need to take account of these trends in order to tackle social exclusion. The National Strategy for Neighbourhood Renewal is an important part of the government's plan to build socially inclusive communities. All local authorities

have a remit to lower 'worklessness' and crime, improve skills, health and housing, and to narrow the gap that exists between the most deprived areas and the rest of the country.

Socio-economic groups

Not surprisingly, the participation rate in sport varies across social groups, as Figure 14.01 shows. Furthermore, the link between gender and social class appears to be increasingly significant when looking at participation rates.

Generally, individuals from the lower socio-economic groups have poorer health and mortality rates than those in the other groups, therefore the health benefits of participation in physical activity are particularly important for this group. This group is very likely to suffer from social exclusion as they have less power, less opportunities for decision making, less disposable income and so on. This can affect what they can afford to do and the quality of life they can expect. The 'working-class **subculture**' can also affect how this group may adapt to what can be middle-class sporting environments. The values that are transferred through the generations can still alienate some people who have been brought up with different values to that of the dominant culture. Feelings of inadequacy, low self-esteem, isolation from major social institutions are all factors that make this group difficult to mobilise.

TASK 14.01

1. How could participating in sport improve the quality of life for an individual who suffers from social exclusion?
2. Why should a government be concerned about a number of citizens being socially excluded?

Attitudes	Access	Programme
• Stereotyping	• Facilities	• Range of activities
• Lack of confidence	• Times of opening	• Inappropriate for ability
• Lack of self-motivation	• Transport	• Inappropriate for delivery style
• Image of sport	• Lack of information	• Quality of provision
• Family/personal relationships	• Official procedures	• Too competitive
• Cultural norms	• Fees	• Not enough fun
• Lack of interest	• Lack of childcare facilities	
• Too competitive	• Lifestyle	
	• Health	
	• Education	
	• Socio-economic status	
	• Other competing activities	

Table 14.03 General barriers to participation in sport

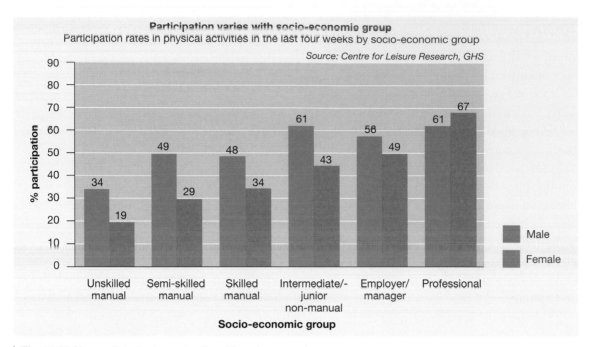

Fig. 14.01 How participation in sport varies with socio-economic group

KEY TERMS

Gender:
used by sociologists to describe the cultural and social attributes of men and womn, which are manifested in masculinity and femininity

Subculture:
an identifiable group within society whose members share common values and have similar behaviour patterns

Ethnic groups:
people who have racial, religious, linguistic and/or certain other traits in common. Where a group forms a minority in a population, the term 'ethnic minority group' is used

REMEMBER!

For the purpose of this specification, ethnic minority groups refer to those people residing in the UK. Many students mistakenly refer to these groups as if they still lived in another country.

Ethnic minority groups

'Sports Participation and Ethnicity in England, 1999–2000' was a survey by Sport England to better understand the extent and causes of inequity in sporting opportunities for certain groups in the population and ways to overcome them. The findings have particular relevance to the active communities programme, which aims to extend sporting opportunities for all.

Defining ethnicity

Defining ethnicity is fraught with problems, as it is almost impossible to identify a whole group and presume they will have similar experiences. This is particularly so where religion, culture, values, language, generation, age, **gender**, length of residency in a country and nationality all play a part in creating considerable diversity of experiences, expectations, way of life and behaviours. However, for the purposes of a national quantitative survey, people have been classified into these 'broad **ethnic groups**':

• White	• Pakistani
• Black Caribbean	• Bangladeshi
• Black African	• Chinese
• Black other	• None of these (17 per cent) became 'Other'
• Indian	

The findings of the survey showed that for ethnic minority groups, the overall participation rate in sport is 40 per cent compared to 46 per cent national average. Only the 'Black other' group (60 per cent) has participation rates higher than the population as a whole. Black Caribbean, Chinese, Pakistani and Bangladeshi were lower than the national average. These figures were similar for women from the same groups. However, the gap between men's and women's participation is greater among ethnic minority groups than it is in the population as a whole (see Fig. 14.02).

Reasons for low participation rates

Reasons given for constraining factors in participation are similar to the population as a whole, for example work/study demands, home and family responsibilities, lack of money, laziness and so on, but some also quoted negative experiences in sport due to ethnicity. These instances were higher for the 'Black other' men and less relevant for the Chinese section of the population. Indian (31 per cent), Pakistani (21 per cent) and Bangladeshi (19 per cent) women in particular have a lower involvement in sport than the national female average of 39 per cent.

Sporting patterns are also different for different ethnic groups, for example participation rates in football among all ethnic groups is higher than the national average, whereas for swimming it is lower.

Within a multicultural population, sport needs to be sensitive to the barriers that impact on these groups and provide types of activities that appeal to them within environments that are accessible and welcoming. So what activities are popular with ethnic minority groups?

Ethnic preferences

There are a number of instances where sports have relatively high levels of participation among certain ethnic minority groups. These include:

- weight training among Black males
- running/jogging among Black other males and Black Africans, which is higher than the general male population
- badminton by Chinese men
- cricket by Pakistani, Black other and Indian
- basketball among Black Caribbean and Black African.

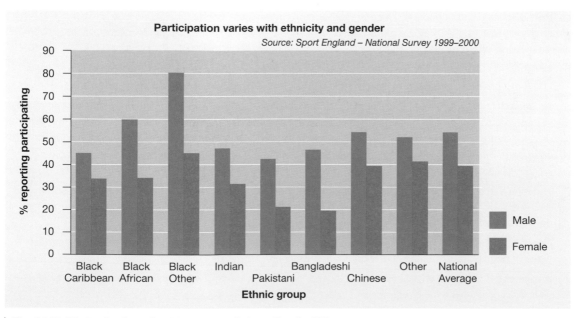

Fig. 14.02 Ethnic minority participation is generally lower than the UK average

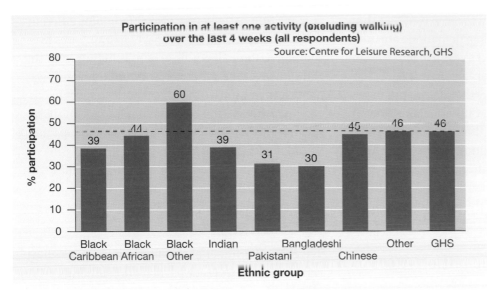

Fig. 14.03 Participation in sport by ethnic groups

An important result of the survey is the complexity of the whole issue. There is considerable variation in the levels of participation between different ethnic groups, between men and women and between different sports. The results also challenge the stereotypical view that suggests that low levels of participation in sport by certain groups are more a reflection of culture and choice rather than other constraints such as provision, affordability and access.

TASK 14.02

Why do you think cricket is popular among the Pakistani and Indian communities?

HOT LINKS

www.sportdevelopment.org.uk/html/ethnicity2000.html

Term	Definition
Stacking	Refers to the disproportionate concentration of ethnic minorities in certain positions in a sports team, based on the stereotype that they are more valued for their physical skills than for their decision-making qualities. An example would be placing Black players in outfield positions in baseball
Centrality	According to Grusky's theory of centrality, this restricts ethnic minority groups from more central positions, which are based on coordinative tasks, requiring decision making and social interaction
Labelling	An approach that focuses on the way in which agents of social control, such as teachers, attach stigmatising stereotypes to particular groups of people. These can then have a self-fulfilling prophecy. An example can be a teacher having lower educational expectations of Black children compared to White children, or girls compared to boys in the field of sport. Children take these expectations on board and behave accordingly – the implication being that the prediction was always true
Channelling	The idea that teachers and coaches will channel children from ethnic minority groups into certain sports that they feel they are most likely to succeed in. It can also involve them channelling them into sport rather than down the academic route
Attitudes/ prejudice	Opinion, bias or judgement formed without due consideration of facts or arguments. For example, certain types of people are sometimes not made to feel welcome in a sports centre
Racist attacks	If someone is attacked, physically or verbally, and feels they were targeted because of the colour of their skin, this constitutes a racist attack

Table 14.04 Examples of racism in sport

The issue of racial discrimination was touched on and although the results were variable, at its highest, as many as one in five said that they had had a negative experience in sport related to their ethnicity. This should be a concern of policy makers.

Solutions to the lower participation rates from ethnic minority groups

- Sport policies that are sensitive to and respectful of other cultures – this can mean providing single-sex sessions for Muslim women, changing facilities and physical educational programmes in schools.
- Use of policy planning, race relations advisers and customer care.
- Information should be available about sport provision in a local area.
- Clubs should be supported but integration not forced.
- People from ethnic minorities from the local communities to be trained as sport leaders and sport development officers.
- Greater media coverage to raise awareness of ethnic minority sports and role models.
- Campaigns to eliminate racism.

Kick it Out is football's anti-racism campaign. The brand name of the campaign – *Let's Kick Racism out of Football* – was established by the Commission for Racial Equality and the Professional Footballers' Association (PFA) in 1993. Kick it Out works throughout the football, educational and community sectors to challenge racism and work for positive change. The campaign is supported and funded by the game's governing bodies including the players' union (the PFA), the FA Premier League, the Football Association and the Football Foundation.

HOT LINKS

www.kickitout.org

Internationally, Kick it Out plays a leading role in the Football Against Racism in Europe (FARE) network and has been cited as an example of good practice by the European governing body UEFA, the world governing body FIFA, the Council of Europe, the European Commission, European parliamentarians and the British Council.

Female participation

Statistics show that for most sport and physical activity, participation is higher amongst men. Swimming and keep fit/yoga are notable exceptions.

Changing trends in female participation can be difficult to track fully due to a lack of up-to-date comparable data. Using the information contained in the 1996 General Household Survey, however, it appears that participation rates are relatively static, with modest increases in some activities (see Fig. 14.04).

Those are the statistics – we now need to account for them.

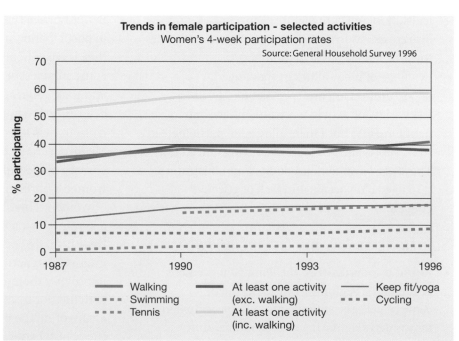

Fig. 14.04 Trends in female participation

Reasons for lower female participation rates in active recreation

- Domestic role: women still bear the greater burden of domestic work, reducing the time they have for leisure.
- Social stereotyping: society is still less positive about female sport participation in comparison to males. This is because the characteristics associated with sport tend to match society's view of masculinity rather than **femininity**. Examples are being competitive, assertive, achievement orientated and so on.
- Sport traditionally the preserve of males: sport was established and controlled by men and this led to situations where women were actively discouraged from participating in sport.
- Less media coverage: there has traditionally been less media coverage of female sport. This does not raise the profile of women's sport and there are fewer role models for women to aspire to.
- Traditionally less money and power: women generally earn less money than men and occupy fewer positions of power in society and in the workplace, and consequently in sporting institutions where decisions are made.
- **Sexism**: discrimination can be overt, as in legislation and club membership clauses, and also covert, as in society's more negative attitudes towards female participation.
- Evidence of inequalities in sporting opportunities: unequal provision of facilities, less variety of activities – women have had to fight long and hard to be allowed to participate in some sports such as football, boxing and rugby. There are fewer female coaches/administrators, restricted club access and lack of effective childcare.

Solutions to low participation rates

- **Equal opportunities**: the feminist movement began at the beginning of the twentieth century with the suffragettes and the campaign for women's rights. It gathered momentum when women won the right to vote in 1917.

KEY TERMS

Femininity:
characteristics associated with being a woman

Sexism:
the belief that one sex is inferior to the other, and is most often directed towards women

Equal opportunity:
the principle and practice of providing all people with the same chance to participate, in this context, in recreational and sporting activities

Women have fought for equal rights since this time. In the present day, organisations, such as national governing bodies, must create and deliver equal opportunity policies following the Sex Discrimination Act 1975 and in line with government policies. The Women's Sport Foundation has been established to raise the awareness of inequalities in female sporting provision and provides guidelines for organisations involving female sport participation.

- More facilities for women: facilities should be made accessible to women offering women-only sessions where appropriate and combined with more effective childcare facilities.
- Better links between schools and clubs: the drop in participation amongst young women when they leave education is dramatic. This has serious consequences for later participation in sport and their general health. The government is determined to improve links between schools and clubs to help lower this 'post-school gap'.
- Media coverage: more and better quality media coverage of female sport should help to widen women's horizons and promote positive images of women. This should create positive role models for women to aspire to.
- Health-related activities: women are very interested in activities that are geared towards improving their general health and conditioning activities for toning the body. Women should be aware of all the possibilities in their area and the health benefits of sport participation should be promoted.

Sex means the biological aspect of a person, either female or male. Gender roles refer to what different societies and cultures attribute as appropriate behaviour for that sex. Gender roles therefore carry social expectations that can be very difficult to fight against. These can vary from culture to culture and can change over time within a culture. An example would be the contrast between the ideal image of a woman in the UK and the old Eastern bloc ideal image of a woman. In the latter, they appreciated the strong woman who could do heavy manual work, and this is also emphasised in the popularity of female shot putters. In this country, we have revered the dainty and delicate female, one who is physically slim and emotionally vulnerable. In modern-day sport, this means that sports such as tennis, gymnastics and so on receive more social acceptance than sports requiring more 'masculine' orientated features.

TASK 14.03

1. Make a list of the characteristics you associate with the terms 'femininity' and 'masculinity'.
2. Now list the words you feel demonstrate the ability to succeed in sport.
3. Which gender role is the sporting success model most similar to?

Historically, sport was always seen as a male preserve as they developed and controlled sports while women have had to fight hard to achieve similar opportunities. This immediately suggests that men discriminated against women and there are many instances of this, one notable example being the banning of female football by the Football Association in 1921. Many reasons given for these limitations or restrictions have been based on medical grounds and the idealistic image of femininity, which was strengthened in the nineteenth century. This led to many stereotypes and myths developing, particularly regarding the medical problems women would encounter if they participated in sport too strenuously. These myths existed well into the twentieth century.

In the present day, opportunities for women to participate in sport have increased greatly due to greater independence via more disposable income and transport, availability of more sports, clubs and competitions, more media coverage and women in positions of responsibility in sport organisations. Also, all organisations have to face the responsibility for improving opportunities for women as part of their social and legal responsibility.

Sex Discrimination Act 1975

This Act made sex discrimination unlawful in employment, training, education and the provision of goods, facilities and services, that is, a female should be treated in the same way as a male in similar circumstances. However, competitive sport is excluded by Section 44 of the Act. Separate competitions for men and women are allowed where 'the physical strength, stamina or physique puts her at a disadvantage to the average man'. Successful appeals have been made where discrimination has occurred towards female referees. Private sports clubs can also legally discriminate under Sections 29 and 34 of the Act.

The Women's Sport Foundation

The Women's Sports Foundation is the UK's leading organisation dedicated to improving and promoting opportunities for women and girls in sport and physical activity. They are committed to improving, increasing and promoting opportunities for women and girls – in all roles and at all levels – in sport, fitness and physical activity through advocacy, information, education, research and training. They campaign for change at all levels of sport through raising awareness and influencing policy.

HOT LINKS

www.wsf.org.uk

It was originally set up in 1984 by women working in sport who were concerned about the lack of sport and recreation opportunities for women and girls, and the low representation of women in sports coaching, sports management and the sports media. WSF became a registered charity and company limited by guarantee in 1997.

- At present, the Women's Sports Foundation is funded primarily by Sport England.
- They have a quarterly newsletter – Women in Sport.
- They also receive a small amount of additional income via other grants, donations and supporter subscriptions for the magazine and information resources.

Since 1984, the Women's Sports Foundation has been involved in a variety of projects to promote women's sport. These have included:

- the Women's Sports Foundation Awards for Girls and Young Women
- training for Britain's top sportswomen on working with the media, attracting sports sponsorship, employment opportunities in sport and recreation, and receiving benefits from sports science support
- the National Action Plan for Women's and Girls' Sport and Physical Activity (1999–2001)
- Women into High Performance Coaching Project
- Women Get Set Go initiative, which is a personal development course intended to provide a springboard for women into sports leadership, whether as coaches, administrators or officials
- production of a variety of women and sport resources including posters, information packs, photographic exhibitions and fact sheets.

The factor that seems to have the greatest impact on female participation is the growing emphasis placed on health and fitness and the toned, slim stereotypical female form.

Football is the number one sport for girls and women. There are now 61,000 women competing in clubs affiliated to the Football Association (FA), and there is also a similar increase in the number of girls' football teams, which are developing within schools. There are 40,000 more under-14 girls playing at school than ten years ago. One problem holding back the number of girls taking up the sport, however, is the lack of career prospects. There are still only approximately nineteen England-based professional players. The FA has put in place a series of initiatives to increase opportunities.

- In 1997, it launched its Talent Development Plan for Women's Football.
- Establishment of 42 Centres of Excellence to develop 10–16 year olds.
- Nineteen Women's Football Academies – 16 years and over.
- In 2001, the National Women's Player Development Centre was launched in Loughborough University – for the most promising.

TASK 14.04

Why is aerobics considered more socially acceptable for women than body building?

Fig. 14.05

Fig. 14.06

Disability and participation in active recreation and sport

A national survey by Sport England (2000) revealed lower levels of participation in sport amongst the young people with a disability compared with the rest of the population (see Fig.14.07). The most popular sports for the young disabled are horse riding and swimming, where participation levels are higher than in the overall population of younger people. However, these are sports that tend to organise events specifically for people with disabilities. Participation in other sports alongside the non-disabled is low.

'Disability sport' is a term used to suggest a more positive approach towards the participation in sport of disabled people. It includes people with a physical, sensory or mental impairment. The term 'disability' is used when impairment adversely affects performance. Other terms used are handicapped sport, sports for the disabled, adapted sport, wheelchair sport and deaf sport. Competitive sports have either been designed specifically for the disabled, such as goalball for the blind (see below), or have been modified such as volleyball and wheelchair basketball and tennis.

Goalball is a three-a-side game. The aim is to score a goal by rolling the ball along the floor into your opponent's goal. All players wear eyeshades to ensure that everyone is equal when it comes to visual perception. The features of the game that enable visually impaired people to play include:

- the ball has a bell inside
- the playing court has tactile markings.

Internationally, goalball is played in 87 countries, is a paralympic sport and has European and World Championships. In Britain, the British Blind Sport (BBS) is the organisation that is responsible for the sport.

Adapted sports

Although many sports have been developed specifically for disabled people, the majority of disabled people participate in mainstream sports. If a sport is adapted, it is essential that the activity is recognisable as the original sport it is being associated with.

Adaptations may be needed for one disabled person and not for another. For example, in tennis, wheelchair users are allowed to let the ball bounce twice before playing it, whereas for the non-wheelchair user tennis player who is deaf, this would not be permitted.

Sports can be adapted by changing aspects such as the rules, equipment, role of players, environment playing area, time or duration. The following are examples of adaptations needed for two specific sports.

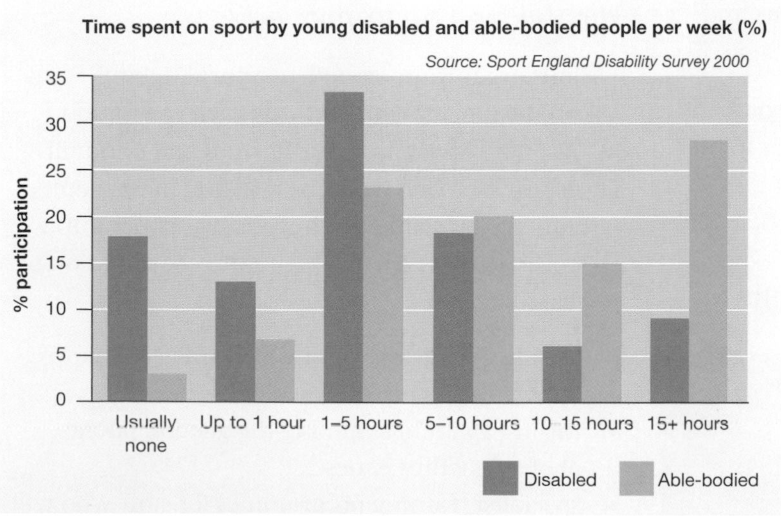

- Wheelchair basketball: the rules, height of the ring and court size are identical. The only adaptation is in the dribble rule: two pushes and one bounce replaces the 'bouncing while travelling' rule in ambulant basketball.
- Swimming: some technique rules can be more flexible for some classifications and visually impaired people may need a tap on the head to let them know they are nearing the end of the lane.

Time spent on sport by young disabled and able-bodied people per week (%)

Source: Sport England Disability Survey 2000

Fig. 14.07 Young disabled people have a low rate of participation in sport

TAKE IT FURTHER

1. In groups, research different sports that have been adapted for disabled people. Remember to consider outdoor and adventurous activities.
2. Consider a game of rounders. Discuss how this game could be adapted for children with disabilities.

Inclusiveness

There have been many improvements in trying to integrate disabled people into mainstream sport as well as recognising in some instances that segregation is the more appropriate option. The key word is **inclusiveness**, which is a belief or philosophy that all people should have their needs, abilities and aspirations recognised, understood and met within a supportive environment. Inclusiveness does not only include people with disabilities, but also those who may suffer difficult social or economic circumstances, such as people from low socio-economic backgrounds. We have already made mention of the government's policies to challenge social exclusion. An inclusive approach is being developed by:

- putting the individual at the centre of its policies
- recognising and supporting diversity by striving to meet the widest range of needs
- seeking to achieve the best 'match' between provision and the needs of the individual
- providing staff training and development
- liaising with other relevant organisations and fostering 'joined-up thinking'.

Integration in this context relates to the able-bodied and the disabled taking part together in the same activity at the same time, while **segregated activity** means people with disabilities participating among themselves. There are advantages and disadvantages with each approach. With

KEY TERM

Inclusiveness:
inclusiveness recognises diversity of needs and does not necessarily mean integration or segregation

integration, the disabled participant may not be able to participate fully and the able-bodied players may find it unchallenging. Safety issues would have to be addressed. However, it can help the disabled person feel more included in society and can help raise their self-esteem when they achieve success. Segregation, on the other hand, reinforces the notion of being different from the rest of society but could be the best option in some cases. Participants may actually achieve more in this environment.

Functional **classification** is an integrated classification system that places emphasis on sport performance by disability groupings rather than by specific disability (Fig. 11.00). This has enabled disability sport to move on from its rehabilitation base to developing elite competitive sport.

KEY TERMS

Integration:
the act of incorporating individuals into mainstream society

Segregated activity:
an activity carried out away from the main group

Classification:
an attempt to group sports competitors to enable fair competition

How can opportunities for people with disabilities be improved?

Various organisations such as Sport England, Disability Sport England, the English Federation of Disability Sport, local authorities and national governing bodies have supported and implemented various projects aimed at improving opportunities. However, there is a need for greater coordination of policies:

- raising awareness among the disabled about opportunities already available
- raising awareness among the general public about disability issues
- specialist training programmes for staff who will be involved

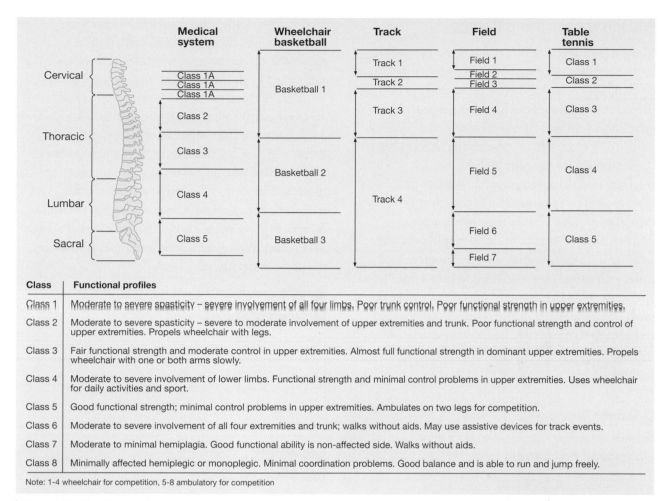

Class	Functional profiles
Class 1	Moderate to severe spasticity – severe involvement of all four limbs. Poor trunk control. Poor functional strength in upper extremities.
Class 2	Moderate to severe spasticity – severe to moderate involvement of upper extremities and trunk. Poor functional strength and control of upper extremities. Propels wheelchair with legs.
Class 3	Fair functional strength and moderate control in upper extremities. Almost full functional strength in dominant upper extremities. Propels wheelchair with one or both arms slowly.
Class 4	Moderate to severe involvement of lower limbs. Functional strength and minimal control problems in upper extremities. Uses wheelchair for daily activities and sport.
Class 5	Good functional strength; minimal control problems in upper extremities. Ambulates on two legs for competition.
Class 6	Moderate to severe involvement of all four extremities and trunk; walks without aids. May use assistive devices for track events.
Class 7	Moderate to minimal hemiplagia. Good functional ability is non-affected side. Walks without aids.
Class 8	Minimally affected hemiplegic or monoplegic. Minimal coordination problems. Good balance and is able to run and jump freely.

Note: 1-4 wheelchair for competition, 5-8 ambulatory for competition

Fig. 14.08 Disability groupings

Source: Disability Sport England

- making access to and within facilities more manageable
- adapting even more sports.

Disability Sport England

The aims of Disability Sport England are to:

- provide opportunities for disabled people to participate in sport
- promote the benefits of sport and physical recreation by disabled people
- support organisations in providing sporting opportunities for disabled people

- educate and make people aware of the sporting abilities of disabled people
- enhance the image, awareness and understanding of disability sport
- encourage disabled people to play an active role in the development of their sport.

The following seven National Disability Sports Organisations are recognised by Sport England:

- British Amputees and Les Autres Sports Association
- British Blind Sport
- UK Deaf Sport
- British Wheelchair Sports Foundation
- Cerebral Palsy Sport
- Disability Sport England
- English Sports Association for People with Learning Disabilities.

National governing bodies

Many national governing bodies have been required to democratise their sport. This means to open sport up to all sections of society. One example is the Lawn Tennis Association, which has developed inner city tennis schemes. How can national governing bodies of sport try to achieve equity in sporting opportunities for the priority groups?

They need to develop specific policies to specifically target groups via community projects and in particular need to meet government policies such as 'best value' and neighbourhood regeneration if they are to receive much needed lottery funding. They also need to target funding at the grass roots level of sport and elite sport as they each serve the needs of the other. Attempts need to be made to make facilities accessible/affordable/attractive (the three 'A's), but this alone is not enough.

Changes in the structural aspects such as admission fees, membership clauses and cost all need to be considered. Attitudes within the sport need to change with positive campaigns to get rid of discrimination. They need to raise awareness through publicity and advertising. Active participation is important but national governing bodies also need to make sure their employment opportunities within the institutions are not restrictive in terms of colour/race/ethnic origin and so on. Much has already been said about the value of having more people from these sections of society in decision-making positions and the role models they create for others.

TAKE IT FURTHER

Choose a governing body and try to discover what policies it has regarding equity issues. You may find websites a useful source of information. An example could be the Lawn Tennis Association, the All England Netball Association and the Football Association.

APPLY IT!

Lawn Tennis Association: 'Many tennis clubs are working with our team to become more physically accessible for wheelchair users, and they are also creating a more welcoming attitude to encourage disabled people to participate.'

HOT LINKS

www.lta.org.uk
www.england-netball.co.uk
www.thefa.com

ATHLETE PROFILE

For a horseball player, owning a horse is not a necessity but it is a decided advantage, although interested individuals can borrow a horse (guidelines produced by the BHA). Rochelle Plumb has always had access to her own horse. Membership to the BHA is approximately £30–£45 a year, so it is the upkeep of a horse that is the biggest barrier to the sport for most people.

'Access to facilities and coaching are the biggest problems people face,' says Rochelle, 'as currently there are still not very many clubs in the country, though new ones are starting up all the time.'

The sport has the advantage of being quite new and does not have a traditional gender segregation, enabling males and females to participate together.

Refresh your memory

Revision checklist

Make sure you know the following:

▷ It is generally accepted that the national and local governments have a responsibility to improve the opportunities the population as a whole receive in participating in recreational and sporting activities

▷ Equal opportunity – the principle and practice of providing all people with the same chance to participate in recreational and sporting activities

▷ Prejudice – an opinion or attitude, especially an unfavourable one, based on inadequate facts, often displaying intolerance or dislike of people due to race, religion, gender or culture. If a prejudicial attitude was acted upon it would be called discrimination

▷ Stereotype – a standardised image or concept shared by members of a social group whereby certain behaviour traits are associated with particular types of individuals or groups. This usually involves negative images/expectations relating to gender, race and people with disabilities

▷ General barriers to participation include:

  • society's attitudes, such as stereotyping and image of sport

  • access to sport, such as accessibility of facilities and sufficient information

  • programmes of activities such as the range of activities offered and at different levels, such social and recreational as well as more competitive

▷ People from low socio-economic groups generally have less financial security and participation in sport may not be a priority. Yet these groups are also most likely to suffer from combined problems, such as poor health and social exclusion. Sport could be a benefit to them in acquiring new skills and raising self-esteem as well as making them more inclusive within their society

▷ Ethnic minority groups are people who have racial, religious linguistic and/or other traits in common and who form a lower percentage of the population. Issues such as racism and stereotyping can affect participation rates. Campaigns such as 'Kick it Out' are solutions aiming to solve the problem

▷ Females participate less than males due to the traditional view that sport is more manly, as well as more personal issues such as lack of time. The Sex Discrimination Act (1975) and increased media coverage aim to improve these issues

▷ People with disabilities covers groups of people with a physical, sensory or mental impairment which adversely affects participation in recreational and sporting activities

▷ Sports can be modified or adapted to enable people with disabilities to enjoy successful participation. Rules and sometimes equipment can be changed. People with disabilities can either participate separately, that is, segregated from the able bodies section of the population or integrated, that is participate with able bodies people. There are advantages and disadvantages to each

▷ Each sport has its own national governing body to administer and organise on a national level. Another duty they have is to ensure their sport is adhering to the equity laws set by the government. In order to receive lottery funding many of them have to have equity policies as a stated aim

Revise as you go

1. Explain the terms 'equal opportunity' 'discrimination' and 'prejudice' with reference to sport participation.

2. What does the term 'stereotyping' mean and how does it affect participation in sport?

3. What is a target or priority group?

4. Name three target groups identified by Sport England.

5. What is 'upward social mobility' when referring to successful sport participation?

6. How can positive sporting role models be influential in society?

7. What is meant by 'inclusion' with reference to sport participation?

8. What are the three main aims of Sport England?

9. Outline the difference between integrated and segregated sport.

10. Explain the term 'adapted' sport.

11. What is the role of Disability Sport England (DSE) in relation to participation in physical recreation?

12. Suggest barriers people with a disability may face when participating in a sport.

13. State three strategies that a sports club may introduce to attract more disabled people.

Get the result!

Examination question

Physical Education and Outdoor Education are considered worthwhile experiences for children and young adults.

a) How does the *National Curriculum for Physical Education* encourage children to develop an appreciation of sport, beyond that of merely participating as a performer? (2 marks)

b) Using suitable examples, explain what is meant by the terms *outdoor education* and *outdoor recreation*? (2 marks)

c) What *educational* and *recreational* values might a child gain when participating in outdoor and adventurous? (4 marks)

d) Why might young adults give up physical activity when they leave school? (4 marks)

Model answer

Student answer

a) In Key Stages 4, if you are not a particularly able performer you can take on the role of official or coach which allows people to be involved with sport without playing.

b) Outdoor education is where you learn basic survival skills like map reading and compass work which can then be used in sports like orienteering. Outdoor recreation is just recreation outside, e.g. playing football in the park, cycling or running.

Examiner says

Maximum marks are achieved here for highlighting two roles of official and coach.

Examiner says

No marks are achieved here as the student has not clearly stated that learning map and compass skills occurred within an educational setting such as a school/college. Also the use of football as an example of outdoor recreation is incorrect. Examples such as skiing were needed and also the understanding that this occurs within a person's free time.

c) The educational values that a child will gain from outdoor
   activities is the effect people will have on the outdoors,
   like pollution. They will learn to respect the environment
   in which they live. The child will also learn teamwork as
   many activities consist of more than one person for safety
   reasons. It will give the children the chance to explore out
   of their normal environment as they may escape to the
   countryside, as many people live in urban areas.
   The recreational value they will learn is that these
   activities are fun and they can also get fit while having
   fun.

d) Young adults may give up physical activity when leaving
   school because it isn't compulsory anymore and so they
   don't need to take part. Many go into work and so will
   not have much leisure time in which they can play sport.
   Another reason is they may not have the money to be able
   to go to the gym, whereas in school it was free.

Examiner says

Common mistakes

- Students should always give more points than needed in order to increase the chances of obtaining maximum marks. For example in d) only three points were made so the maximum four marks could not be achieved.

- Where there are two clear aspects to a question students must clearly state which one they are referring to and not expect the examiner to sort their answer out for them. For example, this was done well in c) where the response clearly stated which were educational and which were recreational. Failure to do this can result in many marks lost.

- When specific examples are asked for, students often fail to comply with this requirement. This was done well in b) though the lack of understanding of the content let them down.

Examination question

The government is using sport as a means of addressing wider community issues such as reducing crime rates.

a) State two other ways in which a community could benefit from improved sport and recreation provision. (2 marks)

Participation rates in sport and physical recreation activities among some groups in the United Kingdom tend to be lower than the national average.

b) Account for the lower rate of participation in physical recreation and sporting activities by ethnic minority groups in the United Kingdom. (3 marks)

c) Indoor games such as badminton are popular among women. Suggest reasons why female participation is relatively high in this sport. (3 marks)

d) How can school physical education departments increase participation rates among minority groups? (4 marks)

Model answer

Examiner says

The student begins by mentioning benefits to the individual rather than benefits to the community, as required by the question. Therefore no marks for team spirit. However, the maximum two marks were achieved for 'improve health' and 'socialise' as the response has been further developed and positive marking means the whole answer is read and credited if correct.

Student answer

a) It encourages children to get involved in clubs and they then get the benefits of team sport and spirit. People will do more exercise in general, which will improve health and therefore strain on the NHS. It will also encourage people to take an active role in their community and to socialise.

b) Ethnic minority groups have a lower participation rate in physical recreation in the UK. This may be for a number of reasons. They have fewer role models in professional sport so assume they will not be good themselves. They could worry that they could get socially discriminated against. There could be poor provision of sport in their local communities and it could also be considered

Examiner says

Maximum marks are achieved for 'fewer role models' 'worried about discrimination' and 'expectation of society'.

socially unacceptable for women of certain religions to participate.

c) Female participation is high in badminton because it can be played at any time of day to suit women. Gyms will have women only days and many sports centres will have women only days. Also there are more role models. It is a way of keeping fit and healthy. The game can also be played just for fun and doesn't have to be competitive.

d) Schools should try and encourage those groups to join clubs and teams. They should try and get famous people of the same religion or race to promote sport. They should mul e a wide range of sports available so they can find something they can enjoy. If they succeed this will boost participation throughout their communities at all ages.

Examiner says

Only 1 mark was achieved here for 'way of keeping fit and healthy'. References to 'any time of day' was considered too vague; reference to more role models was incorrect as was 'it doesn't have to be competitive'.

Examiner says

Three marks were achieved for 'join clubs and teams' 'get famous people of the same religion' and 'range of sport'.

Student tips

- If section a) had begun with the word 'list' instead of 'state' the first response of 'team spirit' would have been taken and therefore not credited. This does not happen very often but students need to be aware of it.

- When referring to women and sport, students often say sports such as badminton are 'not competitive'. This is clearly incorrect as to play a game of badminton requires competition. Students need to be much more precise in what they are trying to say, for example, the intensity of the competition can be dependent on the attitude the women bring to the game. Similarly reference to 'not physically demanding' is not credited as a worthwhile answer.

UNIT 2

Analysis and evaluation of physical activity as a performer and/or in an adopted role/s

LEARNING OBJECTIVES:

By the end of this chapter you should be able to:

▶ understand the requirements of the practical assessment

▶ select your optimum activity considering all relevant factors

▶ understand how you will be assessed

▶ analyse your own performance identifying strengths and weaknesses

▶ formulate a plan to optimise your performance.

Introduction

The practical coursework is your opportunity to demonstrate your skills in two of the three optional roles of performer, coach/leader or official in your chosen activity or activities. You have the opportunity to dictate how well you do because you know exactly the areas in which you will be assessed.

The purpose of this chapter is to outline how you will be assessed and help you to understand the requirement of the published specification. It is not intended to inform you how to become a better technical performer, coach/leader or official. There are many more resources available to help you with the specific knowledge of each activity and it would not be feasible to attempt to outline all the details required for each one in this chapter. You should read relevant coaching manuals and rule books as well as watch appropriate videos to enhance your knowledge and understanding of your own activity.

The chapter will outline advice on assessment and preparation for the moderation, the roles you are expected to master and details of how to analyse your performance. Many of you will relish the opportunity to master the skills previously developed through Physical Education lessons,

the GCSE course and extra-curricular activities. However, the requirements of the course at AS level demand a technical competence via demonstration and execution through conditioned practices rather than playing in a competitive situation. Both of these require practice and concentration to achieve high marks.

The aim of the practical coursework component is to assess not only the physical skills and application of strategies and tactics, but to bring together all the various theoretical components allowing the optimisation of performance. The task facing you is to use your knowledge and understanding of the theoretical aspects of the course to identify weaknesses in performance, possible causes and use the acquired knowledge to address the faults.

Table 15.01 outlines the AQA Examination Board requirement for AS and A2 levels of study. It is useful to have some understanding of the A2 course because if you develop a clear understanding of the correct technique during the first year of study, it will make your studies easier the following year.

AS level	A2 level
Demonstration of skills in two out of three roles; • Practical performer • Coach/leader • Official/referee	Demonstration of skills in one role • Practical preformer • Coach/leader • Official/referee
Demonstration of core skills in isolation and conditioned practice	Assessment is based on performance in a competitive situation or equivalent
Roles may be assessed in: • one activity • two activities	See the individual specification criteria for exact assessment requirements
The only restriction is that you may not be assessed in the same role in two different activities	Plus an analysis of the weaknesses of performance when compared to an elite performer, possible causes of the weaknesses and solutions Practical performer – assesses their own performance Coach/leader – assesses another performer Official/referee – assesses their own performance

Table 15.01 Requirements for AS and A2 levels of study

HOT LINKS

Obtain a copy of the practical specification and make notes on the exact requirements.
Visit the AQA website. www.aqa.org.uk

Structure of the course and preparation advice

This element of the course aims to develop many skills and prepare students to fulfil a number of roles. Figure 15.01 outlines such roles.

In order to complete each of these roles successfully, time must be devoted to practice and development of knowledge about the rules, scoring systems, tactics, strategies, technical skills, specific terminology, physical preparation, psychological requirements and any other areas that may hinder or promote performance.

It may be easier to view this section of the course as progressive, with the foundation skills and knowledge being laid during the AS year and the refining and optimising of performance occurring during the A2 year. Many of the skills developed via practices at AS level will be examined in more detail during full competitive situations at A2 level.

Many students often neglect the practical element of the course and tend to focus on the theoretical aspects. However, a large percentage of the final marks are allocated to this section, up to 40 per cent. Therefore time should be devoted to developing the skills required from the onset of the course and not left until close to the final assessment or moderation.

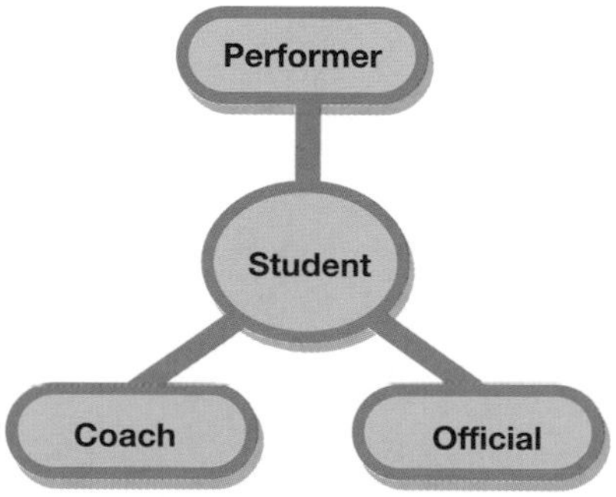

Fig. 15.01 Outline of roles that students will fulfil

To fully understand the nature of performance and how to facilitate improvement, links should be made with the theoretical components as frequently as possible. Individual strengths and weaknesses should be identified and, as the course progresses, possible causes and corrective measures can be implemented.

The selection of activities must be carefully considered, as there may be circumstances that may affect your chances of development. In addition to your own experience, other factors may include the time available to complete extra training, the opportunity for extra curricular activities, the accessibility of facilities and resources plus the expertise of teachers and coaches.

The nature of assessment requires a demonstration or applied knowledge (depending on your chosen roles) of named core skills related to a specific activity, the difficulty of which gradually increase due to the requirement of executing effectively in more pressurised or demanding situations.

KEY TERMS

There are several key terms that need to be outlined in order to fully understand the assessment procedure:

skills in isolation:
the demonstration of specific core skills, which will be compared to a correct technical model (see later for full explanation)

conditioned practice:
the demonstration of core skills and some tactical awareness in a more pressured practice situation, but not a full game or equivalent competitive situation

competitive situation:
demonstration of core skills, strategies and tactics, the application of the psychological and physiological qualities needed within a fully competitive environment or appropriate alternative. This is not actually assessed until the A2 year of the course

The activities available for assessment are outlined in Table 15.02. The categories are subdivided to allow for easier application of the

Category 1		Category 2	Category 3
Association Football	Lacrosse	Athletics	Dance (Contemporary/ Creative/Ballet)
Badminton	Mountain Activities	Olympic weightlifting	
Basketball	Netball	Swimming	Diving
Boxing	Orienteering		Gymnastics
Canoeing/Kayaking (Moving/Inland water)	Rowing and Sculling		Trampolining
Climbing	Rugby Union/League		
Cricket	Sailing/Windsurfing/Kitesurfing		
Fencing	Skiing/Snowbarding		
Gaelic football	Softball/Baseball/Rounders		
Goalball	Squash		
Golf	Table tennis		
Handball	Tae Kwon Do		
Hockey (Field/Roller/Ice)	Tennis		
Horse Riding	Track/Road cycling/Mountain biking		
Judo	Volleyball		
Karate	Water polo		

Table 15.02 Activities available for assessment

criteria. You do not have to choose a particular combination of activities. The purpose of dividing the activities into groups will become clear as you continue to read through the chapter and begin to understand how you will be assessed.

The marking of the practical activities is conducted by continual assessment. This allows for ongoing development of performance and caters for students who may have an 'off day' during a moderator's visit.

To facilitate development, the various skills need to be analysed to identify personal strengths and personal weaknesses. More detailed advice to complete this process is outlined in the next section.

TASK 15.01

- List possible activities that may be selected based on your experience and strengths.
- Outline the opportunities that will allow skills and performance to develop outside normal lesson time.
- Select the activity to be assessed and highlight the core skills to be assessed.

Each activity is different in terms of core skills; examples from different categories are shown below in Figures 15.02–15.05, which illustrate the diverse nature of each activity.

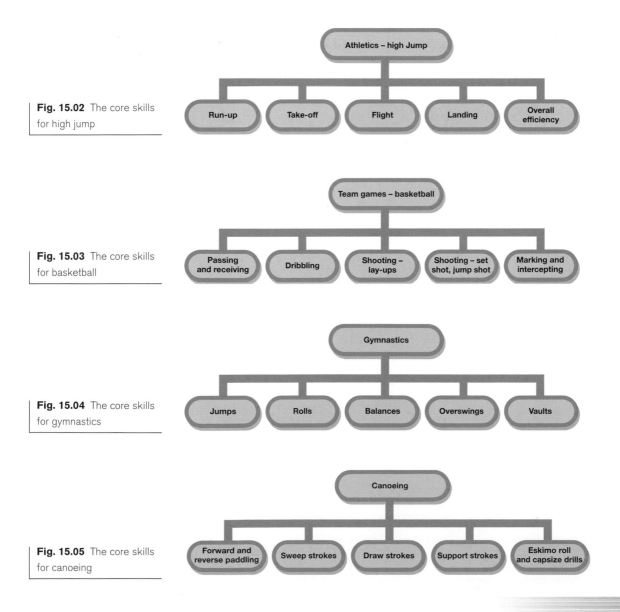

Fig. 15.02 The core skills for high jump

Athletics – high Jump: Run-up | Take-off | Flight | Landing | Overall efficiency

Fig. 15.03 The core skills for basketball

Team games – basketball: Passing and receiving | Dribbling | Shooting – lay-ups | Shooting – set shot, jump shot | Marking and intercepting

Fig. 15.04 The core skills for gymnastics

Gymnastics: Jumps | Rolls | Balances | Overswings | Vaults

Fig. 15.05 The core skills for canoeing

Canoeing: Forward and reverse paddling | Sweep strokes | Draw strokes | Support strokes | Eskimo roll and capsize drills

Once this process has been completed for all the core skills, time should be devoted to rectify faults or develop an awareness of the correct techniques or rules related to each one. The assessment is based on competence of performance in comparison to a correct technical model (see next section for further details) and marks are awarded to subroutines of the skill as well as end result. For example, the subroutines for a squash stroke may be the grip, footwork and preparation, shot positioning and timing, follow-through and recovery, and finally effectiveness (see Fig. 15.06).

To develop the necessary skills and tactical awareness required, time must be given to practice or observation of practice. It is of no use to simply read books or watch videos informing you how to complete the skills correctly. They may be useful as a reference resource but there is no substitute for actually performing or analysing the skills.

Training sessions are always easier with others not just because it is more sociable but they can actually help to improve your performance by observing and coaching. If the practice takes place with another student who has limited knowledge of the activity, outline the identified weaknesses of the skills and prepare a sheet of the correct techniques and coaching points required.

However, if time can be spent with a teacher or another student who is experienced and is able to identify your weaknesses, this may be of greater benefit. Allocated time for development may be available either during lessons or extra-curricular activities.

Further time for development may take place at a local club and the expertise of their coaches and officals may be utilised. If this is the case, it may be advisable to inform them of the specification criteria so that they are aware of your aims and the specific skills that need to be developed.

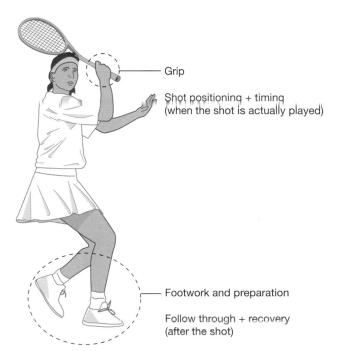

- Grip
- Shot positioning + timing (when the shot is actually played)
- Footwork and preparation
- Follow through + recovery (after the shot)

Fig. 15.06 The subroutines of a squash player

When developing your personal skills, do not try to change everything at once or expect a huge improvement in performance overnight. The process may take months or years to complete. Many elite performers/coaches/officials strive to make minor modifications to their technique/knowledge/ performance in order to achieve the optimum performance. The aim of the AS/A2 course is not to make you compete at this level but to be competent performers. Try to remember that when developing your practical performance.

Assessment procedures

The school/college will be assigned an external moderator to ensure the marking criteria are applied correctly by the teachers when compared to recommended national standards. The moderation may involve either:

- one school/college
- a group of schools/college
- video evidence.

The moderator may not see all the activities being offered by the school/college due to time restrictions, availability of facilities or numbers involved. However, the assumption must be made that they will observe any possible combination of activities and as a consequence you should be fully prepared. This may involve not only the actual practical performance but also any analysis of performance requirements. The best way to prepare for the moderation is to start practising the core skills as early in the course as possible and give yourself the opportunity to experience as many conditioned situations as possible to develop your skills.

The moderation usually involves both AS and A2 students. Consequently, it may be easy to lose focus and concentration. Many students assume the moderator is not watching them because they are at the other end of the sports hall or far side of the playing field. They may be assessing you at any time.

A common error during the moderation visit involves a lack of concentration during the demonstrations of the core skills. Many students appear to not apply themselves fully and produce weaker demonstrations compared to their actual ability. This may be due to the misconception that they are easy, do not require much attention and are less intense compared to the conditioned practice or competitive situation.

REMEMBER!

Make the effort to dress appropriately and 'look the part'. This will at least give the moderator the impression that some preparation and thought have been given to the assessment rather than simply turning up on the day.

The nature of physical activity inevitably involves mistakes being made during performance; it is almost unavoidable. Even performers at the highest level make errors of judgement or are influenced by the environment, occasion and opponents. If mistakes are made, do not worry about them, redirect your attention and concentrate on the task ahead. The moderator will look at the overall performance, not just one small part.

If the selected activity is a team game or one that involves other performers, do not try to be the centre of attention all the time. The assessment is based on your ability to fulfil a role within a specific position. Marks may be lost because of the inability to implement certain tactics, strategies and systems of play.

The moderator may require the analysis of your own performance and a comparison with another student. If this does happen, further advice is outlined in the next section covering all aspects of preparation for this assessment.

Analysis of skills and performance

As the course progresses, there will be a requirement to analyse the performance of yourself and others in greater detail. In order to successfully achieve this, a coaching cycle should be used ensuring a consistent approach; an example is shown in Figure 15.07.

Fig. 15.07 A coaching cycle

When the coaching and analysis process occurs, there are many factors that may need to be considered and knowledge of each must be established if the outcome is to be successful. Many students can identify basic faults in technique and performance but not expand their responses with the use of detailed technical information or appropriate terminology. Figure 15.08 highlights some of the knowledge that may be required to successfully complete the coaching cycle.

As you can see, the knowledge base required to be an effective coach who is able to observe and analyse performance is wide ranging and varied. During the course of your studies, you should aim to improve each of them.

REMEMBER!

Understanding each element is crucial if the coaching process is to be effective and actually develop skills and their application.

- *Performance* – the actions of the performer either in isolation, practice or competitive situation.
- *Observation* – the actions of the performer are watched either by another person or video recorded.
- *Analysis* – the actions of the performer are assessed. Notes should be taken when possible to highlight key strengths and weaknesses.
- *Evaluation* – the actions of the performer are compared to a correct technical model, competent performer or past performances.
- *Planning* – possible causes of weaknesses are identified and corrective measures devised to eradicate the problems. These may be in the form of physical practices, physiological adaptations or psychological preparation. It is also important at this stage not to neglect the strengths of the performer but to maintain a level of training to ensure they do not decline at the expense of improving the weaknesses.
- *Feedback* – the identified training adaptations are discussed with the performer and implemented during the forthcoming performances.

TASK 15.03

For your selected activity, place in rank order the types of knowledge on Figure 15.08 and assess your own strengths and weaknesses as a coach.

Fig. 15.08 Knowledge required to complete the coaching cycle

Diagram showing "Required knowledge base" at centre connected to: Technical models, Strategies and tactics, Physiological factors, Socio-cultural factors, Effective observational skills, Psychological factors, Rules and regulations, Specialist terminology.

Technical models

Often reference will be made to your performance compared to your knowledge of a 'correct technical model'. This term refers to the performance of a skill that is considered to be of a very high standard. There may actually be several variations of a skill and different performers may have their own individual peculiarities but still be highly successful. Similarly, as many activities become exposed to scientific and technological support, alterations in techniques are becoming more common as actions and techniques are refined.

As a consequence, it is advisable to base your comparisons on the most recent information or a performer who is generally accepted as being close to the norm. The technique of many international competitors may be considered unique and inadvisable to coach to developing athletes. For example, the technique of the former South African bowler Paul Adams and the running style of former Olympic and World Champion 400 metre sprinter Michael Johnson are unlikely to be actively encouraged among younger performers but are highly effective for them personally.

REMEMBER!

There are many resources for appropriate technical models, often published by the national governing bodies. Suitable sources may include:
- coaching manuals
- photographs
- instructional videos
- CD-ROMs
- the Internet
- television recorded performances with expert commentary
- live events.

When studying and developing an awareness of each skill, refer back to the specific subroutines identified previously. A thorough knowledge and understanding of each phase of the skill is vital if the observation and analysis process is to be effective. For each skill, make diagrams and notes of the key points for each subroutine. Initially, concentrate on the major technical points, including the correct terminology, but later, once these are well learned and easily recognised, develop an awareness of the more advanced technical points.

TASK 15.04

Research and find relevant resources to identify the key technical points or rules for each of the core skills. A useful aid to developing this understanding is a chart containing all the basic information for each subroutine of the specific skill. Often an A3 piece of paper divided as shown in Table 15.03 can be easily constructed and contain all the information required.

Subroutine 1	Subroutine 2	Subroutine 3	Subroutine 4	Subroutine 5
Diagram or photographs of this phase				
Correct technique Include two or three points				
Common faults Include two or three points				
Corrective practices				
Include one per fault				

Complete a chart for each core skill using the resources identified above.

Table 15.03 A specific skill can be divided into subroutines

Observation advice

When observing any performance, the various viewing angles may provide different information about the effectiveness of performance. Imagine when watching a sporting event on television the numerous camera angles employed by the editor and the different impression and information that is produced by each. It is now common practice in many high-level sporting events to use such technology to aid referees in their final decision. This approach should be employed to aid your observation and analysis.

Different views give very different perspectives and the aim of the observation should be identified clearly. The actual execution of skills may require a position as close to the action as possible from the side, front and rear, while the observation of tactical awareness and effective implementation may require a location further away. However, a view from behind the field of play may provide different information compared to one from the side or elevated in a stand. It may be advisable to vary your position to maximise the information upon which to base your judgements.

EXAM TIP:

When observing, either live or from video evidence, make notes to remind you of specific instances or actions. Divide the observation sheet into sections covering the areas required. For example, when observing a game, the sheet may consist of sections for attacking skills, defensive skills, tactics and set plays.

Analysis of personal performance

Before any personal development of skill and technique can occur, your own performance must be analysed and evaluated. This can be achieved in a number of ways:

- teacher/coach observing performance and providing feedback
- another student observing performance and providing feedback
- video recording of performance and personal analysis.

If possible, the third is in many ways the most useful as you can see the faults (via visual guidance) and develop a better understanding of the exact modifications needed. Video footage is also useful as a means of stopping the action and making specific comparisons to the technical model, which may be more difficult during live or full speed actions.

Once the performance has been analysed, the next stage in the process involves the evaluation of the effectiveness of its application either during conditioned practices or competitive situations. For game activities, these are often split into the following sections.

- effectiveness of attacking skills
- effectiveness of defensive skills
- effective implementation of strategies and tactics
- effective implementation of physiological and psychological factors that affect performance.

Other activities have alternative categories which are more appropriate, for example swimming and athletics may require the comments to be based on two events and gymnastic events on agilities and twists. Detailed requirements need to be obtained from the specification criteria.

TASK 15.05

Observe and analyse your personal performance in the selected two roles for the various core skills and conditioned practices.

TAKE IT FURTHER

Once this process has been completed, a structured programme should be followed to develop the identified weaknesses in the skills or enhance your effectiveness when analysing the skills in context. Frequently assess your development either via a teacher/coach or by video recording again. Do not just assume because practice is taking place an improvement will occur — you may be practising the wrong technique, giving the wrong advice or interpreting the rules incorrectly!

Requirements of a practical performer

You are being assessed in your ability as a performer in the selected activity and will be required to demonstrate a mastery of sport-related skills both in isolation and conditioned practices. During the conditioned practices you will also be assessed in your tactical awareness and ability to participate in set plays, as well as show your analysis and evaluation skills to critically appraise your performance, suggesting how it could be improved.

Category 1 activities

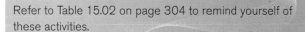

REMEMBER!

Refer to Table 15.02 on page 304 to remind yourself of these activities.

For the demonstration of the five named core skills in isolation there are 25 marks available. You need to fully understand the criteria to ensure you are able to access all the marks. For example, if the core skill is 'passing' you will be required to show a range of passing techniques to be awarded full marks not just one or two methods.

There are 15 marks awarded for application of those core skills in the conditioned practice are mainly subdivided as follows:

- attacking situations
- defensive situations
- set plays or specific situations.

Each of these areas are worth 5 marks.

For some activities these subdivisions may be different and you need to refer to the published specification for full details. These activities include canoeing/kayaking, climbing, horse riding, mountain activities, orienteering, rowing and sculling, sailing/wind surfing, skiing/snowboarding and track/road cycling.

The final 10 marks are awarded for:

- Your ability to implement and follow the rules, your effort and efficiency.

- Your ability to analyse your performance and suggest appropriate measures to improve performance.

Each of these areas are worth 5 marks.

Category 2 activities

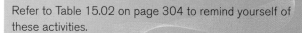

REMEMBER!

Refer to Table 15.02 on page 304 to remind yourself of these activities.

The difference to the Category 1 activities is that due to the nature of those listed in Category 2 you only have to demonstrate two events, strokes or lifts.

Each one is subdivided into three specific subroutines and awarded up to 5 marks each, making a total of 15 marks per event and 30 marks in total for your demonstrations.

In terms of the conditioned practice requirement you only have to demonstrate your ability in one event, and this is assessed out of 12 marks. The final marks, worth up to four each are awarded for:

- your knowledge of the rules, strategies and effort
- your ability to analyse your performance and suggest appropriate measures to improve performance.

Category 3 activities

REMEMBER!

Refer to Table 15.02 on page 304 to remind yourself of these activities.

The final category is very different compared to the previous two categories due to the very diverse nature of the activities listed. In order to fully understand the requirements of particular activity you should read the specification criteria carefully. Most of the advice offered in the previous pages of this chapter can then be adapted to ensure you can access all the marks.

Requirements of a coach/leader

If you are being assessed in this role you will be required to observe, analyse and suggest improvements a performer can make to their core skills/techniques. This will be a test of your understanding of the relevant techniques and basic tactics depending on the situation, as well as your ability to ensure all the participants involved are safe and that you can implement key elements of the theoretical aspects of this section in a practical situation. For example, you must understand how to provide effective feedback, select the best teaching style and modify the method of guidance used to ensure learning takes place. The final aspect of the assessment will involve you evaluating your own performance and suggesting aspects that you too could improve upon to become a better coach/leader. Remember this role is worth a total of 50 marks.

Category 1 activities

REMEMBER!

Refer to Table 15.02 on page 304 to remind yourself of these activities.

You will be assessed in your ability to analyse and evaluate the strengths and weaknesses of a performer in a variety of named core skills in isolation and suggest corrective practices. This is worth 25 marks – 5 marks per named core skill. For example, in Association Football the named core skills for an outfield player are; passing and receiving, dribbling and moving with the ball, shooting, heading (attack and defence) and finally tackling and jockeying a player. You will be expected to analyse a variety of specific techniques within each of those groups and provide specific feedback to the player about their performance using specialist technical vocabulary.

The second section of marks assesses your ability to analyse the core skills/techniques, not in isolation but during conditioned practices or a modified game situation. Another 15 marks are available for the following criteria, each of which is worth 5 marks.

- Ability to analyse the relevant skills/techniques during attacking phases of play.
- Ability to analyse the relevant skills/techniques during defensive phases of play.
- Ability to analyse the relevant skills/techniques during set play phases of play.

For each of these areas you should be able to comment on basic strategies and tactics, outlining what the performer did well and what they did poorly. Comments should also involve the impact of the performance on other players or the outcome of the activity.

Some of the activities will have alternative criteria if those highlighted above are not relevant. For example, mountain activities and horse riding do not have attacking and defensive phases of play, therefore an alternative aspect of the sport will be assessed. You should check the assessment criteria carefully to ensure you understand which aspects of the activity you need to develop knowledge of.

The final 10 marks (each of which is worth 5 marks) are awarded for your:

- Ability to communicate effectively with the performer to implement change as required.
- Ability to analyse your own personal performance as a coach/leader.

The first bullet point refers to your ability to implement the various theoretical aspects of coaching you have studied to produce an effective performance from the person you are working with. For example, are your instructions and feedback clear and accurate?; do you use the appropriate methods of guidance?; do you use the correct teaching style?

The second bullet point assesses your ability to evaluate your own performance and suggest ways in which you could become a better coach/leader. It is very hard to become a perfect coach! Ask yourself does the 'perfect coach' actually exist? There are numerous examples of good quality, experienced coaches and leaders saying they didn't get everything right, whether they are refering to tactics, preparing their athletes in terms of fitness or generally not making a decision quick enough to cause a change, which may have affected the final result. Bear this in mind and don't think you have to be perfect. There is always room for improvement. You may like to ask yourself 'does the performer understand me?', if not, why not.

Category 2 activities

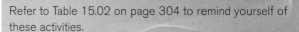

REMEMBER!

Refer to Table 15.02 on page 304 to remind yourself of these activities.

The requirements within this category are similar to Category 1 but rather than analyse five core skills/techniques you are now required to develop your knowledge of two events. For example, from the sport of athletics you may choose the high jump and hurdles, or swimming the front crawl and the butterfly stroke.

Your ability to analyse and evaluate a performer's strengths and weaknesses are worth 15 marks per event (30 marks in total).

The remainder of the marks are awarded for your effectiveness within a conditioned practice/modified competition. However, you only have to analyse one event and comment on three named core skills/ techniques which are clearly outlined in the criteria. For example, if you specialised in the high jump, the three core skills would be:

- run-up
- take-off
- flight and landing.

If you chose swimming and the front crawl the three core skills would be:

- starts, turns and finish
- head action, breathing action and body position
- arm action and leg action.

The awarding of marks for this section in Category 2 activities is slightly different. There are a total of 20 marks available, with each sub-section worth 4 marks.

Therefore there are 12 marks available for your analysis of the event based on the three core skills as outlined above, plus an additional 8 marks for your:

- ability to communicate effectively with the performer to implement change as required
- ability to analyse your own personal performance as a coach/leader.

The advice outlined in the previous section relating to these two bullet points also applies.

Category 3 activities

REMEMBER!

Refer to Table 15.02 on page 304 to remind yourself of these activities.

The third category requires exactly the same skills of analysis and evaluation. Due to the different nature of dance there are specific requirements which are outlined in the criteria which refer to the performance and choreography of a solo sequence, worth 30 marks and 20 marks respectively. You are able to offer a variety of genres depending on your own strengths and personal interests.

The other activities have 25 marks available for analysis and evaluation of the demonstration of core skills. A further 15 marks are available for your ability to assess a performer during a conditioned practice or modified competitive practice.

The final 10 marks (each of which is worth 5 marks) are awarded for your:

- ability to communicate effectively with the performer to implement change as required
- ability to analyse your own personal performance as a coach/leader.

Requirements of an official

If you chose to be assessed in this role you will be required to fulfil three main objectives. The first involves you demonstrating your ability to apply the rules relating to the various core skills both in isolation and within conditioned practices. The second aspect of being an official requires you to show you have a good understanding of the requirements and expectations associated with the role. For example, an awareness of safety issues and the ability to apply the rules fairly and consistently. The final aspect assesses your ability to apply the the correct scoring systems and justify the decisions made to players and other officials as required.

Remember the skill of being an official is to be fair and consistent. The nature of sport relies on officials, referees and umpires making decisions immediately to ensure fairplay and the safety of all participants. Officials do not get every decision correct and at the elite level they are increasingly aided by new technology. For example, just look at how the introduction of technology is now such an important aspect of many sports and often final decisions are referred to the fourth official for clarification or confirmation. Therefore, bear this in mind when developing the skills required to be an official – you cannot get every decision correct, but try to get as many right as possible.

Although each of the different activity categories may have slightly different requirements the structure is broadly the same. More detail will be outlined in terms of the mark allocation in the specific sections below, but the following bullet points show the main skills you will need to develop.

The first section of marks focuses on the core skills, general awareness of requirements for an official and personal preparation. This includes;

- The ability to explain any relevant rules relating to the named cores skills.
- The ability to demonstrate an awareness of safety issues relating to equipment, players clothing and the playing area.
- The ability to understand and explain the scoring and/or judging system.

- The ability to undertake the various roles associated with the activity.
- The ability to be physical and mentally prepared to officiate and be suitably equipped.

The second section of marks relates to your ability to execute the knowledge shown above in a conditioned practice or modified competitive situation when officiating the named core skills.
This includes:

- the ability to apply the rules or judging criteria correctly
- the ability to be consistent
- the ability to communicate decisions correctly
- the ability to demonstrate a rapport with the performers to maintain fairplay
- the ability to analyse and evaluate you own performance and suggest appropriate methods to improve.

As you can see from the lists above you will be assessed in a similar manner to how you would evaluate an official is you were watching a sporting contest.

The following information outlines in more detail how the marks are awarded depending on the nature of the activity.

Category 1 activities

REMEMBER!

Refer to Table 15.02 on page 304 to remind yourself of these activities.

25 marks are available (5 per sub-section) for the first group of bullet points outlined above.
25 marks are available (5 per sub-section) for the second group of bullet points outlined above.

Category 2 activities

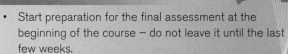

> ### REMEMBER!
>
> Refer to Table 15.02 on page 304 to remind yourself of these activities.

30 marks are available (5 marks per sub-section). The additional 5 marks are available because you have to outline the rules relating to two events rather than five core skills.

20 marks are available (4 marks per sub-section) for the second group of bullet points outlined above.

Category 3 Activities

> ### REMEMBER!
>
> Refer to Table 15.02 on page 304 to remind yourself of these activities.

25 marks are available (5 per sub-section) for the first group of bullet points outlined above.

25 marks are available (5 per sub-section) for the second group of bullet points outlined above.

> ### REMEMBER!
>
> - Start preparation for the final assessment at the beginning of the course – do not leave it until the last few weeks.
> - Learn the correct techniques and rules for the chosen activities.
> - Take time to analyse your strengths and weaknesses.
> - Set realistic targets for performance development.
> - Evaluate progress regularly and revise targets.
> - Look for the links between the theoretical aspects of the course and personal practical performance.
> - Keep notes updated regularly and use them as a revision resource.
> - Enjoy it – the practical aspect of the course is supposed to be fun!

Index

Bold page numbers indicate a definition of the term.

Italic numbers indicate an illustration or table.

Nesta and Rob would like to thank Ffion, Ellie, Rees and Cai for their patience during the writing of this book. Also, thanks to Rochelle and Claire for taking the time to share their sporting experiences.

Graham would like to thank his family, friends and colleagues for their patience and support during this project.

Texts cited in this book are as follows:

Claxton, G., Expanding the capacity to Learn, British Education Research Association, 2006

Huizinga, J., *Homo Ludens*, Beacon Press, 1964

Mortlock, C. *The Adventure Alternative*, Cicerone Press, 1984

Mosston, M., Ashworth, S., *Teaching Physical Education*, Merrill, 1986

Piaget, J., *Play and Imitation in Childhood*, Norton, 1962

Torkildsen, G., *Leisure and Recreation Management*, 1983

The authors and publisher would like to thank the following individuals and organisations for permission to reproduce photographs:

p2 BR © PA Photos/AP Photo/Jason DeCrow; **p2 BL** © Corbis/Jean Christophe Bott/EPA; **p4** © PA Photos/John Walton/ EMPICS Sport; **p6** © PA Photos/Glyn Kirk; **p8** © PA Photos/AP Photo/Steve Yeater; **p9** © PA Photos/Tom Theobald/Zuma Press; **p10** © PA Photos/AP Photo/NZPA, Wayne Drought; **p12** © Alex Potemkin/Istockphoto; **p15** © Getty Images/Andy Lyons; **p19** © Getty Images/Dorling Kindersley; **p23** © Corbis/Tim de Waele; **p31 ML** © Getty Images/Bob Thomas; **p31 BR** © Paul Johnson/Istockphoto; **p33** © Rex Features/Kip Rano; **p45 BL** © Getty Images Michael Steele; **p45 BR** © Rex Features/ Photosport International; **p50** © Getty Images/Al Bello; **p63** © Getty Images/Gary M Prior; **p66** © Getty Images/Joel Saget/ AFP; **p78** © Rex Features/Greg Allen; **p89** © Getty Images/AFP Photo/Miguel Rojo; **p93** © Corbis/Damir Sagolj/Reuters; **p113** Action Plus; **p130** Photolibrary; **p131** © PA Photos/AP Photo/Francois Mori; **p132 BL** Alamy Images; **p132 BR** Corbis; **p149 BL** Action Plus; **p149 BR** Action Plus; **p152 ML** Corbis; **p152 MR** Action Plus; **p153TL** © PA Photos/AP Photo/Al Goldis; **p153 TC** © PA Photos/Adam Davy/EMPICS Sport; **p153 TR** Corbis; **p154 TL** © Getty Images; **p154 TR** © PA Photos/AP Photo/ Roberto Candia; **p165 BL** © PA Photos/John Walton/EMPICS Sport; **p165 BC** © PA Photos/AP Photo/Thomas Kienzle; **p165 BR** © PA Photos/AP Photo/Keystone, Urs Flueeler; **p170 T** © Action Plus/Glyn Kirk; **p170 B** © Empics; **p180** © PA Photos/AP Photo/Michael Probst; **p185** Corbis; **p188** © Getty Images; **p189** © Getty Images; **p190 BL** © Corbis/Scott Wohrman; **p190 BR** © PA Photos/AP Photo/Steve Yeater; **p202 TL** Getty Images; **p202 TR** © PA Photos/AP Photo/Michael Sohn; **p204 TR** © PA Photos/AP Photo/John Cogill; **p207** © Corbis/Image Source; **p208** © PA Photos/John Walton/EMPICS Sport; **p209 T** © Corbis/ Andrew Wong/Reuters; **p209 B** © PA Photos/AP Photo/The St. Petersburg Times, James Borchuck; **p290 L** © Getty Images/ Christof Koepsel/Bongarts; **p290 R** © Getty Images/Stone/Lori Adamski Peek; **p236 T** © Getty Images/Dave Nagel; **p236 B** © Alamy Images/Steven May; **p239** © Rochelle Plumb

The authors and publisher would like to thank the following for permission to reproduce copyright material:

P293 Fig.14.08 Disability sport classifications reproduced with permission of Disability Sport England

Crown Copyright material is reproduced with the permission of OPSI/HMSO and the Queen's Printer for Scotland

Every effort has been made to contact copyright holders of material reproduced in this book. Any omissions will be rectified in subsequent printings if notice is given to the publishers.